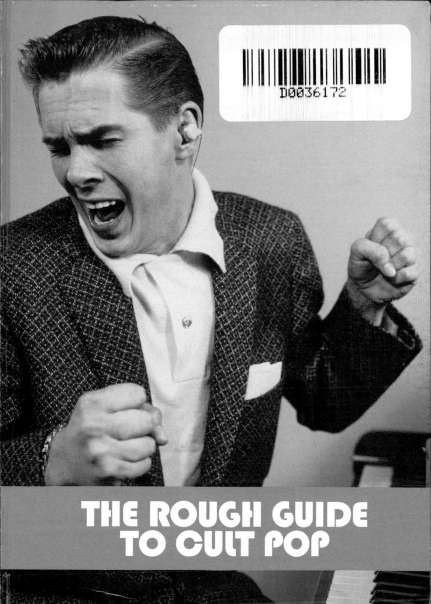

D0036172

THE ROUGH GUIDE
TO CULT POP

"Strange how potent cheap music is"
Noel Coward

There is, as Noel Coward knew better than anybody, nothing strange about the lure of 'cheap' music. Popular music is the soundtrack to our lives and loves: whether we've just checked into heartbreak hotel or been touched for the very first time. For many of us, it's the music we have actually been listening to when we ought to have been lending our ears to something more weighty.

For three minutes, or less, we can enter a parallel universe where there's a better-than-even chance that if we ask a girl to dance she might say, yes, she can boogie – but it takes a certain song. A world of extreme pain and joy, yet where everything is temporary, written in the sand. A world where nothing is real, where we can shout "Awalopbopaloobop Alopbambboom!" and not be obliged to explain ourselves.

Pop is as powerful a force today as it was when it was invented back in the 1950s by any or all of the following: Elvis Presley, Bill Haley, Sam Phillips, Johnnie Ray or Big Joe Turner. You could also make a case that popular music, as we know it today, was invented by **Bing Crosby**, a consummate vocalist and technological pioneer. Without his illusion of intimacy, pop could never have been the same – although **Louis Armstrong**, **Fats Waller** and **Louis Jordan** can all claim to have assisted at the birth because pop, whatever the myth says, wasn't created overnight when a chubby bloke called **Bill Haley** sang Rock Around The Clock.

Whoever or whenever or whyever it was invented doesn't really matter. What matters is that it exists. We've all heard the complaints that we're living in an age of manufactured meaningless pop, but that lament is as old as pop itself. Pop was invented, to quote Frank Sinatra, by "cretinous goons" and this "rancid aphrodisiac" has, according to the snipers, been in continuous deterioration ever since. The perfect snook to such attitudes was cocked by writer Fran Liebowitz in 1978. "There are two kinds of music," she mocked. "Good music is music that I want to hear. Bad music is music that I don't want to hear."

Ol' Blue Eyes would have been mystified by the appeal of **Funkytown**, the 1980 disco hit by Lipps Inc. But for sheer economy, it is a thing of pop beauty. Driven by an urgent beat and an irresistible, limpet-like synthesizer hook, it bursts into

🐦 Rock'n'roll the "poor old" Johnnie Ray way

glorious life as lead singer **Cynthia Johnson** zaps out, "Well, I talk about it, talk about, talk about, talk about… moving." Whatever Cynthia's been talking about is irrelevant. You're caught up, intrigued and having fun which has, after all, always been the point. As **Nick Hornby** notes in *31 Songs*, pop songs don't have to be innovative or important to be great, and popularity is not in itself proof that an artist or a song is flawed. As **Nik Cohn** put it, in *Awopbopaloobop Alopbamboom*, the best pop does "what Bogart and Brando and Monroe have done in films – it has to be intelligent and simple, carry its implications lightly and it has to be fast, funny, sexy, obsessive and a bit epic." Or, at least, do more than one of those things.

This book is for people who still find **Wham! Rap** a bit of a laugh all these years later, can't get that Kylie riff out of their heads, and yield to no one in their admiration for singers and bands officially classified as minor. So whether your idea of a great songwriter is **Noel Coward** or **Noel Gallagher** (see p206) you should find something here to amuse.

Noel Coward wrote London Pride, one of the few drinks not in front of Liz Taylor

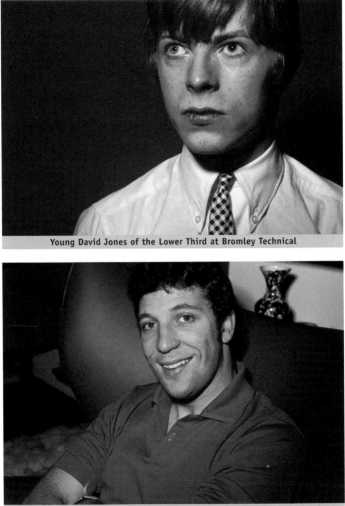

Young David Jones of the Lower Third at Bromley Technical

Thomas Woodward of Pontypridd, rebranded Jones after the 1963 movie

Early days Every pop act has a past, when their unlined faces were lit by nothing more than the untrammelled optimism of youth

Raw early Kylie: Aussies called her "the singing budgie"

v

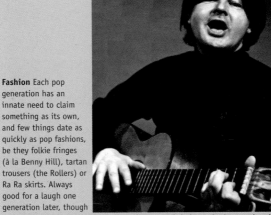

Fashion Each pop generation has an innate need to claim something as its own, and few things date as quickly as pop fashions, be they folkie fringes (à la Benny Hill), tartan trousers (the Rollers) or Ra Ra skirts. Always good for a laugh one generation later, though

"Take me disappearin' through the smoke rings of my mind"

Who got to wear the red shirts was always a sore point in The Monkees

Edinburgh council estate chic, circa 1974

Liam Gallagher takes Mr Tambourine Man rather too literally

Movies Despite being shy, introverted types, pop stars have been astonishingly keen to put on some fancy dress and light up the screen

Sheik, rattle and roll: you have to admire Elvis for keeping a straight face

Bak 'Ome: Slade get ready for dress down day at Wolverhampton Social Club

Saturday Night Fever brought disco to the masses – and damn near killed it

Blimey, Ozzy looks a bit rough... oh hang on, it's a video

Courtney Love indulges in some deeply anti-social behaviour...

...along with Jimi Hendrix, Ray Davies and Harry Nilsson

Life's a drag As ye smoke, so shall ye reek

"Rrr-Regals" growls Eartha. Her heart belongs to daddy, but will he want it?

Finger-clickin' good: a dapper Stevie Wonder, in a suit that made fans see red

Following suit
Although rock music has become associated with non-corporate scruffiness, pop music – especially black pop – has always stayed within the realms of showbiz, and hence shown a penchant for cutting a certain dash

Donovan modelled himself on Napoleon – the XIVth

The Jacksons' suits were so bright you just had to wear shades

The Village People – never leave gay men unsupervised near a dressing-up box

Mud in their 1970s finery. No wonder they were forever Lonely This Christmas

You're not going out dressed like that The broad tent that is pop music has always found room for those who thought if it was worth doing well, it was worth overdoing

Sonny & Cher: no coincidence that Sonny's only solo hit was Laugh At Me

Swimwear The Itsy Bitsy Teeny Weeny Yellow Polka-Dot Bikini is an essential part of any credible pop chick's wardrobe, just ask Geri

Debbie suddenly realised the tide wasn't so high today

Is Beach Boy Brian Wilson Surfin' USA? God Only Knows

Mungo Jerry's records on Pye came with free chops

Hair! From a rock'n'roll quiff through hippiedom to punk, hair has been as much about rebellion as style. Pile it high...

Blonde on blonde: David Sylvian (Japan), Dolly Parton...

...Van Halen's David Lee Roth and Wizzard's Roy Wood

ZZ Top: natural blondes if ever we saw two

Style challenge: Ken Dodd was all eyes and teeth and hair

The (very young) Bee Gees were all teeth and hair and eyes

And Shane MacGowan: all eyes and, erm, hair

Love at first bite
Being a successful pop star means spending hours in the dentist's chair having those pearly whites scaled, filled and polished. Usually

After winning Eurovision, Sandie Shaw prepares for a visit from Imelda Marcos

Eurovision Step into the parallel pop world that is Eurovision, where fashion takes a back seat and ripping your skirt off counts as a dance routine. And where songs like Rock Bottom, Don't Play That Song Again and Why Do I Always Get It Wrong? (all UK entrants) all sound horribly prophetic

Clodagh Rodgers buttons up for Eurovision glory

Bucks Fizz's patriotism was as subtle as Cheryl's and Shelley's make-up

Because the knight: Sir Elton dwells on all the things Nikita will never know...

Singer/songwriters
If you have something
to say and you want to
be the one who says it
(or sings it), become
a singer/songwriter.
Then everyone will know
that you're serious,
won't they?

...while Jarvis Cocker sports a different class of suit

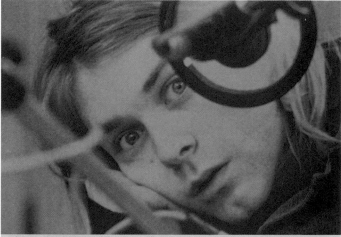

Nirvana summed up confusion and alienation, and the tunes weren't bad either

Gilbert O'Sullivan's idea of a treat was to climb a tower. And throw himself off

Cover story The right sleeve can do wonders for a record and a cardigan

The Mothers Of Invention's classic spoof of The Beatles' Sgt Pepper sleeve

The Small Faces, Elvis Costello and Supertramp: all paid homage to past styles

Ike & Tina Turner: Ike played on Rocket 88, arguably the first rock'n'roll record

Strange brew: Bob Wills's Western Swing mixed blues, jazz and Tin Pan Alley pop

Roots: Pop and rock'n'roll have always been, as Blue Mink put it in 1969, a great big melting pot into which were mixed blues, gospel, country and jazz

With Fats Waller, nobody ever shot the piano player

After inventing scat singing, Louis Armstrong takes a well-earned rest

Contents

1. Genres 3-102
From actors who have tried to make it big as pop stars to
the misunderstood role played by zombies in pop music

2. The Talent 103-174
The geniuses, muses, mavericks, bit players and backroom
boys without whom pop wouldn't be where it is today

3. The Lists 175-200
Welcome to a pop pickers paradise!
All the essential pop trivia and much more! Not aarf!

4. The Number Ones 201-252
The stories behind 40 very different British chart toppers.
And the greatest No. 2 ever.

5. Wired For Sound 253-266
"Slide the needle in the groove":
how technology, of all kinds, has shaped pop music

6. Unchained Melodies 267-282
Great stories about pop music
which didn't fit in anywhere else

7. Ephemera 283-312
Great pop artefacts: from Nancy Sinatra's walking boots
to rare historic records and Michael Jackson's sleeping bag

8. Pop Goes To The Movies 313-324
Your A to Z guide to what happens when
Tinseltown and pop music collide

9. The Final Countdown 325-333
Fifty glorious years of pop music
digitally compressed into a virtual nutshell

The Credits

Text editor Paul Simpson
Contributors Helen Rodiss, Victoria Williams, Jo Berry, Richard Pendleton,
Mark Ellingham, John Aizlewood, Lesley Turner, Steve Morgan, Simon Kanter,
Lloyd Bradley, Kath Stathers, Ann Oliver, Nick Moore, Sam Upton, Ian McLeish,
Derek Harbinson, Dave Burton, Steven Morewood
Production Ian Cranna, Michaela Bushell, Caroline Hunt, Chas Chandler
Picture editors Dominique Campbell, Jenny Quiggin
Main cover pic Mick Rock 1977, 2003, www.mickrock.com
Thanks to Jon Wilton and Julian Ridgeway, Redferns, Hulton Getty, Cathrine
Keen, Julia Bovis, Mark Ellingham,
Lindsay Fryatt, Colour Systems, Simon Kanter, Laurence Down
Picture adjustment Link Hall
Cover design by Jon Butterworth
Designed by Sharon O'Connor and Jon Butterworth

Printed in Spain by Graphy Cems

Dedicated to Jack Simpson, Miles and Nat, the Rodisses, Gavin, Howard,
Jerry Schilling, Leiber & Stoller, David Albert Cook, Aunt Mimi,
Thomas Wright Waller, Noah Kaminsky,

Publishing Information
This edition published October 2003 was prepared by Haymarket Customer
Publishing for Rough Guides Ltd, 80 Strand London, WC2R 0RL

Distributed by the Penguin Group
Penguin Books Ltd, 27 Wrights Lane, London W8 5TZ

©Rough Guides/Haymarket Customer Publishing 372pp, includes covers
A catalogue record for this book is available from the British Library
ISBN 1-84353-229-8

THE MUSICS

The pop music universe – from actors to zombies

A real Bay City roller: Madonna Louise Ciccone, the girl from Bay City, Michigan

Actors

Actors don't need much persuading to make a record; others fancy themselves as rock musicians (**Bruce Willis** and **Johnny Depp**). But for every Kylie Minogue there are hideous failures like **Anita Dobson**, **Dennis Waterman** and **Eddie Murphy**. Every actor about to make a record should listen to Somethin' Stupid by **Amanda Barrie** and **Johnny Briggs** (aka Alma and Mike Baldwin from *Corrie*).

★And the nominations are...★

Are You Being Served Sir? John Inman 1975 novelty spin-off, panto prison beckoned.

For All Time Catherine Zeta-Jones From 1992, when she was John Leslie's arm candy.

Old Rivers Walter Brennan with The Johnny Mann Singers This curiosity, sung by one of Hollywood's most prolific and respected supporting actors, barely troubled the charts in 1962, but as far as obscure songs from obscure actors go, it's hard to top.

She's Like The Wind Patrick Swayze Passable ballad well sung. To his credit, he turned down an album deal after this *Dirty Dancing* track was a hit.

Something Outta Nothing Letitia Dean and **Paul Medford** Bury it on Arthur Fowler's allotment with Better Believe It by Sid Owen and Patsy Palmer.

Wand'rin' Star Lee Marvin A great song from *Paint Your Wagon*, delivered with true gravel. The double A-side of this track is I Talk To The Trees, sung by **Clint Eastwood**.

Alcohol

Research suggests that from **three to 20 per cent** of popular songs are devoted to Mister Booze. The finest in the genre include **Whiter Shade Of Pale** (see page 249), **Dean Martin**'s classic version of **Waylon Jennings**'s **Little Ole Wine Drinker Me** (never a UK hit) and Jeff Beck's 1972 hit **I've Been Drinking Again**, on which Rod Stewart sounded suitably hungover. **Dr Feelgood** broke the Top 10 in 1979 with **Milk And Alcohol**. None quite match the zest of **Mario Lanza**'s **Drinking Song** (No.13 in 1955) with its chant of "Ein, zwei, drei, vier/Nip your stein and drink your beer." Some of the best songs – eg Louis Jordan's **What's The Use Of Getting Sober? (When You're Gonna Get Drunk Again)** – predate pop music. Oddest of all is **Slim Dusty**'s tragic **A Pub With No Beer**, No.3 in the UK in 1959.

Pop has given us a song for enough varieties of booze to stock a small bar. Those brands celebrated include cider (**The Wurzels**' ooh-aarh Una Paloma Balanca homage **I Am A Cider Drinker**, No.3 in 1976), lager (**Splodgenessabounds** with **Two Pints Of Lager And A Packet Of Crisps Please**), tequila (The Champs' No.5 hit **Tequila** in 1958, the **Eagles**' **Tequila Sunrise**), whisky (**Thin Lizzy**'s **Whiskey

Songs about actors

Marilyn Monroe isn't the only screen idol to inspire hits. Robert De Niro's Waiting helped **Bananarama** meet the great man. They were drunk and may have thrown up over him. That'll teach him to be so inspirational. We preferred **Kim Carnes**'s Bette Davis Eyes, **Haysi Fantayzee**'s John Wayne Is Big Leggy and **Roxy Music**'s 2HB, a song dedicated to Bogart and pencils.

In The Jar), even lilac wine (Elkie Brooks's 1978 hit in which she cries "Why is everything so hazy?" – presumably the stuff had corked). **Sailor**, a bubblegum Roxy Music, hit No.2 in 1975 with **A Glass Of Champagne**, although, from the costumes and video quality, any girl accepting the offer probably got Asti Spumante. Roxy themselves spoke of "Canadian club love" in Mother Of Pearl. The best drinking song? **Chumbawamba**'s **Tubthumping** just for the list: "He drinks a whisky drink/He drinks a vodka drink/He drinks a lager drink/He drinks a cider drink." A soft female voice then croons "Pissing the night away." Sublime.

★**Recommended**★ English Drinking Songs by **AL Lloyd** (Topic) is an album which almost reeks of beer, with titles like **Drunken Maidens** and **When Johnson's Ale Was New**.

Ambient

This trendy yet elusive musical genre has had negligible chart impact – unless you think **Lieutenant Pigeon**'s **Mouldy Old Dough** (a surprise No.1 in 1972) invented it rather than **Brian Eno**. Eno discovered ambient in hospital, when he was too ill to turn the music up and had to strain to hear it. He began twiddling on albums like **Music For Airports**. Working with **David Bowie**, **David Byrne** and **U2**, Eno has spread ambient's influence. Ambient electronic, the beatless trance music of **Aphex Twin** (who hit No.16 with **Windowlicker** in 1999), is still very popular.

★**Recommended**★ Music For Airports **Brian Eno** (EG); Piano Works 1 & 2 by **Erik Satie** (Angel), the French composer who started all this – in a way.

America

Uncle Sam dominated the British charts in the 1950s, leading with **Elvis Presley**. But since the counterblast of the British beat invasion, America has never quite regained its old supremacy, although some artists – notably **Madonna**, Diana Ross and **Michael Jackson** – have racked up hundreds of weeks on the UK singles chart. In the 1970s the British and American pop cultures spun apart, as two rock'n'roll messiahs were crowned: **David Bowie** in the UK and **Bruce Springsteen** in the US. Even Madonnna hasn't wielded the same kind of transatlantic clout as Elvis and The Beatles. But Britain has cherished certain American acts seen as marginal in their own country – **Scott Walker**, **Cher**, **Dean Martin** and Dean Friedman...

Andover

Home of **The Troggs** and therefore of caveman rock. Drummer **Ronnie Bond**, bass player **Pete Staples** and singer **Reg Presley** all came from here. If you haven't been to this town off the A303, love isn't all around (despite the title of Reg's best-known ballad), sheep are. The Troggs' first hit was the three-chord monster **Wild Thing** (it had flopped for the Wild Ones) while the lust-fuelled (and banned) **I Can't Control Myself** caused a stir, proof of the youthful rage that growing up in a town so quietly prosperous can inspire? *Wild Thing* (on Collectables) is still their best album.

Animals

Once, all you had to do to get on British TV was **stick your hand up an animal's backside**. In 1982, **Keith Harris**, of the frizzy receding hair and fixed carpet-salesman grin, hit No.4, his hand up a coy green duck, with **Orville's Song** – and we all pined for **Disco Duck**, No.6 in 1976 for **Rick Dees & His Cast Of Idiots**.

Songs about dogs always get a hearing – from the day Elvis stood up at a county fair and sung Red Foley's tearjerker **Old Shep**. Lobo's **Me And You And A Dog Named Boo** was a hit in 1971, and **Peter Shelley**, the power behind Alvin Stardust, reached No.3 with **Love Me Love My Dog** in 1975. But **Your Bulldog Drinks Champagne** wasn't a UK hit for **Jim** (Spiders And Snakes) **Stafford**. Top dogs in pup pop, despite the claims of **Lita Roza** with (How Much Is That) Doggie In The Window? – No.1 in 1953 – are the **Baha Men** with **Who Let The Dogs Out**.

El's rival **Pat Boone** has made the best single about a mouse, **Speedy Gonzalez** (No.2 in 1962). **Michael Jackson** takes home all the cheese with **Ben**, the greatest song ever written about a boy's love for a rat. Other species to chart: gibbons (**The Goodies**:"Do, do, do the funky gibbon"), kangaroos (**Rolf Harris**) cats (crept to No.2 with **Mud** in 1973) and **The Chipmunks**, an American trio in which all three parts were sung, speeded up, by **Ross Bagdasarian**, hit No.11 in 1959, and his son took the act and a **Macarena** cover into the charts in 1996 . Scary. The lion slept to No.1 with **Tight Fit** (see page 221) but **Lulu**'s **I'm A Tiger**, No.9 in 1968, had more feline grace. Horses are a genre of their own (see Horses), as are Sheep. Honest.

Answer records

In **Big Mama Thornton**'s **Hound Dog** a woman reproves her useless spouse. This upset **Rufus Thomas**, who cut **You Ain't Nothing But A Bear Cat**, with the riposte, "You might purr pretty kitty, but I ain't going to rub you no more."

Most answer records are naff and don't chart. **LaVern Baker**'s Phil Spector-produced **Hey Memphis**, a reply to Elvis's **Little Sister**, was better than most – Baker and Presley dug each other's music – but didn't chart. Wanda Jackson's response to Jimmy Webb's hit was to the point – **By The Time You Got To Phoenix** – but dull. **Patti Page**'s gorgeous **Tennessee Waltz** was partly a response to the fact that if a nearby state had a song called **Kentucky Waltz**, Tennessee better have one too.

Some artists have to answer their own songs. **Buddy Holly** pulled it off, just, with **Peggy Sue Got Married**, sequel to his own **Peggy Sue**. But following **Lesley Gore**'s **Quincy Jones**-produced No.1 **It's My Party** with **Judy's Turn To Cry** sabotaged Gore's career. The most celebrated answer record may be **It Wasn't God Who Made Honky Tonk Angels**, a response to the country classic **The Wild Side Of Life** (a minor hit for **Tommy Quickly** in 1964 and a Top 10 hit for **Status Quo** in 1976), with its line "I didn't know God made honky tonk angels." Kitty Wells, Dolly Parton and Marianne Faithfull have all disputed divine intervention.

AOR

In the 1980s Adult Oriented Rock described bands like **Heart** or **Toto** who played 'proper' rock music with professional musicianship, sold albums by the million and packed stadiums. Think Dire Straits' **Brothers In Arms**: if you don't own it by now, you never will. But AOR went AWOL in the 1990s and is now officially MIA.

Art

Groups like **The Moody Blues** and **Emerson, Lake & Palmer** were inspired by **Sgt Pepper** to expand rock's sonic universe, creating art rock. Sounds self-important but art, through Andy Warhol and Richard Hamilton, inspired Roxy Music, David Bowie and German experimentalists **Can** (best album: **Future Days**).

Art pop includes the good (sloppy) **Vincent**, a 1972 No.1 for **Don McLean**, and the bad **Matchstick Men And Matchstalk Cats And Dogs**, a 1978 No.1 for Brian & Michael, the nadir of LS Lowry's career (luckily he was dead by then). **10cc**'s **Art For Art's Sake**, with the cry "money for God's sake", was more fun, as was **Boney M**'s **Painter Man**, No.10 in 1979 (Creation's original stalled at No.36 in 1966).

Australia

To crash the UK chart as an Aussie, be horribly cheery. You don't have to say "G'day cobber!" but your demeanour should imply this is a distinct possibility. This sunniness unites tall, yodelling **Frank Ifield**, bearded funster **Rolf Harris** and small, non-yodelling, unbearded **Kylie Minogue**. When **Jason Donovan**, hot in the late 1980s (his first six hits hit the Top 10), stopped being cheery we tired of him.

The Australian act of the 1960s – bigger than Ifield – were acoustic folk rockers **The Seekers**. They had two No.1s in 1965, their songs (especially **Georgy Girl** and **The Carnival Is Over**) hummed by those who don't know the

Ah the innocence of youth

group. Though **Sherbet** hit No.4 in 1976 with **Howzat**, the big Aussie success story of the era was Melbourne-raised **Olivia Newton-John**, a proto-Kylie, the girl next door who became a sex kitten with **Grease** and **Physical**, racking up three No.1s.

Even **Men At Work** had to give a passing nod to the cliché to hit No.1 in 1983 with the vastly underrated **Down Under** – "I met a strange lady, she made me nervous" one of many fine lines just too subtle for us Brits. They did better than **Mental As Anything** (No.3 in 1987 with the foot-tapper **Live It Up**). More credible, till Michael Hutchence's lurid death, were **INXS**, No.2 in 1988 with **Need You Tonight**. By then Britain was awash with Oz's soapy singing wannabes. The most durable, Kylie, has gone from girl next door to virtual sex toy. Her half-decent hits include **Can't Get You Out Of My Head**. Gloomy **Nick Cave** allied with Kylie for the No.11 **Where The Wild Roses Grow**. **Natalie Imbruglia** hit No.2 with **Torn**, looking like a very acceptable cross between Suzanne Vega and Kylie. There's no place here for Rolf Harris – his appeal is explored on page 130.

Austria

Austria produced one trendy young musician. But since **Mozart** died rock-star young, this country has inspired more hits (chiefly Ultravox's **Vienna** and Falco's

Vienna Calling) than it has created. **Falco** (another classically trained child prodigy who died too young) had four hits in 1986. The best (fittingly), **Rock Me Amadeus**, got to No.1. Mozart hit No.5 in 1971 with part of his Symphony No.40 In G Minor, thanks to Argentina's orchestra leader **Waldos De Los Rios**.

Ballads

A ballad is a melodic, lyrical piece sung at a slow tempo. This could be Renee & Renato's **Save Your Love** (No.1 in 1982) or Tammy Wynette's **Stand By Your Man** (No.1 in 1975). The charts were full of them. Hold on, they still are; Words, Seasons In The Sun and How Deep Is Your Love? are being remade almost daily.

Traditional pop history suggests rock has reigned since the 1950s, but the Top 100 UK chart acts include **Frank Sinatra** (No.10), **Tom Jones** (No.16), **Roy Orbison** (No.19), **Shirley Bassey** (No.22), **Perry Como** (No.23) and **Pat Boone** (No.30).

Some of the No.1 ballads in the 1950s were as fine as **Stranger In Paradise** (**Tony Bennett**), many weren't – Tin Pan Alley was low on ideas. Yet from 1959 to 1963 rock, not the ballad, was out of fashion. In 1964, Beatlemania at its height, two **Burt Bacharach** songs (**Anyone Who Had A Heart** and **There's Always Something There To Remind Me**) hit No.1. In 1966 Ol' Blue Eyes had his second No.1 with **Strangers In The Night**, grabbing a third in 1967 (**Somethin' Stupid**) with daughter Nancy. Glam rock and punk, memorable or moronic, ruled the 1970s, but singer/songwriters of varying degrees of soppiness multiplied and **George Harrison** wrote the standard, **Something**. In the 1980s ballads as fine as **The Winner Takes It All** – and as awful as **Ebony And Ivory** – topped the charts.

In 1981 post-punker **Elvis Costello** reached No.6 with **A Good Year For The Roses**, a country ballad which brought genre (and ballad) back into fashion. Thirteen years later Costello

Frank Sinatra rocked, even as a kid

sang with **Tony Bennett** on MTV Unplugged and the classic American songbook was back in vogue. In 1996 Dean Martin's death promoted the re-release of **That's Amore**, which peaked just outside the UK Top 40, and in 1999 Andy Williams's **Music To Watch Girls By** slid into the Top 10 aided by a TV ad, and Costello crept into the Top 20 with his take on **Charles Aznavour**'s 1974 No.1 **She**. Meanwhile the power ballad (think Bryan Adams emoting) had become an essential part of the arsenal for any stadium rock band.

★**Recommended**★ **Tony Bennett**'s I Left My Heart In San Francisco (CBS) is his most satisfying album, richer than many compilations. On the same principle, try Sinatra's In The Wee Small Hours (Capitol). **Charles Aznavour**'s 20 Chansons D'or (EMI) is good too.

Banned

Pop songs are usually banned for obscenity (**Love To Love You Baby**), politics (**Give Ireland Back To The Irish**), or suspicion of promoting drugs (John Denver's **Rocky Mountain High**). But they have also been banned as morbid (Mike Berry's **Tribute To Buddy Holly**) or (Rosemary Clooney's **Mambo Italiano**) for what US network ABC called not meeting "standards of good taste".

Those seeking tititlation – singles too sexy for us to hear – should see X-rated, this focuses on the more high falutin' stuff. Kinda. Too many records have been banned for too few reasons (ie bureaucratic stupidity) to list here. But a few weird bans are worth noting (the **Louie Louie** saga is explored on page 269). Country singer **Webb Pierce** had his 1955 hit **There Stands The Glass** banned by DJs for condoning heavy drinking, while Nervous Norvus's novelty **Transfusion** was banned on US radio because, NBC said, "there is nothing funny about a blood transfusion."

In 1967 **Verve Records** cut eight bars from Frank Zappa's **Let's Make The Water Turn Black** over fears that the pad on which the song's mama takes orders in the café was slang for sanitary towel. In 1968 DJs in El Paso banned **Bob Dylan** singing his songs– they couldn't understand him – but still played covers of his songs.

For the BBC, references to Northern Ireland would get a single blacklisted (Macca's **Give Ireland Back To The Irish**) or shunned (The Police's **Invisible Sun**). Auntie's finest moment (not) was the ban of the Sex Pistols' **God Save The Queen** in the Queen's silver jubilee year, 1977. Officially it reached No.2, but many believe the chart was fixed to keep Rod Stewart's **I Don't Want To Talk About It** at No.1 and spare Her Maj's blushes. In 1984 **Relax** was eventually banned all the way to No.1. Rave act **The Shamen** had their drug-fuelled single **Ebeneezer Goode** (No.1) banned on radio. Even MTV balked at scenes of sadomasochism, homosexuality and cross-dressing in Madonna's **Justify My Love** video.

Doubtless the resultant publicity was a complete surprise to Ms Ciccone.

Today songs and artists get played until some group demands they be banned or the broadcasters get nervous – often because a certain event (eg 9/11) is said to have changed the public mood. After the terrorist attacks, the largest owner of US radio stations sent out a list of 'banned' songs, including Billy Joel's **Only The Good Die Young** and Jerry Lee Lewis's **Great Balls Of Fire**. The same principle led **Radio 1** to ban Phil Collins's **In The Air Tonight** during the first Gulf War.

The oddest event in the annals of banned pop occurred in 1980 in Iowa, when a **church group burned records** by The Carpenters, John Denver and Perry Como. Burning easy listening classics has not caught on, nor has it given the artists much street cred. Almost as strange was Sir Cliff's decision to ban his own 1975 single **Honky Tonk Angel**, when he realised what honky tonk angels were. Crumbs!

Belgium

Belgian pop is often summed up in two words: **Plastic Bertrand**. But the world's smallest federal nation has given us **Jacques Brel** (see page 110) and a lot of chart acts with names like Telex or Technotronic. The record label **Les Disques Du Crepuscule** – a kind of low-countries offshoot of Factory Records – made Brussels fashionable on the underground scene. To most Brits, Belgian pop comes down to four words – **"Ca plane pour moi"** – our collective surprise at seeing a Belgian 'punk' on **Top Of The Pops** has engraved the song on our memory.

Birmingham

Monotony is a charge often levelled at Britain's second city and at Brum rock – why, the very term sounds like an insult. But without Birmingham there would have been no **Spencer Davis Group** (or Steve Winwood), no **The Move**, no **Moody Blues**, no **Wizzard**, no **UB40**, no **Dexy's** and no **Electric Light Orchestra**. OK, **The Diary Of Horace Wimp** didn't enrich our lives, but The Move brightened up the late 1960s, promoting a record with what was effectively a dirty postcard of **Harold Wilson**, then prime minister. Led by Carl Wayne, Ace Kefford and Roy Wood, they made such fine records as the snarling **Fire Brigade**. Wood then flirted with ELO before fronting Wizzard, who were wizard for a while, **See My Baby Jive** was so infectious you forgot Wood's hair. Almost.

The Moody Blues gave up R&B, looked solemn and sold 50-million albums. **Go Now**, their first No.1, was catchy, vaguely political and a cover of an American soul record. Then singer Denny Laine left (he'd end up in Wings). They're famous for **Nights In White Satin**, though it only got to No.9. Their album titles (To Our

Putting up their gloves

Pugilism and pop are just two ways to escape from the wrong side of the tracks. Apart from Prince Buster, **James Brown**, **Chris Isaak**, **Lee** **Dorsey** and **Screamin' Jay Hawkins** all gave up boxing for pop (although Hawkins also tried to make it as an opera singer).

Children's Children's Children, On The Threshold Of A Dream, Journey Into Amazing Caves) say it all. **ELO** had their moments (**Roll Over Beethoven**, parts of **A New World Record**) before leader Jeff Lynne decreed that every song had to feature spurious backing vocalists and orchestration. ELO's dependency on The Beatles sounds finally became so blatant it was like musical stalking.

UB40 made two fine albums in the early 1980s (**Signing Off** and **Labour Of Love**) and the angry double A-side single **One In Ten/King**) before making reggae oldies with machine-like precision; US success and dullness coinciding. **Dexy's** were truly great, for a while: **Geno** was one of the 1980s finest No.1s.

★**Recommended**★ **The Move**'s **Shazam** (on import on JVC Japan) is rather fine.

Blues

Blues was one of the partners – country is the other – in the merger which made rock'n'roll. Yet the legends who inspired British acts like Eric Clapton and Mick Jagger (**Muddy Waters**, **John Lee Hooker**, **Howlin' Wolf** and **BB King**) have spent 44 weeks on the UK singles chart between them, less than **The Glitter Band**.

Alexis Korner, a trad jazz veteran (and later a DJ), was British blues' patron saint, forming, in the early 1960s, a group called **Blues Incorporated** which, at different times, would include **Charlie Watts**, **Jack Bruce** and **Long John Baldry**, and attract the likes of **Mick Jagger** and **Keith Richards** to its concerts.

The Stones, named after a Muddy Waters song, had their second UK No.1 with Howlin' Wolf's **Little Red Rooster** in 1964. They played what was later called British R&B because their music was faster, rockier, with more emphasis on guitars than traditional blues, though it owed something to American fast jump blues, pioneered by the likes of **Big Joe Turner**.

Soon the charts were full of blues bands: **The Pretty Things** (who made the Stones look handsome), the **Animals** (whose **House Of The Rising Sun** is discussed on page 212), **The Yardbirds** driven by Clapton's guitar, **Manfred Mann**, **Spencer Davis Group**, **Them** (with Van Morrison) and **Chris Farlowe**, who hit No.1 with the

Jagger-Richards song **Out Of Time** and has remained out of time ever since.

But The Yardbirds went pop (Clapton quit, invented blues-rock with Cream and went solo) and Baldry went pap, giving up the blues for sobalong ballads. The Animals and Spencer Davis split. Fleetwood Mac, the **Peter Green** edition, stuck to the blues with **Need Your Love So Bad**. But by 1970 British R&B was all but dead. Reggae and soul became the most influential black musics of the 1970s. Clapton has returned to the blues with albums like **Unplugged**, but one of the last blues singles to reach the Top 20 was **The Blues Brothers**' **Everybody Needs Somebody To Love**, No.12 in 1990.

★**Recommended**★ R&B From The Marquee (Decca) has the best of **Blues Incorporated**. The Demention Of Sound (Feedback) is a fine set of rarities from the 1960s blues boom.

Boxing

Pugilism, like pop, has always given working-class kids a shot at upward mobility, albeit of a kind. Which may explain why, for example, reggae giant **Prince Buster** was a boxer. **Muhammad Ali** inspired British vocalist **Johnny Wakelin** to cut two singles – **Black Superman** and **In Zaire** ("See the rumble in the jungle… in Zaire") – which both reached the Top 10 in the 1970s. Hard to see Audley Harrison's fights inspiring hits, though he could remake **Eye Of The Tiger**, the *Rocky* theme, No.1 for Survivor in 1982 and No.28 for **Frank Bruno** in 1995.

Boy bands

The Beatles were arguably the first boy band. Since then the ride into pop hell has had its pleasures, provided by **The Monkees** (often), **New Kids On The Block** (sometimes), **Take That** (less often) and **Curiosity Killed The Cat** (almost never). Making boy bands may be the one manufacturing industry in which Britain still leads the world. But boy bands have given us **Mike Nesmith**, **Robbie Williams** and **Our Kid**. Remember them? These talented Scouse schoolkids hit No.2 in 1976 with **You Just Might See Me Cry**. Their manager used all the days they were legally allowed to work as kids to book them into somewhere like Great Yarmouth, so, by the time they wanted to cut a new single, they had no working days left to spare. Anybody who saw the lads troop back to school might have just seen them cry.

Brackets

Why do so many songwriters need parentheses? Is **Natural Woman (You Make Me Feel Like)** better for almost having to be read in reverse? Yet The Monkees

Alternate Title (Randy Scouse Git) wouldn't be the same without the brackets. Elvis only resorted to parentheses four times. The Beatles racked up 17 No.1s without a parenthesis in sight. Norwegian Wood (This Bird Has Flown) is one of their best songs never to chart, though it might have been more impressive if it had stood, magnificent and mysterious, as plain old Norwegian Wood. The Stranglers threw out a grammatical challenge with their first hit (Get A) Grip (On Yourself).

Brazil

Many Brazilian albums bear the words "Disco e cultura". Not a tribute to disco, it means "Records are culture." In other words, football isn't Brazil's only universal language. Yet Carmen Miranda, Astrud Gilberto and Sergio Mendes have paid for global success with the charge that they have sold out. This was hard on Carmen, who may have worn a basket of fruit for no obvious reason, but who also recorded 275 Brazilian songs (her Brazilian Recordings, on Harlequin, is classy samba). She even sang a samba They Say I Come Back Americanized in

Carmen Miranda does the floral dance

which she notes "I know there's a rumour about that I've lost my rhythm and hot-blooded temperament" (it scans better in Portuguese).

Brazil is best known for bossa nova, a sunny 1960s variant of jazz which sounded like Copacabana beach set to music. The boom was fuelled by American saxophonist Stan Getz and Brazilian guitarist Joao Gilberto, who combined on Desafinado (No.11 in 1962). Getz then cut The Girl From Ipanema, with Joao's soon to be ex-wife, Astrud, singing. This reached No.5 in the US, in the UK it was heard more often than bought. Brazilian conductor Julio Medaglia noted: "She sings so horribly, it couldn't get any worse." Mendes faced similar criticism after the success of Never Gonna Let You Go (a No.45 hit in 1983).

Brazil has also inspired some memorable pop songs. Copacabana is mainly memorable as a work of kitsch, but Mike Nesmith's Rio will always be in fashion.

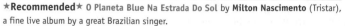
★Recommended★ O Planeta Blue Na Estrada Do Sol by Milton Nascimento (Tristar), a fine live album by a great Brazilian singer.

Brill Building

If you think of rock and pop history in terms of significant buildings, a few obvious shrines spring to mind: **Sun Studios**, **Abbey Road**, the **Motown studio**. Yet the **Brill Building** in New York has been as influential as any of these.

The 'Building' is actually three separate addresses spread over five blocks of Broadway. **1619 Broadway** – the Brill Building itself – flourished in the late 1950s and early 1960s, and was where the publishing of blues and Southern rockabilly artists (including **Elvis Presley**) were handled. This is where **Doc Pomus** and **Mort Shuman** worked, and where **Leiber & Stoller** wrote **Hound Dog**.

By the mid-1960s, the action had shifted to 1650 Broadway. It has no name, just a number, but the inscription above the door reads "The best-known address in the entertainment field." **Don Kirshner** (The Monkees mastermind) had his empire here. A long list of jobbing writers (**Gerry Goffin** and **Carole King**, **Barry Mann** and **Cynthia Weil**, **Neil Diamond**, **Neil Sedaka**, **Jeff Barry** and **Ellie Greenwich**) sat in cubicles to churn out hits. **Paul Simon** still has an office here.

The third Brill address was 1697 Broadway, where the black acts were based. **Al Kooper** says in his memoir, **Backstage Passes & Backstabbing Bastards**, the few white people who had office space there felt obliged have one R&B hit. This is where **The Tokens** – "Jewish as the driven snow" – wrote **He's So Fine** for **The Chiffons**.

Brill's trademark was crowd-pleasing candyfloss like Perry Como's **Magic Moments**, but Brill writers also crafted **Natural Woman (You Make Me Feel Like)**, **You've Lost That Lovin' Feeling**, **Stand By Me**, **Will You Still Love Me Tomorrow?**, **River Deep Mountain High** and **One Fine Day**. Rock'n'roll's birth usually stresses its links to country and blues, but Brill has probably produced more No.1 hits than any other place in pop history.

★**Recommended**★ The Brill Building Sound, a K-Tel box set, doesn't have the Spector hits but has 74 fine tracks. **Dionne Warwick**'s From The Vaults (Ichiban) is divine.

Bristol

Eddie Cochran died near Bristol, but in recompense the city has given us pianist **Russ Conway**, songwriters and serial group members **Roger Cook** and **Roger Greenaway**, the great **Robert Wyatt**, the not-so-great **Nik Kershaw** and the grating **Sarah Dallin** and **Keren Woodward** of **Bananarama**. For all the groups which have sprung from here, like Massive Attack, you don't find critics – not even **Julie Burchill** who was born here – talking about a Bristol sound.

Britpop

Although Britpop is now consigned to the same dustbin as "Cool Britannia", the rivalry of **Blur** and **Oasis** (and the eccentric, commercial genius of **Pulp**) made the UK single charts matter in a way they hadn't done since the Beatles-Stones rivalry. Other acts – such as **The Charlatans**, **Suede**, **The Verve** and **Supergrass** – brought an edge to pop with such hits as **North Country Boy**, **The Drugs Don't Work** and **Alright**. Their brand of intelligent, guitar-based music with catchy melodies and strong hooks meant that, for a while, pre-teens had some intelligent pop to listen to. Megolamania, internecine rivalry and creative burn-out took their toll but, from 1993 to 1997, the charts fizzed with an energy rarely seen since the 1960s.

★**Recommended**★ Britpop, apart from its debt to The Beatles, began with **The Stone Roses**' self-titled debut album (Silvertone), which would grace most music collections.

Bubblegum

In the late 1960s the business of making hits seemed beneath many rock acts, and the subtleties of some of their music was lost on younger singles buyers. Astute producers (notably **Jerry Kazenetz** and **Jeff Katz**) were quick to market musical escapism. Acts such as **The Monkees** (see page 144) and **Tommy James & The Shondells** offered simple, well made, enjoyable pop rock. James's chief claim to fame, apart from producing one of the decade's great dance singles with **Mony Mony** (No.1 in 1968), was that one single – **Mirage** – was created by playing its predecessor – **I Think We're Alone Now** – backwards.

James and The Monkees were too smart to be pure bubblegum. Aiming at pre-pubescent kids, Kasenetz-Katz struck gold with a series of simplistic hits by fictitious groups with daft names. The definitive bubblegum single is **Yummy Yummy Yummy**, a No.5 hit in 1968 for session musicians billed as Ohio Express, although some prefer **Simon Says** by the 1910 Fruitgum Co. (same writers and session men), a No.2 the same year. Both hits had a hook so simple and compelling you remembered it before you'd heard all of it, a cheerful lyric and a bright, disposable sound. The first bubblegum chart-topper was **Dizzy**, sung and co-written by **Tommy Roe** (later returned to the top by **Vic Reeves**). This was soon followed by The Archies' **Sugar Sugar**, a 1969 smash which The Monkees had turned down but which soul great **Wilson Pickett** later covered.

Punk finally deflated bubblegum, but **Talking Heads** covered a 1910 Fruitgum Co. song and Squeeze adopted **Quick Joey Small** (No.19 for The Kasenetz-Katz

Singing Orchestral Circus in 1968) – a fantastic pop-rock song about a jailbird on the run. Still reviled, bubblegum helped save pop from its own pretensions.

★**Recommended**★ Bubblegum Hit Pack (BMG) has most of the major hits.

Calypso

Day-oh! Calypso, originally the music of the carnivals from Trinidad, was briefly in vogue in the 1950s when sung by **Harry Belafonte** and, erm, **Robert Mitchum**, whose seminal 1950s album, **Calypso Is Like So**, actually includes a few rock tracks. Nobody sings calypso like Mitchum – and that's probably a blessing.

Belafonte assimilated calypso, folk and jazz to create a distinct, yet commercial, music. **Island In The Sun** reached No.3 in the summer of 1957. He hit No.1 at Christmas with **Mary's Boy Child**, later pepped up by Boney M, but by 1961 he was losing a UK chart war with **Bernard Cribbins** over **There's A Hole In My Bucket**. Yet his music lives on, with **Banana Boat Song** (his first hit) launching a thousand covers and spoofs). Performers like Lord Kitchener popularised the music in concert in Britain but calypso has not returned to the singles chart.

"OK, take six. There's a hole in my bucket, my bucket, dear Liza, dear Liza"

★**Recommended**★ Miss Calypso (Scamp) by **Maya Angelou**, the singer who later became a poet and novelist, has more than novelty value.

Canada

Canada has produced two global pop stars (**Shania Twain** and **Bryan Adams**), one MOR monster (**Celine Dion**) and several national monuments: **Neil Young**, **Joni Mitchell**, **Leonard Cohen** and **Gordon Lightfoot**. Lightfoot had a gravelly voice and played a folksy guitar, but his beautiful **If You Could Read My Mind** stalled at No.30 in 1971. Joni Mitchell has only had one hit herself, but she wrote Matthews Southern Comfort's **Woodstock** (No.1 in 1970), so she's ahead of Cohen, whose **Suzanne** is in that unfortunate category: songs you thought were hits but weren't.

Canadian acts have often played minor supporting roles. In 1974 **Bachman-Turner Overdrive** stuttered their way to No.2 with "B-b-baby, you ain't seen nothing yet" – we ain't seen nothing since. In 1983 **Men Without Hats** reached No.6 with **Safety Dance** ("You can dance if you want to…" – that's big of you, thanks very much). And in 1993 Crash Test Dummies rumbled their way to No.2 with the mysterious (not to say pretentious) **Mmm Mmm Mmm Mmm**.

The vogue for **Alanis Morissette**'s confessional music and **KD Lang**'s torch 'n' twang (Madonna called her the reincarnation of Elvis) may have passed. But Bryan, Shania and Celine sell enough to have earned international abuse. **Phil Spector**, tempted into the studio by Celine's voice, stalked off saying: "The people around Celine are just interested in making hits, no matter how repugnant."

Shania's exposed midriff, her marriage to her svengali **Mutt Lange** (producer of **AC/DC**), and the release of alternate versions of her albums (one for country fans, one for pop fans) have appalled many. Yet the duo have created classic pop songs (**That Don't Impress Me Much, Man! I Feel Like A Woman!**) and some smug pap. Shania's mixing of genres, and her ability to sell a lyric, might one day be respected. In the meantime, the Canadian government's policy of requiring radio and TV to play a certain proportion of Canadian talent is paying off with a new generation of sparky young acts, especially in the alt.country field.

★**Recommended**★ Bryan Adams's Reckless is fine, melodic, radio-friendly pop rock.

Cars

Even before the arrival, in 1977, of **The Cars**, with their sleek, new wave pop rock, cars cropped up in pop almost as much as affairs of the heart did. Before **The**

Beatles invited us to Drive My Car, Elvis had assured us There's No Room To Rhumba In A Sports Car in the movie *Fun In Acapulco*. And, in 1971, Janis Joplin begged the Lord to buy her a Mercedes-Benz. There were all those trips Don McLean made to the levee in his Chevy (American Pie) and all those trips Johnny Cash took to make his car One Piece At A Time. A Cadillac (as with Elvis) fired Bruce Springsteen's imagination. Madness dragged one of the world's most famous car marques into an (almost) rhyming couplet – "I like driving in my car/It's not quite a Jaguar." A high-speed Maserati was blamed by Joe Walsh for his lack of a driver's licence in Life's Been Good. Gary Numan was less brand-specific in Cars ("It's the only way to live/In cars"), a UK No.1 in 1979, while Prefab Sprout tried to convince The Boss there's more to life than Cars and Girls. From an almost endless list, the final word goes to surf-rock band The Malibooz, for the magnificently titled Santa Drives A Super Stock Dodge…

Cartoons

The Archies define cartoon pop perfection. Created by Don Kirshner when The Monkees (his previous hit) got ideas of their own, they were the ultimate manufactured group. The TV series (based on the Archie comics and animated by Hanna-Barbera) was a hit, but Sugar Sugar proved hard to reproduce, despite the help of Brill Building writers Jeff Barry and Andy Kim. The project lasted three years, but the anonymous singer Ron Dante (also the voice on the Cufflinks' Tracy, No.4 in 1969) went on to bigger things as Barry Manilow's producer.

Josie & The Pussycats never had a hit, but the cartoon girl band (created by Hanna-Barbera after The Archies)were more gifted than some real groups of the era (their 1970 recordings are on Rhino). The Simpsons (Homer's blues parody Born Under A Bad Sign has merit) and South Park have had novelty hits, while Damon Albarn's animated Gorillaz turned down Brit awards. Oh, and The Beatles' Yellow Submarine wasn't bad – but then they were real(ish).

Celtic

Most artists get accused of making the same record over and over again. Enya (or Eithne Ní Bhraonáin) might not see that as a flaw, sticking, as she does, to a mystic Celtic/new age sound which seduces fans and bores critics. With Clannad, she had had a No.5 hit with the evocative theme to the TV spy series Harry's Game in 1982. She split from the family group but returned in 1988 with the surprise No.1 Orinoco Flow, her trademark. Enya's new-age aura made her a novelty in a decade where the charts were full of flashy careerists. Her success (and the critical respect already accorded to Van Morrison and bands like The Chieftains) may have smoothed the way for **The Corrs**. We still prefer Dexy's **Come On Eileen** though.

Charity

Songs for good causes started off well. **Do They Know It's Christmas?** was compelling – if simplistic – and the Bowie/Jagger version of **Dancin' In The Street** was agreeably camp. But just as charity shops threaten to take over our high streets, fund-raising pop songs are now two a penny. The American Live Aid single **We Are The World** was sent up by a Texan group called **Culturcide**: "They're not the world/They're not the children/They're just bosses and bureaucrats and rock'n'roll has-beens." Sounds harsh – until you watch the We Are The World video.

★**Recommended**★ **Culturcide**'s Tacky Souvenirs Of Pre-Revolutionary America (CS).

Children

One of the strangest pop phenomenons of the 1980s – and there were many – were the **Mini Pops**. Seven British children aged between six and nine, they imitated chart acts such as Culture Club, Kajagoogoo and Survivor by dressing in the same clothes and plastering themselves in make-up. Between 1982 and 1989 this group released seven albums, with titles like *Mini Pops Magic* and *Mini Pops Wanna Have Fun*. Today such flirtatious displays of underage sexuality would incite a **Daily Mail** campaign. But, in days gone by, the public loved to see the likes of little **Jimmy Osmond** grinning his way to chart success. While America had the Osmonds and the Jacksons, Britain had the **St Winifred's School Choir**. Their single There's No One Quite Like Grandma held the coveted Christmas No.1 spot in 1980 and holds a similar rank in most people's Top 10 Worst Records lists.

The first child pop star was shrill-voiced curly-headed **Shirley Temple**. Just six when she had her first hit– **Baby Take A Bow** – she soon earned $300,000 a year. Despite her part in **On The Good Ship Lollipop**, the world held no grudges – when the dimples vanished she became a diplomat. No drug habits, fatalities, mental illnesses, lost royalties or bitter recriminations afflicted Shirl. Which brings us to **Musical Youth**. Their story sums up the perils of being a multi-million-pound business when you're barely old enough to tie your shoelaces. Their 1982 single **Pass The Dutchie** sold five-million copies. Aged between nine and 14, Musical Youth were the first black artists on MTV, the biggest reggae group in the world for a while and counted The A-Team's **Mr T** as a close friend.

They soon regretted leaving the pubs and clubs of Birmingham. "Fun Boy Three tried to talk to us about the business," said singer **Dennis Seaton** once. "But we were asking them, 'Are you going out with Bananarama?'" Brothers Patrick and Junior Waite developed mental problems – not helped by their drug habits – with Junior sectioned and Patrick (after run-ins with the law) dying of heart failure in 1993. The remaining members are barely on speaking terms.

Musical Youth's fall is a familiar tale. **Frankie Lymon**, the 13-year-old singer of 1956 doo-wop hit **Why Do Fools Fall in Love?**, overdosed on heroin in 1968. Winner of the 1973 **Opportunity Knocks** final aged ten, **Lena Zavoroni** became famous and anorexic, dying in 1999 from complications linked to the disease. **Billie Piper**, the youngest person to enter the charts at No.1, wed Chris Evans. **Michael Jackson** may yet face a fate worse than Chris Evans. The moral? If you want a happy, well-balanced adult life, avoid the charts as a child. Still, with events like **Stars In Their Eyes Kids**, it's only a matter of time before we hear a shrill seven-year-old belting out "Fame!" Mini Pops: The Reunion? It could happen…

Christmas

When **Bing Crosby** crooned **White Christmas** in the 1942 movie **Holiday Inn**, he created a showbiz institution. No.1 in the US for 11 weeks in 1942, White Christmas is the best-selling Christmas song ever. Crosby didn't want to record it at first, fearing he'd be accused of commercialising Crimbo. When **Elvis** covered Bing's standard the latter's version prompted Irving Berlin to try to ban it.

Leiber & Stoller offered a less sentimental take on Yuletide with Elvis's **Santa Claus Is Back In Town**, a howled, bluesy classic in which Santa swaps reindeer for a black Cadillac. **Phil Spector** used his trademark 'Wall of Sound' on **A Christmas Gift For You**, reworking classics like Rudolph The Red Nosed Reindeer alongside Darlene Love's magnificent **Christmas (Baby Please Come Home)**. But, with the exception of Harry Belafonte's **Mary's Boy Child** in 1957, there were no Christmas-themed No.1s in the 1950s and 1960s, just the odd Top 10 hit (Brenda Lee's **Rockin' Around The Christmas Tree**).

Glam rock marked a revolution in the Christmas song. Slade's **Merry Christmas Everybody**, Mud's **Lonely This Christmas**, Wizzard's **I Wish It Could Be Christmas Every Day** (No.4) and Elton John's **Step Into Christmas** (No.24) made it clear Santa would come down the chimney in platforms. More traditional, although quirky, was Jona Lewie's **Stop The Cavalry**. The Christmas tradition of the strange double act began when **David Bowie** appeared on Bing Crosby's TV special in 1977, duetting on an intriguing **Little Drummer Boy**, Bowie getting real pathos in his voice as he pines for "peace on earth". In 1980 **Kate Bush** did something very original, releasing a Christmas single (**December Will**

Be Magic Again) you didn't have to get drunk on sherry trifle to like. After Wham!'s **Last Christmas** and Band Aid's **Do They Know It's Christmas?** came Cliff Richard's arm-swayers **Mistletoe & Wine** and **Saviour's Day**. Thank God for **Shane McGowan** and **Kirsty MacColl**'s **A Fairytale In New York**, a No.2 in 1987.

For future Christmas No.1s, give us Spinal Tap's **Christmas With The Devil?**, Half Man Half Biscuit's **All I Want For Christmas Is The Dukla Prague Away Kit** or Keith Richards's touching **Run Rudolph Run**. And, for a festive album, how about **North American Air Defence Tracks Santa** (1962) in which festive music is interspersed with reports on Santa's whereabouts and whether he will be targeted by missiles? Even Phil Spector couldn't top that.

★**Recommended**★ The hits are on **The Best Christmas Album In The World Ever** (Virgin) But treat yourself to **Phil Spector**'s A Christmas Gift For You (ABKO).

Comedy

If a record like **Benny Hill**'s **Ernie (The Fastest Milkman In The West)** reaches No.1, it's a good sign pop is in a fallow period. This section ignores animated comedy records (see Cartoons) and spoofs (see Spoofs) to focus on such tomfoolery as **The Ying Tong Song**, a No.3 for The Goons in 1956 (and No.9 in 1973). American comic Allan Sherman is best known for **Hello Muddah, Hello Faddah!** but his blues take on King Louis XVI (**You Went The Wrong Way Old King Louie**) is funnier. Sadly, he never got to do a Jewish parody of **My Fair Lady**.

Transistor Radio was an affecting Benny Hill novelty, a No.24 hit in 1961 and arguably funnier than his No.1. For all his nudge-nudge faults, Hill's mickey-taking could be very witty (the proof: his *Ultimate Collection* on Castle). **Goodbye-ee!** for **Peter Cook** and **Dudley Moore** was so popular they got to perform it on *ReadySteadyGo!* (a clip is on the RSG Vol.1 video).

They're Coming To Take Me Away, Ha-Haaa! was the only hit for Napoleon XIV who, in real life, was recording-engineer **Jerry Samuels**. A disturbing, if not grating, account of a man being taken away (ha-ha, hee-hee) by those nice young men in their clean white coats, this No.4 hit is backed by **!aaah-aH, yawA eM ekaT oT gnimoC er'yehT** – yes They're Coming To Take Me Away… backwards.

Guy Marks's **Loving You Has Made Me Bananas**, No.25 in 1978, came out of nowhere, with its old-time Tin Pan Alley feel, curious lyrics about a dad who suffered from the shipfitter blues and unique chorus of "**Oh your red scarf matches your eyes**…" It was probably quirkier than Monty Python's **Always Look On The Bright Side Of Life**, No.3 in 1991, although looking on the bright side of death "even as you take your terminal breath" is especially fine.

The Barron Knights have been excluded from this section – for making a record called **Heaving On A Jet Plane**. Rolf Harris and Peter Sellers, on the other hand, so bestride this genre that they are profiled on page 130 and page 159 respectively.

★**Recommended**★ **Half Man Half Biscuit**'s **Back In The DHSS** (Probe) is just hilarious.

Country

Disco excepted, few popular music genres have been shown as much disrespect as country music. What could claim, at its roots, to be the white man's blues, has been caricatured as full of steel guitars and squeaky fiddles, rhinestone cowboys, right-wing rednecks in cowboy hats and dolly birds in sparkly costumes.

The original **Jimmie Rodgers**, the 'father of country music', who died of TB in 1933, has shifted fewer records in the UK than Pinky & Perky. **Hank Williams**, the greatest-ever country singer, never had a UK hit himself. **Johnny Cash** has had two UK Top 5s, while **George Jones**, feted as the greatest living country singer, has never had a UK hit single. But detwang the songs and you might have yourself a hit, hence the bizarre coupling of Spanish balladeer **Julio Iglesias** with eccentric country stylist **Willie Nelson** to produce the Top 20 hit **To All The Girls I've Loved Before**. Nelson, despite huge critical acclaim, has never matched this, even his famous cover of Elvis's Always On My Mind floundering at a lowly No.49 in 1982.

Country sweetened itself with The Nashville Sound in the late 1950s, with orchestration and angelic backing singers which purists called a sell out. It did sell: in the early 1960s the **Everly Brothers**, **Jim Reeves** (see page 157), **Floyd Cramer** and **Marty Robbins** made regular forays into the UK Top 30. Today's country acts make similar adjustments. **The Mavericks** took **Dance The Night Away** to No.4, a song more **Herb Alpert** than country. Shania Twain's new album **Up!** appeared in three versions, the country mix not available officially in the UK. You can see why the camouflage is necessary by glancing at the UK singles chart. **Michael Holliday** hit No.1 covering Marty Robbins's **The Story Of My Life**; **Tom Jones**, **Engelbert Humperdinck** and **Whitney Houston** all took popped-up country songs to No.1.

Real British chart-toppers by country acts have been rare. The first country act to do so was yodeller **Slim Whitman**, No.1 for 11 weeks with **Rose Marie** in 1955. He has been followed by: Floyd Cramer's **On The Rebound** (1961); Roger Miller's **King Of The Road** (1965); Jim Reeves's **Distant Drums** (1966) – the first UK No.1 written exclusively by a woman, Cindy Walker; **Stand By Your Man** (1975) though Tammy Wynette wasn't amused when **Michael Parkinson** pointed out that, with her third divorce due that year, she hadn't lived up to the song; and **Kenny Rogers** (**Lucille** and **Coward Of The County**), the only country act to have two UK No.1s.

Johnny Cash is depressed by his lack of chart success in the UK

Country novelty songs have done well. **JJ Barrie**'s No.1 cover of Melba Montgomery's **No Charge**, the riposte of a mother faced with her boy's bill for household chores, was parodied by **Billy Connolly** – No Chance (No Charge) – before he spoofed Wynette's **D.I.V.O.R.C.E.** to go to No.1. The Bellamy Brothers had their best UK hit with **If I Said You Had A Beautiful Body (Would You Hold It Against Me)**, centred on a Groucho Marx witticism, which made No.3 in 1979.

The success of albums like the soundtrack to **O Brother, Where Art Thou?** (and artists like **Gillian Welch** and **Alison Krauss**) has thrown the spotlight on rootsier country, especially bluegrass, akin to early blues and old American folk music, a reminder that country is more varied than critics allow. Some re-evaluation is long overdue. **Bonnie Raitt** isn't country, but her 1991 album **Luck Of The Draw**, usually billed as a fusion of blues and rock, has a countryish tinge. You hear a lot about the poetry of the blues, but one of Raitt's lines on this album is straight out of Hank Williams: "Why the angels turn their backs on some is a mystery to me."

★**Recommended**★ For a different entry point try Waylon Jennings, Willie Nelson, Jessi Colter and Tompall Glaser on **Wanted! The Outlaws: 1976-1996 20th Anniverary** (RCA), with lost bonus tracks not on the original release, or **Drunk & Nutty Hillbillies Foolin' With The Blues** (Indigo). For male country singers, try **Glen Campbell**'s **My Hits And Love Songs** (Capitol) or **Johnny Cash**'s **American III: Solitary Man** (American). For female singers **Patsy Cline**, **The Patsy Cline Collection** (MCA), a four-CD set, is essential. **Emmylou Harris**'s **Wrecking Ball** (Grapevine), with inspired arrangements by Daniel Lanois, is very listenable.

Coventry

Home to **Terry Hall**, **Hazel O'Connor**, **Pete Waterman** and… **Vince Hill**, who had a No.2 hit with **Edelweiss** in 1967. Vince started in The Raindrops alongside such notables as **Jackie Lee**, whose big hit was **White Horses**. Hill's contribution to the Coventry scene is often neglected as locals talk up The Specials, **Selecter** and the **2-Tone** sound. The Specials weren't the city's first chart-toppers – that honour belongs to **Lieutenant Pigeon**, whose 1972 No.1 **Mouldy Old Dough** was recorded in a Coventry front room and featured the artist's mother.

Cover versions

Sometimes it seems there are no new songs. But then, before The Beatles, writing songs was left to people who had a talent for it (see Brill Building). The cover version, as old as Tin Pan Alley, usually falls into one of five categories. We've filled in a few for each, but there are so many to choose from, you can add your own.

★The "Why Bother?" cover version★

Ain't No Sunshine **Michael Jackson** Sorry, but Bill Withers will always sing his song best.
Isn't She Lovely? **David Parton** A No.4 hit, Stevie Wonder's original never made the charts.
Smells Like Teen Spirit **Abigail** Utterly pointless version of Nirvana's 1991 classic.
You've Lost That Lovin' Feelin' **Cilla Black** Cilla could have saved her breath.

★The "Make It Your Own" cover version★

Always On My Mind **Pet Shop Boys** The boys certainly gave it that 1980s hi-energy twist.
Killing Me Softly **The Fugees** Very, very cool indeed.
Lady Marmalade **Christina Aguilera, Lil' Kim, Mya and Pink** Labelle was never this raunchy.
You've Got A Friend **Brand New Heavies** James Taylor's version just isn't funky enough.
Gangsta's Paradise **Coolio featuring LV** For once, Stevie Wonder is truly outdone. Coolio's song is based on Wonder's Pastime Paradise from the *Songs In The Key Of Life* album.
Kiss **The Art Of Noise featuring Tom Jones** Tom's cover of Prince's hit revived his career.

★The "Didn't Know It Was A Cover" cover version★

Pure and Simple **Hear'Say** Released by Girl Thing the year before Popstars mania hit.
Nothing Compares 2 U **Sinead O'Connor** A Prince song, originally recorded by The Family.
I Heard It Through The Grapevine **Marvin Gaye** Yes, it's one of the all-time classic Motown hits, but the grapevine reached Gladys Knight & The Pips first.

★The "Always Good For A Hit" cover version★

The Tracks Of My Tears A hit for **Smokey Robinson & The Miracles** in 1979, **Linda Ronstadt** in 1976, ex-Zombie **Colin Blunstone** in 1982 and **Go West** in 1993.
You'll Never Walk Alone **Robson & Jerome** You can always rely on Liverpool fans buying this, as they did for **Gerry & The Pacemakers**, **Elvis**, **The Crowd** and even **The Three Tenors**.

★The "It'll Make People Laugh" cover version★

Achy Breaky Heart **Alvin & The Chipmunks** Sometimes a song gets the cover it deserves.
Wonderwall **Mike Flowers Pops** and Mr Tambourine Man **William Shatner**

Cowboy

You don't get many hits about cowboys these days. The last was probably **Where Have All The Cowboys Gone?** by **Paula Cole** in 1997 – one of those records that was ubiquitous rather than bought, despite Cole's generous offer to do all the laundry if her cowboy paid the bills.

But in the 1950s songs of gunfighters, horses and beans filled the charts. Yet many of these songs are brutally honest about the West. In **Johnny Cash**'s **Don't Take Your Guns To Town**, recklessness proves fatal. Another song, **Boot Hill**, is named after Tombstone's cemetery. And in Eddy Arnold's **Partners**, he says chillingly "The food ran low so I killed my friend/What else was there to do?"

Some cowboy songs are drippily sentimental: about the bond between men, between man and horse ("Oh there never was a hoss like the Tennessee stud…") and, rarely, between a man and his girl (**High Noon**, a No.7 hit for Laine). **Marty Robbins** penned some fine ballads about love gone wrong. **Devil Woman** reached No.5 in 1962, though the lesser-known **Ribbon Of Darkness** is better. Yet the cowboy songs people remember are Laine's No.6 hit, the rolling, rolling, rolling **Rawhide**. In the 1970s Glen Campbell took the cowboy to the big city with his No.4 hit **Rhinestone Cowboy**. Sadly the best cowboy song, Willie Nelson's **Mama Don't Let Your Babies Grow Up To Be Cowboys**, never even charted in the UK.

The neglect that the western half of country and western has suffered is ironic. Pioneers like **Bob Wills & His Texas Playboys** began, in the 1940s, to fuse country, folk, blues and jazz, anticipating the 1950s fusion that created rock'n'roll.

★**Recommended**★ Eddy Arnold **Cattle Call** (Bear) is worth buying for the multi-coloured golfing socks sported by Eddy on the cover, and the songs are pretty good too. The **Essential Marty Robbins** (Columbia) has the great gunfighter ballads and **Ribbon Of Darkness**.

Cricket

Apart from Sherbet's **Howzat** (No.4 in 1976) cricket has made less impression on the pop charts than the England cricket team has made on the cricket World Cup. Folk legend **Roy Harper** wrote the seminal song **When An Old Cricketer Leaves The Crease**, **Elton John** was at the crease on the sleeve of **Greatest Hits II** and **Rory Bremner** spoofed Paul Hardcastle's **19**. Even **Ian Botham** hasn't had a novelty hit. Cricket's finest moment on the singles chart is its appearance in the chorus of **10cc**'s No.1 **Dreadlock Holiday** ("I don't like cricket, oh no, I love it").

Dance

Friedrich Nietzsche noted, "We should consider every day lost in which we do not dance at least once." Still, Germany's most notorious philosopher never had to sit down on the dance floor in a line of make-believe rowers and chant "**Agadoo-doo-doo**". Dance music has come on since the days of **Black Lace** (who also had a hit called Superman, another concept with which Nietszche was not unfamiliar). The founding fathers of dance music, **Danny Rampling**, **Paul Oakenfold** and

Nicky Holloway, chose the Balearic island of **Ibiza** as their holiday destination, but returned with far more than a suntan. They found Ibiza buzzing with a strange fusion of sounds, soul, electronic beats, even Italian disco.

On their return from Ibiza Rampling opened Shoom, Oakenfold Spectrum and Holloway The Trip. Within months 'rave' culture was born. Abhorred by police, parents and the media, rave died in the mid-1990s and house went back to clubs.

Even the best DJ can't produce a decent track without a decent starting point. Knowing what will become a dance classic isn't easy. How did Armand Van Helden know singer/songwriter Tori Amos's **Professional Widow** would be the 1990s dance anthem? Or that, with tinkering, Faithless's **Insomnia** would get even better? Faithless are one of the most imaginative dance acts, alongside Orbital (named after the M25), Apollo 440, FC Kahuna and Basement Jaxx. No.1 releases by Danny Rampling et al are thin on the ground, but acts such as Fatboy Slim and Armand Van Helden have popularised a more commercial brand of dance music.

★**Recommended**★ Northern Exposure: Expeditions (Incredible), mixed by **Sasha & John Digweed**, excels. **Faithless**'s Reverence (Cheeky) fuses house, blues, reggae and soul.

Dance crazes

"Hey everybody gather round/Listen to that bongo sound!" That's the authentic sound of the **Clam**, a shortlived dance craze inserted into one of Elvis's 1960s movies. The Clam was fairly simple – it involved walking up and down a ridge of sand and rubbing shoulders with your significant other. **The Hucklebuck** was more taxing, which may be why, despite being popularised by **Chubby Checker**, it never caught on. The choreographers instructions began "back rock, shuffle step, step half pivot right, triple turn half right", and after 11 more sequences like that you'd mastered the Hucklebuck and snapped your calf muscles.

Dance crazes have punctuated pop history. The **Jive** dominated dance halls in the 1950s, but in the 1960s, fuelled by the **Twist**, crazes were invented, became popular and died at breakneck speed. The 1960s also saw the **Limbo**, the **Pony**, the **Fly**, the **Mess Around**, and the Freddie, created by **Freddie & The Dreamers**.

Noel Coward had whined in the 1920s: "Down with the modern dance!… Down with the shimmie shake". You wonder how Noel felt when he first heard the hippy hippy shake. Most of these crazes (the **Dog**, the **Mashed Potato** and the **Frug** – not as rude as it sounded) made you feel more danced against than with, going against the point of dancing as the perpendicular expression of a horizontal desire.

The pace of innovation (or hype) slowed in the 1970s, although in the last 30 years we have hustled to **Van McCoy**, breakdanced, lambada'd and got lost halfway through the **Macarena**, stood around for a bit and then joined in the final chant of "Oh, Macarena!" as if we knew what we were doing all along.

Denmark

The nation that gave us Hamlet and Kierkegaard has never brought to pop the clout it has brought to suicidal indecision and existentialist philosophy. **Sannie Charlotte Carlson**, who called herself Whigfield in honour of her favourite teacher, kicked off her chart career with the Eurodance No.1 **Saturday Night**. But soon Carlson was back to being big in mainland Europe. **Aqua** (see Europop) have done as much for Denmark's musical reputation with their Barbie record as Danny Kaye's **Wonderful Copenhagen**, a No.5 hit in 1953. Greatest Danes of all are the Baron and Baroness, **Nina & Frederick**. They were a real baron and baroness who slummed it by recording such classics as **Little Donkey**.

Disco

Today the very word 'disco' sounds like an expletive, so low has the critical stock of the 1970s essential genre fallen. Even the 1970s revival hasn't helped restore the credibility of a genre that was dominated by producers (like **Giorgio Moroder**) and created relatively few enduring stars (**Rose Royce** and **Chic**). Yet in some ways, disco was a return to rock'n'roll's roots, with a healthy emphasis on the beat and a recognition that dancing lay at the root of popular music's appeal.

Originally disco records (a reaction against the bloated, burned-out hulk of prog rock) were designed with one aim in mind – to keep crowds at clubs in New York on the dance floor for as long as possible. But the real stars of disco – like the Jackson Sisters' fantastic **I Believe In Miracles** or Sylvester's gospelly **Mighty Real** – were black and soulful. Outsiders soon cashed in, creating all sorts of watered-down trash. The movie **Saturday Night Fever** spread the sound to the masses, but it was this emasculated, soulless cuckoo – as opposed to the joyful, spiritual original – that hijacked the name. The feeling that disco was a svengali's medium (think **Frank Farian** with Boney M or **Jacques Morali** with Village People), the association with unapologetic homosexuality (long before it was acceptable, let alone trendy) and the fact that so many established acts (the Bee Gees, Rod Stewart, even The Rolling Stones) exploited the sound didn't help disco's cause.

But claiming that disco sucked per se was as daft as saying the blues sucked. The genre did create one truly gifted act, **Chic**, who had a genuine groove going and influenced funk, dance and hip hop. Nile Rodgers's rhythm guitar and Bernard Edwards's bass lines have been reproduced, ripped off and paid homage to countless times. After a decade where the average rock lyric was full of pretention, it was good to hear a band who felt it was enough to rhyme "le chic" with "le freak".

★**Recommended**★ C'Est Chic (Atlantic). Check out the Mastercuts series of compilations.

Doo-wop

Bo-bo bom-bom-a-bop-a, dang-a-dang-dang, yip-yip-yip-yip-yip-yip-yip-yip, changety-changety-changety-chang-chang… You can understand why, as a genre, doo-wop has been seen as lacking a certain gravitas, but rock's vocal range would be nowhere near as wide without groups like the **Orioles** (whose It's Too Soon To Know, a 1948 hit in the US, is often cited as the first real doo-wop record), The Chords ("Sh-boom, life is but a dream…") and Dion & The Belmonts. When Dion woh-oh-ohed his way into Runaround Sue, a No.11 in 1961, he displayed more energy than almost anyone else in that year's ennui-laden singles chart.

Doo-wop was all about the interplay of a vocal group, with each singer taking a different part to weave together an unmistakeable sound. The backing singers weighed in with nonsense noises like doo and, er, wop, hence the genre's name. Doo-wop's roots go back to vocal groups like **The Mills Brothers** in the 1930s, but its trademark vocal noises were soon absorbed into rock and soul – its influence on the **The Beach Boys** is obvious. Doo-wop is one of the most democratic forms of pop – you don't even need to buy a guitar – and its influence lives on. **The Darts** (**It's Raining, The Boy From New York City**) brought the sounds back into the UK chart in the 1970s, even if they weren't wholly serious. Billy Joel paid homage to doo-wop with **The Longest Time**, which deserved better than to stick at No.25 in 1984. You can also hear doo-wop's echoes in mainstream acts like Hall & Oates.

★**Recommended**★ For a long, delightful residence in doo-wop heaven, buy The Doo-Wop Box Vol.1 (Rhino), 100 tracks and hardly a dud among them. One of the best but not best known – to the public – R&B doo-wop bands was **The Coasters** and their 1998 Very Best Of (Rhino) is great – their Blue Velvet makes Bobby Vinton's sound as bland as a water biscuit.

Double acts

In pop, two egos are not better than one. Only a few can cope with the cat-fights, sorry, profound creative differences which occur. The duo isn't one of the archetypal rock'n'roll line-ups, although it's a healthy tradition in R&B (Robert & Johnny, Sam & Dave) and The Beach Boys precursors **Jan & Dean** were massively influential, only parting when Jan Berry almost died in a car accident.

Drummer jokes

How can you tell when the stage riser is level?
The drool comes evenly from both sides of the drummer's mouth.
How can you make a drummer slow down?
Put a sheet of music in front of him.
What's the difference between a drummer and a drum machine?
With a drum machine you only have to punch the information in once.
What's the difference between a drummer and a trampoline?
You take your shoes off to jump on a trampoline.

Captain & Tenille, whose biggest hit in the UK was **Do That To Me One More Time**, are a rarity, still married today while **Sonny & Cher** and **Ike & Tina** accepted their decree absolute's long ago. But you don't have to be married to fall out with your singing partner. Having recorded together for 13 years, **Simon & Garfunkel** simply tired of one another. They reconciled briefly in the late 1970s, but a studio album was cancelled: "artistic differences". Absence doesn't make the heart grow fonder if the person who's not around happens to be Art Garfunkel.

Smile

Opportunity knocked

A similar plight befell soul legends **Sam & Dave**. Nicknamed Double Dynamite, on stage they had chemistry, but behind the scenes they were explosive, separating in 1970 at the height of their fame. **Peters & Lee** didn't split, they just drifted apart, saying adios in 1980 and reuniting in 1986 to play holiday camps, before Lennie died of cancer. Their success inspired the singing miners **Millican & Nesbitt**, who made polite versions of such classics as **Vaya Con Dios**. They wore tuxedos which – this being 1973, the year of the three-day week – were designed to reassure middle England that these particular miners wouldn't be cutting off our power supply. And they weren't a patch on America's top duo **Hall & Oates**, the bestselling duo in pop history, even outselling the Bellamy Brothers.

In the 1980s **Wham!** convinced many wannabes the key to chart success was forming a duo comprising of one half flamboyance and the other quiet mystery (think **Pet Shop Boys**, **Soft Cell** and **The Communards**). And then there was Yazoo. **Eurythmics**, the most durable 1980s duo, decided to record together although they were no longer an item. Their hiatus – in 1990 – was due to deflated sales not inflated egos. Stewart then helped wife Siobhan Fahey shun Bananarama to form **Shakespear's Sister** with Marcella Detroit. Their fifth single, **Stay**, hit No.1, but "artistic differences" intruded.

The boy-girl duo became a popular combination with Dollar, although their demise, instigated by the twosome's split off-stage, pointed at the perils in this route. Abused for producing shallow pop songs with teasingly catchy hooks, Roxette became national treasures in Sweden, honoured on postage stamps and calling their greatest hits album **Don't Bore Us And Get To The Chorus**. Duos dried up in the 1990s but bounced back in the Noughties with **Cheeky Girls** and **t.A.T.u** and indie acts such as the enigmatic **The White Stripes**, who may be ex-spouses or siblings. In dance music, acts such as **The Chemical Brothers** (no relation), have found two knob-twiddlers are better than one.

★Recommended★ The Best Of Peters & Lee (Spectrum), be brave; The Final **Wham** (Epic); Elephant **The White Stripes** (Xl); The Original **Jan & Dean** (Disky); The Contino Sessions **Death In Vegas** (Concrete); Like The Deserts Miss The Rain **Everything But The Girl** (Virgin); This Is The Story **The Proclaimers** (Chrysalis); Sacred Songs **Daryl Hall & Robert Fripp** (RCA); and The Best Of Sam & Dave **Sam & Dave** (Rhino).

Drummers

What do you call someone who hangs round with musicians? A drummer. It's an old gag, and, as most of the daftest men in pop have been tub-thumpers, probably a fair one. But the chap at the bottom of the musical food chain deserves respect. Drums are the world's oldest instrument, used through millennia for religious and communication purposes, and every genre of popular music is defined by its beats. Whether it's the swing of jazz and blues, the bop of Merseybeat, the thunder of rock or the relentless pounding of rave – drum patterns determine the songs.

The debate over the world's finest-ever sticksman usually leads to one name: **Buddy Rich**. "The greatest drummer ever to draw breath," noted contemporary **Gene Krupa**. Rich was as unpopular as his technique was astonishing. A short-tempered perfectionist, he was loathed by most colleagues and well known as the man Frank Sinatra hated most in the world. No mean feat.

Better liked, and just as influential, was **Ringo Starr** – although he hardly had Buddy's awesome chops. Stupidly derided as "not even the best drummer in The Beatles", Starr's timing was so impeccable he rarely needed a metronome. He understood the importance of playing what was right for a song and not showing off. The drum sounds he achieved with **George Martin** were revolutionary, too. Almost as great are **Stuart Copeland**, whose reggae-inspired beats powered The

Police, **Roger Taylor** of Queen and **Charlie Watts** – a jazzman at heart, and the only Stone left with dignity intact. A few social-climbing traitors have left the drum stool to front a band, chief among them **Dave Grohl**, who traded being the best rock-thumper around with Nirvana for fronting Foo Fighters.

Most fun though are the holy trinity of rock loons: Bonham, Moon and Wilson. Led Zeppelin's **John Bonham** had, Jimi Hendrix noted, a "right foot like a rabbit" and attacked his kit with unbelievable gusto. But "Bonzo" approached his drinking likewise, and died in 1980 after downing 40 vodkas. The Who's **Keith Moon** played the kit like a lead instrument and drank his great friend Oliver Reed under the table – which proved his undoing. Topping them all was **Dennis Wilson**. The most dysfunctional Beach Boy (sorry Brian), Wilson combined shambling alcoholism with wonderful harmonies and perfect drumming. Once scaling the World Trade Center without a rope for bet, he married five times before falling drunkenly to his death off a boat. Only a drummer…

★**Recommended**★ Led Zeppelin **Led Zeppelin I** (Atlantic), John Bonham at his terrifying best; Buddy Rich **Mercy Mercy** (Live), logic-defying drumrollery; The Police **Zenyatta Mondatta** (A&M), Copeland's seamless blend of reggae, percussion and pop, pity about the songs; The Beatles **Abbey Road** (Apple), possibly the ultimate drum sound.

Duets

In any 'How To Be A Popstar' almanac, the much-thumbed section on reviving your career is guaranteed to suggest finding a nubile partner for a duet. It's been pivotal to the regeneration of the furry-chested **Tom Jones**'s career and been a tactic employed by those two great divas, Barbra Streisand and Elton John.

Elton knows just how to play the duet game, hitting No.1 with both Don't Go Breaking My Heart (with **Kiki Dee**) and Don't Let The Sun Go Down On Me (**George Michael**). Babs has always been a fan of the duet, partly as the vocal equivalent of an Olympic event. On **No More Tears (Enough Is Enough)** she gets the gold and poor old Donna Summer gets the silver.

The duet was a common feature of the Hollywood musical. In the 1930s **Judy Garland** and **Mickey Rooney** seldom stopped crooning on-screen. But movie duets didn't hit the charts until Bing's romantic single True Love (sung with Grace Kelly) from *High Society*, went platinum, reaching the Top 5 in the UK and US.

Since then, movie-related duets have only sporadically found audiences. In 1978 **John Travolta** and **Olivia Newton-John** reached No.1 on both sides of the Atlantic with **You're The One That I Want**, (the Arthur Mullard-Hylda Baker version stalled at No.22). As chart-topping winsome twosomes go, this was only really matched when Nicole Kidman and Robbie teamed up on **Somethin' Stupid**.

The duet isn't solely about flagging careers and novelty turns. The combination of **Kenny Rogers** and **Dolly Parton** was a veritable world summit of teeth and hair as they sparkled through **Islands In The Stream** in 1983. Diana Ross was happy to tangle tonsils with Lionel Ritchie on **Endless Love** and Marvin Gaye on **You Are Everything**, although Gale's duets with **Tammi Terrell** (especially **If I Could Build My Whole World Around You**) are more satisfying. The public probably assumed 'Jennifer Warnes and' was actually Jennifer's full name; thanks to her duets with **Joe Cocker** on **Up Where We Belong** and Bill Medley on **(I've Had) The Time Of My Life,** Jennifer will always be that girl who sung with so-and-so.

Today the duet is more popular than ever. Eminem added a new dimension with his 1999 hit **Stan**. Most viewers thought the girl in the video was an actress, not Eminem's singing partner **Dido**. The idea of being an unrecognised pop star hasn't caught on (though **Dean Friedman** tried the same trick with a UFV – unidentified female voice – in his No.3 1978 hit **Lucky Stars**). Duetting with dead people (KD Lang and Roy Orbison, Robbie and Sinatra, Natalie Cole and her dad Nat) is very fashionable, but seems too close to a musical seance for comfort.

★**Recommended**★ This is a list of the best, the most unusual and the so bad they need to be heard to be believed: **Islands In The Stream** **Dolly Parton & Kenny Rogers** is on Parton's **The Ultimate Collection** (RCA); **Don't Know Much** **Linda Ronstadt & Aaron Neville** is on **The Very Best Of Linda Ronstadt** (Rhino); **The Skye Boat Song** **Des O'Connor & Roger Whittaker** is on **The Very Best Of Roger Whittaker** (Spectrum); **I've Got You Under My Skin** **Frank Sinatra & Count Basie** is on **Sinatra At The Sands** (Reprise); **Dancing In The Street** **David Bowie & Mick Jagger** is on **The Best Of Bowie** **David Bowie** (EMI); and **Hand In Glove** **Sandie Shaw & The Smiths** is on **Hatful Of Hollow** (WEA).

Easy listening

This can describe almost any kind of soft soothing music, be it **Acker Bilk**'s saxophone doodling **Stranger On The Shore** or the syrupy sounds of **Andy Williams** singing **Home Lovin' Man**. The focus here is on such masters of orchestral maneuvres as **Ray Conniff**, **Percy Faith** (his theme from the movie **A Summer Place** was No.2 in 1960) and **Mantovani** (who had four Top 10 hits including a No.1 with **The Song From The Moulin Rouge** in the 1950s). Orchestras have never had it so good, although **Henry Mancini** (Moon River) and Simon Park (**Eye Level**, TV theme, No.1 in 1973) have had their moments. TV and movie themes have often given easy listening sounds a kick up the charts. Ennio Morricone's **Chi Mai**, the theme to a BBC biopic of David Lloyd

George, is a case in point, as it soared to No.2. Morricone has created some classic movie and TV themes and Chi Mai isn't one of them. Hugo Montenegro's harsh, evocative theme to **The Good, The Bad And The Ugly** was a surprise No.1 in 1968.

★**Recommended**★ Morricone's **A Fistful Of Sounds** (Camden) is very easy to listen to.

Europop

Hooray! Hooray! It's A Holiday
Boney M.
Ribbons Of Blue

The mighty-fine Boney M

Catch all term for lightweight, slick and often daft pop music produced in Europe. Epitomised at its best by **Abba**, (and at its worst by **Aqua**, who spawned **Barbie Girl**), Europop has intermittently influenced the UK charts. **Boney M** epitomised **Eurodance**, lightweight, slick and often a bit daft pop you could dance to. Created by German record producer **Frank Farian** (who later masterminded **Milli Vanilli**), Boney M consisted of four West Indians who had served as session singers in Germany. Marcia Barrett, Liz Mitchell, Maizie Williams and Bobby Farrell, who was always exposing his naked chest, were one of the 1970s most consistent chart acts even if in the US they never got past No.11 (with their first single **Daddy Kool**). Most of their biggest hits were remakes but Boney M still sold millions of singles; no Europop act has come close since.

★**Recommended**★ **Night Flight To Venus** (BMG) **Rasputin**, with its stunning use of balalaikas and rhyme (Rasputin/love machine), is just one of many highlights.

Eurovision

Europe's greatest annual musical melodrama isn't really about pop music, as **Ronnie Hazlehurst** made clear when he conducted the orchestra for Britain's 1977 entry with an umbrella. The first contest, in 1956, was held and won by Switzerland, who pipped a cheery Belgian entry **The Drowned Men Of The River Seine**. The event peaked in the late 1960s and early 1970s when real pop stars like Sandie Shaw, Olivia Newton-John, Cliff and Abba entered; in Abba's case twice – the Swedish panel rejected their 1973 effort **Ring Ring**. In 1969 a young **Elton John** offered his song I Can't Go On Living Without You as the UK entry but **Boom Bang A Bang** was preferred with, Elton admitted, good reason.

Although Eurovision has had a string of chart hits (including nine No.1s), it

The sound of Eurovision

Binge bong, binge bong, boom bang a bang, boom boom boomerang, bana, bana, la, la, la, a-ba-ni-bi, diggi loo diggi lee, didai didai dai, ring a ding girl, sing sang song, pump pump, voi, voi, oui, oui, oui, oui, opera, opera, opera, opera, opera, opera... (The Turkish entry in 1983 consisted entirely of the word "opera" repeated over and over: all the other noises here are either titles or hooks of Eurovision entries).

hasn't created that much great pop. **Nel Blue Dipinto Di Blue,** which came third for Italian singer **Domenico Modugno** in 1959, was sublimely recast in English as **Volare. Waterloo** is OK on record but isn't as much fun if you're not marvelling at Agnetha's outfit. **Puppet On A String** is good enough to boom bang a bang on about. But Eurovision did give 150-million people their first glimpse of **Riverdance.** After that, you're left with some daft song titles, beautifully biased voting and live performances, ranging from the sublime (Abba) to shambling incompetence (UK's point-less 2003 entry, Jemini's **Cry Baby**).

★**Recommended**★ The Story Of Eurovision (BR) has 40 tracks. You've been warned.

Exeter

This posh, slightly dull city gave us **Tony Burrows**, the voice behind **Love Grows, United We Stand, Gimme Dat Ding, Beach Baby** and others too monotonous to mention; 18 of them are on the 1996 compilation **Love Grows** (Varese).

Families

It seems such a good idea. Get together with your brothers and sisters, form a band, have some hits, make a mint and keep all the money in the family. Sadly, not all kin are as harmonious as the Von Trapps. The **Osmonds** are all still pals (and probably swapping toothbrushes), but we all know what the Jackson 5 led to.

Ma, and pa, and kids too is fine for a while, but the generation gap usually kicks in. **The Dooleys** (Anne, Frank, Helen, Jim, John, Kathy were all pure Dooleys and Bob Walsh was married to Anne; Alan Bogan, eighth member of the dizzy troupe, wasn't married to any of them) are the largest family group to chart in the UK. They had two hits people remember and only one worth remembering, **Wanted.**

Pairs of brothers are fruitful but complicated teams. Phil and Don Everly toured happily for 17 years until Phil smashed his guitar on stage and stormed off. (They did reunite for one memorable concert in 1983.) Noel and Liam Gallagher are hardly poster boys for sensible sibling rivalry. Yet Ron and Russell Male, the brothers in **Sparks!**, have always found their band big enough for both of them and **The Proclaimers** have shown brotherly love can endure.

Of course, there are bands that sound like they should be a family but aren't, like the **Thompson Twins** (named after the Tintin characters). Even though the **Ramones** were called Johnny Ramone, Joey Ramone etc, they were not related to each other at all. From a sanity point of view, it's probably better that way.

★**Recommended**★ The Record **Bee Gees** (Polydor), you should be dancing; the Everly Brothers (Cadence); Jump **The Pointer Sisters** (BMG), all the threesome's hits; We Are Family **Sister Sledge** (Atlantic), debut album from four sisters who got started in their opera-singing grandmother's gospel church; ABC **The Jackson 5** (Tamla Motown), it's still hard to resist the upbeat groove of little Michael and his brothers; The Singles **Osmonds** (BR Music), all the sparkly teeth classics and a few Donny and Marie hits; Middle Of Nowhere **Hanson** (Mercury), Mmmbop was the first debut single to reach No.1 in the US and UK at the same time – they could still have a comeback, once they've got the hang of shaving; and Ramones (Sire), not really a family, but you should have this album anyway.

flower power

When Jack Kerouac wanted to be a singer, he wanted to emulate laid-back, stoned jazz crooners like Chet Baker, not Elvis. But when **Bob Dylan** went electric, pop suddenly appealed to the Beat Generation. The real flowering of that change came in 1967, the year of the 'Summer of Love'. It's easy to mock now, but things were very different in the shadow of the draft for the Vietnam War – the genesis of the peace and love movement. Folk singer **Scott McKenzie** hit No.1 with San Francisco (Be Sure To Wear Some Flowers In Your Hair), co-written by John Phillips of The Mamas And The Papas. The quartet were flower-power standard-bearers, trying to create something beautiful as a protest against the ugliness of war; its anti-materialism and heart-on-sleeve naïveté part of the attraction. And then there were the drugs. Flower power mutated into hippydom and psychedelic rock. To quote Nik Cohn, music was "swamped by groups, ugly bastards with beards and matted hair and intense feet, who screamed obscenities at Mister America as he passed."

British attempts at both flower power and psychedelia were quirky at best. The Flowerpot Men (who made No.4 with Let's Go To San Francisco) were hired session men in paisley shirts. The Move (who hit No.5 with I Can Hear The Grass

Grow and No.2 with **Flowers In The Rain**) were nearer the mark, but the quintessential British psychedelic record is Traffic's trippy **Hole In My Shoe** (No.2, later parodied by Neil from the **Young Ones** and, rather more affectionately, by **XTC** in their psychedelic alter ego, **The Dukes Of Stratosfear**). All these hits burst upon the charts in 1967 – as did the Animals' **San Franciscan Nights**, a No.7 – the overkill prematurely ending the hippy phase. The hippy/psychedelia movement was never as intense in the UK as in California, because British youth didn't have as pressing a reason for escapism and wasn't taking the same drugs.

Psychedelic rock, which offered musicians who felt enslaved by the three-minute single the chance to be artists, would be hugely influential through bands like Pink Floyd. The Doors and Jefferson Airplane grabbed the headlines, especially with **Grace Slick**'s interpretation of **Lewis Carroll**'s advice "Feed your head" in White Rabbit, but Arthur Lee's **Love** were genuinely different. They weren't together long but they made two fine albums: **Da Capo** (1967) which mingled perfect pop, proto-punk angst and Utopianism, and the demented, essential **Forever Changes** (1967).

★**Recommended**★ The seminal sound of psychedelic 1967 is still Sgt Pepper. But **Moby Grape**'s self-titled album (San Francisco) is a reminder of what might have been for a promising band. **The Great Society** didn't live to see the big time, singer **Grace Slick** leaving after their debut single to join **Jefferson Airplane** (and taking Somebody To Love with her) but they were real pioneers, and Born To Be Burned (Sundazed) is worth the money. **Jefferson Airplane's** career is best sampled on the drolly titled Worst Of (RCA).

folk

Satirical folk singer **Martin Mull** probably summed up folk best when he told the BBC in 1985: "I was involved in the Great Folk Music Scare back in the sixties, when it almost caught on. It was close for a time, but fortunately…"

Folk music began to make a commercial impact in the mid-1950s when groups like the **Kingston Trio** would excavate some relic like **Tom Dooley** and turn it into such a cheery singalong you almost forget Tom gets hanged. To traditionalists. these acts were anathema. Folk needed an act to reconcile diehards and commercial folkies and it found one in **Peter, Paul & Mary**. They didn't sound threatening, yet, with **Mary Travers**'s radio-friendly but distinctive voice, could steer tougher, political songs like **Blowing In The Wind** near the top of the charts.

Soon Dylan, Joan Baez, Tim Hardin, Judy Collins, Tom Paxton, Buffy Sainte Marie, The Byrds, Sonny & Cher and Donovan would find a niche, with Dylan America's most intriguing pop-cultural force since Elvis. **The Lovin' Spoonful** are best known for **Summer In The City** but the group's leader, John Sebastian, also penned the tender **Darling Be Home Soon** and **Do You Believe In Magic?** with its, well, magical line, "It's like trying to tell a stranger about rock and roll." For **The Mamas And Papas**, writer/co-leader **John Phillips** could drop unsettling insight into a song as commercial as **California Dreamin'**. (In the song, warmth is love "and the preacher likes the cold".) At their worst, says **Nik Cohn**, "they sounded like a hip Ray Coniff." Simon & Garfunkel sold wistful irony, soppiness and loneliness, their breakthrough **Mrs Robinson** covered by **Frank Sinatra** in his **New York New York** Vegas-cabaret style: "And here's to you…[pow] Mrs Robinson…"

In the 1970s singer/songwriters (some, like **James Taylor** and **Janis Ian**, very gifted) took over, Dylan mislaid the plot and **Ralph McTell** moaned on a pub jukebox that he'd like to take us through the streets of London. Folk is vibrant today, witness the rise of **Kate Rusby** (and the posthumous success of **Eva Cassidy**), while **REM** have conquered the world with folk rock. But folk doesn't hold sway over the charts as it did, for a time, in the 1960s.

★**Recommended**★ **Buffalo Springfield**'s self-titled debut album (Atco) proves they really were the finest band ever to be formed after one member (**Stephen Stills**) spotted another (**Neil Young**) driving a hearse on Sunset Boulevard. And for **Peter, Paul & Mary Ten Years Together** (Warner) has their best and worst. The sarcastic **I Dig Rock'n'Roll Music** makes it clear that the reason **Peter and Paul** didn't dig it was because they couldn't bloody sing it.

Football

The heyday of the football pop single, the 1970s, was a lean period for English football and for pop. Qualifying for a World Cup being beyond our lads, they hung around recording studios instead. The best that can be said of fluff like **Kevin Keegan**'s **Head Over Heels** (a No.31 hit in 1979) is that it was no worse than many other exploitation singles of its era. The same applies to **Diamond Lights** (a No.12 hit for Glenn and Chris in 1987). As for the **FA Cup single**, the novelty of seeing your boys grinning their way through **Top Of The Pops** soon wore off.

Football and pop have usually mixed about as well as, well, football and rugby. The honourable exceptions being England's 1990 World Cup collaboration with New Order, **World In Motion**, and the Skinner And Baddiel/Lightning Seeds joint venture **Three Lions**, the theme for Euro 96 and No.1 again in the run-up to France 98, which had lyrics that were vaguely intelligent. But even this isn't quite as great as the urgent, indestructible **Match Of The Day** theme. Sadly, they didn't play it at Cardinal Basil Hume's funeral – as he had originally suggested.

★**Recommended**★ If you must, try **The Ultimate Football Anthems** (Crimson).

France

America has never got why the French love **Jerry Lewis**. And the French have never, despite **Johnny Hallyday**'s best efforts, got rock and roll. French popular music evolved from the cabarets and music halls of Paris and, until Bill Haley rocked the joint, was not that dissimilar to British and American pop.

Performers like **Edith Piaf** (and, less so, **Maurice Chevalier**) were appreciated across the world. Belgian-born **Jacques Brel** has exerted a massive gravitational influence on pop. But other French artists have been regarded as novelty acts (Serge Gainsbourg, **Jean Michel-Jarre**), blonde bombshells (**Brigitte Bardot**, Vanessa Paradis), domestic replicas of international idols (Hallyday, the French Elvis), or a speciality of limited local appeal, the musical equivalent of certain smelly cheeses (**Sacha Distel**). This has begun to change with the rise of electronica acts like **Daft Punk** (No.2 in 2000 with **One More Time**). Two acts are partially exempt from this scorn. **Francoise Hardy** is a cult object, working with the likes of Damon Albarn ("How nice looking is he?" she said of Mr Blur). **Charles Aznavour** (No.1 in 1974 with **She**) was voted the voice of the 20th century by *Time* magazine; a tad OTT, but truer than the British 'Charles Aznovoice' caricature.

Pop stars have been known to parlez Franglais, eg Bill Wyman's ferry-crossing into French patois (**Si Si Je Suis Un Rock Star**) and Labelle's **Lady Marmalade** (sub-titled Voulez-Vous Coucher Avec Moi Ce Soir, the formal 'vous' being very polite). Both deserved, as Bonnie Tyler put it in her 1976 hit, to be **Lost In France**.

★Recommended★ A French Affair is over-priced, and sadly includes Richard Clayderman, but has lots of good stuff. **Sylvie Vartan**, born in Bulgaria, made it in France. Her 1962 album **Twist Et Chante** ('Twist And Shout') is a set of French language covers of pop hits. The best track **(I'm Watching) Every Little Move You Make**, anticipates Sting by 20 years.

Funk

James Brown freed R&B from the restrictions of the 45rpm single and the verse/chorus alternation of the classic pop song. He laid the roots for funk (slang for 'stink') with his insistent **Papa's Got A Brand New Pig Bag**. Soon the groove became everything, giving artists like Brown, **George Clinton** (who created two of the most influential funk acts, Parliament and Funkadelic) and **Sly & The Family Stone**, room to improvise like a psychedelic act. Funk was the emerging hard-hitting sound of the 1970s until disco smoothed off some of the raw edges. Judge funk by chart positions, and its influence in the UK seems minimal. Brown's **Get**

Up (I Feel Like A Sex Machine) didn't even grace the Top 30. But funk's energy, rawness and attitude influenced hip hop and rap. And in the 1990s, white music buyers, turned on by hip hop, rediscovered funk's early classic recordings.

★**Recommended**★ **James Brown**'s The Jungle Groove (Polydor) is the definitive collection of the Godfather's early 1970s funk.

Garage

Garage is a simple word that covers a multitude of styles and artists, but whose key common elements are energy and commitment rather than technical polish. The original garage sound was created by American beat bands in the mid-1960s, many of whom really rehearsed in their parents' garages. The music's primeval energy is best summed up by The Kingsmen's notorious **Louie Louie** (see page 269). This basic rock'n'roll sound encompassed hundreds of bands, stand outs include **? And The Mysterians** (see Symbols) and **Sam The Sham & The Pharaohs**, who, on the cusp of frat rock and garage rock, hit No.11 with **Wooly Bully** in 1965. This 1960s sound is best sampled on the Nuggets compilations on Rhino, in which Patti Smith Group guitarist **Lenny Kaye** had a hand.

The 1980s version of garage is a blacker affair associated with New York's **Paradise Garage** and New Jersey's **Zanzibar** dance clubs. Garage and house, hard to tell apart for a while, shared the same roots – indie black music made for local clubs. New York's garage scene had a soulful, more R&B sound than Chicago's disco-derived cousin, and by the 1990s British passion for this music was funding a host of New York labels. Check out **Blaze**, who recorded and produced club classics under various names and were briefly at Motown (start with **Best of Blaze: 1988–2002**, on Handcut). In the UK, garage evolved into speed (later 2-step) garage, a blend of ragga (crudely put, reggae with digital instruments and gangsta leanings), diva-ish vocal lines and remorseless drum and bass rhythms. Acts like **Artful Dodger**, early collaborators with **Craig David**, made the charts, as did **So Solid Crew** before they became better known for their firearm dealings.

Garage rock returned in the 1980s on indie labels, **The Barracudas** crept into the Top 40 with their energetic, humorous **Summer Fun** in 1980. Garage punk caught on in America in the mid-1980s, guitar-led groups such as **Mudhoney** paving the way for grunge. One hyphenated style we won't see is 'garage-easy listening'.

★**Recommended**★ Divas Of Dance Vol.1 (DCC) is a great starting point. For speed garage, try **Artful Dodger**'s **Re-Rewind** (London). For garage punk, **The Barracudas'** Meantime (Closer) is a minor masterpiece, even if two band members had scarpered by then.

Germany

German pop is a mythologised, dangerous place, like the autobahn, where you might meet **David Hasselhoff** (see page 270). Officially the Germans have no taste in pop, yet they created Berlin's cabaret music, nurtured **The Beatles** in Hamburg (bandleader **Bert Kaempfert** gave them their first studio session), produced **Nico**, whose husky voice enlivened **The Velvet Underground**'s debut and gave us **Can**, too avant-garde for their own good, and **Kraftwerk**, whose 1977 album **Trans-Europe Express** was, said *Mojo* magazine, "the single most important influence on techno from Detroit to Tokyo."

Berlin in the 1970s was almost as much of a pop/rock epicentre as Memphis in the 1950s. **David Bowie**, **Brian Eno** and **Lou Reed** all made pilgrimages there. In a parallel sonic universe, disco maven **Donna Summer** was found by **Giorgio Moroder** while touring Germany in *Hair!*, and German impresario Frank Farian was moulding **Boney M**. Yet to most Britons, German pop in the 1970s and 1980s was exemplified by Eurovision winner **Nicole**'s earnest **A Little Peace**, a No.1 in 1982, and the catchy, nuclear paranoia of Nina, who floated to No.1 with **99 Red Balloons**. Trio's 1982 No.2, **Da Da Da**, was funnier, the assonance in German ("Ich liebe dich nicht/Du liebst mich nicht/Aha") a work of pop art. And **Propaganda**, briefly, gave label **ZTT** some intellectual clout with **A Secret Wish**. The most consistent German hitmakers were **The Scorpions**, who sold more than 20- million records in Europe and reached No.2 with **Winds Of Change** in 1991.

Today all kinds of music find a home in Germany: oompah-intensive schlager, techno, dance, folk, a mellow wimpy rap in which the rap is accompanied by strings and syrupy keyboards, heavy metal and cheesy pop. And some Germans will never leave **Hotel California** or that strain of 1970s West Coast rock.

★Recommended★ **Propaganda**'s **A Secret Wish** (ZTT/Island) is portentous, slightly pompous yet perfect synth-pop, marred only by a ham-fisted retread of Duel called **Jewel**.

Girl groups

Long before **Girl Power** became a slogan, groups of female singers were inspiring acts like The Beatles. The sound was smoother than rock'n'roll, with debts to Tin Pan Alley, doo-wop and R&B. From 1958 (when The Chantels had a US hit with **Maybe**) until the mid-1960s, acts like The Shirelles, The Crystals and The Ronettes, Cookies, The Chiffons and the fabulously named Exciters reigned.

What was new about these groups was the combination of slick harmonies, orchestral production and melodic, hard-to-forget pop songs like Will You Still Love Me Tomorrow?, He's So Fine, Be My Baby and Leader Of The Pack. But the groups, hostage to producers like **Phil Spector** or writers like Gerry Goffin and Carole King, didn't achieve the longevity they deserved. **The Chiffons**, one of the finest groups of any era or gender, only had four UK hits – their biggest, Sweet Talking Guy, reaching No.4 in 1972, long after their heyday. You can see why one of the definitive anthologies of this era is called Growin' Up Too Fast (Polygram).

The Beatles' first album Please Please Me had a cover of Chains, a No.50 hit for Cookies in 1963, but the lads' success ended the girl groups' golden era – though **The Supremes** would amass more UK hits than The Shirelles, The Chiffons and The Shangri-Las combined. In the 1970s The Pointer Sisters offered a soulful variant on the classic sound, Leader Of The Pack reaching No.3 in 1972 and No.7 in 1976; better than in the 1960s. And the sound hasn't died – listen to **The Bangles** and **Blondie**.

★**Recommended**★ The Complete Cookies (Sequel), worth buying for I Never Dreamed.

Glam rock

For most British teenagers growing up in the early 1970s glam rock was a long-overdue dash of excitement, bringing theatricality, glitter and humour back into a rock and pop business grown earnest and self-important. Dubbed 'fag rock', there was a streak of sexual ambiguity, at its widest with Bowie, in the make-up and costumes which didn't play well in America (until **Kiss** arrived). Glam rock could be as infuriatingly repetitive as the worst bubblegum pop (**Gary Glitter**), as well-crafted yet commercial as **T. Rex** or as arty and allusive as Bowie and Roxy.

The key year was 1972, with fine albums from Bowie and Roxy, Mott The Hoople's All The Young Dudes, **Slade** (glam for straights) topping the charts twice, Bolan racking up two No.1s and two No.2s, and the first UK tour by the only true American glam-rock act, **New York Dolls**. By 1976 glam was, like Bolan, virtually dead. Too bad America never got the point.

★**Recommended**★ Marc Bolan/T. Rex's T. Rextasy (Warner) is a must. **Roxy Music**'s self-titled debut and **Bowie**'s Ziggy Stardust ought to be in your collection. The soundtrack to **Todd Haynes**'s movie Velvet Goldmine (Polygram) is another way of getting into the vibe.

Gospel

When the million-dollar quartet (Elvis, Jerry Lee Lewis, Carl Perkins and Johnny Cash) jammed at **Sun Studios**, they mostly sang gospel numbers. Aretha Franklin,

James Brown, Sam Cooke and Lou Rawls all started out singing God's music.

Officially, gospel is only 80-odd years old, the term coined by **Thomas Dorsey** to describe records he issued on his label, although the negro spiritual can be traced to the 1870s. In the 1930s Dorsey unearthed the greatest gospel singer, **Mahalia Jackson**, just as the first great crossover gospel group, **The Golden Gate Quartet**, emerged with a vocal harmony drawing on blues, jazz and gospel. In the 1950s gospel elements would blend into pop. On his 1953 gospel No.1 I Believe, Frankie Laine sounded so fervent he could have met Jesus in the studio. Presley's vocal fervour, like Little Richard's, owed a lot to gospel. And Ray Charles's I Got A Woman, No.1 on the US R&B chart in 1955, is driven by a pounding gospel piano.

In 1960 Elvis cut a gospel album called His Hand In Mine, partly credited with founding contemporary Christian music. His Crying In The Chapel was a rare gospel UK No.1, in 1965. **Norman Greenbaum** emulated Elvis with the divinely inspired Spirit In The Sky (see page 240) in 1970. The next gospel No. 1 was the awful **Lena Martell** with One Day At A Time in 1979. Yet gospel is still influential. Some argue that **Bridge Over Troubled Water** makes most sense as a gospel song – if He is the bridge over troubled water rather than Simon or Garfunkel.

===

★**Recommended**★ Gospels, Spirituals And Hymns (CBS) is the key **Mahalia Jackson** set.

Greece

Any British child who grew up in the 1970s and didn't have to listen to **Nana Mouskouri**'s *Passport* album or **The Roussos Phemonenon** EP was very lucky indeed. **Demis Roussos**, with his high straining vocals (what was occurring inside that tent he wore?) made No.1 in 1976 with The Roussos Phenomenon. It was touch and go, but the phenomenon that was Roussos (ironically he was born in Egypt) soon faded. Mouskouri, who started out with an album of German Christmas songs, was the more versatile talent, a genuinely gifted jazz-pop singer who couldn't help looking like a sensible science teacher.

Greece is often blamed for **Gheorghe Zhamfir**'s panpipes, No.4 in 1976, but Gheorghe was Romanian. Luxembourg is credited with **Vicky Leandros**'s half-decent Eurovision winner Come What May, No.2 in 1972, although Vicky was Greek and had appeared for Luxembourg before (as had Mouskouri). Evangelos Odyssey Papathanassiou, aka Vangelis

The ultimate Nana-rama

(easier to fit on album sleeves), tried to restore Greece's honour by luring Jon Anderson to sing I'll Find My Way Home and penning State Of Independence, Donna Summer's best hit. Vangelis also made No.19 in 1968 with Rain And Tears by his first group, **Aphrodite's Child**; their 666, a concept album based on the apocalypse, had guest vocals from Roussos.

Grunge

Simply put, grunge allied the heavy guitar sound of bands like **Black Sabbath** to the attitude of punk. Early 'heavy' grunge bands like **Mudhoney** enjoyed some UK hits but **Nirvana**, led by Kurt Cobain, made grunge the definitive modern variant of hard rock. Cobain, an iconic figure even before his suicide in April 1994, claimed: "We sound like The Knack and the Bay City Rollers being molested by Black Flag and Black Sabbath." Nirvana started loud but created a melodic strain of grunge; their signature tune, Smells Like Teen Spirit (No.7 in 1991), owes as much to Boston's More Than A Feeling as to punk.

Nirvana's **Dave Grohl** founded **Foo Fighters**, their debut single This Is A Call reaching No.5 and their hook-laden sound positioning them as a hardcore Beach Boys. **Pearl Jam** also emerged from tragedy (Andrew Wood, vocalist with Stone Gossard and Jeff Ament's previous group, Mother Love Bone, also overdosed), making consistent yet minor hits, but selling albums like V by the truckload. Nirvana paved the way for bands like **Green Day** (whose 1994 album Dookie sold ten-million copies), **Offspring** (try Smash on Epitaph) and **Garbage** (sometimes called techno-grunge). But grunge will live in Cobain's shadow for sometime yet.

★**Recommended**★ The seminal albums: **Nirvana**'s Nevermind (Geffen), **Mudhoney**'s Superfuzz Bigmuff (SubPop), **Pearl Jam**'s Ten (Epic), the sound of stadium-filling grunge.

Guitar

The guitar is the one instrument central to rock'n'roll mythology. You can (as **Sun Studios** did) dispense with drums, but without the guitar, rock'n'roll might not exist. Rock's first great guitarist was arguably **Scotty Moore**. His licks inspired Keith Richards, Eric Clapton and Jimmy Page. But **Duane Eddy** was the first axeman to chart regularly on his own. His third record, Rebel Rouser, with a rumbling guitar riff, allied to a raunchy sax and driving beat, convinced **George Harrison** and **John Entwistle** to play guitar. As Nik Cohn says, "He set the standards for instrumental groups for almost five years. The Shadows copied him. So did The Ventures and just about everyone else." Eddy twice hit No.2 (Because You're Young, Pepe), then lost out to the British beat. In the 1980s the **Art Of Noise** recast his Peter Gunn theme.

The Ventures were never big in the UK; we had the **The Shadows** (Apache, Kon-Tiki, Atlantis, Wonderful Land) and **Hank Marvin**, Britain's first home-grown guitar hero (we're ignoring **Bert Weedon** for obvious reasons), made the guitar sound central to pop. **Jimi Hendrix** was a genius but the realisation that his faithful cheered a bum note as loudly as a great one undid him. **Eric Clapton** faced the same trap, Cohn noting: "Announced as God, a small talent for guitar-picking seemed barely adequate." But, disguised as **Derek & The Dominoes**, he created the intoxicating beautiful Layla , No.7 in the UK in 1972 and No.4 a decade later.

The guitar hero – **Jimmy Page**, **Mark Knopfler** (for a time) and **Johnny Marr** – was one of rock's key icons in the 1970s and 1980s, even though synths ruled the charts. The guitar-based sound returned with Britpop and the legacy pops up in surprising places: part of Apache was cut by the funky **Incredible Bongo Band**.

★**Recommended**★ Twang Thang (Rhino), essential **Duane Eddy**; **The Shadows'** Very Best Of (EMI); **Jimi Hendrix**'s Electric Ladyland (MCA); **Eric Clapton**'s 461 Ocean Boulevard (Polydor); and Very Greasy (Elektra), the best of famed guitarist **David Lindley**.

Hampstead

Most acts stress their 'ever so humble' roots, so this upscale area's gifts to pop are often overlooked. Two of Britain's finest female singers are from here – **Marianne Faithfull** and **Dusty Springfield** (the latter from West Hampstead). **Tony Meehan**, The Shadows drummer, was born here. The area has been namechecked in songs by **Al Stewart** (Swiss Cottage Manoeuvres), Donovan (Hampstead Incident) and punk prankster **Johnny Rubbish**, who released the single Living In NW3 4JR.

Heavy metal

Today the cock rock of singers like **David Coverdale** (even some Whitesnake members found the lyrics naff) can seem daft or offensive. But nerdy, white teenage boys needed heavy metal, the term inspired by a line in Steppenwolf's Born To Be Wild, to survive the 1970s. You didn't need rhythm; you could just stand by the wall at your school disco and shake your head. Heavy metal's 'sexism' was, in part, a legacy of the blues – Coverdale's "Lie down I think I love you," is not too far from **Muddy Waters**' "I'll make love to you woman… in five minutes."

The only Top 50 UK singles chart act with a hint of heaviness is **Status Quo**, though bands like Nazareth dented the charts with hard-driving sounds like Bad Bad Boy. And Rainbow strung together three Top 10 singles in a row from 1979 to

1981. Yet heavy metal exerted a gravitational pull on 1970s pop (think **Sweet** with **Blockbuster**; Queen's **Bohemian Rhapsody**, glammed up metal with intellectual allusions). And hard rock bands like **AC/DC** had obvious debts to heavy metal.

The second wave of heavy metal, led by bands like **Iron Maiden** (named after a medieval torture device), formed a punk-inspired back-to-basics movement in the late-1970s. Iron Maiden topped the singles chart in 1991 with **Bring Your Daughter... To The Slaughter**. American pop/metal alloy (from the likes of **Bon Jovi**) and grunge has made life hard for heavy metal bands. The 1970s heyday of bands like Zeppelin now seems like a glorious, mad coda to rock's heroic age. And **Ozzy Osbourne** now has cult status as a rock'n'roll survivor and holy fool.

★**Recommended**★ To get a sense of the genre's finer moments try **Deep Purple**'s **Machine Head** (Warners), **Sabbath**'s **Sabbath Bloody Sabbath** (Warners), **Van Halen**'s **Van Halen 1** (Warners) and **Led Zeppelin II** (Atlantic) – the Zep transcended heavy metal but this is their heaviest album. For more recent work try **Motorhead**'s **Snake Bite Love** (SPV).

Hip hop

Hip hop has come a long way since its birth on the streets of New York's South Bronx 30 years ago. By the time **The Sugarhill Gang** released the first rap single **Rapper's Delight** in 1979, black youths in America's inner cities had been listening to rap music and living hip-hop culture for almost a decade.

Historically, hip hop refers to a cultural movement which includes graffiti and break-dancing as well as the music itself (rap). But the terms hip hop and rap are now almost interchangeable. **Grandmaster Flash & The Furious Five** widened hip hop's audience in 1982 with the single **The Message**. By the mid-1980s **Eric B & Rakim** and **Run-DMC** were helping hip hop cross into popular culture. Today hip hop is popular culture. In the last year, pop stars from Justin Timberlake to Beyoncé Knowles have rushed to work with hip-hop stars. This is a far cry from the genre's roots in the 1970s when **Kool DJ Herc**, the first hip-hop DJ, used two turntables to link sections of songs, known as breaks, to create non-stop music. When he wasn't calling out to his audience over the music (an early form of rapping), dancers known as b-boys and b-girls would show off their latest moves during the breaks, and hip hop was born (see Rap for music recommendations).

Holidays

Like timeshare apartments, the novelty holiday hit (**Y Viva España, Barbados**) is a monster from which no one emerges unscathed. These records were made to be played during the alcohol-fuelled pursuit of skirt or trouser; even young Madonna can't get more inspired than rhyming 'holiday' with 'celebrate' on her No.2 hit **Holiday**. (She did make amends with **La Isla Bonita**, a deserved No.1 in 1987.)

Records about the joys of summer had always been around – Jerry Keller's **Here Comes Summer**, No.1 in 1959, is dusted off annually by DJs trying to cheer up winter-weary Brits. **Brian Hyland** regaled us with tales of a polka-dot bikini, while Cliff chortled smugly that he, Una and the Shads were going on a summer holiday.

Mungo Jerry's **In the Summertime**, No.1 in 1970, though a good record, was a harbinger of horrors to come. With an irresistible jug-band rhythm, dodgy lyrics (if her dad's rich, Mungo Jerry says, take her out for a meal, but "if her daddy's poor, just do what you feel") and big hair, it couldn't fail. Every producer, svengali, impresario and recording engineer thought "I can have one of those!" The 1970s charts were awash with the likes of **Y Viva España** sung, almost against her will, by a Swedish jazz singer called Sylvia. **Typically Tropical**'s 1975 No.1 **Barbados** was a true holiday hit, inspired by studio engineer **Jeffrey Calvert**'s vacation on the isle, **Vengaboys** remade it for their No.1 club anthem **We're Going To Ibiza**.

Other offences committed in the name of the holiday novelty hit include The Tweets' **Birdy Song** (made by **Mikey Foote**, who had also produced the first Clash album) and Chas & Dave's **Margate**, with its irresistibly lurching, "Weeeeee're goin dahn to Margitttt," which didn't deserve to stall at No.46. The best may just be 10cc's **Dreadlock Holiday**, their second and last No.1.

Holland

"I've been driving all night/My hand's wet on the wheel," Dutch pop doesn't get any better than that – at least as far as the rest of the world is concerned. **Golden Earring**'s **Radar Love**, a No.7, caught the imagination in 1973 in a way their first Dutch No.1, **Dong-Dong-Di-Ki-Di-Gi-Dong**, failed to. Earring, one of the best 1960s 'Nederbeat' bands, weren't the first Dutch combo to chart in the UK. **Shocking Blue** came out of nowhere in 1970 with a riff from **Pinball Wizard** to reach No.8 with the striking **Venus** (banally sung by Bananarama) and **Focus** made No.4 with Sylvia. All these were outsold by **Pussycat**, No.1 for a month in 1976 with **Mississippi**. Produced by **Jonathan King**, the only

Confused?
Bands whose names could be their hit singles

Band	Hit singles
Focus	Hocus Pocus
Lieutenant Pigeon	Mouldy Old Dough
Hot Butter	Popcorn
Culture Club	Karma Chameleon
Space	Magic Fly

Dutch thing about it was the band's nationality. Soon the Dutch were so preoccupied by the demise of total football they had no energy to make great pop. In 1984 **Art Company** reached No.12 with Susanna, a song so irritating the French loved it. The best 1980s Dutch band, **Fatal Flowers**, didn't have a UK hit despite being produced by **Mick Ronson**. But the awful Stars On 45 medleys, created by Dutch producer **Jaap Eggermont**, were hits (see Various Artists).

The only Dutch-based act to score six Top 5 singles in a row are **Vengaboys**, but as they were formed by two Spanish DJs and have links to Hungary, Trinidad and Brazil, they transcend national boundaries. We wanted to talk Dutch pop without raking up **The Smurfs**, but it's worth noting, in passing, that they sadly weren't allowed to cover Oasis's Wonderwall. A good sampler of Holland's pop is **Dutch Treats** (Critique), which includes many of the acts listed here.

Horror

Long before **Ozzy Osbourne** bit the head off a bat (even if he didn't, history has printed the legend) and **Alice Cooper** entitled his tour "Welcome To My Nightmare", **Screamin' Jay Hawkins** waved a skull called Henry as he sung such eerie numbers as I Put A Spell On You. Following up with Constipation Blues wasn't a brilliant idea – it didn't get much airplay – but he is a significant figure in rock'n'roll (he has had one UK hit single, Heart Attack And Vine, No.43 in 1993), contributing such macabre classics as Feast Of The Mau Mau.

Welcome to Scream's nightmare

Hawkins's opening trick in concert – emerging from a coffin – was so scary the only way to stop crowds fleeing was for Hawkins to hire boys to drop elastic bands onto people's heads and shout, "Worms!" Welcome to my nightmare indeed. (**Screaming Lord Sutch** would use the coffin trick in the UK.) Climbing out of a coffin would have suited **Boris Pickett**, the Boris Karloff soundalike ("I was working in the lab late one night") on horror spoof Monster Mash. Backed by the Crypt Kickers, Boris's Monster Mash was good, clean, sinister fun. US TV horror-show host John Zacherley was less subtle: his **Dinner With Drac**, complete with tips for laying the table ("Igor, the scalpels go on the left with the pitchforks!"), was banned here.

★**Recommended**★ Voodoo Jive (Rhino), Scream's greatest hits, is horribly amusing.

Horses

Man's second best friend is a country and western hero, **Eddy Arnold** even claiming in song, "You can't hang a man for shooting a woman who's trying to steal his horse" – a very useful travel tip if you're a woman out west. Horses' hooves echoed through the singles chart in the 1950s and early-1960s thanks to Gracie Fields, the Beverley Sisters, and Nina & Frederick (who all had a hit with **Little Donkey**); American instrumentalists the Ramrods (a No.8 hit with **Riders In the Sky** in 1961); and Frank Ifield, who whipped **Mule Train** to No.22 in 1963.

But as the 1960s wore on there was only children's TV theme **White Horses**, No.10 for Jackie Lee in 1968. **The Byrds**' **Chestnut Mare** made No.19 in 1971. (The group hoped the mare in question will "be just like a wife"; that's folk singers for you.) America struck a blow for equine pride with **A Horse With No Name**, a No.3 hit in 1972, in which the singer rides into a desert, letting the horse run free. Eddy Arnold would not approve. The Osmonds started their Top 30 career in 1972 with **Crazy Horses** – which wasn't about heroin or horses, but about native Americans' reaction to the first trains.

The sport of kings should have inspired novelty hits but its most popular icon, **Red Rum**, had the kind of vocal range even a seasoned session singer like **Tony Burrows** would have struggled to recreate in the studio.

★**Recommended**★ Eddy Arnold's Cattle Call (Bear Family) is the best primer.

House

Disco never died in the Windy City, and house music was born in **Chicago**. Chicago had no clubs of any note in the early 1980s – until local entrepreneurs, seeing planeloads of partygoers heading for New York every weekend, installed top New York DJ **Frankie Knuckles** at the city's Warehouse club. Knuckles created a seamless flow of classic dance and disco records, using his own pre-recorded tapes, electronic gadgetry and turntable skills to beef up the beats, creating a single, constant rhythm – the thumping 4/4 beat now synonymous with house. (Locals are split as to the origin of the name: some say it's a contraction of 'warehouse', others say it was the particular blend of music played – as in house wine.)

The first house crowds were black and gay, but other local talents helped create a more inclusive scene. Some were DJs (**Ron Hardy**), others were musicians (**Jesse Saunders**, Marshall Jefferson, Mr Fingers – keyboard player Larry Heard – and soulful singer **Robert Owens**), some were both. There are two contenders for the honour of being the first house record – Z Factor's Fantasy or Jesse Saunders's On And On (Saunders also produced the Z Factor record).

This local scene had existed underground for years before it became hip among British clubbers. By 1987 **Steve 'Silk' Hurley** and **Farley Jackmaster Funk** had had UK hits (Hurley hit No.1 with Jack Your Body). Soon the house beat was applied to pop, a process accelerated by **Madonna**. **Coldcut**, **KLF** and **Technotronic** were among those who took house into the charts; divas (often shortlived) like **Rozalla** kept it there, and acts from the Pet Shop Boys to Shamen drew on it.

Part of the beauty of the original Chicago house was that there were no musical boundaries: the DJ was king, given licence to create. This open-mindedness – and a new musical canvas on which musicians could experiment – led to house fragmenting into myriad synthesized variants. These ranged from deep (uncluttered, with the vocalist emphasised) to acid (squelchy analogue noises and cries of "ac-iiid!") to ambient (the gentler, spaced-out sounds pioneered by the 'discreet music' of **Brian Eno**, often used as chill-out music for the come-downs). In the UK, house became the most significant youth culture since punk, with amphetamine-fuelled all-night raves outraging the *Daily Mail*. House music has never gone away, with acts like **Leftfield** blending in new influences to create new generations of dance music. Disco may be dead, but its genes certainly aren't.

★**Recommended**★ The History Of House Music (Vols.1 and 2) on **K-Tel** has the best of Chicago and New York; for early gems, try the The House Sound Of Chicago (London/ffrr) series. **Virgo**'s deep house EPs Go Wild Rhythm Trax and Game Mania are worth finding.

HULL

The Housemartins (and subsequently **The Beautiful South**) appropriated Hull, but **Ronnie Hilton**, the ballad singer who soared to No.1 with No Other Love in 1956, and **David Whitfield**, another balladeer who had a 1953 No.1 with Answer Me, were born and bred on the Humber. So was **Mick Ronson** who, before he met Bowie (and co-produced Lou Reed's Transformer), played with local garage-rock group The Rats. And, in 1982, a sign in a Hull furniture store gave students **Tracey Thorn** and **Ben Watt** a name for their band: **Everything But The Girl**. The Housemartins, with the album title London 0 Hull 4, played on local pride, though neither lead singer **Paul Heaton** nor bass player **Norman Cook** were born there. When they split,

Cook became **Fatboy Slim** while drummer David Hummings and singer Paul Heaton formed **The Beautiful South**, mixing lilting melodies and sarcastic lyrics. On **Don't Marry Her, Have Me**, Jacqueline Abbot sings: "She has a PhD in 'I told you so'/And you've a knighthood in 'I'm not listening.'"

★Recommended★ As Carry On Up The Charts, **The Beautiful South**'s hits compilation, went platinum five times in its first year of release, you've probably already got it.

Iceland

Bjork, as the only Icelandic pop act with a global fanbase (apart from her old band **The Sugar Cubes**), does her best to span the musical spectrum, offering goth-punk, bebop, trip hop, dance and electronica. The iconoclastic Icelander got her break through a tape of her singing **Tina Charles**'s 1976 disco hit I Love To Love.

★Recommended★ Debut (Elektra) is still Bjork's most satisfying album.

India

India's greatest gift to British pop is, of course, Sir Cliff, born in **Lucknow** in 1940. If you're not an addict we recommend Cliff's **I'm Nearly Famous** (EMI), the most surprising album of the 1970s. What's so surprising about it? Well, that it's good – heck Cliff even sounds like he's got normal, nudge nudge, urges on **Devil Woman**.

India's second-greatest gift to British pop is **Engelbert Humperdinck**. The city of Madras let him go to Leicester where he was raised; Leicester is still wondeing how to return the favour. Madras also gave us **Pete Best**, briefly a Beatle.

Indian pop stars have had little UK chart action. **Alisha** became the Indian Madonna and, prefiguring Madge's Sex period, cut an album in 1990 called **Kaemasutrae**. Alisha's only UK hit, Baby Talk, reached No.67 in 1986.

Four years earlier **Monsoon** (a band run by husband and wife Sheila Chandra and Steve Coe) reached No.12 in the UK with the hypnotically miserable Ever So Lonely. Their 1983 album Third Eye (Great Expectations) is one of the great experiments in fusing the sounds of East and West and kicked off Indipop. Indian pop music has, as you might expect, been dominated by Bollywood musicals.

Indie

The definition of indie is simple, concise and virtually useless. As one fan says on **Amazon**: "Basically, indie bands are musicians on independent labels." Trouble is, in the corporate looking-glass world that is the record industry, a truly independent label may be as rare as herds of wildebeest in Torquay. It would be so much easier if 'indie music' stood for music that came from Indianapolis. Anyway, criticism, schmiticism, let's cut to the music. These albums – if you don't own them all already – will kick-start your indie collection.

★**Recommended**★ **Joy Division**'s **Closer** (Factory), gloomy as Ian Curtis's songs were, he could exercise restraint (live, this wasn't as true, witness his notorious shout before one gig: "You've forgotten Rudolf Hess!"). The line, "The present is well out of hand," in **Heart And Soul** is well understated for an epileptic whose marriage was collapsing. **PJ Harvey**'s **Dry** (Too Pure) is proof there's more to West Country pop/rock than The Wurzels. Try **Teenage Fanclub**'s **Bandwagonesque** (Creation); sometimes the name of the band is a sign of indie intent (names like The Beatles are somehow designed for global domination) but Teenage Fanclub's isn't. The Glaswegian band's affection for pop shines through here. With **The Go-Betweens**' **16 Lovers Lane** (Beggars Banquet) the Aussies went home to make a great, not that pretentious, album citing Plath, Genet and Joyce (James not Yootha).The **Smashing Pumpkins**' **Siamese Dream** (Hut) is an all-but-perfect combo of pop, metal and lullabies. **Magnetic Field**'s **69 Love Song**s (Merge) is classic pop about falling in love and out again. **Guided By Voices Alien Lanes** (Matador) is tuneful and intimate. And on **Once Upon A Time In The East** (NCHCD), by **The Farmers' Boys** (briefly on EMI), these pranksters from Norwich display the lighter side of indie with titles like **Get Out And Walk**.

Infidelity

That point in a love affair where the moon hits your eye like a big pizza pie has provided some fine songs, but it can't beat the moment when **Frankie Laine** shrieks, "Jezzzz-a-bellll!" or **Tom Jones** begs, "Why, why, why Delilah?"

Sometimes you just know what's coming, the definitive version of this awful anticipation being **Ray Charles**'s version of **Crying Time**. But, like The Police (**Every Breath You Take**), you can go mad watching your lover, or, like Dr Hook (**When You're In Love With A Beautiful Woman**), spend your life jumping with every phone call. This pain may start with the thought that your partner's lost that lovin' feelin'. Sometimes it can just be paranoia, as in **Elvis**'s No. 9 hit **Suspicion**. Yet on **Suspicious Minds** he protests his innocence although, live, when he sang, "Honey, I'd never lie to you," he'd often grin to himself and add, "No, not much."

Dion's **Runaround Sue** tells a sad-but-true tale of infidelity yet sounds curiously exhilarated, as if he's glad the lies are over. **Chuck Berry** moans about his **Maybellene** – why can't she be true? And **Kenny Rogers** begs Ruby not to take her love to town. That Jolene must be a looker: young **Dolly Parton** is so worried about her man she begs Jolene, "Please don't take him just because you can."

They should all heed the great **Billie Holiday** in **Don't Explain**, she knows he cheats but right and wrong don't matter when she's with her sweet. **Bobby Vee** even tells his lover to "run to him" if she loves "him" more. If they can't forgive, they should get ironic, like **Willie Nelson** does superbly on **Funny How Time Slips Away**, a song he mostly wrote on his way to work one day.

For the adulterer, life seems simpler. **Billy Paul** is having a ball with **Mrs Jones** although, as they meet every day at the same café at the same time, you fear they'll get rumbled soon. Life's messier for Mary MacGregor who was **Torn Between Two Lovers** in 1976, "feeling like a fool". Fool is one word for it. At least **Gene Pitney** had the grace to say sorry, he was just 24 hours away when he strayed. Wouldn't work in a Tulsa divorce court but it's a great song.

Instrumental

Instrumental hits are often perpetrated by a pianist (see Pianists), a bloke twanging his guitar (to fine effect on Fleetwod Mac's **Albatross**) or **Cozy Powell** drumming himself up to not much of a pitch at all, really, on **Dance With The Devil**.

In the 1950s and early 1960s songs like **Tequila**, a saxophone-led instrumental by Champs, **Rocking Goose** and **Telstar** (see page 243), all went Top 5, **Herb Alpert** (the A in the label A&M) struck gold with his trumpet and tijuana brass, inescapable thanks to songs like **Spanish Flea** (No.3 in 1965). That year he released the album **Whipped Cream & Other Delights**, famous for its cover (a nearly nude model covered in whipped cream) and because all its songs were about food (A Taste Of Honey, Lemon Tree, Yes! We Have No Bananas… one of those was a joke).

Subsequent instrumental hits have often been the work of one-hit wonders such as Focus (or Van McCoy's **The Hustle**), spun off TV, movies (Vangelis's **Chariots Of Fire**) or even ads. The most compelling of all was the theme to **Hawaii Five-O**, (penned by **Morton Stevens**) and, as recorded by The Ventures, part of the essential mix for British discos although it has never graced the charts.

Booker T & The MG's' **Green Onions**, a No.7 hit in 1979, was a work of genuine class and soul by the Stax Studio house band. Mike Oldfield's **Tubular Bells**, album gave him the platform to sell zillions of records and reach No.4 with the festive **In Dulce Jubilo** in 1975. Oldfield's success encouraged the others, notably **Jean-Michel Jarre** whose **Oxygene** was a No.4 hit in 1997. Jarre's records all seem to have names like **Equinox**, **Oxygene**, **Magnetic Field** and **Metamorphosis**, which suggest that marrying Charlotte Rampling has gone to his head.

★**Recommended**★ The Best Of Booker T & The MG's (Stax).

Ireland

Before **U2**, Ireland was in danger of being known, musically, for **Val Doonican**'s rocking chair, **Foster & Allen**'s winsome folk, those always-in-the-mood-for-dancing **Nolan** sisters and its knack of winning Eurovision with songs like **What's Another Year?**. The answer to that – a bloody long time if Johnny Logan's singing.

Val rocked – back and forth

Doonican was always on TV in the 1960s singing that some of his best friends were songs – not songwriters, you notice. His success (five Top 10 hits in the 1960s) smoothed the way for **Dana**, No.1 with **All Kinds Of Everything**. She later ran for the Irish presidency on a strict Catholic ticket but didn't win, probably because we all remember the saucy minx telling us something was cooking in the kitchen (her). You could see the export of such talent as **Boyzone**, **Westlife**, Doonican, **B*Witched** (beware of bands that use punctuation marks in their names), **Chris De Burgh**, **The Nolans**, Dana, Johnny Logan, **Foster & Allen**, **Daniel O'Donnell** and **Rose Marie** as Ireland's revenge for Oliver Cromwell. But Ireland has also given us **U2**, **The Cranberries**, **Thin Lizzy**, **The Boomtown Rats**, **Sinead O'Connor**, **Christy Moore**, **The Chieftains**, **The Pogues**, their unlikely cohorts **The Dubliners** (they allied on The Irish Rover, No.8 in 1987), part of **The Waterboys** and, long ago, The Kennedys, without whom there would be no **Dead Kennedys**.

On this balance sheet **The Corrs** hover precariously in the middle. The sisters are an obvious asset to the Irish Tourist Board, but they can sail too close to the rocking-chair comfort of Doonican. Some more bite, as in their early minor hit **I Never Loved You Anyway**, would be nice. U2 are the one truly indispensable Irish rock band. Five of their albums (**Boy**, **War**, **The Unforgettable Fire**, **The Joshua Tree**, **Achtung Baby**) set a standard many acts don't match once in their careers.

★**Recommended**★ The Chieftains 4 (Shanachie) is a haunting album, worth buying.

Israel

The most dramatic news in recent Israeli pop history wasn't the fact that a transsexual won the **Eurovision Song Contest** but that one of the queens of Israeli pop, **Ofra Haza**, possibly died from the AIDS virus. Haza was a real global star, having enjoyed two hits (the best known **Im Nin'Alu**) with **Paula Abdul** in the

UK and supplied the vocals to **M.A.R.R.S**'s **Pump Up The Volume**. She came second in the 1983 Eurovision Song Contest and is overshadowed abroad by **Milk And Honey** (their **Hallelujah** was No.5 in 1979) and Izhar Cohen (**A Ba Ni Bi**, No.20 in 1978), who both won it for Israel. The enigma of Israeli pop is **Esther Ofarim**. She hit No.1 with **Cinderella Rockafella** in 1968, with one-time hubbie Abi, and sang with **Scott Walker**. Her 1972 self-titled album was produced by Bob Johnston, Dylan's first producer, yet she is still, in UK terms, a one-hit wonder.

★**Recommended**★ **Nash Didan** formed to protect the Aramaic language. This isn't pop, but if you fancy dancing to the language Jesus spoke, try **Nash Didan Idaylu** (Phonokol).

Italy

Italy's biggest pop star of the last decade, both in sheer physical bulk and commercial clout, has been **Luciano Pavarotti**, who had a No.2 hit with the 1990 World Cup theme (as it's now known), **Nessun Dorma**.

Apart from Pav, you're left with such one-hit wonders as **Domenico Modugno** (see Eurovision) and **Gigliola Cinquetti**, No.8 in 1974 with **Go Before You Break My Heart**. Sultry Gigliola (actually a two-hit wonder, her first hit **Non Ho L'Etas** won Eurovision in 1964) was gone before we could break her heart. In the 1980s Gigliola was followed by a former Miss Lido called **Sabrina Salerno**. "I am, how you say, a womanly woman," she declared, and the video of her in a swimsuit left no doubt that was the case. After the Europop sensation that was **Boys (Summertime Love)** – a No.5 in 1988 – the sequel All Of Me didn't do the trick, but then not many British men (this was pre-*Loaded*) had the nerve to handle all of Sabrina. In 1991 the Italian singer **Zucchero** memorably duetted with Paul Young on **Senza Una Madonna (Without A Woman)**, his gruff tones helping take the song to No.4.

Such a marginal role is bizarre given the contribution Italian-Americans like **Frank Sinatra**, **Dean Martin**, **Tony Bennett**, **Perry Como**, **Dion Di Mucci**, **Frankie Avalon** and **Frankie Valli** have made to American pop. Italian-American groups like Dion and the lesser-known **The Mystics** helped pioneer white doo-wop. And **Sophia Loren** duetted her way to No.4 with **Goodness Gracious Me** in 1960. The fact that Italian orchestra leader Marcello Minerbi enjoyed his only UK hit with the theme to **Zorba The Greek** somehow just adds to the national shame.

Japan

For most of the last 50 years Japanese pop and rock has existed in a parallel universe. Yet, just occasionally, musical worlds collide, as they did in 1963 when

Kyu Sakamoto took Sukiyaki to No.6 in the UK and No.1 in the US. What started out as Ue O Muite Aruko (I Look Up When I Walk) was renamed Sukiyaki after the favourite Japanese dish of Louis Benjamin, who ran Pye. A Pye artist covered the song, but the original was picked up by an American station and rush released on Capitol. The single sold millions but that was as good as it got for Sakamoto, who died in a plane crash near Tokyo in August 1985 (he was 43). The most influential Japanese musician since, certainly outside his own country, is another Sakamoto (no relation). Ryuchi started in synth-pop band **Big Yellow Orchestra** (they had a No.17 hit in 1980 with Computer Game), but became tolerably famous in the UK for co-writing the marvellous Forbidden Colours with **David Sylvian**.

Sylvian was the ex-lead singer of, coincidentally, **Japan**. Countless Western artists have claimed to be big in Japan (apart from **Big In Japan**, which didn't last long enough to be big anywhere – bassist Holly Johnson joined Frankie Goes To Hollywood and Ian Broudie formed The Lightning Seeds). But David, voted the "most beautiful man in the world" – by his publicist – really was big in Japan, his androgynous looks and kabuki-style make-up generating teen hysteria. But he collaborated with Ryuchi to great effect on his solo album Brilliant Trees.

Shibuya-kei, a strange refracted Japanese pop which draws on Burt Bacharach, St Etienne and hip hop, may be pop's only genre to be named for a shopping district, the trendy Shibuya in west Tokyo. The genre's key act, **The Pizzicato Five**, have released albums with titles like **The International Playboy And Playgirl**.

Possibly even more bizarre than Japan's own pop music is the effect the country has on Western popsters. The Vapors may have used turning Japanese as a metaphor for masturbation as they soared to No.3 in 1980. A year later Aneka, a tall Scottish woman from a good home, dressed up like a geisha, pined for her Japanese Boy all the way to No.1. And in 1984 Germany's **Alphaville** had a hit with Big In Japan, intended to be a self-fulfilling prophecy. Hiroshima was the unlikely inspiration for OMD's first Top 10 hit Enola Gay, a hummable, danceable, exhilarating record about the first A-bomb. In an act of cultural revenge, the Japanese combo **The Surf Chamblers** released their own take on the James Bond theme and, in its way, it's as compelling as John Barry's.

★**Recommended**★ With apologies for crassness, we point you to The Rough Guide To The Music Of Japan (World Music Network), as unpredictable as the country it celebrates.

Jazz

Jazz's roots go back to the marching bands of New Orleans, but it really became popular in the 1920s when it was seen as a danger to society ("Jazz puts the sin into syncopation"). Yet by the end of the 1920s jazz dominated America and the world. In the 1930s and 1940s most great vocalists learned their trade with swing bands (**Louis Armstrong**, **Sinatra**, **Billie Holiday**, **Ella Fitzgerald**, **Sarah Vaughan**, **Peggy Lee**, **Doris Day**). And the career trajectory of cornet player **Bix Beiderbecke** – a star at 20, at his creative peak at 24 and dead (of drink) by the time he was 28 – would set the template for many rock stars. In the 1940s the most popular musician in the world was probably the band leader **Glenn Miller**.

Yet by the 1950s jazz, due in part to such innovators as **Charlie Parker**, lost its grip on the masses. But in the UK jazz – of the trad kind – was a powerful force. Band leaders like **Chris Barber**, **Ken Coyler**, **Kenny Ball** and **Acker Bilk** and groups like **The Temperance Seven** (they couldn't count, there were nine of them) led a trad-jazz revival in the late 1950s and early 1960s, a revival immortalised on celluloid in the 1962 flick It's Trad Dad. The trad-jazz revival didn't rule the charts for long, but laid the roots for skiffle. Colyer's band provided a musical home for **Lonnie Donnegan**, a huge influence on John Lennon, and **Alexis Korner**, mentor to **The Rolling Stones** and other 1960s British bands.

★**Recommended**★ Up Jumped The Devil (Upbeat) shows **Ken Colyer**'s band at the point where skiffle rose from jazz. Ignore the technical imperfections, it's worth it.

Latin

As we all know, Jenny's from a block somewhere in the New York Bronx, but her music is firmly rooted in Latin pop. It's easy to ridicule **J.Lo** but you can't knock her for helping to popularise Latin music. Her debut On The 6 featured two duets with Latino heart-throb **Marc Anthony**, whilst her sophomore effort J.Lo featured her La Isla Bonita-style Si Ya Se Acabo, complete with flamenco guitar.

Gloria Estefan predated Jenny and the current wave of Latin pop by 15 years. At first with the help of her husband's **Miami Sound Machine**, she scored high in the UK and US charts with her infectious blend of Latin beats and slick American production. Their second English-speaking album Anything For You scored four US Top 10 hits. Gloria soon didn't need a formal backing band. Miama Sound Machine were relegated to sleeve note credits and with the band went the up-tempo numbers, Estefan competing in the ballad market with Celine Dion et al.

Of the new kids on the block, **Enrique Iglesias** is happy to take his fathers crown, whilst **Luis Miguel** and **Marc Anthony** don't really have the hips to take Ricky Martin's crown. When it suits her, pop princess **Christina Aguilera** revisits her Ecuadorian roots, in 2000 releasing the Spanish-speaking Mi Reflejo. Colombian-born **Shakira** won a huge following with her Spanish albums, before signing Gloria's husband Emilio as her manager. **Laundry Service**, her most English album to date, spawned **Whenever Wherever**. Though we admire the girl for holding onto control of her music, she might need to improve her English before she writes the next one, to avoid such as lyrics "Lucky that my breasts are small and humble/So you don't confuse them with mountains."

★**Recommended**★ You may not necessarily get the sentiments behind **Gloria Estefan**'s **Alma Caribena** (Epic), but this Cuban and Caribbean blend will keep your toes tapping.

Liverpool

The first Liverpudlian to dominate the charts was **Frankie Vaughan**, who scored 33 Top 40 hits (including two No.1s; Liverpool as a city has amassed over 50 UK No.1s). But it was Ronald Wycherley (aka **Billy Fury**) who taught many young Merseysiders that pop stardom needn't just be a pipe dream. While Fury replaced Cliff as the British Elvis, Knotty Ash's **Ken Dodd** was having hits with ballads so soggy (**Tears**, No. 1 in 1965 for five weeks), it's a wonder they didn't fall apart.

Although the 1960s was Liverpool's golden era (see Merseybeat), the city has continued to produce pop acts with the same remarkable consistency with which it produces young footballers. In the 1970s **The Real Thing** were the biggest-selling British black group of their day, **Half Man Half Biscuit** became cult heroes and Declan Mark McManus (aka **Elvis Costello**) emerged. In the 1980s the city gave us a panoply of acts of which the following are only the most significant or funny: **Flock Of Seagulls** (legendary haircuts), **China Crisis**, **Teardrop Explodes**, **Icicle Works**, **Echo & The Bunnymen**, **Dead Or Alive**, **The Lightning Seeds**, punk elder statesman **Pete Wylie** and **Orchestral Manouevres In The Dark**. **Holly Johnson**, born in Sudan, spent his formative years in Liverpool, conceiving Big In Japan (with Ian Broudie, later of The Lightning Seeds) and **Frankie Goes To Hollywood**, the latter making their debut in Liverpool's Mr. Pickwicks.

The Liverpool scene isn't as lively today, although **The Farm** and **KLF** carried Merseyside into the charts in the 1990s. But the city continues to produce honest, witty, acerbic music – and **Atomic Kitten**.

Manchester

If Liverpool pop could, with some over-simplification, be summed up by the optimism of **Penny Lane**'s blue suburban skies. Such monarchs of miserablism as **Morrissey** and **Joy Division** have been used to paint Manchester as musically manic depressive. But Manchester pop isn't as easily pigeonholed, varying from the panto posturing of **Freddie & The Dreamers**, to the rawness of **Oasis** and the smooth, occasionally monotonous, pop/soul of **Mick Hucknall**.

In the 1950s local teenagers packed beat clubs such as **Oasis** (the name's just a coincidence) and Twisted Wheel to the gunnels. Local band **The Hollies** found fame in the clubs, naming themselves after the Christmas decorations found in Oasis and breaking into the charts in 1963. **Herman's Hermits** rapidly followed in 1964. Despite the rise of local acts like The Mindbenders, Elkie Brooks, Lyn Paul, Godley & Creme, Roy Harper and the Buzzcocks, only in the late 1970s did Manchester create its own inner-city sound. **Tony Wilson** started **Factory Records** in 1978, eventually signing **Joy Division** (which begat **New Order**), **A Certain Ratio** and later the **Happy Mondays**. His **Hacienda** club, opening in 1982, revolutionised club culture and even made Wilson a minor cultural icon who graced the cover of *Newsweek*. He couldn't, though, coax **The Smiths** onto Factory; their near contemporaries, Simply Red, weren't Tony's cup of tea.

A certain irrational euphoria was at the heart of the Hacienda and the Happy Mondays. The Mondays produced lively, if drug-crazed, music with such lyrics as "Son, I'm 30/I only went with your mother 'cause she's dirty". Often seen in the US as thugs, the Mondays stuck two fingers up at the arty, often pretentious music of the capital, an attitude which inspired rival Mad-chester (a phrase initially coined by the Monday's Shaun Ryder) bands **The Stones Roses**, **Inspiral Carpets** and **The Charlatans**. And, although the Fab Four usually get all the credit/blame, it was The Stone Roses (and Inspiral Carpets, for whom **Noel Gallagher** acted as a guitar technician) who inspired Manchester's biggest band of all, **Oasis**.

Merseybeat

"Love, love me do/You know I love you." Simple yet so memorable, these words marked The Beatles assault on the UK charts and the arrival of Merseybeat. For every Merseybeat act after The Beatles who made it big (**Gerry & The Pacemakers**, **Billy J Kramer**, **The Searchers** and **Wayne Fontana & The Mindbenders** – even if they were Mancs) there were many (**The Olympics**, **Jeannie & The Big Guys**, **The Trends**) who didn't make it all and a few (**Peter & Gordon**, **Swinging Blue Jeans**, **The Merseybeats**) whose flirtation with the charts was all too brief.

With its light-hearted lyrics, insistent beat and bubbly infectious tunes, the Merseybeat sound was rock'n'roll, R&B and **Lonnie Donegan**'s British skiffle all shaken up. The Beatles, as the masters of this bright, new, catchy sound, were also the only act to transcend the genre.

Gerry Marsden and his Pacemakers seemed like potential challengers to The Beatles, scoring three No.1s with **How Do You Do It?** (turned down by Adam

Faith and the Fab Four), I Like It and You'll Never Walk Alone, while Billy J Kramer and The Dakotas scored two No.1s with his wimpy melodic pop. The Searchers, formed in 1957 (three years before the Silver Beatles settled on a line-up and dropped the Silver), took six years to reach the charts, adding a Merseybeat edge to The Drifters' Sweets For My Sweet. They arrived just a year before Merseybeat peaked, but had other hits, notably **Needles And Pins**, and The Byrds would share their reliance on 12-string guitar, even borrowing one of their riffs.

As is often the case, Merseybeat's decline coincided with an exploitation movie, Ferry Across The Mersey. Among the acts who never got on the ferry to stardom were The Liver Birds (no relation to the sitcom) who, to quote *All Music Guide*, "couldn't harmonise to save their lives, but they rocked their asses off."

★**Recommended**★ This Is Merseybeat **Various** (Hallmark) features **Billy J Kramer** and **The Beatles** (including the latter's collaboration with **Tony Sheridan** on Why Can't You Love Me Again?). Merseybeat Nuggets Vol.2 **Various** (Sequel) offers a more obscure selection of artists from **The Chants** to **Tommy Quickly & The Remo Four.**

Mods

The Collins English Dictionary defines the term 'Mod': "A member of a group of teenagers in the mid-1960s, noted for their clothes-consciousness and oppositions to rockers." A Mod (the name derived from modern jazz) wore shrink-to-fit Levi's, desert boots and Fred Perry tennis shirts. Their drugs of choice were amphetamines, the ride the pills induced complemented by their scooters, usually Vespas and Lambrettas. Mods were as fussy about music, swayed by **The Kinks**, **The Who** and **The Small Faces**, the latter named by a girlfriend of **Steve Marriott**, based on their height and the fact that they were faces (faces being the highest-ranking Mods). The Small Faces scored a string of early Top 20 hits (the best known being All Or Nothing), but had to adapt their sound to break the US.

Roger Daltrey, lead singer for their chief rivals **The Who**, was a former Teddy Boy. The Mod club circuit gave them a cult following, though they dropped their Mod suits as they became hard rock icons. Other half-decent Mod bands included **The Creation**, who scored a few minor UK hits (guitarist Eddie Philips probably still ruing his decision not to accept **Pete Townsend**'s offer to join The Who) and **The Action**, the second-best band produced by George Martin in the 1960s, who were much better than many of their rivals and, inevitably, never had a chart single.

The 1960s Mods swapped their Lambrettas for Cortinas, and the Mod mood passed until a late 1970s revival. **The Jam**, complete with stylish outfits and bowl-cut haircuts were the biggest, but there were also **The Lambrettas** and **The Merton**

Parkas (named after their birthplace and the obligatory Mod coat). Only The Jam really made it big, the Mod-revival influence is evident in Blur and Oasis.

★**Recommended**★ Watch **Quadrophenia** rather than just listen to the soundtrack (Polydor) and then stick on **The Jam At The BBC Live** (Polydor). Or, if you've already spread enough Jam throughout your music collection, **The Best Of The Lambrettas** (Dojo).

Movie themes

Canny marketing folk know that a good tune can tempt a few more bums onto seats in the cinema, and a bestselling soundtrack CD move an iffy movie's profits into the black. Sometimes a song exists before the film and becomes an integral part of the story, or the title, as with **Misty** by Errol Garner in **Play Misty For Me** (the movie which also launched Roberta Flack's **The First Time Ever I Saw Your Face**). The movies have inspired some truly great songs. Like…

★**When pop goes to Hollywood**★
Car Wash **Rose Royce** It's 1976 and disco is in the clubs and on the big screen.
Ghostbusters **Ray Parker Jr** A strong funky song to match a terrific movie.
Mrs. Robinson **Simon & Garfunkel** Can you imagine *The Graduate* without it?
Night Fever **Bee Gees** The song that sold a million white suits.
St. Elmo's Fire (Man In Motion) **John Parr** Sadly, no one liked any of John's other songs.
Theme from Love Story **Francis Lai** Not released in the UK as a single, but it has become part of the national consciousness anyway. Altogether now, "Da der der da daaaa..."
Theme from Shaft **Isaac Hayes** The standout from Hayes's soul-soaked soundtrack.
Superfly **Curtis Mayfield** As the only soundtrack album (now on Ichiban) to outgross the movie it was written for, it's worth a listen. Simply much groovier than *Saturday Night Fever*.

Music hall

With a cheeky wink, a risqué aside and a sentimental number to tug the heartstrings, **music hall** packed enough variety and invention into an evening's entertainment to have TV schedulers weeping with gratitude.

Skiffle tried to meld music-hall wit and the rhythm of rock'n'roll, **Lonnie Donegan** celebrating refuse collectors on **My Old Man's A Dustman**. It took The Beatles to make music hall hip, Sgt Pepper being inspired by a Victorian circus poster. The amiable sentimentality of McCartney's **When I'm 64** could have been sung by **Eliza Doolittle**. The Kinks made two nostalgia-tinged Sgt Pepper-inspired albums (**Village Green Presentation Society** and **Arthur Or The**

Decline And Fall Of The British Empire) with one track, **Victoria**, a chirpy yet misty-eyed celebration of the late Queen, part Ray Davies, part Gilbert & Sullivan.

As Britpop searched for an idiom, bands like **Blur** rediscovered The Kinks and The Small Faces and, through them, music hall. Ebullient cockney knees-uppery lives on in songs like **Country House**, the **Summer Afternoon** for Generation X. Pop's music-hall roots became 'official' when artists like **Robbie Williams**, **Space** and **Texas** all combined last year to commemorate the **Noel Coward** songbook on the compilation **Twentieth Century Boy** (Ichiban).

My kinda town

Chuck Berry once said the secret to having a hit was to mention as many place names as possible in a song, because folks in those places were more likely to buy it. He took his own advice: in **Promised Land**, a No.9 hit for **Elvis** in 1975, he namechecks ten towns or cities and six states. Big city or small town, the place where you live, or the place where you're going, whether the road to get there is long and winding or even if it's a rainy night when you get there, is always worth a song. Here are a few of the more intriguing songs named after places.

★Around the world in ten tracks★

Barcelona **Freddie Mercury and Montserrat Caballe** So grandiloquent it really ought to be about Las Vegas, although it wouldn't scan as well when Freddie lets rip in the chorus.

The Boston Tea Party **The Sensational Alex Harvey Band** Idiosyncratic Scottish rocker devised this spaced oddity: a hit single which mentions George Washington's wooden teeth.

Copacabana **Barry Manilow** This is what Bondi Beach needs: Bazza to write a song about how music and passion are always in fashion on Sydney's most famous stretch of sand.

New York New York **Frank Sinatra** The song that makes folks everywhere else suffer from little town blues. But we can take solace from the **Bee Gees** New York Mining Disaster.

Flying Down To Rio **Mike Nesmith** It's only a whimsical notion, something to do with the night, but the song and video are more fun than Duran Duran's Rio.

Fort Lauderdale Chamber Of Commerce **Elvis Presley** A cunningly crafted hook which contains the whole title makes this 1960s soundtrack filler something of a curiosity.

Galveston **Glen Campbell** Seldom has such a great song been written (by Jimmy Webb) about such a nondescript place.

Indiana Wants Me **R Dean Taylor** Just as well really. R Dean may have been the first white singer to have a No.1 on Motown (in the US) but Indiana was soon able to keep Taylor.

First We Take Manhattan, Then We Take Berlin **Leonard Cohen** Ambitious bloke, Len.

Rotterdam **The Beautiful South** It could also be Liverpool or Rome, or anywhere else for that matter: the Chuck Berry principle to perfection.

Spandau Ballet were just a 1980s retread of Village People really

New romantics

When **Malcolm McClaren** created an anarchic, rebellious band to shake the music industry to its core, he didn't think it through. What follows chaos? Order of course, the sleek, styled pop of the **new romantics**. But David Bowie and Roxy Music were partly to blame: Bowie dabbled with the synthesizer on *Low*, while late-1970s Roxy wore suits that **Spandau Ballet** would emulate in their *True* phase. Emerging new wave acts, especially Gary Numan, XTC and The Cars, laid the basis for the new romantic sound. But **Steve Strange**, at his neo-glam club Billy's, launched the look, the scene and the band (Visage) which gave us men in eyeliner, frilled shirts (**Duran Duran**) and hilarious haircuts (**Flock Of Seagulls**).

Duran Duran broke through with **Girls On Film**, their success built on boys on film, or video (they were MTV faves). The songs came second – apart from the fab **A View To A Kill**. Duran's Nick Rhodes (hair bigger than Simon Le Bon's pout) helped take **Kajagoogoo** to No.1 with **Too Shy**. But Kajagoogoo, who personified new romanticism's handsome vacuousness, split, denying us more insights like those in **See My Face** ("Life in the Big Apple moves very fast and so must you").

Spandau Ballet were Duran's real rivals, although they were more alluring visually than vocally, with the exception of **True** (sampled by **PM Dawn**, making it the first new-romantic rap song). **ABC** were wittier than most (see page 105), Human League weren't. The demise of **Japan**, the most intriguing group in the field, marked the point at which new romanticism began to lose its sheen.

★**Recommended**★ Check out the debut self-titled album from **Visage** (apart from Strange, there was also a bloke called **Midge Ure**) on Spectrum.

New Zealand

New Zealand has a proud, if slender, tradition of quirky pop. The start was inauspicious. New Zealand-born drummer **Benny Staples** went all the way to Northampton to join The Woodentops only for their acoustic pop to garner a small cult following, their debut album **Giant** peaking at No.35 in the UK.

As everyone knows, the **Thompson Twins** were neither related nor a duo, but singer and percussionist **Alannah Currie** was a 'kiwi'. Joining the Twins after their debut album, Currie added some vocal variety to such hits as **Doctor Doctor**. The hairstyles have distracted from the oddball lyrics ("Somebody's got their eye on me/Perhaps I should invite him up for tea?") accompanying the Twin's synth-pop.

Split Enz were the first New Zealand band to be vaguely famous. Formed by Tim Finn (little brother Neil joined as a junior member but split to found **Crowded House** with Paul Hester), the Enz – once billed as "New Zealand's raunchiest rock'n'roll band" – are best known for their No.12 UK hit **I Got You**. Crowded House emerged when Neil's big brother Tim dallied too long on his solo career. Tim and Neil have both played in Crowded House, but Neil was the boss. Their biggest UK hit **Weather With You** reached No.7, not bad in a land where if you really took the weather with you everywhere you'd get very, very wet.

Of late, only urban soul outfit **OMC**, who had a UK Top 5 with the one-of-a-kind **How Bizarre**, and **The Datsuns** have made much impact here, the latter's lively garage-punk sound leading critics to bill them as the 'next big thing' in indie rock.

Newcastle

Spawning such pop legends as **Hank Marvin**, **Chas Chandler**, **Eric Burdon**, **Sting** and **Jimmy Nail**, Newcastle-Upon-Tyne has never been what you'd call star struck. In 1975 patrons of the Newcastle City Hall were quite content to hear unknown guitarist **Andy Summers** belt out Mike Oldfield's **Tubular Bells**, rather than the man himself. Spookily, the support band on the night was Summers's future Police cohort Sting, with his band Last Exit. Fast-forward almost three decades and a surprising incident occurred during an Oasis concert at **The Riverside Club**: a fan getting on stage to thump Noel Gallagher. The surprising bits being that only one fan took part in the assault and that Liam wasn't the target.

The Oldfields and the Gallaghers may have a jaundiced view of the city but Lindesfarne liked it so much they wrote **Fog On The Tyne** and, in 1978, wanted to run for home, as fast as they could, as they hit No.10. Progressive rockers **The Nice** (with Keith Emerson in the line-up) produced *Five Bridges*, their 1970 album honouring the five bridges which then crossed the Tyne.

Northern Ireland

In one of her more lucid moments **Mariah Carey** once said, "A lot of people are singing about how screwed up the world is, and I don't think everybody wants to hear about that all the time." The irony of Northern Ireland is that, for all the country has endured, it's been mainland pop stars like McCartney and Sting who have pondered the Troubles, while Northern Irish artists have often taken Mariah's advice although, to be fair, it's hard to see how **James Galway**'s magic flute could offer any great insight into the conflict.

The best-known talent is Belfast-born **Van Morrison**, although the music scene has always been more varied than Vanmania might suggest. **Stiff Little Fingers** (crassly billed as the Irish Clash) perfected pop punk while Derry's finest **The Undertones** wrote **Teenage Kicks**, possibly the best punk song ever. Northern Ireland can claim one-third of early **Thin Lizzy**, founding member guitarist Eric Bell being another Belfast boy. Bell had worked with Van Morrison's **Them** before he joined Lizzy. A key player on **Whiskey In The Jar**, he quit after sabotaging a gig in Dublin due to his dissatisfaction with new streamlined sound. Blues guitarist **Gary Moore** initially played with Lynott in Skid Row, he would later join Thin Lizzy, briefly, and dedicate Wild Frontier to Lynott.

Punk-pop-inspired teen act **Ash** weren't punk enough to give up A-level studies to tour the US with **Pearl Jam**, but they were barely out of school when their first full-length album (**1977**, named after the year of their births) made No.1 in the UK.

Norway

Norway's mean line in death metal (**Taake, Theatre Of Tragedy, The Kovenant**) makes it tempting to focus on Seasonal Affective Disorder. Yet Norway have given the world a-ha, who namecheck Phoebus in their No.1 **The Sun Always Shines On TV**. Seen in the UK as a Norwegian Duran Duran, they have also penned songs about traditional Norwegian subjects, like suicide (**Blood That Moves The Body**).

Norway even won Eurovision – in 1985 with the Bobbysocks, although they were part-Swedish. A pan-Scandinavian conspiracy was also responsible for Aqua's **Barbie Girl** – singer Lene is Norwegian, the rest of the blame goes to Denmark. Still, on that basis, Norway can take 25 per cent of the credit for **Abba**: **Frida** (the redhead) was born in the northern port of Narvik. Of late, the best Norway has had to offer is the young singer/songwriter **Lene Marlin** who had a No.5 UK hit with **Sittin' Down Here** in 2000, and **Röyksopp**, the electronic ambient duo whose **Melody A.M.** (Wall Of Sound) is worth a listen.

novelty

Steve Otfinoski, in his book *The Golden Age Of Novelty Songs*, says good novelty songs "puncture the balloon of pomposity, expose the darker side of ourselves and provide life-affirming laughter in the face of civilisation's pretensions." So that rules out **Timmy Mallett** and **Bombalurina**'s **Itsy Bitsy Teeny Weeny Yellow Polka-Dot Bikini**, Joe Dolce's **Shaddap Your Face** and Chuck Berry's **My Ding A Ling** (with the Average White Band backing), though all three were UK No.1s.

Former railway-station guard **Spike Jones** and his **City Slickers** were one of the first influential novelty acts. Jones (named 'the man who murdered music' after his wacky versions of classics such as The William Tell Overture) caught the public's imagination in 1942 with **Der Fuhrer's Face**.

The 1950s was the golden era of the novelty hit. **Tom Lehrer** had two UK Top 10 albums thanks to lyrics such as "It was I who stepped on your dress, la-la-la/The skirts all came off, I confess, la-la-la." The 1960s had its share of novelty hits – such as **Monster Mash** and the charming **Snoopy Vs The Red Baron** (No.8 in 1967) by **The Royal Guardsmen**, a tribute to the cartoon canine who fantasised about being a World War I flying ace. **Johnny Cash** reached No.4 with **A Boy Named Sue**. Bubblegum made it hard, for a while, to tell what was pop and what were jokes.

In the 1970s former radio DJ **Ray Stevens** had a No.1 with **The Streak** in 1974. It was comedians from thereon in: Billy Connolly (**No Chance, D.I.V.O.R.C.E**), Jasper Carrott (**Funky Moped** and an X-rated version of **The Magic Roundabout**) and **Harry Enfield** (**Loadsamoney** – made with über-producer **William Orbit**). Still, that was preferable to **The Teletubbies Say Eh-Oh!**, **Mr. Blobby** etc etc. (For novelty tracks erring on the side of parody, see Spoofs.)

★**Recommended**★ The Holy Grail of novelty albums, **Dr. Demento 20th Anniversary Collection: The Greatest Novelty Records Of All Time** (Rhino) is pricey at £23.99, but includes **Hello Muddah, Hello Faddah!** by **Allan Sherman** and **King Tut** by **Steve Martin**.

One-hit wonders

For some, three minutes of fame is all they get, although they hang on waiting for the other 12 minutes **Andy Warhol** promised them. Some acts are destined to vanish after one hit (no one's achy heart broke when **Billy Ray Cyrus** vamoosed). In the 1970s **Carl Douglas** wrote a good pop song about kung fu after seeing kids in **Soho** mimick **Bruce Lee**'s moves. **Kung-Fu Fighting** was No.1 in the UK and US, selling **nine-million** copies. But his next hit, **Dance The Kung-Fu**, stalled at No.35 in the UK. It's not clear why **Martha & The Muffins** sunk after **Echo Beach**, No.10 in 1980, when **Bananarama**, natural one-hit wonders if ever we saw three of them, had ten Top 10 hits. The **One-Hit Wonders Hard 2 Get Hits** box set with 150 one-off tracks is a fascinating guide to the fickleness of pop fate.

Even more pitiful than a one-hit wonder is a no-hit wonder. **Jackie Lomax** is the best blue-eyed soul singer never to have a UK hit. His band **The Undertakers** were admired by (and played with) **The Beatles**. **Brian Epstein** agreed to manage him – and died. He signed for Apple, to no effect, joined groups with such dire names as **Badger**, **Heavy Jelly** and **Balls**, and has just released an album via the Net.

Pianists

In the 1950s **Winifred Atwell** was queen of the keyboards. A former **pharmacist**, she scored 22 Top 20 hits, including the honky tonk(ish) number **Black & White Rag** (now the theme tune to **Pot Black**). She had two No.1s, a feat matched only by **Russ Conway**, best known for **Side Saddle** and for losing part of his finger in a bread slicer. In 1972 *Opportunity Knocks* winner **Bobby Crush**, notorious as the writer of **Orville's Song**, tinkled the ivories, but stuck at No.37 with **Borsalino**.

Protest songs

Jazz and blues have long attacked injustice, as in **Billie Holiday**'s **Strange Fruit**, written in 1938 about the lynching of black Americans. Although rockers like **Blue Suede Shoes** protested at life in general, the pop protest song kicked off in the 1960s when artists like **Bob Dylan** wrote and sang songs like **The Death of Emmett Till** (about a race killing). Protest songs were so trendy there was a backlash. Merle Haggard's **Okie From Muskogee** ("We don't smoke marijuana") was a minor US hit in 1969, but by the 1970s pop was reflecting America's turmoil over Vietnam in songs like **Edwin Starr**'s **War (What is it Good For?)**. In the UK **Labi Siffre** was often the solemn guest on the **The Two Ronnies** show, but his songs, especially

(Something Inside) So Strong, protested against apartheid and inequality.

The Jam hit out at racism with their first hit, **Down In The Tube Station At Midnight**, in 1978. At the turn of the 1980s, **The Specials**' anger fuelled **Ghost Town**, **Too Much Too Young** and (as **Special AKA**) **Nelson Mandela**. **Billy Bragg** and **Elvis Costello** both dwelt on social inequality. CND got a surprising plug from **Frankie Goes To Hollywood** with their No.1 **Two Tribes**. Vegetarianism was in vogue in the mid-1980s with The Smiths' album **Meat Is Murder**. Comedian **Denis Leary**'s 1996 single about drink-driving, **Asshole**, is vicious and funny. Right now, though, protest songs aren't getting much of a look in.

★**Recommended**★ Bob Dylan's The Times They Are A-Changin' (CBS); So Strong **Labi Siffre** (China) includes **Nothing's Gonna Change** – Eminem sampled Siffre's **I Got The...** as a base for his **My Name Is...** single and the original riff featured **Chas & Dave** on guitar; **The Specials** (2-Tone); **London 0 Hull 4 The Housemartins** (Go! Discs), has pissed-off workers' classics like **Flag Day** and **Get Up Off Our Knees**; and **Billy Bragg**'s **Back To Basics** (Elektra) is a good intro to his work. Try also **Chumbawamba**'s **Anarchy** (One Little Indian).

Pub rock

Before punk, there was **pub rock**. Pub rock's simple stripped-down sound and DIY approach anticipated punk. Pub rock started around **Tally Ho**, a former London jazz club, the acts playing 1960s rock or R&B, with a slice of country. Some prolific bands such as **Bees Make Honey** and **Chilli Willi** remained unknown. But **Eddie & The Hot Rods** (**Teenage Depression** on Island is their best album) and **Dr Feelgood** started as pub rockers; Kilburn & The High Roads featured **Ian Dury**; **Flip City** boasted **Elvis Costello**; the **101'ers** featured **Joe Strummer**; **Brinsley Schwarz** were fronted by **Nick Lowe**; and **Ace**, with **Paul Carrack** (who later sang lead on **Squeeze**'s **Tempted**) hit No.20 with **How Long**.

Punk

The punk fanzine **Sniffin' Glue** once included three drawings of chord shapes captioned: "Here's a chord, here's another one, here's another one. Now form a band." Punk was a DIY business, a reaction against the establishment, pompous prog rockers, public opinion, the utter futility of many young urban lives in Britain and America in the 1970s and anything else that got in punk's way.

The word punk is related to the Spanish words for prostitutes ('punta' and 'punto'). The music's heyday was 1975 to 1978, its roots go back to such groups as **The Stooges**, whose 1969 self-titled album marked the first stirrings of what

Bob Geldof presses his nose to the floor to see if he can smell a Rat

would be called punk. Punk was also shamelessly manipulated by the likes of **Malcolm McLaren**, who courted the scruffiest, most loutish customers to his and **Vivienne Westwood**'s clothing store SEX. He remade the Sex Pistols, replacing bassist **Glen Matlock** with **Sid Vicious**, who couldn't play a note but looked right.

Few acts changed pop as much as the Pistols, yet, thrilling as Anarchy In The UK is, the songs were secondary – the group were made to enrage and inspire. The cliché that punk was musically limited stands up – till you hear The Clash's Bank Robber, The Stranglers' No More Heroes or the Buzzcocks' Ever Fallen In Love. Punk had many styles: the **Ramones** had bubblegum flavours, **The Clash** worked with reggae singer **Lee 'Scratch' Perry**, the **Buzzcocks** were almost pop-punk and **X-Ray Specs** cheerfully led feminist punk with the cry: "Oh bondage up yours".

Punk was such an almighty clearing of the decks that out of it emerged all kinds of musics: post-punk (**Joy Division**, **The Jam**), new wave (**Elvis Costello**, **The Boomtown Rats**), ska-punk (**The Specials**) pub rock-punk (**Squeeze**), ant music and hardcore, a precursor of grunge. Bands like **Green Day** led a punk revival in the 1990s. Yet punk didn't, oddly, dominate the charts as The Beatles and Elvis had done. Punk's annus mirabilis, 1977, saw one disputed punk No.1 – God Save The Queen (see Banned). And the year's big chart-topper was Mull Of Kintyre.

★**Recommended**★ The sum total of the Sex Pistols' recordings, Never Mind The Bollocks (Virgin), is essential – **NME** voted it the third greatest album of all time. D.I.Y: Blank Generation: The New York Scene (Rhino) sums up New York's punk scene with the Patti Smith Group and less-established acts likes Suicide and Richard Hell & The Voidoids.

Puppets

Pinky & Perky were the first puppet popsters, making a Christmas album in 1961 and hitting No.47 in 1993 with their take on Reet Petite. But **The Muppets** are The Beatles of puppet pop, their vast body of work includes the No.7 hit Halfway Down The Stairs, their bid to revive the EP format – The Muppet Show Music Hall (No.19) – and their No.1 debut album The Muppet Show. Their successors, **The Fraggles**,

Making a pig's ear of pop

hit No.33 with the Fraggle Rock Theme, and **The Barry Gray Orchestra** stalled at No.53 with the Joe 90 theme dance mix. The group **F.A.B.** soared to No.5 with Thunderbirds Are Go in 1990. The Big Breakfast's puppet duo Zig & Zag were No.5 in 1994 with Them Girl/Them Girls, just missing out on a Christmas No.1.

As it happens...

American DJs like **Alan Freed** get to coin terms like "rock'n'roll". British DJs launch darts on the radio...

Dave Lee Travis

A one-time tour manager for Herman's Hermits, DLT was a DJ for Radio Caroline pirate radio. Flushed by his success with radio snooker, he launched darts on the radio before quitting Radio 1 live on-air.

Steve Wright

Contrary to what Chris Evans would have you believe, Steve Wright and his 'posse' brought the 'zoo format' (pioneered in the US by Scott Shannon) to UK radio.

Alan Freeman

"Fluff" started out as an accountant in a timber company in Oz, coined "Not arf!" and "Erm" as catchphrases and never told an awful joke on air.

Tony Blackburn

On Radio Caroline South he pioneered the use of sound effects – well, a sound-effect dog called Arnold – and tried to popularise the tea-cosy haircut, to no avail.

Kenny Everett

Often underrated DJ, fired from Radio 1 for suggesting the wife of the transport minister had bribed her way through her driving test.

Radio

A cheap way to get airplay is to stick radio in a song title or (as in Roxy Music's **Oh Yeah**) in a hook. The list of hits on this theme tells its own story: Radio Radio, Radio, On the Radio, Radio (again), Radio No.1, Radio On, Radio Romance, Radio Musicola, Radio Song and Radio Wall Of Sound. As for the lyrics: "I've got my radio on" says ex-Deacon Blue **Ricky Ross** in, er, **Radio On**. These pale beside Queen's hypnotic, totalitarian **Radio Ga Ga**. Radio goo goo... that's poetry, that is.

Rap

Give **Vanilla Ice** a break. His claim to have been stabbed five times in various gang fights has been disputed. Worse, his real name is **Robert Van Winkle**. But his 1990 UK No.1 **Ice Ice Baby** brought rap to the forefront in the UK. And anyone who gets dissed by **Eminem** (on the track **Marshall Mathers**) has a certain cachet. But please don't lump the highly political **Public Enemy** and the highly talented **Ice Cube** in the same sentence as Mr Van Winkle. Cube's 1990 album **AmeriKKKa's Most Wanted** (Priority) along with PE's **It Takes A Nation Of Millions To Hold**

Us Back (Def Jam) are two of rap's most influential albums.

Nearly a quarter of a century since the first rap hit – Rapper's Delight by The Sugarhill Gang – blasted into the US charts, many rappers have fallen by the wayside. Some, like Tupac Shakur, "kept it real" by dying in drive-by shootings similar to those they rapped about. But rap (or hip hop as the music is also now known) is stronger than ever. Rap started in the 1970s as a way for black and ethnic youth in inner-city America to bond. Today it commands a global audience and is marshalled by a white rapper, Eminem. Since Vanilla Ice's Ice Ice Baby, Will Smith, Coolio, The Fugees, LL Cool J, Puff Daddy, Usher, Nelly and Eminem have all had UK No.1s (Eminem has had four). And Run-DMC, the only rap group to play Live Aid, became the first rap act to have a platinum album, a No.1 album in the R&B charts, an album in the US Top 10 and a video on MTV.

Long before Public Enemy's political rhymes, LL Cool J had mesmerised the masses with a fantastic debut album Radio and the pop-rap hit I Need Love. And Beastie Boys, originally a punk band from middle-class Jewish families, also overcame the rap/pop divide by supporting Madonna on tour in 1985.

The social commentary at hip hop's heart became more controversial in the late 1980s with gangsta rap. Drugs, guns, money, gangs, misogyny, homophobia, turf warfare and death fused to form the most popular form of rap. Gangsta rap's LA pioneers N.W.A. (Niggaz With Attitude) didn't last long but changed rap forever. Their 1988 album Straight Outta Compton (Ruthless/Priority) glorified a criminal lifestyle (tracks like Fuck Tha Police have to be heard to be believed), making stars of Dr Dre and Ice Cube. Dre left NWA in 1992 to form Death Row Records. His first solo album, The Chronic, confirmed he was a great rap producer, launching Snoop Dogg. Meanwhile, in New York, the Wu-Tang Clan brought "the muthafuckin' ruckus", boasted of their "Shaolin sword-style" and warned everyone to "protect ya neck". It was very different from West Coast gangsta rap, but so outrageous it worked: Enter The Wu-Tang (BMG/Loud) is a bizarre triumph, one that the nine Clan members' solo projects have yet to top.

★Recommended★ Ready to Die Notorious BIG (Bad Boy); All Eyez on Me Tupac Shakur (Death Row); and The Marshall Mathers LP Eminem (Aftermath/Interscope)

Reggae

"White kids have lost their heroes; Jagger has become a wealthy socialite, Dylan a mellowed, home-loving man, even Lennon has little to say. So along comes this guy with amazing screw-top hair, and he's singing about 'brainwash education' and loving your brothers and smoking dope. Their dreams live on." This was how

Bob Marley & The Wailers try to sneak off with Jimmy Cliff's instruments

the **NMF** greeted the arrival of **Bob Marley**, reggae's near-saintly figurehead.

In the early 1960s many Jamaicans wanted to cap political independence (granted in **1962**) with musical independence. **Ska** emerged in 1961, picked up from **New Orleans R&B** stations, but within six years ska was out (see Ska) and **rocksteady** was in – Jamaican music, but with an obvious soul influence pioneered by producer **Duke Reid**. A year later reggae was born. At first the term was used to describe a new sound which united the offbeat rhythms and melodies of ska and rocksteady with lyrics full of social and political sentiments. Later reggae was influenced by the political persuasions and mystical elements (not to mention the ganja smoking) of **Rastafarianism**.

The hook of reggae, then and now, is the juddering hypnotic pulse which flows through every track, but reggae drew on many styles. You can hear American rock'n'roll in tracks by **Toots & The Maytals**, while the raw soul of the Memphis-based **Stax** label is evident in **Desmond Dekker**'s work. Sweeter soul can be heard in songs by **The Paragons**. But reggae caught Jamaica's imagination, the lyrics reflecting people's lives and hopes. At first songs were sent to the UK to be pressed, but many records never made it back, being sold to former ska fans in the UK.

The Maytals were probably the first act to use the term reggae in a song (**Do The**

Reggay). Ska veterans with producer **Leslie Kong**, they incorporated rocksteady, and reggae; their single **Sun, Moon And Stars** boasting a strong Rastafarian vibe. **Jimmy Cliff** was another pioneer, his first single **Hattie Hurricane** was a big hit. Cliff starred in the 1972 reggae smash movie **The Harder They Come**, but was too polished to appeal to the largely unemployed, disillusioned masses who embraced reggae, for whom Marley seemed the real equivalent to Cliff's character.

The Wailers changed line-ups often, but Marley and his Rastafarian beliefs were the act's **nucleus**. They flourished as songwriters for US acts such as **Johnny Nash**, but Marley wanted to sing his own songs and have them heard outside Jamaica, so he brazenly strolled into the office of **Chris Blackwell**, head of **Island Records**. What is now called the first reggae album, **Catch A Fire**, was released in 1972. **Pete Tosh** and **Bunny Wailer** quit after internal strife, and the group – now called Bob Marley & The Wailers – played the London Lyceum, striking gold in the UK. The band scored eight Top 40 hits before Marley's death from cancer at 37, his Rastafarian beliefs having stopped him having surgery years earlier.

There is more to reggae than Marley – **The Upsetters**, **Black Uhuru** and Peter Tosh to name but three – but no one as powerful has come along since, and variants such as ragga and dancehall took over the hardcore audience. **Dennis 'Blackbeard' Bovell**'s magnificent **Dub Band** are the pick of the British litter (his lovers' rock **Silly Games** took **Janet Kay** to No.2 in 1979) though **The Police** and **UB40** have used a watered-down reggae to create their sounds. Even if you're not a fan of The Maytals, reggae may well have found a way into your record collection – though hopefully not through **Paul Nicholas**'s **Reggae Like It Used To Be**.

★**Recommended**★ Legend (Island) collects Marley's finest work, including an extended version of **Punky Reggae Party**. The **The Harder They Come** soundtrack is a must. And **Funky Kingston** (Trojan) has plenty of funky titles, such as **Time Tough** and **Pressure Drop**.

Rochdale

For a town of its size, Rochdale has groomed its share of songstresses (and **Johnny Clegg**; see South Africa). The town will be forever identified with **Gracie Fields**, an icon of stage, screen and studio, famous for such novelties as **The Biggest Aspidistra In The World**, though you could argue her song **Will You Still Love When I'm Mutton?** is a precursor of **The Beatles**' **When I'm 64**. Gracie's real name was Gracie Stansfield, a fact that prompted **Lisa Stansfield** to disown her home town's most famous singer, saying Gracie "sings like someone has stepped on a cat." Rochdale has also produced arguably the finest cabaret singer in recent times, **Barbr Jungr**. Good as Lisa is, Jungr's album **Chanson: The Space In Between**

(Linn) shows real soul: it's quirky, intelligent cabaret music of the highest order.

Rockabilly

This wild blend of country and R&B kick-started rock'n'roll almost 50 years ago yet still has an avid following. Rockabilly sprang from America's Deep South – **Bill Haley**'s records seem a bit stagey and **Rock Around The Clock**, purists would say, isn't real rockabilly. The classic rockabilly sound was, in the early 1950s, virtually monopolised by **Sam Phillips** at his **Sun Studios**. (The **Sarg** label in Texas created a more country-tinged variant but never had a national hit.)

At its purest, rockabilly was created on very few instruments: guitars and a double bass, slapped more than plucked, to create beat and echo. This sound is best represented by the early records of Elvis, **Scotty Moore**, **Bill Black** and **The Rock & Roll Trio**, led by **Johnny Burnette**. You can hear Phillips experimenting to create this sound with records like **Jackie Brenston**'s **Rocket 88** on **The Sun Story Vol.1** (Charly). Jerry Lee Lewis, although he broke with rockabilly tradition by playing piano, took over from Burnette as the genre's wild man. The rockabilly sound also shaped early **Buddy Holly** records.

By 1958 rockabilly was history. Most of the early stars had gone pop, retired or died. But Elvis's Sun Sessions, released in the UK for the first time on one record in 1976, helped engineer a revival. **Dave Edmunds** brought rockabilly back to the UK charts in 1979 with such hits as **Queen Of Hearts**, and steered **Stray Cats**, who had three Top 10 hits in the US in 1982/3. In the UK **Shakin' Stevens** made some credible rockabilly before becoming a housewives' favourite. Classic rockabilly also inspired **The Cramps**, who recorded at **Sun Studios** and called their 1986 album **Date With Elvis**. The rockabilly revival is still not dead. **The Reverend Horton Heat**'s music is fierce genuine rockabilly. Only 20 or so tracks stand out, so his **Holy Roller** (Sub Pop) compilation may be all you need to know.

★**Recommended**★ **Elvis**'s **Sunrise** (BMG), a collection of his **Sun Studios work**, is as key to understanding rock'n'roll and rockabilly as **Robert Johnson**'s work is to appreciating the blues. **Rockabilly Boogie** (Bear) has the best of **Johnny Burnette** and more besides.

Russia

Josef Stalin would not be surprised by **t.A.T.u**, the Russian 'lesbian' duo who have appalled millions with their tale of a lesbian affair **I Almost Lost My Mind**. Stalin's henchman **Andrei Zhdanov** had once called Western popular music "**a tumour on the social organism**", and the Soviet state fought long, hard and in vain to keep jazz, pop and rock'n'roll at bay.

The Communists tried to get the young to bop to bizarre officially sanctioned dance crazes derived from the ballet. They created a register for **Vocal Instrumental Ensembles** (Sovietspeak for groups) who made music that promoted Social Realism, and nurtured a **Russian Elvis, Dean Reed** – actually an American Elvis clone who had defected. But Moscow medical students in the 1950s still pressed early Elvis records into discarded **X-ray plates** and sold them. In desperation, Stalin's successor **Nikita Kruschev** allowed rock'n'roll bands to play at a 1957 music festival, not realising they would bring electric guitars with them. **The Beatles**, albeit after a time lag, swept the **USSR**. In 1967 the Kremlin had to send the police to Red Square to stop young Russians twisting the day away.

Punk kicked off in the USSR in 1984 with **Egor Letov**'s band **Grazhdanskaya Oborona** (Civil Defence), reviving at the turn of the millennium. And **Mikhail Gorbachev** handed over to Elvis fan **Boris Yeltsin**. For a better idea of Russian music pop than t.A.T.u, try **Inna Zhelaniya**, a folk-rock singer with a warm but not safe voice; her album **Inozemetz On The Green Wave** is worth a listen.

School

Is there any greater cry of joy in pop than **Alice Cooper**'s "School's out for summer!"? Alice went a bit far with "School's been blown to pieces," (upsetting **Mary Whitehouse**), but he was, in a sense, updating **Chuck Berry**'s **School Day (Ring Ring Goes The Bell)** – covered by **Don Lan** in 1957 – an ode to "Golden Rule" days. Signs of discontent emerged with **The Coasters**' **Charlie Brown** ("who calls the English teacher Daddio?") and **Rock Around The Clock** (featured in the film **Blackboard Jungle** – "A shock story of today's high school hoodlums!").

Generation-gap classics gave way to tamer sentiments – in 1963 **The Beach Boys**' **Be True To Your School** made No.6 in the US; unimaginable in the UK– and school crushes. Songs about carrying books to school abound (eg **The Chi-Lites**' **Homely Girl**, No.5 in 1974), and in 1974 **Barry Blue** (formerly Barry Green and barely out of school himself) reached No.11 with the ballad **School Love**. This, too, has been updated by **The Beautiful South** in **Song For Whoever**, where Paul Heaton declares to the girls in his class, "I love you from the bottom of my pencil case."

A different kind of school crush featured in 1967 when **Lulu** had a US hit with **To Sir With Love** (Lulu had a part in the **Sidney Poitier** movie of that name) – in Britain the song was buried on the B-side of **Let's Pretend**. In 1980 **The Police**'s disconcerting take on pupil-teacher attraction – **Don't Stand So Close To Me** – was No.1 for four weeks (Sting himself had been a teacher), dislodged finally by a nation's pique at his rhyming "**shake and cough**" with "**Nabokov**".

In between, **Pink Floyd** raised blood pressures with their attack on the school system in **Another Brick In The Wall (Part II)**, a transatlantic No.1. Not content with lines such as "We don't need no education" (just an English lesson) they got the fourth-form music class of Islington Green School to sing the last chorus. But **Madness** wrote the finest school song of all (with the possible exception of the **Grange Hill** theme) in **Baggy Trousers**: "Oh what fun we had, but did it really turn out bad?/All I learnt at school, was how to bend not break the rules…"

Science

Don't know much about biology, don't know much about algebra… **Sam Cooke**'s 'ignorance is bliss' in **Wonderful World** could apply to most pop. **Einstein A Go Go**, a No.5 hit for **Landscape** in 1981, uses the name of the 20th century's greatest scientist because… it's got two syllables in it. At the other end of the intellectual scale is **Life**, an obscure 1970s single in which **Elvis** heroically tries to reconcile the Theory Of Evolution and the Bible. Funny thing is, he almost pulls it off.

Pop's dystopian view of science is summed up by **Zager & Evans**' 1969 No.1 **In The Year 2525 (Exordium And Terminus)**. The brackets were a clear sign that there aren't many laughs, just one actually: "In the year 9510, if God's a comin'/He ought to make it by then," as if God was some cosmic commuter stuck on an interplanetary **British Rail**. Pop wasn't always so paranoid about men in white coats. In 1955's **I'm Building A ?? On the Moon** American singer **Weldon Rogers** fondly imagined a utopia where slot machines paid out. The Sputnik launch drove **Ray Anderson** to pen **Sputnicks & Mutnicks**, while the launch of a telecomms satellite prompted **Joe Meek** to celebrate with No.1 smash **Telstar**.

The space race would inspire a weird form of electronic easy listening called **space-age pop**. Yet astronauts were only heroes if they were celebs (**Space Oddity**) or normal blokes. In **Elton John**'s **Rocket Man** the astronaut says, "And all the science I don't understand" before confiding "Mars ain't the kind of place to raise the kids." If you think Mars is tough Elton, try Feltham.

As the 1970s ended, **Gary Numan** fretted that his electric friend had broken down. **Devo,** with robot **Bootji** as a mascot, sang, "Are we not men?/We are Devo!" As two of the band now write songs for kids' cartoons, that should now read, "We are not men, we are Rugrats." **Sarah Brightman** with **Hot Gossip** were cheerier, though they had lost their hearts to a starship trooper. That seems fair enough, the hard bit was accepting Sarah had lost her heart to **Andrew Lloyd Webber**.

After that it's mostly apocalypses, from **The Jam**, **Sham 69**, **OMD** (**Enola Gay**), **Frankie Goes To Hollywood** (**Two Tribes**) and **Sting**, who worried about protecting his little boy from Oppenheimer's deadly toy. The good news, Sting, is that the Russians love their children too – apparently. The bad news, **Fun Boy Three** note, is that **The Lunatics Have Taken Over The Asylum**. But give Sting the last word, as he says in **Walking In Your Footsteps**: "Hey there mighty brontosaurus/Do you have a lesson for us?"

Sci-fi

A Vulcan on vulcanite

In the 1950s the sci-fi pop song lagged behind the sci-fi movie. But flying saucers did inspire **Billy Lee Riley**'s **Flying Saucers Rock'n'Roll**, notable because a) it's good, and b) **Jerry Lee Lewis** played piano on it.

Alien sightings inspired the daft, fun, **Purple People Eater**, a No.12 hit for **Sheb Woolley** in 1958, and **50 Megaton**, in which cheery **Sonny Russell** imagines Earth's destruction by aliens. The Ran-Dells had a small US hit with **Martian Hop**, revived in the UK by **Rocky Sharpe & The Replays** in 1980. **The Byrds**, in their US hit **Mr Spaceman**, begged an alien for a ride. **David Bowie** was with The Byrds: he felt the starman, in his 1972 hit, would like to see us, but was afraid we couldn't cope. But the trio Brownville Station, in **Martian Boogie,** shared a ciggie with a green man at a greasy spoon. All this inspired **The Carpenters** to cut **Calling Occupants Of Interplanetary Craft**, with its chorus: "interplanetary most extraordinary space... craft." The pause before "craft" so long you suspected subliminal advertising for Kraft cheese slices.

Sci-fi has inspired some smashtastic hits, like **Doctoring The Tardis**, No.1 for the **Timelords** in 1988, and **Star Trekkin'** by **The Firm** ("Boldly going forward because we can't find reverse"). But these pale beside **Leonard Nimoy**'s bizarre **Highly Illogical** album. The third time you hear Len's **If I Had A Hammer** you feel in urgent need of a blunt instrument yourself. **Catatonia**'s **Mulder & Scully** was better (No.3 in 1998); almost as good as the *X-Files* theme tune.

★**Recommended**★ Ultimate 50s Rockin' Sci-Fi Disc (Viper)

Scotland

Scotland is often seen as a mystical **Celtic society**, but it's too big geographically and too diverse culturally to be so simplified. Only **Runrig** really merit the Celtic tag, taking Gaelic (impenetrable to most Scots) to the Top 20 with **An Ubhal As Airde** (The Highest Apple) in 1995. While the nation's **Calvinist** licensing and entertainment laws have hindered pop and rock, a large number of influential figures – from **Talking Heads'** **David Byrne** and **Dire Straits'** **Mark Knopfler** to fifth Beatle **Stu Sutcliffe** and **Jethro Tull's** **Ian Anderson** – have been born there.

A far cry from Granny's highland home, it was the rough and rugged urban landscape of **Glasgow** that gave birth to 1950s skiffle king **Lonnie Donegan** and to Scottish rock'n'roll pioneer **Alex Harvey**. (Harvey would resurface in the mid-1970s with his provocative combination of everything from blues and jazz to cabaret and rock: his take on **Delilah** even reached No.7 in 1975.) Thereafter it went pretty quiet until 1974 and the **Bay City Rollers** (remembered for their tartan trousers more than their songs), and their more credible offshoots **Pilot** and **Slik**. Isolated individuals such as **Lulu**, **Donovan**, **Jack Bruce** (the sleeve image of **Disraeli Gears** is Cream climbing **Ben Nevis** while tripping on acid), **Barbara Dickson** and **Gallagher & Lyle** have also made their mark on the charts, along with even more isolated groups like **The Average White Band** (**Arif Marden** produced their hit **Pick Up The Pieces**), **Nazareth** and **Stone The Crows**.

Lest we forget, songwriters **Bill Martin** and **Phil Coulter** wrote the Eurovision hits **Puppet On A String** and **Congratulations**, and the 1970 England World Cup song **Back Home** (traitors!). To be fair, they also gave Elvis his last Top 5 hit while he was alive, **My Boy**. Scotland can also claim Elvis's only visit to Britain; he landed briefly at **Prestwick** in 1960 on his way home from GI service in Germany.

Punk brought Scotland back to life. **The Skids** (and then **Big Country**), **Simple Minds** and **The Rezillos** all hit the charts, as did a few lesser bands. **Owen Paul** (see page 150) was a throwback to the old pop order, while the **Postcard** indie label gave us **Orange Juice** and **Aztec Camera**. Even **Midge Ure** was reborn with **Ultravox**.

Annie Lennox, **Eddi Reader** (with Fairground Attraction) and **Sheena Easton** have followed their own paths to the charts, but the country's main export has been a steady stream of decent guitar bands – **The Proclaimers** (produced by fellow Scot **Gerry Rafferty**), **Deacon Blue** and **Marillion**. Singer **Fish** was so named after his landlady only allowed him one bath a week (he retaliated by spending two hours in it at a time), but the nickname was a blessing – his real name is **Derek Dick**. More recent, more fashionable, entrants to the Scottish hall of fame include **Texas**, **Travis** and Primal Scream frontman **Bobby Gillespie**, although enterprising Scots can be found everywhere. As the author J M Barrie noted, there are few more impressive sights in the world than a Scotsman on the make.

Sheep

Paul McCartney's early solo efforts displayed an unusual fascination with the beasts. **Mary Had A Little Lamb** was his third solo single (No.9 in the UK), while the cover of his 1971 album, Ram, featured Paul with said animal. In 1973 jazzy R&B outfit the **Tony Osborne Sound** had a minor hit with The Shepherd's Song. **The Housemartins**' Sheep, their 1986 debut single, peaked at No.54. Despite hailing from New York, rap duo **Black Sheep** released A Wolf In Sheep's Clothing. And that pretty much sums up the history of sheep in pop.

Sheffield

Joe Cocker, **ABC**, **Pulp**, **Human League**, **Def Leppard**, **Ace**, **Moloko**, **Cabaret Voltaire**, **Autechre**, **Angelic Upstarts**, **Heaven 17**; all have their roots in a city which should be famous for making pop, not steel. Metal manipulation being such a local tradition may explain Def Leppard (something has to), while ABC, Heaven 17 and Human League all made catchy stainless pop. Sheffield has a strong say in techno, through **Robert Gordon**, **Manna**, Autechre and Cabaret Voltaire's **Richard H Kirk**. All this and not a dodgy ballad singer to disown either.

Show tunes

In the beginning there were show tunes. And even today, a song from the stage makes it to the top of the charts usually when the song is big, powerful and easy to belt out in the shower. The mother of all chart-topping stage tunes is Don't Cry For Me Argentina from the musical Evita by Andrew Lloyd Webber and **Tim Rice**, a hit on five occasions. In 1976 it was a No.1 for **Julie Covington** (the benchmark, some would say). Two years later **The Shadows** took it into the Top 10. **Sinead O'Connor** released her cover in 1992, **Madonna**'s movie version followed in 1996 and there was a well-deserved **Mike Flowers Pop** tribute later that year.

★**The songs from the shows**★

Aquarius/Let The Sunshine In **The Fifth Dimension** A Grammy-winning medley from the hit hippy musical Hair, which hit the UK charts in 1969.

Day By Day **Holly Sherwood** This God-themed single from Godspell reached No.29 in 1972.

Send In The Clowns **Judy Collins** Much better known than the musical it was in, A Little Night Music by **Steven Sondheim**, based on one of **Ingmar Bergman**'s lesser-known films.

And I'm Telling You I'm Not Going **Jennifer Holliday** Not a hit in 1982, the remix did better for **Donna Giles** in 1996. Sadly, the musical it came from, Dreamgirls, never came to the UK.

One Night In Bangkok **Murray Head** From Chess, a rare non-ballad show tune to chart.

Maria **PJ Proby** Not the Blondie hit, the West Side Story classic, a No.8 hit for PJ in 1965.

Losing My Mind **Liza Minnelli** (with help from the **Pet Shop Boys**) This 1989 dance hit originated as a torch song in Sondheim's Follies.

Singer/songwriters

The tradition of the singer/songwriter goes back much further than the 1970s – **Noel Coward** (whose classic **Mad About The Boy** reached No.41 for Dinah Washington in 1992) and **Hoagy Carmichael** being cases in point. **Lennon** and **McCartney** were the singer/songwriters behind The Beatles' success, but the term singer/songwriter usually refers to artists who accompany themselves on piano or guitar, with the emphasis firmly on the (often confessional) song.

Bob Dylan popularised the genre, marrying folk and rock and adding personal, if cryptic, lyrics. But the introspective musings or social observations of artists like **Carole King**, **James Taylor** and **Cat Stevens** mean the genre is heavily associated with the late-1960s/early-1970s. Being a singer/songwriter makes it easy to perform (no rehearsals with fractious bandmates or vanloads of amplification and no stadia necessary). But it's a genre that lends itself to albums, so UK singles-chart successes are rare. **Carole King** scored a No.3 hit in 1962 with **It Might As Well Rain Until September**, but made her name penning tracks for others, including **The Loco-Motion** for **Little Eva** (her babysitter at the time). Thanks to schoolfriend **Neil Sedaka**, she joined the **Brill Building** where she met (and worked with) future husband **Gerry Goffin**. Her second album, **Tapestry**, spent six years in the US charts and racked up a UK No.6 hit with **It's Too Late** in 1971. **Carly Simon** also emerged at this time, **You're So Vain** (No.3 in 1972 – see page 282) being her signature song. **Joan Armatrading** (**Love And Affection** made No.10 in 1976) and **Kate Bush** were among the leading British exponents.

Of their male contemporaries, **Paul Anka** was one of the youngest to emerge, penning his 1957 hit **Diana** about his babysitter, **Diana Ayoub**, at the age of 16. **Leonard Cohen** switched from poet to songwriter at just the right time, his earnest expressions of romantic despair (**Famous Blue Raincoat**) proving perfect bedfellows with the personal (if less depressing) songs of **James Taylor** and **Paul Simon**. **Randy Newman**, known today for his **Disney** soundtracks, began as a pop songwriter (**Simon Smith & His Amazing Dancing Bear** for **Alan Price**) before moving on to social comment laced with quirky humour (**Short People**).

Recently **Suzanne Vega**, Tracy Chapman and **Tori Amos** have taken up the baton for women, though the latter has a high production element to her songs. **Billy Bragg** and **David Gray** have since championed the British cause, although the best Brit may be **Nick Drake**. Terminally shy, he made three albums before his sad death in 1974, but has been much namechecked ever since. His guitar playing is exquisite too, as are the arrangements. **Five Leaves Left** is the best start point.

Late For The Sky is the best introduction to Jackson Browne, for the quality, subject matter and the Californian school of singer/songwriters. And, having turned odes to the blue-collar worker into stadium rock, **Bruce Springsteen** has gone back to making unpretentious heart-rending music (on **The Ghost Of Tom Joad**, inspired by the novels of **John Steinbeck** and music of **Woody Guthrie**) which reminded us why he was hailed as the new Dylan all those years ago. .

British singer/songwriters

The 1970s was the era of the singer/songwriter, but not all of them were American.

Elvis Costello

First name from you know who, specs from **Buddy Holly**, but a vision (and voice) all his own. Elvis Costello is a great singer/songwriter. A fine maker of detailed, sophisticated pop songs like Oliver's Army, he has penned some of the finest juxtapositions (his date is filing her nails as they're dragging the lake in Watching The Detectives) in pop. Oddly, on an album like Spike, it's the humour of God's Comic or the emotional directness of Any King's Shilling which moves, not the diatribes against Margaret Thatcher.

Ian Dury

Anything might be in an Ian Dury song: **Gene Vincent**, gardens of Japan, NHS glasses. A former art school teacher, he relied on Chas Jankel (leader of his band The Blockheads) for music, once being

banned (by Jankel) from the making of his own album for interfering. His humour and quirky image made him one of the best reasons to be cheerful in British pop in the 1980s.

Chris Rea

Some of his work is dire (Anyone For Tennis? Us neither) but his third album, *Deltics*, is a gutsy blend of pure romanticism (Raincoat And A Rose), an ode to trains (Deltic) and rocky stuff (Letter From Amsterdam).

Al Stewart

His voice was as thin as Carlisle United's chances of winning the European Cup. And his muse petered out after two albums. But anyone who can begin a song with a line about strolling through a crowd like **Peter Lorre** contemplating a crime (Year Of The Cat) was touched by genius, if only briefly. Stewart's other claims to fame were backing **Tony Blackburn** in a band in the mid-1960s and using the 'f' word – entirely appropriately – on Love Chronicles in 1969.

Ska

Before reggae, there was ska. In the early 1960s Jamaican producers such as **Leslie Kong**, **Clement 'Coxsone' Dodd** and **Duke Reid** created a new sound to replace American R&B acts. The new sound drew on R&B, rock'n'roll, swing, jazz, **calypso** and even **European ballroom** music. When Jamaican folk, or '**mento**', rhythms were added with the distinctive **banjo twang**, ska was born. Pioneers included **Prince Buster** (see page 113), **Don Drummond** and **Desmond Dekker**; the first two were purveyors of ska instrumentals, while Dekker created such classic vocal tracks as The Israelites (No.1 in 1969). Rounding off the original ska quartet was **Derrick Morgan**, a teen star who became a **rude boy icon**.

Even in its youth, ska acts were prolific musicians. Drummond wrote 300 tracks in his brief five-year career (he was gunned down by the family of **Marguerita Mahfood**, his former girlfriend whom, they believed, he had killed). But then in Jamaica and Britain ska fans seemed eager to buy every track by their heroes. This didn't apply in the US, although Dekker did make the Top 10 with The Israelites.

The battle between producer Prince Buster and **Kong** (the elder statesman of ska) helped define the genre. In 1963 Buster's protégé Derrick Morgan defected to his old cohort Kong and '**borrowed**' an instrumental break from one of Buster's songs for his first Kong release. A series of records followed, including **Blackhead Chinaman**, as renowned for their magnetic beats as their scathing lyrics. The battle boiled over in 1966, as rocksteady and the rude boy culture emerged. Morgan/Kong's hit **Tougher Than Tough** told the tale of four rude boys on trial for violent crimes, yet let off by a lenient, unnamed judge. The song began a furious war of words, Buster releasing **Judge Dread**, the magistrate sending the same boys down for centuries. Judge Dread spawned a host of courtroom-soap-style tracks, culminating in Buster's **The Barrister** (credited to The Appeal). The barrister's judgement even made national news. But Morgan had the last word: in **Judge Dread In Court** the notorious magistrate is jailed for impersonating a judge.

During the 1970s reggae superseded ska in Jamaica, but ska had garnered enough of a following in the UK to inspire a wave of ska-inspired, hit-making acts in the late-1970s/early-1980s. **Madness** and **The Specials** combined ska's dance beat with the energy of punk. Of late, US bands such as **No Doubt** and **The Mighty Mighty Bosstones** have promoted a new wave of ska-inspired records.

★**Recommended**★ Immerse yourself in Jamaican music with **Tougher Than Tough** (Island), it has everything from **The Folkes Brothers'** Oh Carolina (as revived by **Shaggy** in 1993) through **The Guns Of Navarone** by **The Skatalites** to Country Boy by **The Heptones**.

Skiffle

Skiffle is in serious danger of becoming the Mrs Rochester of rock'n'roll. Without **Lonnie Donegan** there might have been no **Quarrymen** and hence, no Beatles. Seen in retrospect on television, skiffle can seem entertaining yet quaint but, before **pelvic-thrusting** took over the charts, skiffle was incredibly popular.

The term skiffle was used in the US in the 1930s to describe the blending of blues and **boogie woogie**. In the 1950s, in the UK, it referred to an improvised amalgam of jazz and country blues, often played on simple instruments which could be made out of household implements. And it was simply huge, with Donegan alone racking up three No.1s (the best known being **Does Your Chewing Gum Lose Its Flavour (On The Bedpost Overnight)**). Although skiffle is often defined by its instruments, its attitude may be its greatest gift to rock'n'roll. There was an eccentricity, humour and feeling for the extraordinariness of ordinary people at the heart of Donegan's skiffle which inspired The Beatles. Skiffle would be trampled by beat bands but it survives: Donegan, **Chris Barber** and **Van Morrison** collaborated on an acclaimed album, **The Skiffle Sessions Live In Belfast 1998** (Pointblank), which reached the UK Top 20.

★**Recommended**★ **Lonnie Donegan**'s **Talking Guitar Blues** (Sequel) collects the best of the best skiffle artist.

Soap stars

What do you do if you're a **soap** star and you've already slept with your step-mother and your sister, murdered your best friend in a jealous rage and suffered a near-fatal head injury leading you to forget all of the above? You make a hit single, of course. Just don't expect it to be as good as Elvis Costello's **Pills And Soap**.

★**Simply the best**★

Livin' La Vida Loca Ricky Martin With his rugged good looks, Ricky had a brief stint on American soap **General Hospital**. Luckily good looks are also useful for singing careers.

Can't Get You Out Of My Head Kylie Minogue She has released some decent pop tunes ever since she got out from under the car in **Neighbours**.

As The World Turns Lauryn Hill Hill has had several minor acting roles (including **Sister Act 2**), but before them came a stint on the American suburban soap **As The World Turns**.

Kiss Kiss Holly Valance The **Neighbours** star has given us a great summer anthem.

Torn Natalie Imbruglia More fun than acting alongside **Harold Bishop** in **Neighbours**.

★The worst★

Don't It Make You Feel Good Stefan Dennis There can't be a more disturbing image than a leather-clad **Paul Robinson** from **Neighbours** asking you if it makes you feel good.

Good Thing Going Sid Owen Well, strike that: Ricky Butcher singing **Michael Jackson**.

Every Loser Wins Nick Berry Keeps your granny quiet at family dos but it's still torture.

I Breathe Again Adam Rickitt Songs like this earned Adam (**Nick Tilsley**) a one-way ticket back to **Corrie**.

Wanna Be Your Lover Gayle & Gillian Blakeney One of these Neighbours women (they're twins, who cares which?) was dating **Stefan Dennis**. Didn't they learn from his mistakes?

Soul

Soul is an amalgam of blues (**Otis Redding**, the epitome of soul, called himself a blues singer), old-style R&B, gospel and pop. And as soul's sheer diversity means a complete account would involve trebling the size of this handy pocket-sized book, we'll stick to the purist's idea of soul: post-R&B but pre funk and disco.

Soul music was a natural progression, not one man's invention. The 1950s marked a new awareness within the black community that they should celebrate their heritage, not hide it. So gospel's energy and emotional pull began to infiltrate more traditional R&B styles, thanks to artists such as

Reverend Green – after he quit Cluedo

Sam Cooke (see page 117), **Aretha Franklin** and **James Brown**. **Jackie Wilson** and **Ray Charles** tried more pop-friendly sounds like Charles's I Got A Woman.

"Soul is black" (as **Aretha Franklin** succinctly put it), and this allows for different styles. The south's gritty soul differs widely from, say, the soft soul of doo-wop influenced **Philadelphia**. **Berry Gordy**'s Detroit-based **Motown**, the most successful independent label of its era, brought soul to the masses, initially cashing in on the popularity of girl groups like **Martha & The Vandellas** and later with a range of fully-fledged soul stars including **Marvin Gaye**, **Stevie Wonder**, the **Jackson 5**, **Smokey Robinson & The Miracles** and **The Commodores**.

In Memphis Stax/Volt Records offered an edgier sound, closer to raw R&B. Gordy always had a business plan, but Stax artists were often found by chance. Booker T of **Booker T & The MG's** lived near the studios and, having nothing better to do, began hanging around. **Otis Redding** had been a driver for singer **Johnny Jenkins**, but when one of Jenkins' sessions went awry, the final half-hour was used to record Otis's, **These Arms Of Mine**. **Al Green**, with Willie Mitchell, produced some of the finest Memphis soul, on albums like Let's Stay Together. Other US cities had their scenes. Chicago is more famous for blues but made sweet soul with **The Impressions** (featuring Curtis Mayfield). New York specialised in pop-led sounds such as **Ben E King**, while Philadelphia's sweeter sound was typified by the lush orchestrations of **Philadelphia International**.

Soul has added many strands since the 1960s, with the arrival of funk, disco and modern R&B, but the influence of Cooke, Charles, Brown et al is evident in artists from **Prince** and **R Kelly** to soul divas such as **Mary J Blige** and **Destiny's Child**.

★**Recommended**★ Otis! The Definitive Otis Redding (Rhino) captures the essence of his timeless talent and energy. **Curtis Mayfield** is best found on The Anthology 1961-1977 (Unknown Label). The Definitive Ray Charles (WSM) is an ideal selection. The Very Best Of Aretha Franklin (Rhino) has Chain Of Fools and **Respect** – the track Redding said she stole from him. **The Isley Brothers** drew on gospel (**Shout**, a UK hit for **Lulu**), rawer soul, Motown pop and guitar-led tracks; it's all on the two-volume Isley Brothers Story (Rhino).

South Africa

Despite having its own version of **Pop Stars**, South African music is mostly known for its firm hold on its roots. Rochdale-born **Johnny Clegg**, having settled in South Africa as a child, earned international fame with his second multi-racial band **Savuka**, blending Zulu music and slick European production techniques. Scatterlings Of Africa stuck at No.75 in the UK in 1987, but thanks to artists such as **George Michael** the band won a small, loyal following.

Ladysmith Black Mambazo are the most successful act to come out of South Africa. Appearing on **Jools Holland**'s *Later...* show, Mambazo have become a successful singles and album act in the UK. Back in 1986, **Paul Simon** had been so enamoured by their unique hybrid of Zulu sounds and Christian choral styles that he used them on his UN sanctions-busting album Graceland.

The first South African tune to hit the UK charts was another traditional melody, Tom Hark – No.2 for **Elias & His Zigzag Jive Flutes** and No.28 for **Ted Heath & His Orchestra**, both in 1958. It was also used (with new words) by Brighton post-punk humorists **The Piranhas**, reaching No.6 in 1980.

In 1978 **Clout** made history by becoming South Africa's first home-grown one-hit wonder, with **Substitute** (previously recorded by **The Righteous Brothers**) reaching No.2 in the UK. They were followed in 1982 by **Toto Coelo** with the daft **I Eat Cannibals**. Toto Coelo translates as **Total Asshole**, which probably gave the female trio many a snigger. Lead vocalist **Anita Mahadervan** was the daughter of gameshow host **Bob Holness**.

Spain

The Spanish gave us flamenco music, and, er, the **Macarena**. But then Spain has never been known for pop – **Sylvia**'s **Y Viva España** sung by a Swede. Female flamenco duo **Baccara** topped the UK charts with **Yes Sir, I Can Boogie** in 1977, but apart from the No.8 follow-up, **Sorry I'm A Lady**, that's about as good as it gets. The disco-flamenco of **Mayte Mateus** and **Maria Mediolo** has won few fans outside Spain, Germany and Japan. Less controversial, but equally cheesy, the most popular Latin act of the 1970s and 1980s was a trained lawyer and former goalkeeper for **Real Madrid**. Despite his cornball singing manner, **Julio Iglesias** became a global star, winning over the British in 1981 with **Begin The Beguine**. He decided to focus on Spanish recordings in the 1990s, but within ten years his son **Enrique** was the biggest-selling Latin artist in the world.

Spoofs

"Like a surgeon/Cutting for the very first time…" A good spoof has you laughing out loud. Some records, like **Racey**'s **Some Girls** ("Some girls will," apparently), leave you guessing if they're a spoof or not – the best is **Dr Hook**'s 1979 No.1 **When You're In Love With A Beautiful Woman** which starts: "When you're in love with a beautiful woman, it's hard…" By then Dr Hook had already made a record called **The Cover Of Rolling Stone**, just so they could grace the cover of *Rolling Stone*, and reached No.4 in 1980 with **Sexy Eyes** while founding member **David Sawyer** sported an eye patch. Their first big UK hit, **Sylvia's Mother** (No.2 in 1972), was a parody of teen heartbreak songs so subtle that fans took it literally.

Weird Al Yankovic, the man who gave us **Like A Surgeon** and, well, not too many other good ones really, was more blatant. Spoofs often have to be pretty unsubtle to crash into the charts (think **Billy Connolly**'s **D.I.V.O.R.C.E.**) so parodists can be subject to the same pressures as the legends they're sending up. Make a parody as dead on as **Dickie Davies Eyes**, Half Man Half Biscuit's answer to Kim Carnes's **Bette Davis Eyes**, and you'll never have a hit.

Spoofing pop is not new. Back in the 1940s **Louis Jordan** brought a wit to his brand of jump blues, telling the listener not to take him too seriously. His funniest work may be **Open The Door Richard**, in which Richard denies that he's common, saying, "I know I ain't common 'cos I got class I ain't even used yet." Before Jordan, **Fats Waller** brought a similar irreverence to his music, interrupting the romantic duet **I Can't Give You Anything But Love** with the thought, "Diamond rings? Woolworths ain't got no business selling them." Such tomfoolery marked 1950s rock'n'roll. **The Diamonds**' **Little Darlin'** is a fine spoof of the love songs then in vogue. Then there was **Barry Mann**'s **Who Put The Bomp?**, a send-up of 1960s dance crazes... which became a 1960s dance craze.

For sheer versatility, nobody has topped the **Bonzo Dog** band, led by **Vivian Stanshall**, who could parody almost any artist or genre they fancied but only had one hit, the catchy but patchy **Urban Spaceman**. In the early 1970s **Jim Stafford** had a No.20 hit with **My Girl Bill**, which seems to be about a steamy encounter between two men but turns out to be a heart-to-heart between two men in love with the same girl. **Angus Deayton**, **Philip Pope** and **Richard Curtis** created the **Hee Bee Gee Bees** send-up **Meaningless Songs In Very High Voices**, its deadly accuracy earning airplay in 1980. **Steve Coogan**, as Latin singing sensation **Tony Ferrino**, saw his single **Bigamy At Christmas** ("Think of the man who has two wives/He's in a pickle when Christmas arrives") peak at No.42. But his spoof was so finely observed that, after his TV Christmas special, grannies throughout the land sighed, "Why don't they make singers like that any more?"

★**Recommended**★ **Louis Jordan**'s **Jump Jive** (Music Club) and **Fats Waller**'s **The Very Best Of** (Collectors). The first **Blues Brothers** album (Atlantic) raises a laugh on a dull day.

Surf

Surf music (in its classic American pop 1960s prime) fell into two camps: tracks with rolling instrumentals to evoke the sound of rushing waves, and those using words for the same effect. **Dennis Wilson**, a keen surfer, was amazed no one had thought to write about sun, surfing and easy living. Yet **The Beach Boys** weren't the first band to top the charts with a surf song. Having become friends with 1950s harmony duo **Jan & Dean** the pupils became the teachers, Brian belting out **Surfin' USA** to persuade the twosome to change direction. Jan & Dean asked for the song but Brian held on to it, giving them **Surf City** – which shot to No.1.

On the flipside, **Dick Dale** (who would influence **Jimi Hendrix** with his left-handed, upside-down guitar playing) took up the mantle. Nicknamed the **King of the Surf Guitar**, Dale set about developing sounds and later songs that evoked the noises and feelings he experienced riding the waves, creating the reverb sound (on the groundbreaking 1962 album **Surfer's Choice** and single **Let's Go Trippin'**).

Acts such as **The Chantays** and **The Surfaris** then found success with the instrumentals **Pipeline** and **Wipe Out** respectively. Landlocked groups such as **The Astronauts** and **The Trashmen** also found success, with **The Trashmen's Surfin' Bird** only kept off the top spot by **The Beatles**. But surf music's heyday was brief, its easy-living pop ditties out of synch with a nation reeling from the death of **JFK** and finding escape in the music of Brian's future rivals, The Beatles.

★**Recommended**★ Sounds Of Summer (Capitol) is the best Beach Boys compilation. Better Shred Than Dead: The Dick Dale Anthology (Imports) has all his surfin' classics and more. Surf City: The Best Of Jan & Dean (EMI) is exactly what it says it is.

Sweden

Yet another 'new Abba'

What is it about the Swedes? How have they become the biggest exporter of pop after the US and UK and grasped the essentials of Anglo-American pop/rock in a way that the Finns, the Norwegians and the Danes haven't?

The Spotnicks pitted their rock instrumental style against **The Shadows**. **Hava Nagila** hit No.13 in 1963, but their trademark spaceman suits put Brits off. Yet they would sell **20-million albums**, record over **700 songs** and, with in excess of 100 members, go through more line-up changes than **Deep Purple**

In 1974 **Abba** became the first Swedish act to win Eurovision (leaving Swedish music pundits worried they would forever be linked with cringe-worthy cornball pop – fears not assuaged when **Sylvia Vrethammer**'s **Y Viva España** made No.4 the same year) with **Waterloo**, the launch pad for their nine UK No.1s. Any pop act from Sweden since has been called 'the next Abba', but **Roxette** were the only Swedes to find success overseas in the 1980s with simple infectious melodies (**The Look**).

Without the aid of bad haircuts, **Ace Of Base** released the biggest-selling debut album with **The Sign** in 1993, helped by the unforgettable (even if you wanted to) **All That She Wants**. One of Sweden's finest pop moments, **Crucified** by ultra-camp **Army Of Lovers** (they made **Freddie** look like a wallflower), only reached No.31 in the UK in 1992. Swedish musicians now eschew throwaway pop ballads and Euro-disco. Stockholm-born **Neneh Cherry**'s Cockney twang and avant-garde cred helped her avoid the Abba trap, as did her hip hop dance track **Buffalo Stance**. Her brother, **Eagle-Eye**, released **Save Tonight** in 1998, but became a three-hit wonder.

The Wannadies and **The Cardigans** championed indie rock, while driving, beat group **The Hives** are one of the trendiest bands of the noughties.

★**Recommended**★ Almost all that you want is **Abba Gold** (Polydor). **Your New Favourite Band** (Poptones) contains all **The Hives'** best furious-yet-cocky punk-rock pop.

Swindon

Swindon has had a bad rap over the years, but its pop inhabitants have proved very loyal. Moody Blues singer **Justin Hayward** formed his first band, **The Riversiders**, in Swindon. Supertramp's **Rick Davies** is seen reading the **Swindon Evening Advertiser** on the back of their **Breakfast In America** sleeve. The newspaper had a second brush with fame when celebrated residents **XTC** wore costumes made of old copies on the cover of their 1983 album **Mummer**. XTC used the **Uffington White Horse** on the sleeve of **English Settlement**, baffling American fans who thought the famous chalk-hill cutting was a very bad drawing. Sadly, pint-sized popster **Billie** hasn't yet sung about her Swindon roots.

Switzerland

The Swiss are too busy running banks and voting in referendums to worry about pop. But out of Zurich sprang **Liliput**, who signed to Rough Trade but were strangely happy for punks and didn't catch on. Quirky electronic duo **Yello** are from the same city and had the UK transfixed by the annoyingly catchy **The Race** (No.7 in 1988). **Boris Blank** wrote the music; millionaire **Dieter Meier** sang, wrote the lyrics and, in his spare time, organised and funded the Swiss national golf team.

The Swiss played host to – and won – the first Eurovision Song Contest in 1956, with **Refrain** by **Lyn Assia**. The nation had to wait another 42 years before they won again, with the aid of French-Canadian diva-to-be **Celine Dion**, who triumphed in 1998 with **Ne Partez Pas Sans Moi**. Such incidents apart, Switzerland has also provided homes for tax-evading rock stars.

Symbols

Sometimes the quest to find a band's name can lead to words being abandoned…

★ **Prince** ★ Born with a ready-made pop star name, **Prince/Symbol** was a man of principle and when he began to feel enslaved by **Warners** (the label only allowing him to release one album a year), Prince changed his name to the unpronounceable cryptic symbol which had adorned his 1992 album. Eventually he realised his error and is once again called Prince.

★**Freur**★ This 1980s (smith) band were known by a squiggle (a coloured dot and squiggly line) pronounced Freur, a name they belatedly spelt out when their pleasant take on synth-pop got ignored. A very minor hit (No.59) was achieved with **Doot Doot** in 1983. That would all be a mere footnote in pop history had guitarist **Rick Smith** not (a) gone on to play sessions for – well, well – Prince and (b) reunited with Freur vocalist **Karl Hyde** to form Underworld whose **Born Slippy**, featured in the movie **Trainspotting**, reached No.2 in 1996.

★**? & The Mysterians**★ Long before **Wacko Jacko**, ? & The Mysterians frontman, ?, was the weirdest man in pop. Legally changing his name to ?, no one knew who the Texan really was (it now seems he was either **Rudy Martinez** or **Reeto Rodriguez**), what he looked like (he always wore wraparound shades) or what planet he was from (he once claimed to be from **Mars**). In 1966 he scored a US No.1 with **96 Tears**. Minor hits followed. Thirty years later ? was told by voices to reform the band. Stranger still, the results were actually quite good.

Talent contests

The talent show has been a national institution for four decades. **Opportunity Knocks** (hosted by **Hughie Greene**) gave us its fair share of talented, and not so talented, stars. From the tiny Scottish island of **Bute,** Lena Zavaroni wowed audiences in 1973/74 with **Ma, He's Making Eyes At Me** (a No.10 hit). Her own TV show followed, as did stints opposite Frank Sinatra and **Liza Minnelli** and a performance at The White House for President **Gerard Ford**.

Peters & Lee were a struggling holiday camp act (he was blind, she was blonde) when they entered. They became the first act since The Beatles to top the singles and album charts simultaneously (with **Welcome Home** and **We Can Make It** respectively), in 1973. In contrast, **Berni Flint**'s win made him a one-hit wonder, (**I Don't Want To Put A Hold On You** was No.3 in 1977). **Paper Lace** won in 1974 with **Mitch Murray** and **Peter Callender**'s **Billy Don't Be A Hero** (see page 235).

New Faces (a Saturday evening variant on Monday night's Opportunity Knocks) gave us acts like **Showaddywaddy** and **Sweet Sensation**. Rock'n'roll revivalists Showaddywaddy amassed 23 Top 40 hits, including a No.1 with **Under The Moon Of Love**. Sweet Sensation were a Manchester-based soul band who, in 1974, caught the eye of panelist **Tony Hatch** (see page 132). A No.1 with the remarkably decent **Sad Sweet Dreamer** followed, but the eight-piece were a little too holiday camp to make it big, disappearing as quickly they'd come after one more hit.

★**Recommended**★ The Very Best Of Showaddywaddy (Crimson): all the hits, no fillers.

Techno

To explain techno (or noise, as most parents call it) and its many variants would be a book in itself (in fact it is – **The Rough Guide To Techno**). The more commercial strands, however, seem apt for this Rough Guide.

Today techno is a European phenomenon, with **Germany**, Britain and **Belgium** embracing its frantic, pounding rhythms. Yet it began in Detroit in the early 1980s as funk and computer-generated sounds fused. As **DJ Derrick May** famously put it, "It's like George Clinton and Kraftwerk are stuck in an elevator with only a sequencer to keep them company." Techno is all about experimentation, so **Leftfield** and **DJ Carl Cox** are techno musicians, as are such pioneers like **Juan Atkins** and **Kevin Saunderson**. Techno was popular at raves – dance parties on a large scale, often in secluded areas, advertised largely by word-of-mouth. The spontaneity and secrecy (along with the drugs used by participants to keep them going) angered the authorities. For the full techno experience (in all its forms), ears and eyes need to be challenged. Throbbing rhythms are complemented by laser shows with strobe lighting and computer-generated visuals, a combination made more powerful by hallucinogenic drugs – which are, of course, illegal.

★**Recommended**★ **Underworld**'s Dubnobasswithmyheadman (Junior Boys Own) mixed original Detroit techno with Jamaican dub and rock guitar. **Carl Cox** is one of the most respected techno DJs, and his fine F.A.C.T.: Future Alliance Of Communication & Tecknology, Vol.2 is amazingly well-produced given that it was done in his garden shed. **Aphex Twin** (Richard James to his mum) is one of the most gifted, eccentric techno acts, with Selected Ambient Works 85-92 (Pias America) one of his mellowest recordings.

Tennis

The odd impromptu concert by **Cliff Richard** for rain-soaked crowds at **Wimbledon** aside, tennis and rock'n'roll are hardly what you'd call synonymous. In 1968, when **Cream** released **Anyone For Tennis**, topspin and the overhead smash were far from their minds – "But the rainbow has a beard" were among poet **Pete Brown**'s lyrics, with the song used in biker movie **The Savage Seven**.

The lyrics to the title track of **Chris Rea**'s 1980 album **Tennis** did mention the sport and the now iconic image of the female player scratching her bottom. But it won't be played during a rainswept interlude at Wimbledon; the mysterious line, "Freedom is the man with the red grenade/She ran out of gas, got beat and raped", is followed with "Do you like tennis?" A verbal warning for Mr Rea, wethinks.

John McEnroe is the only rock'n'roll tennis player (though Ilie Nastase is the game's Screamin' Jay Hawkins). Mac's rock star-style tantrums led to the novelty ditty Chalk Dust, The Umpire Strikes Back, but he's a decent rock guitarist (taught by Eric Clapton). When not making charity records with Pat Cash (also on guitar) and Roger Daltrey as Full Metal Racketz, he plays in New York clubs with his own band, The John Smythe Band (named after his second wife, former Scandal lead singer Patti Smythe). And Billie Jean King inspired Elton John to write Philadelphia Freedom in thanks for a tracksuit she gave him. A fair swap.

Trains

"Train I ride/16 coaches long." Elvis reinvented but didn't discover Mystery Train – Junior Parker wrote and recorded it at Sun Studios in the autumn of 1953 – but his mournful, almost ghostly rendering (and the tag about 16 coaches) had strong echoes of Worried Man Blues, a 1930s country/folk ballad made famous by the Carter Family, later covered by Woody Guthrie.

Despite what Billy J Kramer and Burt Bacharach would have you believe, in pop, it's trains and trains and more trains. There's the O-Jays climbing on the Love Train (so, less notably, did Kelly Marie), The Farm boarding the Groovy Train and The Monkees hopping on to the Last Train To Clarksville. There's David Bowie going from station to station in a song which starts with the evocative sounds of a puffing steam train, achieving more pathos than Sir Elton's lament, This Train Don't Stop There Anymore. And then there's Eruption, oddly cheerfully brandishing their one-way ticket to the blues.

What is it about trains? Well, in the 1920s and 1930s, a time when the motor car seemed the preserve of the wealthy (and plane travel the prerogative of movie stars), the train stood, especially in country music, as a symbol of freedom. The singer in Hank Snow's country smash I'm Moving On jumps on a train to escape a pesky girlfriend. Those left behind (the narrator of Mystery Train, the Doobie Brothers' Long Train Running) have often been as eloquent as those jumping on board at the last minute. But the ideal train song, musically and romantically, is Gladys Knight's Midnight Train To Georgia, where both partners get on the same train after LA proves too much for the man.

The decline of public transport is reflected in a decline in train songs. One of the few decent songs of recent vintage is Half Man Half Biscuit's take-off of, "Time goes by when you're the driver of a train." Replacing trains with planes has been great news for travellers, but not for songwriters (Chuck Berry's Promised Land is an honourable exception); as Gordon Lightfoot laments in his classic Early Mornin' Rain, "You can't jump a jet plane/Like you can a freight train."

Tributes

"It's better to burn out than to fade away." Inspired by the antics of **Sex Pistol John Lydon**, this line from **My My, Hey Hey (Out Of The Blue)** was **Neil Young**'s way of paying tribute to fallen stars such as Elvis, **Joplin**, Hendrix and **Morrison**.

Tribute records vary widely. Some artists rehash a song by the artist (more often than not, recently deceased), as with **The Jam**'s **So Sad About Us** (for **Keith Moon**). **Bryan Ferry** initially thought it tasteless to release his version of **John Lennon**'s **Jealous Guy** so soon after his death; some Lennon fans still think it was.

Sir Elton's **Candle In The Wind** (in both the Monroe and Princess Di versions) is the most famous tribute, although its poignancy has been airplayed to death. **We Love You Bay City Rollers** made by, of all people, **Nick Lowe**, was a hit in Japan. Fading 1950s star **Alma Cogan** made **We Love You Illya**, trying to cash in on the **The Man From U.N.C.L.E**, under the pseudonym **Angela & The Fans**.

Elvis has been honoured by everyone from **Belle & Sebastian** (**A Century Of Elvis**) to **Marc Cohn** (**Walking In Memphis**) and **Janice Nicholls** (**I'll Give It Five**). Janice was a panelist on a *Juke Box Jury*-style TV show famous for saying "Oi'll give it five," if she liked a record. Despite such lines as "I love Elvis and his pelvis," this novelty 'hit' was a miss. **Donna Lynn** tried to cash in on Beatlemania, with **My Boyfriend Got A Beatle Haircut** in 1964. Comedy actress **Dora Bryan** made the Top 20 with **All I Want For Christmas Is A Beatle** in 1963, while **The Beatlettes** voiced the opinion of most females with **Yes You Can Hold My Hand**.

The plane crash in 1959 which killed **Buddy Holly**, **Ritchie Valens** and the **Big Bopper** inspired **Tommy Dee & Carol Kay With The Teen-Aires** (the name rolls off the tongue) to pen **Three Stars**, not, alas, as famous as **Don McLean**'s tribute.

In the more politically aware 1960s the assassination of **JFK** was remembered by **The Beach Boys** in **The Warmth Of The Sun** and **He Was A Friend Of Mine** by **The Byrds**. Actor/singer/poet **Richard Harris** recalled the assassination of **Robert Kennedy** with **The Morning Of The Mourning Of Another Kennedy** (albeit seven years on), and **Marvin Gaye** (himself later honoured by **Cyndi Lauper** in her rendition of his **What's Going On**) recorded **Dion**'s **Abraham, Martin & John** as a tribute to Abraham Lincoln, Martin Luther King and the Kennedy brothers.

In the 1970s the unusual tributes included **Jim Morrison**'s **Brian Jones's "Chlorine Dream"** in an Ode To LA While Thinking Of Brian Jones, Deceased; two years (to the day) later, Morrison died in a bathtub of water. Lou Reed's **Andy's Chest** commemorated the holes in Warhol left by three bullets from the gun of Factory acolyte Valerie Solanas.

Ian Dury & The Blockheads paid homage to a rock'n'roll pioneer in **Sweet**

Gene Vincent. **Dexy's** hit No.1 in 1980 with **Geno**, a homage to soul singer Geno Washington, namechecking Jackie Wilson and Johnnie Ray in other hits. **REM** honoured comedian **Andy Kaufman** in **Man On The Moon**, while **Puff Daddy/P Diddy**/whoever scored a UK No.1 with **I'll Be Missing You**, a tribute to the rapper **Notorious B.I.G.** (on which he was accompanied by Biggy's wife, **Faith Evans**).

Trip hop

Trip hop originated in England as a successor to acid house in the mid-1990s, taking in **acid jazz** and **funk**, breakbeat and **hip hop**. For the purist, **Portishead**, **Tricky** and **Massive Attack** represent trip hop proper; the drum beat of hip hop combined with strong, often female, vocals.

Massive Attack's roots lay in **The Wild Bunch** (alongside Tricky). **Daddy G Marshall** and **Andrew 'Mushroom' Vowles** teamed up with graffiti artist **Robert Del Naja** and, with Soul II Soul's Nellee Hooper, they produced **Blue Lines**, recruiting Shara Nelson to sing soulfully. This paved the way for trip hop acts.

Portishead have a noir-ish side to their music. Led by former job-scheme pub singer **Beth Gibbons** and producer **Geoff Barrow**, they brought a melancholy and cool jazz tinge to trip hop; their debut album, **Dummy**, launched trip hop in the US. The gritty element of trip hop came from former Wild Bunch member Andrew Thaws (aka **Tricky**). Having provided key raps on *Blue Lines*, he recruited teenage singer Martina – their **Maxiquaye** was a No.3 album in 1995. Trip hop had arrived. Trip hop has since been applied to various acts, such as **Sneaker Pimps**, **Death In Vegas** and **Morcheeba**, and has even drawn on rock'n'roll – with the Lo Fidelity Allstars' **How To Operate With A Blown Mind**.

★**Recommended**★ Trip hop's holy trinity would be **Portishead**'s **Dummy** (Go Discs), **Tricky**'s debut **Maxinquaye** (Island) and **Massive Attack**'s **Mezzanine** (Wild Bunch).

Turkey

Forget **Eurovision**, the Turkish capital's new name gave **The Four Lads**, Frankie Vaughan and **They Might Be Giants** a hit with **It's Istanbul Not Constantinople**.

Ukulele

Delve deep enough and you find that without the beautiful twanging sound of the ukulele we may not have Pink Floyd, Jimi Hendrix or even The Clash. **George Formby** was a diminutive 'cheeky chappie', with a loveable, buck-toothed grin, obligatory catchphrase ("Turned out nice again") and a dictionary full of innuendos. Forced to take up the ukelele by his missus, it proved the perfect accompaniment to his double entendres on songs like **With My Little Stick Of Blackpool Rock**. His biggest hit, **When I'm Cleaning Windows**, was reworked and reissued in 1994 (and in 1996) by Stock, Aitken & Waterman act **2 In A Tent**.

The ukelele was the first instrument played by **Peter Frampton**, **Syd Barrett** and **Del Shannon**. And, at 13, **Jimi Hendrix** was given one to play by his dad. **George Harrison** used the ukulele to preview songs from his last album, **Brainwashed**, to his producers. And The Clash's **Joe Strummer** earned his stage name strumming the ukulele as a busker on the London Underground.

Various artists

Technically, various artists is a cast of thousands on a charidee single (see Charity). But some of the strangest pop artefacts were made by Dutch producer **Jaap Eggermont**, who made good money in the 1980s from his **Starsound** and **Stars On 45** compilations. How, we're not sure. The idea that a few session singers could do a better job of Beatles tracks than **The Beatles** is too fantastical to comprehend, yet **The Best Of Stars On 45** contains a Fab Four medley (as well as Abba, Stevie Wonder and The Supremes). Eggermont had a knack for timing, his first Beatles medley single was released a day after the killing of John Lennon.

Wales

Welsh pop, sponsored by Denim

In the late 1990s British music critics proclaimed that the UK charts were being invaded from an unusual direction: Wales. Bands such as **Stereophonics**, **Catatonia** and **Super Furry Animals** were taking music back to basics with simple yet catchy guitar rock tunes. The press had obviously forgotten that despite being a relatively small country, Wales had already produced the following:

Ricky Valence He topped the charts with **Tell Laura I Love Her** – though it was the only hit for the boy from Ynysddu (Caerphilly).

Harry Secombe Best known as a Goon and presenter of *Songs Of Praise*, this Swansea lad scored a No.2 hit in 1967 with **This Is My Song**. That said, in the genre known as 'Welsh singers with big voices,' Harry suffers a total eclipse compared to **Bonnie Tyler** (the first Welsh artist ever to top the US charts), **Tom Jones** (the

16th-biggest UK chart act ever) and **Dame Shirley Bassey**.

John Cale Born in Garnant, Cale was crucial to The Velvet Underground and produced **Squeeze**'s first album and **Patti Smith**'s **Horses**.

Badfinger The first band to sign to The Beatles' Apple Records (and the only world-class band on the label apart from the Fab Four) came from Swansea and gave the world some fine albums (**No Dice**) and **Nilsson**'s No.1 **Without You**.

Shakin' Stevens Forget the No.1s, Shaky (real name Michael Barratt) actually made some decent rock'n'roll, like **Marie Marie**. One of the Top 40 UK chart acts, he was last seen in the corner of an Indian restaurant in Virginia Water.

Manic Street Preachers Possibly the originators of the Welsh revival.

The Alarm From Rhyl, although they never complained, The Alarm released one of the most passionate albums in rock, **Declaration**.

Gorky's Zygotic Mynci Carmarthen's finest recorded a lot in their native tongue and were rewarded with no big hits but a cult following.

Wales has also had a spiritual impact on pop music. In 1967 Mick Jagger, The Beatles and Marianne Faithfull all headed to Bangor to sample the **Maharishi**'s transcendental meditation. Didn't they have a lovely time the day they went to…

★**Recommended**★ The Best Of Tom Jones (Polygram) is a must. As is **Shirley Bassey**'s This Is My Life (EMI). Shirley hails not from Tiger Bay but a place called Splott, across the water; anyway, this is vintage Shirl. For prime dame Cerys (Matthews) try the rootsy Cock A Hoop (Blanco y Negro). For prime Shakin', 16 Rock'n'Roll Greats (RCA) is the best.

Weddings

Love and marriage go snugly together in the Sinatra standard but, in pop, it's love which hogs the limelight. The trip down the altar has been the subject of surprisingly few great pop songs. **Russ Hamilton** hoped for big things in 1957 with the self-penned **Wedding Ring**, inspired by his girl, but it stuck at No.20. In 1963 **Elvis** backed a daft A-side, Kiss Me Quick, with the seminal – in wedding pop terms – **Something Blue**, in which El is best man (and something blue) as his girl marries another. **Julie Rogers** took **The Wedding** (La Novia) to No.3 in 1964, and the same year **The Dixie Cups** reached No.22 with **Chapel Of Love**, later remade by **Bette Midler**. **Labelle** had a US R&B hit with the powerful **Down The Aisle**. Possibly because of this flurry, Britain had tired of nuptial records by 1965, Julie's **Hawaiian Wedding Song** stalling at No.31 although The Fifth Dimension reached No.16 in 1970 with **Wedding Bell Blues**.

The best, in nuptial pop, was to come when **Yvonne Fair**, a Motown singer, made No.5 in 1976 with a stunning cover of the best wedding ballad, **It Should**

Have Been Me (on her deleted 1976 album **The Bitch Is Black**). At the sillier end of the genre, **Godley & Creme** made the Top 10 with the camp **Wedding Bells** in 1981, which **Elton** out-camped with **Kiss The Bride**, a No.20 hit in 1983. Four years later Billy Idol's **White Wedding** soared to No.6 and became a bit of an albatross. In 1996 Cliff's cover of **The Wedding** stumbled to No.40. And then there is **The Wedding Present**, whose music would bring an edge to any wedding.

Weepies

Pop songs can bring back sad times and teenage angst with a single riff. That riff could be from **Blame It On The Boogie** if that was playing when you got chucked by the love of your life. But some songs go all out to pull on your heartstrings.

★Start your sobbing★

All By Myself Eric Carmen A self-pitying classic, featured in the film *Bridget Jones's Diary*.
Baby Of Mine Bonnie Raitt First sung by Mrs Jumbo in *Dumbo*. We defy you not to well up.
Drive The Cars (No.5 in 1984, No.4 in 1985) At Live Aid in 1985 footage of the Ethiopian famine was set to The Cars' track, instantly embedding it in the national conscience.
Nothing Compares 2 U Sinead O'Connor (No.1 in 1990) The saddest break-up song ever?
Patches Clarence Carter (No.2 in 1970) Clarence is a blind soul singer whose brand of sexy soul often sounds like Lenny Henry taking the mick, but he hit big with this stirring tale of a son called to his dying pappy's bedside to be told, "Patches, I'm depending on you son."
Sometimes It Snows In April Prince His pal died and he wrote a song about it. It's a killer.
Green Green Grass Of Home Tom Jones (No.1 in 1966) Elvis cried when he first heard this; millions of blokes have pretended they had something in their eye since.

Weybridge

Birthplace of the **Nashville Teens**, who never quite fulfilled early promise. Managed by **Don Arden**, this 1960s sextet signed to **Decca** for seven-eighths of a penny per record sold, meaning if each member were to make a modest £1,000, they needed to sell 1,600,000 records. Their first release, **Tobacco Road**, a No.6 hit, marked the pinnacle of their career; £1,000 is still a long way off.

Whistling

The holy trinity of whistling pop are: **Bryan Ferry** pursing his lips on **Jealous Guy**, Otis's coda on **(Sittin' On) The Dock Of The Bay** and **Whistling Jack Smith**'s novelty No.5 **I Was Kaiser Bill's Batman** (courtesy of Roger Cook and

Roger Greenaway), the whistling hook supplied by the Mike Sammes Singers. Mind you, Morrissey shows off his whistle to good effect in **How Soon Is Now?**

Woking

Woking gave British pop Status Quo's **Rick Parfitt**, **Peter Gabriel** and **Paul Weller**. The Jam jammed at Weller's house on **Stanley Road**.

Wolverhampton

The 'N Betweens became **Slade** after recruiting the windswept-looking (but Walsall-born) **Noddy Holder** in Beatty's coffee shop on the high street. **Goldie** was born here. **The Charlatans** first got together in Wolverhampton.

Worthy Farm

Thirty-two years since **Michael Eavis** was inspired by the **Bath Blues Festival** to use his own dairy farm to similar effect, Worthy Farm, Pilton, Somerset is still the home of the famed **Glastonbury Festival**. Revellers were treated to **Marc Bolan & T. Rex** in 1971 for just £1. In 1993 the Waterboys honoured the festival – a legend in its own mud – and town with the imaginatively titled **The Glastonbury Song**.

X-rated

Pop music thrives on records that were banned, censored or bowdlerised all the way to No.1. **Madonna** was the chief advocate of sex in pop but not the first. Fifty years ago, **Shake, Rattle And Roll** had to be sanitised for the masses – the line about the sun shining through the woman's low cut dress simply had to go – although, oddly, references to the singer rolling his eyes and gritting his teeth stayed. Comedian **George Formby** wrote the words to **My Little Ukulele** which, revamped by **Joe Brown & The Bruvvers** in 1963, was banned as risqué. Four years later **The Rolling Stones** were accused of "championing promiscuity", (not Mick, surely!) and Jagger changed the lyrics from **Let's Spend The Night Together** to **Let's Spend Some Time Together** so the group could play *The Ed Sullivan Show* on US TV. Chinese officials recently asked for the whole song (plus Brown Sugar, Honky Tonk Woman and Beast Of Burden) to be cut from The Rolling Stones' tour when it reached China.

The most famous X-rated record, **Je T'Aime**, the orgasmic 1969 No.1, is discussed on page 251. (Seven years later the groans inspired Donna Summer's producer **Giorgio Moroder** to release Love To Love You Baby, with Donna's groaning also deemed unsuitable for innocent ears.) In 1970 John Lennon and Yoko Ono released Open Your Box, a B-side to Instant Karma, with the words "open your legs" guaranteeing a ban. Radio 1 DJ **Mike Read** would not have approved – in 1984 he publicly snapped Relax in half, calling it "overtly obscene". Oddly, the BBC didn't ban the equally explicit Love Come Down by Evelyn Champagne King (No.7 in 1982) or Lou Reed's Walk On The Wild Side (No.10 in 1973). George Michael, poor lad, was too blatant with I Want Your Sex (perhaps the BBC had noticed its release number: Epic Lust 1), although it was only banned pre-watershed. (For more lewd, crude or verboten records, see Banned.)

★**Recommended**★ Welcome To The Pleasure Dome (ZTT/Island) by **Frankie Goes To Hollywood**. There's also **Judge Dread**'s Early Years (Cleopatra). Dread was a Kent DJ, **Alex Hughes**, who made 11 records of innuendo set to reggae, all banned by the BBC (a record).

Yodelling

The Swiss are not wholly to blame for yodelling. Country legend **Jimmie Rodgers** made the Blue Yodel records which popularised this vocal style, in which the singer instantly switches to falsetto and back again. Slim Whitman briefly made yodelling popular in the UK with hits like Rose Marie (No.1 in 1955) but it fell out of fashion, despite **Frank Ifield**'s attempt tried to revive it in the 1960s. Even *The Sound Of Music* couldn't make Britons yodel (**Laurie Anderson** also tried on Big Science). Folk singer **Jewel** started out yodelling with her dad as a tribute to her Swiss heritage but, as a platinum-selling artist, has ceased to yodel. She may have been wrong: the soundtrack to O Brother, Where Art Thou? sold millions, a double helping of yodelling on We're In the Jailhouse Now certainly helped.

Zombies

The Zombies are one of the most underrated bands in pop. After becoming only the second British beat group to score a US No.1, their melodic, creative pop was all but ignored in the UK. Keyboard player **Rod Argent** would found Argent, while singer **Colin Blunstone** recut the band's big hit She's Not There every few years. **The Eyeliners**, a New Mexico post-punk outfit, tried to get us to Do The Zombie, while the **Cranberries** reached No.14 in 1994 with Zombie. Zombies danced in Michael Jackson's Thriller video. And in Finnish director **Mika Kaurismaki**'s movie Zombie And The Ghost Train (1991), Zombie the bass player gets a chance for redemption with a band called **Harry And The Mulefukkers**.

THE TALENT
Geniuses, mavericks, muses, bit players
and backroom boys

The artist formerly known as Larry Lurex loved being called Queen: "It's ever so regal"

> "When we started, we wanted to be famous. I mean, what a stupid thing to want. We actually wanted fame, fortune and probably all to live in one house with a fire pole in the middle"
> *Andy Partridge, XTC*

ABC
Perfect pop purveyors

For one album, *Lexicon Of Love*, ABC made purveying perfect pop sound as easy as, oh go on then, ABC. The songs were simultaneously rousing and knowing, but it couldn't last and, apart from the odd track like **When Smokey Sings**, it didn't. But for one album and one year (1982), ABC had panache, popularity and a lot of other things beginning with 'p'.

Martin Fry (vocals), Mark White (guitar), Stephen Singleton (saxophone), David Palmer (drums) and Mark Lickley (bass) were aided and abetted, if not partially transformed, by the technical studio wizardry of producer **Trevor 'Buggles' Horn**. Manchester-man Fry had met White and Singleton, both Sheffield lads, when interviewing them about their experimental electronic band Vice Versa for his rock fanzine *Modern Drugs*. Having accepted their invitation to join their band as a vocalist, Fry promptly took over and changed their entire artistic direction towards glamorous pop.

Their first hit, **Tears Are Not Enough**, was driven by Fry's Thin White Duke-influenced vocals and relentless determination never to resist a rhyming opportunity. This started out conventionally enough (tears/souvenirs) but soon progressed to the wittily elaborate (Astaire/millionaire) and the just plain over-ambitious (trash is/fascist). But then, in the world of **Lexicon Of Love** everything was temporary, even a marriage proposal could end up in the waste disposal.

Supply and demand remained in perfect balance throughout 1981/82 with the album spawning such hits as **Poison Arrow**, **The Look Of Love** and, best of all, the gorgeous, overblown, romantic complaint **All Of My Heart**, probably the perfect summary of a weary fatalism straight out of the Bryan Ferry school of songwriting. But their second album, **Beauty Stab**, essayed a sudden swing in the opposite direction – from sparkly showbiz to gritty reality, with a heavier, guitar-based sound and, perhaps fatally, an attempt to rhyme grumble with apple crumble.

Band members (and fans) defected, and the law of diminishing returns has mostly applied ever since. Fry was seriously ill in 1986 with Hodgkinson's disease but teamed up for a last hurrah with White in 1987 on the glorious **When Smokey Sings**, their biggest hit in the US. At the time of writing, Fry was leading a version of ABC on the 1980s revival circuit.

Lexicon Of Love has been re-released with bonus tracks, many of which aren't a bonus at all

Essential purchases The Lexicon Of Love and, if you're still not satisfied, move on to **Absolutely**, a compilation which will have a lot of duplication but will give you a decent smattering of the band's other hits.

Underrated The Lexicon Of Love has been re-released on CD with lots of bonus tracks, many of which aren't a bonus at all, including a slowed-down, jazzy version of Poison Arrow (aka The Theme From *Mantrap*). It's hated by most critics but it's perfectly in keeping with their brand of 'don't take me too seriously' romantic angst. **Beauty Stab** is probably worth another listen.

You've been warned 1991's **Abracadabra** probably won't reach out and grab ya.

Stuart Adamson — Dreams stay with you

When news of Stuart Adamson's suicide in a Hawaiian hotel room emerged on 16 December 2001, it was hard to believe the ex-Big Country frontman, whose swelling, widescreen music espoused the simple things in life – hope, pride, love, compassion, family, the great outdoors – could have valued his own life so lightly.

Resplendent in their trademark checked shirts – and aware of the bandana's fashion potency well before gangsta rap – Adamson and **Big Country** (named after a line in the Roxy Music song **Prairie Rose**, which the band covered) had, for a time in the 1980s, trembled on the verge of greatness, despite dividing opinion among pop's cognoscenti. Some saw them as genuine contenders for the crown captured by U2; others saw their honest, working man's ethic as, well, naff. If it was, and with hindsight some of the promo videos and artwork don't look too clever, the band's appearance at Live Aid – Adamson also appeared on Band Aid's **Do They Know It's Christmas?** – offers ample proof of their currency in 1985.

The flailing 'bagpipe' guitars of Dunfermline-raised (and proud of it) Adamson and former nuclear-submarine cleaner Bruce Watson, backed by the precise rhythm section of former session-men Tony Butler and Mark Brzezicki, came to the nation's attention with their 1983 debut album **The Crossing**, which sold three million copies. The Big Country sound was highly distinctive – so vividly outdoors it should have included **a free campfire**. It also rang a defiant note in the early Thatcher years – a Celtic folk-punk rallying cry against the pomp and circumstance of their smooth, yet vacuous, New Romantic contemporaries.

Adamson cut his teeth in the charts with post-punk outfit **The Skids**. Their biggest hit, 1979's guitar-driven **Into The Valley** (currently bookending Sky Sport's football coverage), sketched a convincing template for what came next. Big Country's success was swift and sure. A string of anthemic hits, including Fields Of Fire (400 Miles), In A Big Country and the memorable ballad **Chance** – "He came like a hero from the factory floor, with the sun and moon his gifts/But the only son you ever saw, were the two he left you with" – struck a popular chord, though its oddly singalong chorus – "I never felt so low" – now seems to offer a chilling portent of Adamson's fate.

Increasingly out of synch with the times, Big Country finally called it a day in 2000. Adamson relocated to Nashville, Tennessee in 1997, where he started a new project, **The Raphaels**. But he had battled drink and depression as a youth, and sadly his demons returned. He'd already disappeared on the eve of a British tour in 1999, and his body was found three weeks after he'd vanished for a second time.

Big Country might now seem little more than a footnote, but their longevity and sales of more than ten million (all first four albums went gold) ensure a place in history. As Adamson sang on **In A Big Country**, the rousing opener to *The Crossing*: "Dreams stay with you/Like a lover's voice fires the mountainside/Stay alive."

Essential purchases The spiky Skids debut **Scared To Dance** is a showcase for Adamson's guitar playing. For Big Country, it's **The Crossing**, a bold, windswept melodrama with Chance, 1000 Stars and the epic ballad The Storm standing out.
Underrated Come Back To Me, from 1984's **Steeltown**: a lovelorn ballad from a female point of view. Not too many blokes can take that on and succeed.
You've been warned One Great Thing, used for a garish Tennent's beer TV advert, spoils much of the good work on 1986's **The Seer**, which featured Kate Bush.

Adam Ant
Don't step on that Ant

If prizes were given for self-confidence, **Stuart Goddard** – aka Adam Ant – would have cleaned up. In 1977, infatuated with the **Sex Pistols** (who had made their debut supporting his band two years earlier), the 22-year-old Goddard jacked in his design course, assumed the Ant name and took to the stage sporting a leather fetish mask. Unfazed by the poor reception of his 1979 debut, **Dirk Wears White Sox**, and having Pistols guru Malcolm McLaren then hijack his musicians for Bow Wow Wow, he returned triumphantly with a new band and **Kings Of The Wild Frontier**.

With sterling contributions from guitarist Marco Pirroni, 'Antmusic' – a bizarre melting pot of rock'n'roll riffery, Burundi drums and pop hooks – was fresh and new. His time in design obviously hadn't been wasted either – his look was native American meets The Gay Hussar with a dash of pirate chic.

As **Antmusic** exhorted, the public did indeed "unplug the jukebox and try another flavour". Adam & The Ants amassed nine hits and 91 weeks on the chart in 1981 – a run not bettered until Oasis in 1996. Despite the poster chic that won the hearts of millions of teenage girls, there were enough subversive touches to sweeten the pill for the discerning. The next album, **Prince Charming**, spawned consecutive No.1s with **Stand And Deliver** and the title track, though the focus elsewhere lacked the earlier sharpness and the album was critically mauled.

Embarking on a solo career, Ant was back at the top of the pile with **Goody Two Shoes**. More Top 10 hits followed with Friend Or Foe and the **Phil Collins**-produced Puss 'n' Boots. But increased competition, notably from Duran Duran and Wham!, and a failed bid to make it in the movies (he'd appeared in Derek Jarman's **Jubilee** in 1977), cost him dear. Nineteen eighty-five's ironically named Vive Le Rock – and a puzzling performance at Live Aid – was followed by a five-year hiatus from the Top 75. In January 2002 Ant was sectioned under the Mental Health Act, months before he was due to appear on a 1980s nostalgia tour. He was later taken into custody after stripping off in a London café. We may have to wait some time before he belts out once more that "ridicule is nothing to be scared of."

Essential purchase **Kings Of The Wild Frontier** is the sound of a man with a plan. Not 100 per cent quality, but worth it for Dog Eat Dog, Kings Of The Wild Frontier and the yodelling menace of Killer In The Home.
Underrated Friends, from the **Antmusic** EP – a satirical gem aimed at liggers and the only song to namecheck Nobby Stiles, Mr Spock and The Woodentops.
You've been warned **Don't Be Square (Be There)** from *KOTWF*. Don't even ask.

Burt Bacharach — Mister songman

One song illustrates just how great Burt Bacharach is – **Arthur's Theme**, his collaboration with **Christopher Cross**. Mawkish, phony, incomprehensible (getting caught between the moon and New York City – what was that all about?), this song was a massive hit, a MOR virus transmitted over the world's airwaves. Yet such is the quality of the rest of Burt's work, we have forgiven him for it. At his best, which usually means when he was working with longtime-partner **Hal David**, Bacharach was responsible for complex, subtle yet radio-friendly ballads which made so much other pop feel musically and emotionally one-dimensional.

He sprang out of the **Brill Building** school of pop but soon surpassed his old teachers. Chiefly responsible for identifying the talent in one of **The Drifters**' backing singers, a certain **Dionne Warwick**, Bacharach positioned her as one of the most distinctive female vocalists of the late 1960s with classics like **Do You Know The Way To San Jose?** Dionne has never sounded as seductive since Bacharach and David stopped writing and producing her material. But in the 1970s Burt fell out with Dionne, David and his first wife Angie Dickinson, and out of favour (he vanished, for the most part, from the top of the charts).

Happily the lounge music revival has led to a long overdue reappraisal and, in a wonderful collaboration with **Elvis Costello** (the album *Painted From Memory*), a real return to form. Besides, Bacharach has created too many classic songs – I'll Never Fall In Love Again, Make It Easy On Yourself, Trains And Boats And Planes, I Just Don't Know What To Do With Myself and Walk On By to name but five – to be ignored for long. As a songwriter, he has had five UK No.1s, and his appearance on the cover of the **Oasis** album *Definitely Maybe* shows his influence has percolated through to some surprising places. He is, in **Jimmy Webb**'s words, "the great innovator of popular melody… a breath of fresh air to those who had tired of schmaltz but could not completely surrender to rock and roll."

Essential purchases The Look Of Love (Rhino, 1998) has most of the classics, alongside such oddities as **Bobby Goldsboro** singing Me Japanese Boy I Love You.
Underrated Any Day Now, an achingly beautiful, lesser-known David/Bacharach composition, sung as country/soul by Elvis on **From Elvis In Memphis**.
You've been warned Living Together, his 1973 album, is music to iron to.

Blondie
Peroxide pop punk

A product of the New Wave movement that grew up around the CBGB club in New York, Blondie were formed by **Deborah Harry** and boyfriend **Chris Stein** in 1974, borrowing their arthouse aesthetic from Andy Warhol and their name from truck drivers who had shouted, "Come on blondie, give us a screw!" at Harry.

The debut album *Blondie,* was **the perfect New Wave album**, arch pop culture references and urban ennui neatly reconciled in energetic three-minute singles. But it was Harry who gave it an edge, striding through the set like a starlet gone bad. The second album, *Plastic Letters*, brought more of the same, and **Denis**, the first UK chart entry, was only beaten to No.1 by Abba's Take A Chance On Me.

The third album **Parallel Lines** was more pop than punk. And while the disco-influenced **Heart Of Glass** was the final indignity for some, it gave Blondie the first of six No.1s and is the best song on the band's best album. Its inconsistent successor *Eat To The Beat* has its moments too, not least with **Atomic** (another No.1) – though as producer Mike Chapman later observed, the band's escalating drug intake meant that it could easily have sounded like "the product of seven sick minds". But pop is never good enough for 'artists' and two concept albums followed. *Autoamerican* (set in a dystopian, car-dominated future) takes itself too seriously, although it has a certain ruined grandeur, some hooky, melancholy music and **Rapture** is an inspired experiment with an emerging art form or a grating novelty, depending on your point of view. *The Hunter* is simply wacky: an ill-starred attempt to marry paganism and sci-fi. After its failure the band fell apart, though **Maria** was a surprise No.1 hit for a reformed line-up in 1999.

Essential purchases Both **Parallel Lines** and **Eat To The Beat** have an agreeable mix of hits and equally good but less well-known material.

Underrated **Autoamerican** contains some overlooked work such as The Hardest Part, the story of an armoured car heist that errs on just the right side of camp.

You've been warned The Hunter: Harry's frightwig and stare on the cover say it all.

Jacques Brel Satire, pathos, brothels

The name Jacques Brel might be less well known in Britain than Jean-Claude Van Damme – the other **famous Belgian** – but French speakers have this prolific songwriter right up there with Lennon and McCartney. In fact they'd probably put him well above, because he refused to write in English and only gave two live performances to the English-speaking world. Translations of his songs, however, have been sung by everyone from **Scott Walker** and **Marc Almond** to **Westlife**.

Brel wrote **intensely poetic songs**, usually about love and friendship but also about his homeland, death, misogyny and the bourgeoisie. And it is difficult to translate them into English without losing much of the clever wordplay and pathos that give them their depth. The poet and singer **Rod McKuen** had a go, and although purists sniffed, his versions brought Brel a wider audience. Seasons In The Sun (albeit

All's Brel that isn't well

a bizarrely emasculated version of the vitriolic original) was a No.1 for Terry Jacks and then Westlife, and If You Go Away was a Top 10 hit for, of all people, **New Kids On The Block** in 1991. (It's also been recorded by Tom Jones and Frank Sinatra.) David Bowie and Leonard Cohen both name Brel as one of their **greatest influences**.

At the height of his fame, in 1966, Brel quit the music business and took up acting in spaghetti westerns, eventually directing two of his own. He then bought a boat, sailed around the world and went to live in Hiwa-Oa in the South Pacific – the island where the painter Gauguin lived and is buried. He returned to France in 1977 and, having said nothing to his record label about the lung cancer that was slowly killing him, recorded one final album called simply *Brel*. In 24 hours it sold 650,000 copies, eventually selling more than two million. He died in 1978 at the age of 49.

> At the height of his fame, Brel bowed out and took up acting in spaghetti westerns

The novelist **Julian Barnes**, a huge Brel fan and Francophile, summed up his oeuvre wittily if a tad simplistically: "He sang of the north, of getting drunk (in the north), of sexual betrayal (and getting drunk, as a result, in the north), of being widowed (and discovering, on the day of the funeral, that you have been betrayed, and therefore getting drunk – probably in the north – as a result)."

Essential purchases The final album Brel encapsulates his style. Sung in his low, gravelly voice, this is a rough album full of mood, emotion and passion. Brel made only one comment about it – that he didn't like the cover design. The double album of **Amsterdam: The Best Of Jacques Brel** is the best compilation with all his hits.
Underrated Even if musicals aren't your thing, **Jacques Brel Is Alive And Well And Living In Paris** is a fine way to get acquainted with Brel. Ironically, it was written in the 1970s when Brel was far from well and living in the South Pacific.
You've been warned His balladic style (and his refusal ever to do more than three takes of a song) means his albums are all very much in the same vein and all have something to offer. Only the diehard fan needs to collect all his albums and only the determined melancholic needs to listen to more than one album at a time.

Kate Bush
Queen of English eccentricity

When 19-year-old Kate Bush walked into a recording studio for the first time in the summer of 1977 she had already written 50 songs. "She sat down at my piano," recalled producer Andrew Powell, "and said, 'I've written this new song – what do you think?'" The song was **Wuthering Heights** – written, according to pop legend, one moonlit night and on which, as Bush said, she did her "witch impression".

It was a strange, even perverse, debut but the song's very oddness meant it was more than just any old No.1. (Astonishingly EMI had suggested that James And The Cold Gun should be her debut single.) Over the years we grew accustomed to the eccentricity and the range of her subject matter. She would sing about incest (The Kick Inside), the persecution of freethinkers (Cloudbusting) and even dinner with Adolf Hitler (Heads We're Dancing).

The Bush voice has remained a barrier to many; it was no accident that at the end of 1980 she was voted both 'most liked' and 'least liked' in a *Sunday Telegraph* poll. But what sounded mannered to some was seductively unique to others. She could, as her engineer Haydn Bendall told *Mojo*, do the opposite of Geri Halliwell: "She was using her voice in a **completely unashamed** way. You wouldn't get Ginger Spice doing that. She might take her clothes off but she'd never really be naked, whereas Kate could be naked without taking her clothes off."

Bush is too English to have enjoyed consistent success in America. Her only Top 40 Billboard single was **Running Up That Hill** (which she reluctantly agreed could be renamed because radio stations wouldn't play it under its original title Deal With God) and she is probably still best known in the US as the woman who provided the "angelic soprano" on Peter Gabriel's Don't Give Up.

In an increasingly corporate music world her limited appeal Stateside put more pressure on her as, partly influenced by Gabriel, Bush became **more ambitious** and experimental. To be fair, some of the critically revered experiments (parts of *The Dreaming* and even some of The Ninth Wave, the concept half of *Hounds Of Love*) are hard to listen to. But she always seemed to follow her own muse until 1993 when she retired into motherhood. She is said to be working on new material but don't hold your breath.

> **Bush was simultaneously voted Britain's 'most liked' and 'least liked' vocalist in 1980**

Influences She grew up listening to (and liking) artists such as Bryan Ferry and David Bowie partly because unlike, say, the Stones, they sang in an accent that was **recognisably English**, not American. Gabriel has also made a powerful impact. Tori Amos is just one of many female singers to cite her influence.

Essential purchases **The Kick Inside** (which, apart from Wuthering Heights, includes The Man With The Child In His Eyes and the sublimely sexy Feel It) and **Hounds Of Love** would improve any record collection. Her greatest hits **The Whole Story** is another route into Bush's private musical world but it does feature an irritating and pointless update of Wuthering Heights.

Underrated **The Sensual World**: not as much of a shock as *The Kick Inside* and not a tour de force like *Hounds Of Love*, but an album whose appeal endures and which features her most beautiful, touching song, **This Woman's Work**. Kate has written some of **the greatest twisted pop songs** of the last quarter of a century: Breathing, Army Dreamers and Babooshka to name but three.

You've been warned The Dreaming is not to everyone's tastes, and it's not just because Rolf Harris is playing **didgeridoo** while Percy Edwards is doing bird noises. Sometimes the production and experiments overwhelm the songs.

Naked without taking her clothes off

Prince Buster — Reggae's original rude boy

As well as being a boxer, Muslim minister, sound-system operator, record business and jukebox entrepreneur, teacher and rabble-rousing critic of his government, Prince Buster also found time to **invent ska**. During the run-up to Jamaican independence in 1962, he wanted records for his sound system that were more intrinsically Jamaican than the popular American-style R&B. He set up a recording session that combined his regular musicians with the Rastafarian Count Ossie and his master drummers, borrowed the 4/4 time of army marching bands and grafted it on to an R&B framework to create Oh Carolina, widely acknowledged as the first ska record.

Prince Buster was drawn into the Jamaican music business as a teenager in the 1950s, when he intervened in a fight between Coxsone Dodd (a Kingston sound-system supremo and owner of the legendary Studio One label) and employees of his rival Duke Reid. A **locally successful pugilist**, Buster saw off Dodd's attackers and was taken on as his minder. From there he used his innate understanding of music and crowd-pleasing to branch out on his own and record some of Jamaican music's best-known songs – Al Capone, **Madness**, Ghost Dance, Orange Street…

"The hills are alive..."

An astute businessman, Buster wasn't slow to recognise ska's international possibilities. He frequently recorded and toured in Britain where he became a mod 'ero. Following a London gig in the early 1960s, he stopped at a tea stall on the Thames Embankment where a group of Mods approached him, any violent thoughts submerged by their admiration for his skinny Brooks Brothers-style suit, and subsequently escorted him on tour with a phalanx of scooters. As a result his Blue Beat releases and **effervescent stage shows** came to define ska in the UK, influencing artists from Georgie Fame (Buster taught him to play ska and Fame guests on several records) to the 2Tone acts over a decade later – Madness took their name from his song title and their first single, The Prince, was a tribute to him.

Today Prince Buster remains active, touring Europe, America and the Far East, and recording in the state-of-the-art studio in the grounds of his Miami home.

Essential purchases Prince Buster's Fabulous Greatest Hits features Madness, Al Capone, Judge Dread, Ghost Dance and Wash Wash so no problems with the Trade Descriptions Act. **Prince Buster Live On Tour**, recorded in Britain in 1967 without the benefit of post-production, is ska at its rawest, most rollicking best.
Underrated *Ska Boogie – Jamaican R&B, The Dawn Of Ska* (various artists) charts the often overlooked evolution of embryonic ska from xeroxed R&B. This set, containing many of Buster's productions of artists from his Wild Bells, Voice Of The People and Record Shack labels, proves it was a vibrant, inspired music.
You've been warned *Big Five:* **nudge-nudge rock steady** that soon gets tedious.

David Cassidy
Talented teen idol

If two tribes went to war in the early 1970s, it was odds-on that the conflict would be over the respective merits of David Cassidy and **Donny Osmond**. In those tumultuous decades, finding a British teenage girl who liked both was about as easy as finding a boy who supported both Leeds United and Chelsea.

Although Osmond has arguably had the longer-lasting career, Cassidy had the more **distinctive vocal talent**. That this wasn't recognised at the time had a lot to do with hipper-than-thou rock journalism and a natural suspicion of made-for-TV groups like The Partridge Family, who first brought Cassidy to the public eye. It probably didn't help that his first smash, **I Think I Love You**, was premièred in an episode where Cassidy bathed in tomato juice after being sprayed by a skunk.

Played today, the songs are eminently listenable and **cunningly crafted** to stick in the memory as quickly as possible. But then composer-impresario Wes Farrell did draft in the writing talents of **Brill Building legends** Barry Mann, Cynthia Weil, Gerry Goffin and, er, Rupert (Escape) Holmes. And apart from Cassidy and his screen mum (and real-life stepmom) **Shirley Jones**, the musicians on the records were the same Wrecking Crew who had played on countless West Coast pop hits.

The catchiest hits (Could It Be Forever, How Can I Be Sure?, I'll Meet You Halfway) are **crying out to be rediscovered** by the next winners of *Pop Idol*. On the best songs, such as solo hit Daydreamer and **Some Kind Of A Summer**, he offers a subtler, richer experience than Donny. Both lost their hold on teenage girls in the mid-1970s, but Cassidy has kept touch with both music (his version of I Write The Songs; a collaboration with George Michael on The Last Kiss) and **acting** (roles include that of a sleuth in the weird US TV series *David Cassidy - Man Undercover*). His double album of classic hits and what the sleeve notes for such affairs invariably refer to as "new favourites", *Then And Now*, was a big Christmas hit in the late 1990s.

Essential purchases *David Cassidy & The Partridge Family* **The Definitive Collection** is excellent value with 20 tracks which perfectly showcase the best of their work (the apparently throwaway, but brilliantly engineered, pop) and the worst (when David tries to convince the world that he rocks). Of his proper albums, **The Higher They Climb The Harder They Fall** is more than decent.
Underrated For soppy (but not soggy) early-1970s pop, Cassidy's **Cherish** album is hard to beat. **Some Kind Of A Summer** is actually a cleverly constructed pop song about life on the road.
You've been warned From 1976 to 1990 his albums can be hard to listen to.

Cher

Even Cher's real name sounds a bit daft: Cherilyn Sarkasian LaPier. But then Cher – the possessor of **one of the huskiest, most distinctive voices in pop** – is a woman who has, at various times, seemed to epitomise first the 1960s flower child and the most bombastic excesses of 1980s American 'adult-oriented rock'. A talented Oscar-winning actress, she has spent half her public life wishing to be taken seriously, yet starred in a video (for the **Diane Warren**-penned **If I Could Turn Back Time**) with half the US Navy and without half her underwear.

Her music has never quite garnered as much attention as her private life. In the mid-1960s she appeared as the partner and protégé of her hubby Sonny Bono with their smash **I Got You Babe**, in which Cher's vocal just manages to steal the limelight from **Sonny's trousers**. And that's how it's been ever since: trivialities (her latest toy boy, the sexuality of her offspring, speculation about which entertainment legend she's slept with) distracting from the fact that she has a cracking voice which can work wonders with the right material directed by the right producer. (And, yes, hard to believe it may be, but the right material can sometimes be written by Diane Warren.)

Gypsies, Tramps And Thieves, a massive hit in the early 1970s, may just be Cher's best solo single. Dismissed at the time as pop-rock schlock, it has since been recognised as a classic, with Cher's vocal driving the unusual lyrics and nailing the key line, "But every night the men would come around and throw their money down..." The album of the same name (originally released as *Cher*) may be her most coherent solo album, with the hit matched by The Way Of Love, either about a woman's love for another woman or about a woman saying goodbye to a gay man.

Her longevity would probably have astonished Bono, or Phil Spector, who produced some of her first discs. There have been times when the musical pickings have been lean (at which point Cher has headed to Hollywood), but every few years she releases a classic performance, her vocal even saving **Believe** (the biggest-selling single ever by a female artist in the UK) from monotony.

And she spits out the words of such made-for-radio guff as **Just Like Jesse James** with **such conviction** you'd think she was delivering an eternal truth about the human condition, rather than just bolstering Warren's bank balance. Cher has been written off, derided and ignored more often than Madonna (and often with greater cause), but she's still in there singing.

Essential purchases The best album is **Gypsies, Tramps And Thieves** (MCA,1971) For a hits compilation, try **The Greatest Hits** (Elektra, 1999).
Underrated **Bittersweet Love Songs Collection** (MCA, 2000) is an unusual collection presenting Cher as a torch singer. And it works.
You've been warned **The Best Of The Casablanca Years** is a greatest hits collection from a decade (the 1970s) when she had hits only with the disco community.

Rosemary Clooney — The jazz singer

These days the late Rosemary Clooney is chiefly famous in Britain for being **George Clooney's aunt**. But in the 1950s she was briefly one of the most popular female vocalists in the world. One of her hits, Mambo Italiano (No.1 in 1954), was even banned on American radio for being too saucy.

Clooney was a **contradictory figure**: an actress who starred as the good girl in conventional showbiz slush like *White Christmas*, and a singer who rose to fame before rock'n'roll and should, by rights, have been made irrelevant by it. Yet she was independent enough and, for an entertainer of her era, committed enough to campaign for **Robert Kennedy** in his doomed run for the US presidency in 1968.

Clooney grew up in Kentucky in the 1930s, making her singing debut on a Cincinatti radio station in 1941. Her first big hit, Come On-A My House (co-written by the American novelist **William Saroyan**) came in 1951, but she soon began to chafe at the restrictions of stardom, insisting her hit "sounded more like **a drunken chant** than a historic folk art form." She married the actor **José Ferrer**, enjoyed more hits (Mambo Italiano was easily the biggest), but soon disappeared from the charts to devote herself to personal appearances.

The shock of witnessing Kennedy's death triggered problems with drugs and alcohol, leading to a **nervous breakdown**. But nine years later she re-emerged as a jazz singer, and over the next 20 years she reinvented herself as one of America's best interpreters of jazz-based material. She died in 2002, aged 74, but those final albums form the most impressive part of her legacy. Her pop performances are not without their moments, and are all sung with her sense of commitment, but songs like Botch A Me (Ba Ba Baciani Piccina) soon lost their appeal. On numbers like It Might As Well Be Spring, Blues In The Night and Half As Much, however, her easy, emotional depth puts a **distinctive stamp** on great American songs.

Essential purchases There's no substitute for **Songs From The Girl Singer**, a two-CD retrospective.
Underrated Do You Miss New York? is perfect for a night in Manhattan, even if you live in Essex.
You've been warned Beware of compilations full of schlock like **Where Will The Baby's Dimple Be?**

> Clooney insisted her hit "sounded more like a drunken chant than a historic folk art form"

Sam Cooke
The man who invented soul

The album title which proclaimed Sam Cooke as the inventor of soul was a tad over the top. He has as good a claim as anybody, but soul, like country and blues, was not created by one performance or performer. That said, the grit and feeling Cooke brought to his finest work in the early 1960s made them sound deeper and more significant than most pop records of that era.

Like his fellow Mississippian Elvis Presley, Cooke was a singer with **gospel roots** whose commercial music was often regarded, by guardians of public morality, as profane. It is hard now, too, to listen to Cooke without remembering his strange death – **shot in a motel** after being accused of being too familiar with a woman who turned out to be a prostitute. He was just 33 and, some 18 months before, had made his finest album, *Night Beat*: 37 minutes and 35 seconds of mature popular music which lit the way for successors like **Marvin Gaye**. Otis Redding's Sittin' On The Dock Of The Bay would not sound the same without Cooke's example.

Cooke had started out as the star of a gospel vocal group called **The Soul Stirrers**, and he would bring that control, passion and commitment to bear when cutting such secular classics as **Cupid**, Chain Gang and You Send Me. Cooke could sing sweet and raunchy, scat, improvise, even yodel if he thought it necessary. But, after rehearsing in the studio – as he so often did with Lou Rawls – he would sing pop songs in such a way that, whatever the lyric might say, it's hard not to detect a note of sadness which seems to prefigure his untimely end.

Cooke was always **more than a singer**. He wrote many of his best hits (like Cupid) and drove the recording process. As he took control, his music got better and he became a crossover star, breaking out of the 'chittlin' circuit' of black concert venues to play the top nightclubs and Las Vegas. With *Night Beat* he proved that pop albums didn't have to be built around a hit single and packed with filler material. His music was growing more confident – witness his posthumous hit A Change Is Gonna Come, a fine song about the **civil rights movement**. Then, however, he was shot in those suspicious circumstances – Elvis was just one of many who didn't believe the official story about that night.

Today Cooke's music still sounds fresh; whether you believe he or Ray Charles invented soul music, you can't deny that he made **great music** which was full of soul.

Essential purchases The Man And His Music (a 1986 RCA compilation) is the ultimate collection. *Night Beat* is the best of his secular solo albums.
Underrated Jesus Gave Me Water (Ace, 1993) is the definitive collection of his gospel music with The Soul Stirrers.
You've been warned His live set Sam Cooke At The Copa is for completists only. His ballads and folk songs are well sung but some of his more soulful material is missing and the band is a bit antiseptic.

The Cure   Pantomime dames of the apocalypse

For post-punk nihilists, The Cure had an odd start. In their original incarnation, **Easy Cure**, they signed to a German label after winning a talent contest. The label unwisely tried to turn them into a pop group, and Easy Cure walked out.

After dropping the 'Easy,' the band were picked up by Polydor offshoot Fiction who released the first single, **Killing An Arab** (an Albert Camus tribute whose title caused a minor stir), in 1978. Recorded at the height of punk, it's dominated by jagged guitars, but Smith's voice, broken and plaintive, sounds like nothing else on earth. The first album, **Three Imaginary Boys,** was released the following year, with a suitably edgy sleeve that replaced the band with electrical appliances.

It wasn't until A Forest reached a modest No.31 that The Cure first appeared in the singles charts. Its ethereal gloom set the tone for the next singles, particularly Charlotte Sometimes, a goth masterpiece of doomed beauty and ruined elegance. But the public didn't care for such miserablism and the band returned to more tuneful songs: the catchy, offbeat romanticism of **Let's Go To Bed** and **The Lovecats** gave them the first of four Top 10 singles, and showed Robert Smith as an inventive lyricist – "strange as angels" is one of pop's more memorable similes.

A revised line-up and the almost chirpy **Kiss Me, Kiss Me, Kiss Me** turned the band into unlikely stadium-fillers. The price was that they became a caricature of themselves as agreeably barmy goths, with Smith as a **pop Edward Scissorhands in smeared lipstick**. Disintegration returned to darkness, but allied to lushly beautiful arrangements, though the video to Lullaby (at No.5, still their most successful single) showed their curious humour was still intact: Smith sings while being eaten by a spider that looks oddly like a giant pudenda. Freud, anyone?

The pop sensibility of **Wish**, The Cure's finest album, outraged the black-clad diehards, but won many new fans. Friday I'm In Love, an exuberant love song, reached No.6, while A Letter To Elise is one of their most intoxicating songs. Since then, however, the band has struggled to recapture earlier form.

Essential purchases Two singles collections, **Staring At The Sea** (Fiction) and **Galore,** cover the band's history. As a stylistic whole, **Wish** is easily the best album.
Underrated Kiss Me, Kiss Me, Kiss Me is often overshadowed by *Wish*, but it has some delicious moments – Just Like Heaven is worth the price alone.
You've been warned The Top: while Caterpillar is a minor Cure classic, you're unlikely to see any of the other tracks featuring on a 'best of' compilation.

Neil Diamond   A solitary man

Almost 40 years after his first hit as a singer (Cherry, Cherry) and as a songwriter (**I'm A Believer** for The Monkees), Diamond's Vegas-style concerts are still sell-outs. Perhaps it's something to do with those mesmerising sequinned shirts (who makes them is a key FAQ on Neil's official website), but he certainly knows how to play to his audience with that deep New Yorker's crooner voice.

Yet his break into music had nothing to do with his voice (although rubbing shoulders with a teenage **Barbra Streisand** in the local chorus as a schoolboy has since paid off). After his parents bought him a guitar as a teenager, his heart was never in the pre-med course at New York University (he won his place on a fencing

The Diamond geezer in a rare moment of sartorial sobriety

scholarship). Only six months before graduation, he took a $50-a-week songwriting job with Sunbeam, and in 1966 he signed as a singer with Bang Records while still working as a **songwriter**.

After hits with Cherry, Cherry and Solitary Man he moved to Uni Records in 1968, where he made his name with songs like **Sweet Caroline** and **Cracklin' Rosie**. A string of hits followed, including Song Sung Blue, but the quality control went awry. Some tracks didn't make much sense (I Am I Said), some were mushy (Forever In Blue Jeans, **You Don't Bring Me Flowers**), and a few were just rubbish (most of *The Jazz Singer*; he starred in the awful remake). Yet although he's always had a weakness for rhymes so obvious you know them in advance (eg marry me/carry me), he can be agreeably cynical, as when asking you to pour him a drink so he can tell you some lies (**Love On The Rocks**).

In his heart, Diamond may see himself as a wandering troubadour in the grand tradition of Roland, Woody Guthrie and Hank Williams, but he's **too schlocky** to be a real folkie and too city-boy to be country. Although Urge Overkill's cover of his Girl You'll Be A Woman Soon graces the soundtrack of **Pulp Fiction**, he's still unfashionable. A pity really because he's crafted some great pop songs, a fact noted by such acts as Elvis Presley, The Monkees, Johnny Cash, Cliff (he wrote one of Sir Cliff's best B-sides, an underrated classic called **Just Another Guy**) Bobby Womack, reggae group The Ethiopians and UB40 (Red Red Wine).

Essential purchases Classics: The Early Years is a fine compilation of his early work in the late 1960s. After that, it's the 1991 compilation **Glory Road**.
Underrated Tennessee Moon: just six songs too many to be a great country album.
You've been warned Sincere it may be, but **Jonathan Livingston Seagull** is not for the fainthearted. 1992's **Greatest Hits** has awful live versions of early material.

Fats Domino
The real king of rock?

It's easy for the British to get very smug whenever the history of rock'n'roll is told. Invariably, reference will be made to the music's role in ending racial segregation in America, a point often reinforced by clips of a fat, white Southern sheriff standing in front of a sign saying, "Whites only served here" and denouncing rock'n'roll as "animalistic nigra music".

For Britons, the comfort zone lasts for about as long as it takes to flick through the 1950s pop charts. You soon realise that Britain, on the whole, preferred its rock and rollers as white as Elvis, or as Daz white as **Tommy Steele**. The three greatest black rock and rollers of the 1950s (**Chuck Berry**, **Fats Domino** and **Little Richard**) did not scrape one No.1 hit between them in their heyday. Eventually, in 1972, Berry would top the charts with the tacky novelty My Ding A Ling, instead of the stunning **Johnny B Goode** or **You Never Can Tell**.

Of the three, Little Richard was the most flamboyant (a prototype Muhammad Ali, he once declared: "I'm the same as ever: loud, electrifying and full of personal magnetism") and Berry was the wittiest, but it was **Antoine 'Fats' Domino** who, **Elvis Presley** declared, was "the real king of rock and roll". The number of Domino records in El's personal collection is proof this was no mere soundbite. He also probably outsold his rivals, shifting 50 million records by the end of the 1950s. Not bad for a man who, critics insisted, had the **vocal range of a cricket**.

Domino was born in New Orleans and gravitated to the piano at that precise point in the city's history where boogie woogie, percussive barrelhouse blues and jump blues were coalescing into something the world would call rock'n'roll. His first US hit, produced by his longtime-partner **Dave Barthomolew**, was **Ain't That A Shame**, although it took a bland-as-white-bread **Pat Boone** cover to haul Domino's version up the charts. His best songs had the simplicity of genius

(Blueberry Hill, I'm Walkin') and, while his vocal talents were limited, he could talk his way through a song like **Walkin' To New Orleans** to wondrous effect. Domino always sounded not too fussed about the job, just happy to have a good time, an attitude perfectly expressed in his Blue Monday, a less apocalyptic precursor of the **Boomtown Rats** I Don't Like Mondays. In concerts the most energetic thing he ever did was shove the piano across the stage for his finale.

In the UK he was a consistent maker of mostly minor hits – only **Blueberry Hill** made the Top 10. But his influence – especially on British beat bands – was deeper than his sales suggested. **Mick Jagger** drew on his vocal style, noting "Fats Domino really influenced me when he said 'You should never sing lyrics out very clearly.'" In the late 1960s he made a minor comeback with an album of covers called **Fats Is Back**, including two Beatles songs (**Lovely Rita** and **Lady Madonna**, the latter a homage to Domino by Lennon and McCartney). Even **Cat Stevens** surprised a Royal Albert Hall crowd in 1975 with an affectionate take of **Blue Monday**.

Essential purchases For some, the greatest hits will suffice (we recommend **Simply The Best**, WM 860052). For others, nothing less than the Bear Family box set **Out Of New Orleans** (with 100 of his songs recorded for Imperial) will do.
Underrated Fats Is Back is lesser known than his classic 1950s recordings but is a brilliant revamp of the classic Domino sound, presided over by producer **Richard Perry**. The 1961 single **It Keeps Rainin'** never made the Top 20 on either side of the Atlantic but shows Fats's voice and piano at their most hypnotic.
You've been warned Fats spared us his take on acid rock, folk and heavy metal so just be careful of sound quality. On some albums, notably **My Blue Heaven** (EMI America, 1990) the hits are reproduced with their true pitch. In the 1950s they were often speeded-up when mastered. The 'slower' versions take getting used to for those who recall them first-time around, but they're better.

David Essex
Out of style for a while

David Essex is an easy man to underrate. These days he looks less like a rocker than like someone who is soon to be drafted into panto. Like the football team he supports (West Ham), his story is often seen as one of unfulfilled promise, and promise there was – as his debut hit, the self-penned **Rock On**, proves.

Born David Albert Cook, of **gypsy stock** (hence the 'Romany Romeo' tag he received in the tabloids as a teen idol) in Plaistow in 1947, he started playing the drums at the age of 14. After a variety of singles on a variety of labels stiffed in the 1960s, his manager **Derek Bowman** suggested he try acting. He proved a natural, soon gaining a lead role in *Godspell*, and stardom beckoned. He made two of

What every teenage girl wanted in the 1970s: to see David's etchings

Britain's best rock movies (*That'll Be The Day* and *Stardust*) with producer **David Puttnam** saying, "The camera just fell in love with him." **Rock On** was a Top 5 hit in the UK and then, sometime in the summer of 1973, he was staying at a hotel in the Midlands when the doorman tapped him on the shoulder and told him he was **No.1 in America**, a feat David Bowie would wait two years to emulate.

More hits followed, and if none of them were quite as striking or as original as Rock On, many had real merit. His first UK No.1, **Gonna Make You A Star**, was an amusing take on the music scene with self-mocking lines: "Is he more, too much more than a pretty face?" (to which his backing singers respond, "I don't think so…"). Stardust, Lamplight, **Hold Me Close** (his second No.1), all of which he wrote, gave the lie to that. In 1978 he gave one of his finest vocal performances as Che Guevara in the musical *Evita*, delivering **Oh What A Circus** with exactly the right blend of tenderness and bitterness. Even the Latin bit sounded good.

He also wrote the words and music to **Silver Dream Machine**, but to less effect. Me And My Girl (Nightclubbing) was something of a return to form (and roots). A Winter's Tale, an attempt to grow up, sounded more MOR than mature but was horribly catchy. And that, after a decade or so, was pretty much it.

He would do other stuff, including a musical based on *Mutiny On The Bounty* with Catherine Zeta-Jones and tons of good work for charities in Africa. But like Cliff and Barry Manilow, he seemed to have been taken hostage by an avid female fan base from which he has never really escaped. The last greatest hits compilation tells the story: 11 of the best tracks were recorded before 1982. And the misguided 1989 remake of Rock On simply pales beside the original.

Essential purchase **Greatest Hits** (Mercury, 1991) is the best place to start. You might just want to ignore the second half – and those yellow socks on the sleeve.
Underrated **Rock On** is still one of the more listenable early 1970s pop-rock LPs.
You've been warned **Silver Dream Machine**, movie or album, is not something you'd buy for anyone you were intending to speak to again.

Marianne Faithfull — A rose with thorns

Marianne Faithfull is one of the few British singers who, in the course of her erratic career, has ventured into territory occupied at different extremes by **Petula Clark** and **Nico**. Yet she runs the risk of being known for posterity for what she is alleged to have done with a Mars bar at the behest of rock satyr Mick Jagger.

A convent-educated English rose, Faithfull was a reluctant singer, coaxed into the limelight by **Rolling Stones** manager Andrew Loog Oldham. (Jagger and Richard wrote her 1964 debut hit As Tears Go By.) But she proved a fast learner, and for most of the 1960s she enjoyed parallel careers as Britain's pre-eminent rock chick (she starred, clad in leather, in a French flick *Girl On A Motorcycle*) and a delicate chanteuse (she sounded like Britain's answer to **Françoise Hardy**). Oldham produced some of her finest work, with her versions of House Of The Rising Sun and Greensleeves especially notable, and she is also shown to good effect on the Jackie De Shannon-**Jimmy Page** (yes, *that* Jimmy Page) collaboration In My Time Of Sorrow. At the same time, her covers of such Pet sounds as Downtown were, at best, pointless.

> **Faithfull has recorded a relevant, creative album more recently than her old muckers, the Stones**

Being Jagger's girlfriend clearly influenced the second phase of her career, even if the collapse of the relationship aggravated her dependence on drugs. In 1969, her song **Sister Morphine** (written with Jagger and Richards, and which the Stones recorded for *Sticky Fingers*) proved to be a precursor of the edgy, angry material which comprised most of her 1979 transformation, the magnificent **Broken English**. She wrote most songs herself, the stand out being the graphic accusation of infidelity, Why'd Ya Do It? (based on a poem by playwright Heathcote Williams). And, for a privileged lass from Hampstead, she delivers a terrific cover of John Lennon's **Working Class Hero**.

Faithfull has since ventured into the artier domain of Billie Holiday, Kurt Weill and Tom Waits. Her **new persona** (a feminine version of Keith Richards's wasted elegance) has been helped immeasurably by the fact her now-husky voice has dropped at least an octave since the mid-1960s – quite possibly due to exceeding the recommended daily intake of alcohol and other stimulants.

Nothing she's done since has quite matched *Broken English*, partly because she hasn't always, pardon the pun, remained faithful to her reinvented self. But her albums have always been intriguing, usually offering at least one masterpiece. Her 1987 release **Strange Weather** is full of delights, not least her gut-wrenching remake of her own hit As Tears Go By. You can argue that she has recorded a relevant, creative album far more recently than her old muckers, the Stones.

Essential purchases Broken English and **Strange Weather** are her most satisfying albums. Her career as a demure, female hit machine in the mid-1960s is probably best revisited on the Deram compilation **Marianne Faithfull**.
Underrated Check out her version of Kurt Weill's Ballad Of A Soldier's Wife (on **Perfect Stranger: The Island Anthology**), and 1978's **Faithless** album, her first with her new world-weary voice, has a countryish feel.
You've been warned Dangerous Acquaintances, a step back from *Broken English*, lingers in the memory about as long as it takes to say As Tears Go By.

Bryan Ferry

Pop's resident vampire

Julie Burchill, rock criticism's queen bitch, used the release of Roxy Music's greatest hits album to tear Bryan Ferry apart in *New Musical Express*. But, in closing, she admitted: "This music is a **precious relic**, not relevant anymore. But at their best, Roxy Music were better than David Bowie, than the Supremes, than the Doors, than the Sex Pistols, than anyone I imagine I will ever hear."

This is the kind of ambivalence Ferry, the eternally upwardly mobile miner's son from Washington in Tyne and Wear, attracts. Fans of the early Roxy panache and wit mourn the fact that the man who (with **Brian Eno**) was responsible for some of pop's cleverest and most satisfying sounds, seemed ultimately to have no greater ambition than to become the world's greatest lounge singer.

> **Bryan Ferry is a genuine maverick – a man who can combine roses and potatoes in one couplet**

The white dinner jacket (originally a joke), the fact that Ferry looks as if he spends all his waking hours in smoky nightclub situations, his forays into easy listening – all have obscured the fact that he is **one of Britain's greatest songwriters**. As he says in Do The Strand, all styles are served. If you want disposable yet durable brokenhearted pop, try Dance Away (the vital line: "She's dressed to kill and guess who's dying?"). If you want a song about the mechanisation of life and love, try **In Every Dream Home A Heartache**, covered by **New Order** and devised long before **Talking Heads**' Once In A Lifetime . If you want a soundtrack to seduction that isn't Barry White, try his 1980s solo album *Boys And Girls*. If you want a work of grandiloquent, self-mocking, pseudo-romantic whimsy loosely inspired by the Eurovision Song Contest, seek out A Song For Europe on *Stranded*. And if you want "mashed potato schmaltz", he's done plenty of that too.

Roxy Music were a creation of **glorious eccentricity**, a beat combo with glam-rock trimmings and arty pretensions, whose music and presentation looked backwards and forwards. Ferry wrote most of the songs but Roxy would never have been as magically different without Eno reinterpreting the sound and nudging Ferry away from the mass market, or the talents of Phil Manzanera, Andy Mackay and Paul Thompson. Through alchemy, they created **two of the most influential albums** of the early 1970s: their self-titled debut and the essential *For Your Pleasure* which, Q magazine noted, still sounds like the future three decades after it was made, and is Ferry's (and **David Bowie**'s) favourite Roxy album.

Eno quit after *Pleasure* but its follow-up, *Stranded*, was as good, if not better. By then Ferry had begun his **controversial solo career** with *These Foolish Things*. He had wanted to cut an album of songs from the **Cole Porter** era but lacked the nerve (in fact, he waited almost three decades to make *As Time Goes By*). But his take on Bob Dylan's **A Hard Rain's Gonna Fall** appalled traditionalists and, in pre-*Pin Ups* 1973, the very idea that a serious artist should want to do an album of other people's songs was considered to be inherently dodgy.

Despite one more cracking album, *Country Life*, and one so-so effort (*Siren*, which paled beside the magnificence of its singles **Love Is The Drug** and **Both Ends Burning**), Roxy were **defunct** by the mid-1970s. Ferry's solo career hit the skids commercially with his moving, elegiac album *The Bride Stripped Bare*, the press being more interested in his failed romance with Jerry Hall. **Roxy reformed** in 1979 in what seemed like desperation and recorded *Manifesto*, not as strong as the title track and Dance Away would suggest. Two albums in even more melancholy vein followed (*Flesh And Blood* and *Avalon*), with the John Lennon tribute Jealous Guy giving them their only No.1 hit. *Avalon*, the last proper Roxy Music album, is a gorgeous, seductive work capped by the title track (in which Ferry brings just the right note of **world-weary ennui** to his voice when he sings "I'm so tired"). Roxy split again, but Ferry's solo effort *Boys And Girls* feels like a companion piece to *Avalon*. Though dismissed as "mild green Ferry liquid", it repays relistening.

Ferry has never been as significant since, although all of his solo efforts have some merit. *As Time Goes By*, his belated album of 1930s classics, was a powerful reminder of his talent as a vocalist. The experience seemed to fire Ferry's muse and *Frantic*, on which he worked with Eno, may be his most credible solo album. But Ferry remains a **genuine maverick**, with one of the most idiosyncratic voices and songwriting sensibilities in pop. Only he could combine roses and potatoes in a romantic couplet (**If There Is Something**) and get away with it.

Influences Ferry was initially inspired by US soul acts like Sam & Dave and Otis Redding, yet his work also shows a fascination with the legacy of Cole Porter, Bob Dylan and Edith Piaf. In turn, Roxy have influenced a variety of acts, from Big Country to David Sylvian, Tin Machine and Pulp.
Essential purchases For Roxy Music, it's the **first four albums** and **Avalon**. **The Best Of** is the best of numerous compilations. Of Ferry's solo work, **These Foolish Things**, the lovelorn **The Bride Stripped Bare**, **Boys And Girls** and **Frantic**.
Underrated *The Bride Stripped Bare,* especially his emotive rendering of the Irish folk song **Carrickfergus**; the title-track of **Bête Noire**, his most nakedly romantic performance; **Mother Of Pearl**, his meisterwork on *Stranded*; Both Ends Burning from **Siren**, a stirring anthem for eternal romantics; and his quirky version of the country classic He'll Have To Go (on **The Essential Performances**).
You've been warned **In Your Mind** is for completists only.

Billy Fury

The king of British rock'n'roll

Marty Wilde, Vince Eager, Johnny Gentle, Dickie Pride, Duffy Power – these were just dress rehearsals for 1950s British impresario **Larry Parnes** before he created his masterpiece, Billy Fury. The search for a British Elvis had long preoccupied pop svengalis like Parnes, and Fury, despite Cliff's claims, was as close as they got.

Fury, a Liverpudlian deckhand by the name of Ronald Wycherley, swung his hips as if he meant it (he got banned in Ireland). On self-penned blues/rock tracks like **Since You've Been Gone**, Fury's sound was reminiscent of Elvis's Sun sessions. He was also a classy pop crooner, witness the recently revived (for a car ad) **Wondrous Place**, a mysterious number which belongs in a David Lynch movie. And **Halfway To Paradise** is a classic sulky rock'n'roll love song, sung with real urgency and played with a staccato rhythm reminiscent of Johnnie Ray.

Naturally moody and reticent (which added enormously to his appeal), Fury didn't like people much, preferring birds and horses – he even co-starred with his own racehorse in the movie **I've Got A Horse**. Ironically, four Liverpudlians who had once tried to serve as his backing band would end his reign as a chart king. Poor Fury didn't have the best of luck either. Eddie Cochran had pledged to help him tour America but then died in a car crash. A mini-comeback ended in 1983 when his heart packed up – he was 42 when he died, the same age as Elvis.

Still, **Keith Richards** described the 1960 album *The Sound Of Fury* (with Andy White, the drummer on Love Me Do, and guitarist Joe Brown) as "one of the pivotal rock'n'roll albums". Georgie Fame's The Blue Flames backed Fury for a while, and **John Lennon** famously asked for his autograph. His best music still sounds fresh even if the orchestration, at times, can sound about as subtle as the idea of naming a class of rock'n'roll singers after human emotions.

The look of Fury

Essential purchases The Sound Of Fury (issued by Decca with ten extra tracks in 1988) and **The Best Of**, a good mid-price introduction.
Underrated His last British Top 10 hit, In Thoughts Of You, is very classy pop indeed, once you get past the pianist with metal gloves.
You've been warned Shun slushy **Billy** (1963).

Born to be mild

Billy Fury excepted, the British rock'n'rollers of the 1950s were united, in the main, by the fact they had less of the real Elvis in them than footballer Frank Worthington.

Adam Faith had the ambition and the acting talent, but not the voice. Marty Wilde had looks, but less vocal finesse than daughter Kim. Tommy Steele blew his chance with Rock With The Caveman. Cliff Richard showed some verve with his greasy debut Move It, but soon moved into cleaner-scrubbed territory. Johnny Kidd's 1960 No.1 Shakin' All Over was in the Eddie Cochran class, and Crispian St Peters impressed with You Were On My Mind in 1965 – but then declared he was a better singer than Elvis and a better songwriter than Lennon or McCartney. Dave Berry, later covered by the Sex Pistols, was as close as we got to Gene Vincent, (ie not very close at all).

Not a very glorious record, is it? Respect, though, goes to Cuddly Duddly (real name Dudley Heslop) who, backed by the Redcaps, gave rock'n'roll a West Indian flavour and was rewarded for his originality with not one Top 40 hit.

Bobbie Gentry
Southern-fried belle

The middle of the road was a dangerous place for female singers in the late 1960s and early 1970s. Dusty Springfield, Lulu, Clodagh Rogers, Mary Hopkin and Sandie Shaw were pigeonholed so badly as to obscure what made them different. The clichéd career trajectory: become famous, enter the Eurovision Song Contest, host a TV variety show and perform a similar range of Bacharach-lite ballads.

Being Mississippi born and bred, Gentry (real name Roberta Lee Streeter) escaped Eurovision but was otherwise straitjacketed so ruthlessly that, by the late 1970s, she had to find another career – in TV production. It was a pity because, had she arrived in the mid-1970s, she could have been as successful as Dolly Parton – even if she lacked Parton's most obvious attributes. Drawing on country, folk and blues (and taking her stage name from the Charlton Heston-Jennifer Jones movie *Ruby Gentry*), she wrote her own first hit, a moody slice of southern gothic called Ode To Billie Joe that topped the US charts in 1968, and the rawer Mississippi Delta (earmarked as the original A-side). But such daring made her record label nervous and she adopted a cosier personality to keep them happy.

It paid off commercially: as her own work took an artistic back seat, she topped the charts with her sultry, knowing version of Bacharach & David's I'll Never Fall In Love Again, and had another minor MOR hit with their **Raindrops Keep Falling On My Head**. But the British public, with a perversity that challenges the image of the 1960s as the golden age of popular music, preferred Sacha Distel's version, even though it was as fresh as nine-year-old brie.

Her only other hit was All I Have To Do Is Dream, from an album of duets with **Glen Campbell**. After that, it was guest slots on Saturday evening TV and, finally, her own show. A brief marriage to Jim (My Girl Bill) Stafford can't have helped morale. She was briefly rescued from obscurity when her first hit inspired the movie *Ode To Billy Joe*, but the TV industry's gain was our loss – as is immediately apparent if you listen to her tragically overlooked 1969 album *Touch 'Em With Love*, a soulful country companion to *Dusty In Memphis*. Still, Ode To Billie Joe remains one of the darkest, most mysterious records ever to top the US charts.

Essential purchase The Best Of Bobbie Gentry has all the hits and a bit more.
Underrated On Touch 'Em With Love the best of her own songs (like Seasons Come Seasons Go) stand comparison with Burt Bacharach and Jimmy Webb.
You've been warned The duets with Glen Campbell, at their worst, sound like the offensively inoffensive music played during hotel breakfasts across the world.

Rolf Harris — From a land down under

"Oooh it makes me wonder... How does it affect you blokes?" For anyone who survived the early 1970s, when progressive rock was venerated, the one-time junior backstroke champion's cheerily irreverent version of Led Zeppelin's **Stairway To Heaven**, complete with bad jokes and goofs, is a very good joke indeed. Harris once told Q magazine that he had pioneered world music. Certainly the Australian entertainer, artist, cartoonist, musician and *Animal Hospital* host has been responsible for some of the strangest records ever to see the Top 20.

Born in Perth in 1930, he moved to England aged 22 and found work as a TV cartoonist, storyteller and artist who, in 1956, had his work exhibited at the Royal Academy. But Rolf was homesick and he became a regular at the Down Under Club, where he began singing and wobbling a warped Masonite board to create strange noises. His first hit, Tie Me Kangaroo Down Sport, was first recorded in his bathroom with a tiny tape recorder. Originally called Kangalypso, it was Rolf's tribute to **Harry Belafonte**, whose hit Hold 'Em Down included the lines, "Don't tie me donkey down there, let him bray, let him bray." Harris made the donkey into a kangaroo and created an Australian calypso which became a Top 10 hit in

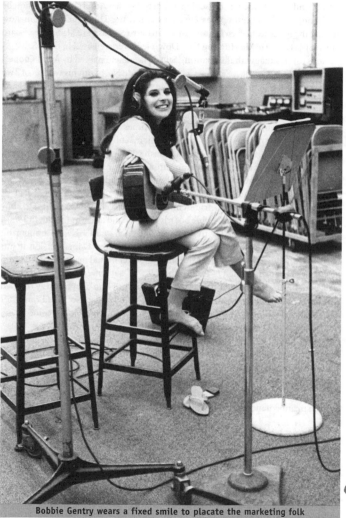

Bobbie Gentry wears a fixed smile to placate the marketing folk

the UK and No.3 in the US, outselling a watered-down Americanised version by Pat Boone. (A Dutch group has covered his hit, the Dutch accents somehow making the lyrics seem even funnier.) Two answer records (Tie Me Surfing Board Down Sport and Tie Me Hunting Dog Down Jed) were released in the US.

Harris topped that with the chanting **Sun Arise**, later covered by **Alice Cooper**, which got to No.3 in 1962. Seven years later he made No.1 with his version of Two Little Boys. If the record seemed inescapable, it was because it stayed in the charts for 24 weeks, and boys of the right age (and men of the right level of sentimentality) found the line, "Did you think I would leave you dying?" made the hair stand up on the back of their necks, sometimes against the owner's wills.

Luckily Rolf had no ambition to become a hit machine, contenting himself with popping up in surprising places, like Kate Bush's experimental LP **The Dreaming**. (He also became a pal of a group of four up-and-coming lads from Liverpool via their shared producer **George Martin**, although they didn't invite him to guest on their experimental album *Sgt Pepper*.) Though his music was laughed at or ignored, Harris retained a frightening ability to persuade Brits to buy stylophones, didgeridoos or wobble boards (55,000 sold after his first hit in 1960).

In the 1990s Rolf returned with his cover of **Stairway To Heaven**, a minor hit much funnier and easier to listen to than the Australian Doors' version it was released with. Harris only heard the original song after he had made his version, and he wasn't impressed, telling *Q*'s **Tom Hibbert** it was "a namby-pamby bloody awful song", but his cover and other modern classics did earn him a rapturously received spot at the **Glastonbury Festival**. Ooh, it makes you wonder. Not a bad career for a man who calls himself "just a novelty-type guy doing weirdo bloody comedy."

Essential purchase The Definitive Rolf Harris contains 23 tracks including all his early hits, a version of Tie Me Hunting Dog Down Jed and Stairway To Heaven.
Underrated At The Court Of King Caractacus, produced by George Martin, is a clever, breathless variation on a song he found in a book of songs for boy scouts.
You've been warned Rockin', Rollin', Ramblin' by 'King Rolf'. The Stairway To Heaven treatment meted out to Satisfaction, Walk On The Wild Side, Wild Thing…

Tony Hatch — The original Simon Cowell

Long before **Simon Cowell** hitched his waistband several inches higher than is medically advisable and become the pantomime villain of *Pop Idol*, a man called Tony Hatch did a very similar job on another ITV talent show, **New Faces**. But Hatch was a man of vast and puzzling – if sometimes appalling – talent; a man capable of composing and producing a song as lovely as **Joanna** (or as classic as

Downtown), who also found it in his heart to record, for patriotic reasons, **Bruce Forsyth** singing I'm Backing Britain. (He also produced novelty numbers by Norman Vaughan, Kenneth Cope, Benny Hill and Sue Nicholls – *Coronation Street*'s Audrey.) As if all that weren't enough, he also wrote (with his wife Jackie Trent) the themes to **Neighbours, Emmerdale** and **Crossroads,** the last given a gentle twang by Paul McCartney and Wings in the 1970s. (Shamefully, Macca made it slightly worse.)

Partners Tony and Jackie

But Hatch was always more than a hack. Growing up in the 1940s, he took up the piano at four. At ten he was in the school choir, and he discovered Mantovani at 14. He left school at 16, joined a music publisher and, after a couple of years national service arranging music for the Coldstream Guards, never looked back.

His first hit as a producer was **The Searchers**' Sweet For My Sweet in June 1963, quickly followed by Sugar And Spice (which he wrote under the name Fred Nightingale). His work with Petula Clark was even more rewarding: **Downtown** was the first disc by a UK solo artist to top the US charts. One of the most sung songs in pop, it has been covered by everyone from The KLF to Billy Preston and David McCallum. **Don't Sleep In The Subway** was another seductive slice of late-1960s pop, and he also hit No.1 in 1965 with his songwriting partner Jackie Trent's big ballad Where Are You Now (My Love)?. The pair married in 1967.

Hatch worked with an amazing variety of talent, but his greatest moment is **Scott Walker**'s version of **Joanna**, written for the film of that name but dropped in favour of Rod McKuen. Much of the other pop he produced and/or co-wrote is listenable, though some is risible. Many songs, like Petula Clark's **Sign Of The Times,** are almost too infectious. The hook is **ruthless,** the backing so bright and breezy you almost forget it's actually not that good a song. He was never the same force in the 1970s – too much slagging people off on *New Faces* perhaps. He has now parted from Trent and all but parted company with the music business.

Essential purchase Call Me: The Songs Of Tony Hatch (Castle, 2002) has 68 of them. This may feel like 61 too many, but there are few compact compilations.
Underrated Sad Sweet Dreamer by Sweet Sensation was actually quite a decent 1970s commercial soul hit in the manner of the Stylistics.
You've been warned Yoko by **Tony & The Cherry Children** is a dubious tribute to Yoko (Daughter of the rising sun/Who's sweet and kind and having fun) and the most irritating musical abuse of children in pop before Clive Dunn's Grandad.

The Ink Spots

Every generation of parents has complained of the latest teen sensation ("but all their songs sound the same…"), but never has that complaint been more justified than with The Ink Spots. Almost every song began with a plonking guitar intro, and cut to a falsetto vocal followed by a spoken intro, delivered in a voice so deep it seemed to come from the centre of the earth, before the falsetto returned for the closing crescendo. Only occasionally did the Ink Spots stray from this format, notably on the classic Java Jive and a couple of songs recorded with a young upstart called **Ella Fitzgerald**.

This black vocal harmony group only ever had one hit on the UK singles chart (Melody Of Love, a No. 10 hit in 1955), but they had a massive influence on acts from Elvis to The Beach Boys. And, by splitting and regrouping so often that even their most fervent admirers struggled to remember which group was the real Ink Spots, they personified the great schismatic tradition in pop and rock which would see acts as diverse as Bucks Fizz and Fleetwood Mac (to name but two) break-up and reform with new members in sometimes competing line-ups.

The Ink Spots (who met as porters in the Paramount Theatre in New York) were hugely popular in the 1930s and 1940s, their sound paving the way for the 1950s **doo-wop** boom. The first line-up was Jerry Daniels on lead vocals, Orville 'Happy' Jones on bass vocal, Charlie Fuqua (baritone) and Ivory Watson (second tenor). Illness forced Daniels to leave the band and it was with his replacement, Bill Kenny, that the classic Ink Spots sound was created.

Kenny's keening vocal soared to great effect on such Stateside hits as When The Swallows Come Back To Capistrano and **Whispering Grass** (later covered by the unlikely duo of Don Estelle and Windsor Davies). Bass singer Jones's nickname, Happy, seems especially ironic given that it was his role to deliver the spoken, often accusatory, monologue. On the classic **Do I Worry?**, he asks, "Do I worry when the ice man calls?" He does indeed, leaving the listener wondering if his girlfriend is really two-timing him or if Jones is merely very paranoid.

Their biggest gift might have been to deliver this material with a straight face but on a handful of songs, notably Duke Ellington's **Don't Get Around Much Anymore** and If I Didn't Care (covered in the 1970s by David Cassidy), they surpassed themselves. And Java Jive and Into Each Life Some Rain Must Fall (which features Fitzgerald) are terribly addictive. The group broke up in the 1950s with Watson launching his own act, The Brown Dots, a split which would enable countless groups to masquerade as The Ink Spots. Kenny also had a solo US hit – the sincere gospel of It Is No Secret – covered by, among others, Elvis Presley. But in the end The Ink Spots deserve respect because, even if their songs did sound the same 80 per cent of the time, as their records show, it didn't really matter.

Influences Bill Kenny's tenor set the pattern for hundreds of singers and groups: doo-wop, The Platters and even The Beach Boys wouldn't have been the same without them. But probably their most powerful influence was on Elvis Presley, who recorded two of their songs on the single he cut for his mother in 1953. He'd also imitate bassist 'Happy' Jones's talking bridge on Are You Lonesome Tonight?
Essential purchase The compilation The Best Of The Ink Spots is the essential starting point. After that, it really depends on the extent of your appetite for the remarkably consistent musical experience offered by The Ink Spots.
Underrated Java Jive is arguably the greatest song ever about coffee and tea, and certainly the best to rhyme waiter and percolator. The Ink Spots' version is definitive.
You've been warned Just make sure whatever you're buying is by the authentic line-ups (either Daniels/Jones/Fuqua/Watson or Kenny/Jones/Fuqua/Watson).

Leiber & Stoller
Black wannabes

When critics accuse Elvis of stealing the blues from black musicians, Hound Dog is often cited as an exhibit for the prosecution. But the song which was a hit for Big Mama Thornton in the R&B chart in 1953, and for Elvis in the pop chart three years later, was actually by two white songwriters whose similarly ambiguous relationship to the unofficial colour bar gave pop some of its greatest songs.

Jerry Leiber had met Mike Stoller in Los Angeles in 1950. A pair of preppy college kids, they were as black as the Waltons, but both had come into contact with R&B at an early age, and, in the words of Jerry Leiber, "wanted to be black". While still in their teens they started writing songs for black artists, and within months Jimmy Witherspoon recorded Real Ugly Woman. Leiber had met Lester Sill, sales manager for Modern Records, several months before, and his contacts proved instrumental in getting their songs recorded. But after one submitted to Capitol came back sounding like a 1940s swing band, the duo started their own label, Spark, along with Sill in 1954. The pair had already worked with The Robins, an R&B vocal group, and now The Robins recorded a series of songs that became instant classics, including Smokey Joe's Café and Riot In Cell Block 9.

Free from A&R men, Leiber and Stoller developed a reputation for slick, catchy songs with wit that fell just the right side of parody, and when Elvis covered Hound Dog in 1956, they were well-placed to exploit the rock'n'roll boom. Both hated Elvis's version, seeing him as an idiot savant, but their attempted revenge, Love Me (an ironic take on country ballads) backfired when Elvis made it a hit.

This was followed by many songs for Elvis's early movies, but Leiber and Stoller quickly became disillusioned with the Elvis organisation (though not with Elvis.) They wrote the soundtrack to *King Creole*, but loathed the title song, and the camp lyrics of **Jailhouse Rock** suggest a satirical intent. This, though, was largely lost on the teen audience and it went to No.1 in the UK and the US.

Leiber and Stoller's relationship with Atlantic, where they started working as independent producers in 1955, gave them the control they needed and **The Coasters** gave them a string of hits including Searchin', Yakety Yak and Charlie Brown. With its innuendo and impeccable arrangement, The Clovers' **Love Potion #9** is close to being the perfect Leiber and Stoller pop song, but Stand By Me and Spanish Harlem (written for Ben E King), showed they could forego irony when they wanted to. They left Atlantic in 1964 to start their own label, Red Bird – home to girl groups like the **Shangri-Las** and the Dixie Cups – but it closed abruptly amid rumours of run-ins with organised crime. Their careers tailed off as the 1960s ended, although in the early 1970s they produced Stealers Wheel (Stuck In The Middle With You) and co-wrote **Pearl's A Singer** for Elkie Brooks.

It would be easier to like Leiber and Stoller if they didn't already like themselves so much, but it's hard to argue with their back catalogue. From their offices in New York's mythical hit factory, the **Brill Building**, they wrote songs that shaped popular music and inspired a young wannabe called **Phil Spector**. In the words of one music journalist, Leiber and Stoller were "almost as hip as they thought they were."

Essential purchase The King Of Rock'n'Roll, the Elvis box set covering the 1950s, has some of their best-known work. The songs written for The Coasters and The Drifters can be found on a range of compilations.

Underrated Big Mama Thornton's original version of **Hound Dog** is worth revisiting, and has aged better than many of the classics.

You've been warned Elvis's recording of **Three Corn Patches** shows the extent to which all three protagonists' careers had gone into decline by the mid-1970s.

Dean Martin   The icons' icon

Dean Martin was the man whom both **Elvis Presley** and **Frank Sinatra** aspired to be. He was also the only actor who consistently made Jerry Lewis look funny on screen. And in the 1980s, when Martin had retired into a kind of alcoholic twilight, a group of Hollywood actors (led by Mickey Rourke) would form a club called **Sons Of Dean Martin** in their idol's honour.

The appeal might not be immediately apparent when you listen to his records. Dino Paul Crocetti, to use his real name, always contrived to sound so relaxed he

The other ones in bands

Mikey Graham, Boyzone

When Boyzone weren't boys any more they split, and all sorts happened. Little Stephen Gately came out of the closet, Ronan Keating embarked on a strangely successful solo career and found Westlife, and Keith Duffy entertained us more in *Celebrity Big Brother* than he had in Boyzone. Shane went racing cars and Mikey got himself a part in the new movie *Hey Mr DJ*, alongside none other than Mike Reid. Mikey once admitted he condoned smoking cannabis for medicinal purposes. From a member of Boyzone, that was akin to admitting to clubbing seals in his spare time. Shane says his ideal lady "has small breasts and dyed hair". Thanks for that, Shane.

John Deacon, Queen

John, with his fluffy hair, was always 'the other one' to Freddie Mercury, Roger Taylor with his girl's face and the other bloke with the massive perm. Bass players were often 'other ones', but none more so than Mr Deacon. Still, why should he care? He's got a first-class honours degree in electronics, six kids and, according to his website, likes to drink tea. He also says he doesn't like any band or singer in particular, and that he likes a bit of everything. How exciting!

John Keeble, Spandau Ballet

There were the Kemp twins (everyone fancied Martin), Steve Norman on sax with his floppy blond hair, Tony Hadley looking all grown-up on vocals, and then there was John Keeble, sat out the back on the drums. John is now married to a lady called Flea, drinks milk and Stella, though perhaps not together, lists foie gras and sirloin steak as his favourite foods and has lots of tattoos and peroxide hair.

Roger Taylor, Duran Duran

Roger Taylor, unrelated to **Andy Taylor** or **John Taylor** of the same band, chucked in his drumsticks for wellies, giving up music for married life on a farm. A hit with the ladies because of his moody stance in photos, Rog wasn't posing – he really was as fed-up as he looked.

Ian McLagan, The Faces

The one on drums was left marooned when **Ronnie Wood** and **Rod Stewart** split the Faces in 1975. But he has survived as a session musician, releasing albums with the word 'bump' in the title roughly once every decade.

A true mafia favourite

Now that Francis Albert Sinatra has left the building, the truth can be told. The mob's favourite singer was not Ol' Blue Eyes but **Jimmy Roselli**, who grew up in the same part of Hoboken, New Jersey, as Sinatra, in the same era and dealt with the same local godfathers.

But Roselli was, at least by his own account, not as amenable as the late Francis Albert, and his career suffered as a result. Still, his refusal to play the game didn't stop **John Gotti** hiring him to sing at his son's wedding. Another mobster, Larry Gallo, was even buried with a Roselli record in his hands.

His only UK hit was his standard When Your Old Wedding Ring Was New which reached No.51 in 1983. Roselli, aka 'Ol' Brown Eyes', insists his old rival Sinatra held his career back. With characteristic generosity, he calls Frank "a jealous piece of shit who would have given up his whole career to be a don."

Roselli may have had the edge, with his two-octave range, over Frank when it came to traditional Italian music, hence his popularity with the wise guys. But even Jimmy has to admit that Frank could sing.

might have been singing in his bath rather than in a recording studio. Many of his records are characterised by the same somebody-wrote-this-song-so-I-might-as-well-sing-it attitude *Variety* said typified his Vegas concerts. But it's easy to be deceived by a vocal style which hovers between laid-back and lackadaisacal.

Martin may have felt more at home on a golf course than he ever did in a recording studio but in between movies, Las Vegas concerts, TV shows and some serious womanising, he cut some classic ballads – many paying homage to the Italian music he had grown up with, others anticipating the country renaissance of the late 1970s. His rendition of **Waylon Jennings**'s Little Ol' Wine Drinker Me has achieved cult status, while his signature tune Everybody Loves Somebody knocked The Beatles off the top of the American singles charts in 1964.

Dino's recording career never really fitted with any great plan for chart domination. He produced some sizeable hits with songs like That's Amore and Volare in the 1950s. In the 1960s he hit a minor groove with Everybody Loves Somebody and a string of soundalikes, the most blatant of which (You're Nobody Till Somebody Loves You) sounded as if the original hit had just been rearranged on a primitive computer. At the same time, as Dean 'Tex' Martin, he recorded fine versions of such country classics as **Gentle On My Mind** and **Born To Lose**.

In the UK, his hits spanned 16 years (although only **Memories Are Made Of This** occupied the top spot, in 1956). In 1998, three years after his death, a BBC documentary about his life and times helped turn yet another compilation (*The Very Best Of Dean Martin*) into an instant bestseller. A second volume and an album of love songs proved popular if less lucrative, but Dino's success inspired such hip lounge compilations as *Music To Watch Girls By*. The Rat Pack was back in fashion, almost 40 years after its heyday, yet strangely this time King Rat wasn't Sinatra but Dino, the dean of swank.

Essential purchases **The Very Best Of 1** (EMI) **and 2** (Capitol) are a must, as is **Hurtin' Country Songs** (EMI, 1999) often available at a discount.
Underrated His **Baby It's Cold Outside** (with the Andrews Sisters) is light, frothy and effortlessly sexy – ie the complete opposite of the Tom Jones/Cerys Matthews version. And **Rio Bravo** recalls Saturday afternoons in the 1970s when a western, often starring Dino, was always on BBC2. And it rhymes Spanish and vanish.
You've been warned You can find some seriously dodgy compilations out there. **Baby It's Cold Outside** is cheap but only for fans who feel their collection isn't complete without a crackly version of A – You're Adorable.

Dino, the original lounge lizard, in an unusually vertical pose

Kenneth McKellar

Mac The Knife

Are you Scottish? Fortysomething? Then the name Kenneth McKellar will immediately bring to mind an immaculately groomed vision in kilt, velvet dress jacket and frilly jabot, giving it **Will Ye No Come Back Again?** or My Ain Folk on *The White Heather Club*. Sassenach TV viewers only had this musical maelstrom of **tartanalia** inflicted on them once a year at Hogmanay. But anyone north of the border had to face it at teatime every week – braving regulars Andy Stewart, 'Dixie' Ingram's highland dancers and concrete-barneted songbird Moira Anderson without the benefit of pre-midnight beverages to soften the impact.

The half-hour show was broadcast from 1958 to 1967 and was a *Top Of The Pops* for those who liked their pop music with a couthy edge. McKellar's Scottish songs were a mainstay but he had more strings to his bow than peddling sentimental teucherama. Before taking the BBC's tartan bawbee, McKellar, born in 1927, had sung Albert Herring and Macheath for **Benjamin Britten**, as well as recording some of the best Handel this side of Gigli with Thomas Beecham and Adrian Boult. **Sir Alexander Gibson** also tried to persuade

> **McKellar had spent time in music halls and used that training to write sketches for Monty Python**

him to join the Scottish Opera. But from then on tartan beckoned, with a career as one of that professional class of Scottish singers referred to by Billy Connolly as **"singing shortbread tins"**.

One of the least edifying moments in his career in popular entertainment was the UK entry in the 1966 Eurovision Song Contest, singing a ballad called **A Man Without Love** which, inevitably, became his one and only British hit. McKellar came 9th, and the next year's entry was Sandie Shaw with Puppet On A String. But there was also one curious episode in his career which didn't involve tartan or shortbread – or even singing. McKellar, who had spent time stalking the boards of the Glasgow music hall in comedies, put that training to good use – by writing sketches for a certain late-1960s TV comedy show called **Monty Python's Flying Circus**…

Essential purchases *The Very Best Of Kenneth McKellar* (Spectrum) has all the tartan classics like **The Skye Boat Song** at budget price. The *Decca Years* box set has much more of the same (plus O Sole Mio), also for less than a tenner.
Underrated Try **Handel: Messiah Arias And Choruses** (on Decca Eloquence) for a sample of McKellar's tenor voice at its best.
You've been warned **A Man Without Love**: his Eurovision Song Contest entry, though hopefully it will be impossible to find by now.

Yvonne Elliman

Listen to Yvonne Elliman's definitive version of the Rice/Lloyd Webber song I Don't Know How To Love Him and it's easy to believe this one-time session singer is better than she really is. It's rare to hear a singer combine such power and purity of tone on one song, and none of the famous singers who have covered this ballad since have come close. Sadly, she never quite matched that performance again.

Hawaiian by birth, Elliman had come to England to sing at a folk club in Chelsea, which is where **Tim Rice** and **Andrew Lloyd Webber** found her. After *Jesus Christ Superstar* she worked with **Pete Townshend** (who played guitar on her biting cover of his classic I Can't Explain), supplied backing vocals on **Eric Clapton**'s I Shot The Sheriff and later delivered cracking versions of the Gibb brothers' Love Me and If I Can't Have You.

You can find these on *The Best Of Yvonne Elliman* (Polygram, 1997), which neatly rounds up her best stuff and, because she was good but not great, is really the only Yvonne Elliman album that fans who aren't obsessed need to buy.

Mel & Kim   Never quite respected

The time: 7pm. The date: 2 April 1987. The programme: *Top Of The Pops*. On one of the three stages in the studio, two East-End girls adjust their flat-brimmed gaucho-style hats, bolero jackets and oversized gold half-moon earrings and get ready to launch into the new No.1, the song by which they will be remembered.

Respectable was a turning point not only for the Appleby sisters, but for their mentors and production team **Stock, Aitken & Waterman**. The three middle-aged producers had already tasted success with their unashamedly formulaic approach to pop. But it wasn't until Mel & Kim gave them their own first No.1 that they could justifiably stick two fingers up to the sneering music establishment, opening the floodgates that would see them amass upwards of 100 Top 40 hits in seven years.

The song, with its familiar 1980s theme of doing your own thing and not caring what others think, fitted Mel & Kim perfectly. Born five years apart within the sound of Bow Bells, the pair recorded demo tapes in their bedroom as teenagers. At one point they planned to send one to producer **Quincy Jones**, but gave up after a call to Directory Enquiries failed to result in his address.

Getting fresh for the weekend

True to the SAW ethos, Respectable was recorded in under a day and had the girls singing the immortal chorus: "Tay tay tay tay t-t-t-t-t-tay tay/Take or leave us/Only please believe us/We ain't never gonna be respectable." Mel, at least, was true to her word. A couple of years before she'd posed nude for *Mayfair* men's magazine, but such lurid revelations in the tabloids only added to the sisters' appeal. Respectable stayed in the charts for 15 weeks, and became No.6 in the top hits of 1987.

The album *F.L.M.* (it stands for **Fun, Love, Money**) went straight to No.1 across Europe and the video for Respectable (modelled on the street scenes from *West Side Story*) picked up an award at the Montreux Pop Festival. It was in Montreux, two years later, that Mel's deteriorating health first became evident when she left in a wheelchair. The official story was that she had a slipped disc, but news soon broke that she was having treatment for **spinal cancer**. She died in January 1990.

Mel & Kim's career may not have reached the heights they deserved, but for a while in the mid-1980s they were one of the greatest pop acts this country had to offer, and with Respectable had one of the greatest pop singles of the decade.

Essential purchase That's The Way It Is: *The Best Of Mel & Kim* is your best bet for all the hits plus a hint of Kim Appleby's solo recordings.
Underrated Showing Out (Get Fresh At The Weekend) is pure 1980s pop joy.
You've been warned Most 1980s remixes were little more than a junior engineer with one finger on the s-s-s-s-scratch button. Mel & Kim's are no exception.

Melanie
Look what they did to her song

In 1970 Melanie Safka recorded a song called **What Have They Done To My Song, Ma?** Today, the title seems prophetic. First the **New Seekers** (the 1970s pop band manufactured on the dubious basis that the retirement of The Seekers left a void in entertainment which had to be filled) had a debut minor hit with their own conventional pop treatment of the song. Four years later, Melanie's US No.1, **Brand New Key**, would be transmogrified by, of all acts, **The Wurzels**, who topped the UK charts with their comic retread **Brand New Combine Harvester**.

Today Melanie is in serious danger of being best known for her involuntary association with the Wurzels, her braying cover of the Stones' Ruby Tuesday (or, as she sang it, "Roo-bay Toos-day") and an image of cloying tweeness. It would be tragic if this were to obscure, for example, the knowing, Weimar-style cabaret which influenced her debut LP, 1969's *Born To Be*, which includes some pretty scary songs.

Born in Long Island, New York, in 1947, she is the daughter of Ukrainian-Italian parents. Without wishing to indulge in national stereotypes, it's fair to say her career has been marred by a tendency to **overdramatise**. But her intense, brooding style served her well in the Greenwich Village of the 1960s and at Woodstock, inspired by which she wrote the hymnal **Lay Down (Candles In The Rain)**.

Her image – as the kind of singer/songwriter-cum-chanteuse who helps lovelorn students make it through the wee small hours – has also overshadowed the fact that, at her best, she wrote some very **sharp songs**. "Gamblin' is illegal in the state of mind I'm in," she notes in The Nickel Song, and in What Have They Done To My Song, Ma?, she says, "If the people are buying tears, I'll be rich someday." The people did buy Melanie's tears, especially in her early 1970s heyday, but not in sufficient numbers to make her rich. But she continues to have a devoted following and has lucratively recorded the theme for the US TV series *Beauty And The Beast*.

Melanie might have been more successful if she'd been content to mellow into a singer/songwriter in the vein of James Taylor or Carole King. But Melanie is never afraid of a song and gives each one her all, which works beautifully on **Candles In The Rain** but is frankly **hard to listen to** on, for example, her cover of Dylan's Lay Lady Lay. Still, it's hard not to feel that the government should pass a law obliging everyone wanting, say, Phil Collins's latest to buy Melanie's greatest hits instead.

Essential purchases Best to start with **The Very Best Of** (Camden). **The Good Book**, with a wondrous version of Phil Ochs's Chords Of Fame, is her best album.
Underrated Her 1976 album **Photograph**, was released past her commercial peak but is one of her best, with the feverish Save Me just one of the highlights.
You've been warned Too many budget releases contain **inferior versions** of her classics, as well as outtakes which were never intended for release.

George Michael
Tortured pop star

In 1982 Wham! (the exclamation mark was added when US band Wham sued) became one of Britain's most successful pop bands, as Hertfordshire schoolboy pals Andrew Ridgeley and Yorgos Panayiotou (aka George Michael) traded the social comment (and **soul boy** leather jackets) of Wham! Rap for the sunny tunes and tight shorts of Club Tropicana and Wake Me Up Before You Go-Go.

Aside from Careless Whisper, which George and Andrew wrote when they were just 19, all Wham!'s songs were written by the young half-Greek singer/songwriter (many believe extrovert Andrew was brought along mainly as a confidence-booster for his shy pal), so it came as no surprise when, in 1986, they announced Wham! were over and George Michael was to embark on a solo career.

His first solo album, *Faith* (on which he wrote, arranged and produced each song), followed in 1987, with the cover – George hiding under his **leather jacket** – the first sign that he, even as a new solo artist, was weary of pop stardom. A heavy hint followed with his second solo album, *Listen Without Prejudice Vol. I.* The single Freedom 90 had a Michael-less video in which his words were lip-synched by models while props from his Faith video exploded in the background.

After that album's disappointing sales, Michael started appearing in the papers more often than the charts. First he **sued Sony Records** to get out of his contract (he lost and bought his way out). Then *Older*, his next album of often sombre but perfectly crafted tunes, didn't sell well. But it was his visit to a public toilet in a Beverly Hills park in 1998 that had the tabloids dancing with glee: he was **arrested** for propositioning an undercover cop, after which he came out as gay on TV and satirised his arrest on the song and video Outside. Since then Michael has kept a low profile after an unsubtle exercise in political comment (Shoot The Dog) destroyed his fan base in America. But George hasn't given up, making his first appearance on *Top Of The Pops* for 17 years to perform Don McLean's anti-war song The Grave. It's either horribly sincere, or a desperate bid for 'relevance'. An odd fate for a singer/songwriter once talked of as the new **Elton John** and a singer who could hold his own working with **Queen**, **Mary J Blige** and **Aretha Franklin**.

Essential purchases Best bet is **Ladies & Gentlemen: The Best Of George Michael**, though for his earlier tongue-in-cheek pop it's **Wham! The Final**.
Underrated Faith: Less preachy and far sexier than **Listen Without Prejudice Vol.1**, thanks to tracks like Hard Day, the slinky Father Figure and I Want Your Sex.
You've been warned Shoot The Dog: shunned by virtually every radio station, not so much for its politics but because it was so bloody awful.

The Monkees
The best boy band ever

After the Fab Four came the Fabricated Four. The advert for "four insane lads aged 17-21" in *Variety* paid off for TV producers **Bert Schneider** and **Bob Rafelson**. The producers wanted to create a TV series based on The Beatles' antics in **Help!** (the Richard Lester movie disliked by the Fab Four) and the four lads they selected were diverse enough. **Peter Tork** was a well-known folk musician and, though he wasn't a drummer, possessed the sleepy dopiness that marked Ringo Starr's public persona. **Mike Nesmith**, heir to the Tippex millions, had already released records as Michael Blessing and, cast as the quiet George Harrison figure, is still the only rock guitarist to look cool in a bobble hat. **Mickey Dolenz**, the ersatz Lennon, had been a TV child actor, as had expat Mancunian (and Macca equivalent) **Davey Jones**, who'd once played Ena Sharples's nephew in **Coronation Street**.

Soon, with session musicians playing on the records, they were selling millions of records (their album *More Of The Monkees* outsold *Sgt Pepper* in the 1960s). Their manic TV show was launched on the BBC in 1966: by November 1967, they'd had a No.1 (**I'm A Believer**), and three more Top 5 hits, including **Daydream Believer** and Dolenz's Alternate Title (its original title was Randy Scouse Git, an **Alf Garnett** phrase from *Till Death Us Do Part* that had tickled Dolenz). Yet by the end of 1968 (and a tour in which they tried to encourage **Jimi Hendrix** by taking him as the support act) their heyday was over. Artistically frustrated, the band collaborated in their own decline with the ambitious but incomprehensible movie *Head*.

Yet the fabricated four have retained their appeal. They inspired the **Banana Splits** (Bingo was a closer match for Dolenz than the Monkee was for Lennon) and the Banana Splits, in turn, inspired **The Dickies** and, bizarrely, **REM**, whose presiding genius **Michael Stipe** announced the Splits were

> The Monkees have inspired the Banana Splits, the Sex Pistols and football fans

a bigger influence on the group than The Beatles. And the **Sex Pistols** (just as fabricated in their own way) cut I'm Not Your Stepping Stone.

Nesmith's interim credible solo career peaked in the UK with the hypnotically indecisive **Flying Down To Rio** but his Pacific Arts company did pioneer the pop video. Call it karma, but The Monkees later became MTV staples, attracting a new generation and, inevitably, leading to an awful reunion. Their most famous hit, **Daydream Believer**, also became a football anthem, the lines "Cheer up Peter Reid…" directed at the erstwhile Sunderland boss. Part of The Monkees' charm is the songs (often by **Carole King**, **Neil Diamond** and **Nilsson**), but much of what makes them great is that they knew they weren't great and never really tried to be.

Essential purchases The **Greatest Hits** album (subtitled *Here They Come…*) is worth considering, although it omits a few of their better album tracks. Devotees may not feel satisfied until they own the 1998 **Anthology** (Rhino, 1998) box set.
Underrated Some **Mike Nesmith** songs (especially Circle Sky, The Girl I Know Somewhere and You Just May Be The One), and some album tracks and B-sides (such as the soulful Goin' Down), deserve greater recognition.
You've been warned Shades Of Gray: The Monkees waxing philosophical, it's sentimental, simplistic and dirge-like. And avoid the original **Head** album, because of the movie dialogue and music.

Jim Morrison

"You want to see my cock, don't you?" Eight of the most famous, and possibly fatal, words in rock history. Jim Morrison's invitation, to a crowd at a concert in Miami in March 1969, was received enthusiastically. But it left him exposed to **indecency charges** which exacerbated his paranoia. He soon fled the US, and the end came for real in July 1971(he was just 28) after a mammoth binge of alcohol and heroin.

Morrison is a hard man to be dispassionate about. A self-indulgent military brat (his father was a US admiral), he took himself and his poetry incredibly seriously, a pompous (almost self-parodying) trait he shared with the rest of The Doors. Yet his admirers take him more seriously still. The 30th anniversary of his death saw a near riot at his grave in Paris. In essence, Jimbo accelerated the rock'n'roll cycle of **success, disillusion and death** with the aid of booze, drugs and sex. In five years he effected a mental and physical collapse which others took decades to accomplish; he came to fame ten years after Elvis but by 1971 was already porkier.

Musically, there's no clear consensus either. His most famous lyric, **Light My Fire**, was soon adopted by middle-of-the-road crooners: the later, Latin-tinged retread by **José Feliciano** was a much bigger hit in the UK than The Doors' original. His biggest UK hit while still alive, **Hello I Love You**, bears a striking resemblance to The Kinks' All Of The Day And All Of The Night. But **The Doors** weren't really about singles and their albums mostly stack up, though much of their appeal lies in Ray Manzarek's innovative keyboard work. Shorn of rhythm and music, Morrison's musings can sound as coherent as his suggestion that the cover of Strange Days should feature 30 dogs because "it's symbolic – and dog is God spelt backwards."

But you couldn't write such morbid, oedipal magnificence as The End if you weren't completely convinced of your own importance. Besides, as **Apocalypse Now** showed, Morrison's nightmares echoed the nightmares of wars and assassinations which soured the 1960s. This arrogance, which produced the jazzy, ominous sound of **Riders On The Storm**, the bombastic When The Music's Over, and a fine version of Alabama Song, was also the weakness: quality control wasn't a priority. But nobody has, before or since, **fused poetry and rock** to such effect.

Essential purchase If you only want one, opt for either of the greatest hits compilations or **The Doors** (Elektra), one of the greatest rock debuts of all time.
Underrated Waiting For The Sun: mellower than much Doors stuff, this 1968 release contains half a great album, with The Unknown Soldier a masterpiece.
You have been warned An American Prayer is for fans of the poetry only.
The Doors box set is only worth the price if you must have absolutely everything.

Jim Morrison: what a cult he turned out to be

Nilsson

In 1969 Nilsson appeared on the German TV show *Beat Club* to perform his first global hit, **Everybody's Talkin'** (the theme to *Midnight Cowboy*). Gawky, gauche and wearing an impossibly tight pair of trousers, he clutched the mic as if for dear life and, when it came to the "waaaa" passage of wordless vocalising, twisted his hand in a gesture which in certain repressive regimes in Latin America at the time would have led to his immediate arrest. It was an astonishing performance. Naïve, nervous and definitely not cool. Anybody seeing him for the first time would have found it hard to credit that this American singer/songwriter was a favourite of **The Beatles,** who regarded his 1967 album *Pandemonium Shadow Show* as comparable to their own *Sgt Pepper*.

But then with Harry Nilsson nothing was quite as it seemed. The list of genres in the excellent *All Music Guide* website gives you some idea of his idiosyncrasy. It lists him as contributing to "vocals, piano, album rock, psychedelic pop, baroque pop, pop/rock, soft rock, pop". To which you can add country and easy listening, and the soundtrack to the animated children's film *The Point*. Yet while others found success

He wasn't the mornin' DJ

Would **Harry Chapin** have become famous if he'd been born in the UK? It's hard to see him writing his famous song (which starts "I am the morning DJ on WOLD...") if the DJs he'd woken up to were of the calibre of Andy Peebles or Simon Mayo.

That was almost Harry Chapin's only stroke of luck. Born in Greenwich Village in 1942, he sang in a local choir but wanted to make documentaries. In 1968 he made the Oscar-nominated *Legendary Champions* about boxing legends. By 1971 he'd rediscovered music and soon had his first hit, Taxi,

a six-minute narrative epic. His third album *Short Stories* made him, thanks to the epic tale of the WOLD DJ, and the follow-up (*Verities and Balderdash*) was good – if didactic.

By the late 1970s his vogue had faded, due to his liberal politics and what some saw as his heavy-handed arrangements and moralising. He didn't live to see his star fade, dying in a car crash in 1981. He left behind the most distinctive canon of work by a singer/songwriter this side of Harry Nilsson. If you want to hear why many mourn his loss, pick up *The Essentials* on Rhino.

with his songs (eg **The Monkees** with the unsettling Cuddly Toy), his own hits were the work of others: **Everybody's Talkin'** was by folk-rocker Fred Neil, and his only No.1 in the UK, **Without You**, was a cover of a **Badfinger** album track.

Born in Brooklyn in 1941, Nilsson started out as a singer (before he ruined it, he had a three-and-a-half-octave voice) and as a **songwriter** (including some with **Phil Spector** for The Ronettes), selling his first songs to The Yardbirds, The Monkees (also enthusiastic early fans) and Three Dog Night. His first album tells the story of the rest of his career. He could deliver perfect and/or intelligent pop (his cover of The Beatles' She's Leaving Home) yet offer something far weirder, such as his retelling of the Ten Commandments in Ten Little Indians.

In the next seven years he would variously release an album of Randy Newman covers; a souvenir of a **lost weekend in LA** with his drinking buddy and one-time producer John Lennon; covers of such classics as As Time Goes By; and an album on which old people close a song by declaring, "I'd rather be dead than wet the bed."

He was probably more of a true rebel than most rock'n'rollers, refusing to perform in concert and restricting himself to the occasional TV appearance. He sang like a man addicted to cigarettes and **alcohol**, and the lifestyle did eventually catch up with him. He retired partly through ill health and died of a massive heart attack in 1994. But the grittiness of his voice made his performance of such tear-jerkers as Without You all the more affecting. Equally, his version of **Mr Bojangles** is much darker and more appropriate than the usual triumphant reading the song has been given by everyone from Sammy Davis Jr to Robbie Williams.

Essential purchases **Best Of** is a decent budget-priced collection. For a single album, you may want to start with **Nilsson Schmilsson**, although those intrigued by 1960s psychedelic pop should snap up **Pandemonium Shadow Show**.
Underrated **A Little Touch Of Schmilsson In The Night** – a classic American songwriter takes on classic American songs, and wins. Most of the time.
You've been warned **Skidoo** may be the album you want to come to last.

Hazel O'Connor   Seriously cool for a time

Is Will You? the perfect song? Possibly. It has everything you want – excitement, pathos, a feeling of anticipation and then recklessness. For a teenager, scared of life and love, especially love, it's the permission you need to be nervous, clumsy and completely unsure of whether someone fancies you or not. Hazel O'Connor deserves a place in pop history for that one track alone.

Before she blasted into the charts in 1980, seemingly from nowhere, O'Connor had already travelled (**crossing the Sahara** before she was 18), learned several

living next door to Ozzy

In 2002 **Owen Paul** was unwittingly thrust back into the showbiz stratosphere courtesy of Mrs Ozzy Osbourne. A classic episode of the reality TV show saw Sharon launch the contents of her fridge into the garden of her noisy neighbour... none other than the Glasgow-born singer, last seen forgetting to mime to his first (and only) hit, My Favourite Waste Of Time, on *Top Of The Pops* in 1986.

Football was Owen Paul McGee's first love but then big brother Brian's band, Johnny & The Self-Abusers, became **Simple Minds** and sibling rivalry persuaded the

15-year-old to quit Celtic's youth team and have a crack at being a pop star. Snapped up by Sony, his debut single Pleased To Meet You bombed, but then came MFWOT.

Championed by Radio 1's **Peter Powell** it was an instant summer smash, only kept off the top slot by Doctor & The Medics' Spirit In The Sky. But follow-up hits failed to materialise and it was a series of successful business ventures rather than record royalties that saw Paul able to afford a mansion next door to Ozzy and Sharon. But don't expect to see his new album *About Time* on the next Ozzfest.

languages along the way including Japanese and Arabic (partly down to her stints as a dancer in Tokyo and Beirut), and even made the usual young wannabe's mistake of having a series of topless photos taken. When she was 'discovered' for her role in the movie *Breaking Glass*, O'Connor had actually already signed a recording contract, but she was still so broke that she was working on her record company's switchboard.

After the success of the movie and the album, plus an autobiography that was released, with Kenneth Branagh-style precociousness, before she turned 25, O'Connor's life spookily started to imitate her art and she soon disappeared from the charts and the national radar. She now lives in Ireland, but she's still singing, still recording, still touring, still blonde, still cool. Her music has deepened and the albums keep coming. She has mellowed, too, towards *Breaking Glass*, which she once saw as a handicap as she tried to escape the hype surrounding it.

Hazel O'Connor was the real thing. After several years when the charts were full of shouting, snarling lads, she blew them away with songs about feelings, influenced by punk, but not a slave to it. She wasn't manufactured, or kept afloat by management or stylists (although a bit of business advice might have done her some good as she only ever got two per cent of the royalties for her recording work, rather than the mega-bucks you – or, more to the point, she – might have expected). She made mistakes in her private and professional life, but she rocked and sang as the coolest woman on the planet. And if that was only for a short time, it was most certainly worth it.

Essential purchase Breaking Glass (Spectrum) the soundtrack to the movie, it has all of O'Connor's most memorable singles on it, most notably Will You?, Eighth Day and D-Days.

Underrated Albion: from 1981, a very good selection of songs, even though the best is a cover of Lou Reed's Men Of Good Fortune.

You've been warned On **To Be Freed** (Sony, 1993), she moves towards a more soulful style – but never actually gets there.

Prince   Imp of the perverse

Prince Rogers Nelson was the most controversial, prolific and influential talent of the 1980s. The breakthrough albums **Purple Rain** and **1999** – the former the soundtrack to his semi-autobiographical feature film – established the artist who became a squiggle as a true international star. However, a public dispute with record company Warner Brothers a decade later, the subsequent scrawling of 'slave' on his cheek, and the advent of that unpronounceable symbol, withdrew Prince from the mainstream music industry. Whether this liberated his creativity or was merely an act of commercial suicide is open to debate. Although few now hear Prince's new music, only distributed via the Internet or through independents, he remains truly creative and prolific.

That wasn't how the Prince story was supposed to end. He is the talent Terence Trent D'Arby aspired to be. He is more musically gifted (if less charismatic) than Madonna. And he has written some of the best-crafted pop songs of the past 20 years – Sinead O'Connor's **Nothing Compares 2 You** for example. He also, as **Alexander Nevermind**, wrote Sugar Walls for Sheena Easton, taking the Morning Train girl from Belshill and making her into a sex symbol, which makes him one of pop's great alchemists. His classic **Kiss** also led to **Tom Jones**'s second career.

Sadly, his reinvention as the infamous squiggle has meant that such decent songs as **The Question Of U** have been overlooked. The fact that he's decided to become a Jehovah's Witness won't do much for his street cred either, although 2001's *The Rainbow Children* is, it can safely be said, the best Jehovah's Witness album ever. His conversion also presumably means an end to such insights as, "Sex isn't all I think about, it's just all I think about with you."

The artist formerly known as a genius

Essential purchases 1984's **Purple Rain** is one to get, and especially 1987's **Sign O' The Times** – Prince's greatest album and arguably the essential album about the late 1980s. **The Hits/B-Sides**: you'll find no hits-only Christmas compilation (that's the less-inspired *Very Best Of Prince*) here; *The Hits 1* and *2* include his classics and his finest album tracks.

And don't dismiss the *B-Sides* album – he has written more great songs than any record company could release.

Underrated The Truth (1998) is probably his finest album as the symbol; it's an acoustic collection of original material only available as a bonus to the NPG triple CD out-takes album **Crystal Ball**.

You've been warned The Black Album (1988, released 1998) was originally scheduled for released by Warners in 1988 but it was replaced by **Lovesexy** at the last minute. When it was finally released, those who hadn't bought the previously sought-after bootleg discovered why it wasn't issued in the first place.

Queen
The drama, darlings

The band who brought guitar rock back from counter-culture into the musical mainstream was formed in 1970. **Freddie Mercury**, having left the latest in a string of bands, joined old pals **Brian May** (guitar) and **Roger Taylor** (drums). (Taylor and Mercury had shared another interest: flouncing around the streets of posh Knightsbridge in full drag together.) The line-up was completed in 1971 by bassist **John Deacon**, recruited by May and Taylor at a **teacher-training college** disco. And while the singer may have changed his name from **Faroukh Bulsara** to disguise his roots in Zanzibar, it didn't take long for the exotic to come out in Queen's music.

The first album, *Queen*, appeared two years later. It wasn't a massive hit, but it sowed the seeds of success with such songs as **Seven Seas Of Rhye** – concise, tuneful enough to be a Top 10 hit and fiercely energetic in contrast to much of the elaborate, laboured prog rock around it. Other hits and the album *Sheer Heart Attack* followed, but Queen's crowning glory came with **Bohemian Rhapsody** in 1975, which at almost six minutes long should have bombed but, helped by a film clip which was one of pop's first videos, it became one of the greatest singles ever, remaining No.1 in the UK chart for nine weeks, helping the album *A Night At The Opera* go platinum. The band's other classic, *A Day At The Races*, swiftly followed.

By 1977 Queen had moved on to such stadium anthems as **We Will Rock You** and We Are The Champions (*News Of The World*). An early sign of future critical derision came in 1979 when **Rolling Stone** dubbed their album *Jazz* as "fascist". To taking-it-all-too-seriously rock musos, there was something very unsettling about a band which could sing so enthusiastically about fat-bottomed girls.

In 1980 *The Game* propelled them to US stardom with such hits as **Another One Bites The Dust** and **Crazy Little Thing Called Love**, in which Queen do The King. But the theme to *Flash* was bombastic nonsense and began a decline which even **Under Pressure** (with David Bowie), Radio Ga Ga (which had crowds clapping like they were at a Nuremberg rally) and I Want To Break Free (with its **marvellously camp** video) couldn't disguise. At a time when old-fashioned entertainment was deemed at odds to great music, Mercury's theatrical prancing in an ermine cloak, thrusting in a skintight jumpsuit or sipping champagne during concerts was anathema to critics. But in 1985 Queen (well, Freddie really) stole the show at Live Aid, displaying more genuine charisma than any other act.

On 23 November 1991 Freddie Mercury announced he had AIDS. The next day he was dead. Bohemian Rhapsody/These Are The Days Of Our Lives was swiftly re-released to raise funds for the AIDS charity Terrence Higgins Trust, entering the UK chart at No.1, and raising more than £1 million. By December, Queen had **ten albums in the UK charts**.

Queen are still with us. Their biggest hit inspired the funniest scene in Mike Myers's **Wayne's World**. The musical *We Will Rock You* (co-written with **Ben Elton**) hit London's West End, and the Queen Symphony (by **Tolga Kashif**) was recorded by the Royal Philharmonic Orchestra. Nobody has combined high-octane melodrama with knowing self-parody like Queen and Freddie Mercury. He combined, **Simon Napier-Bell** thought, "the strutting male chauvinism of the Middle East, the shiny silk costumes of the male hero in Indian movies, the twisting lower abdomen and endlessly moving hands of a Persian belly dancer, and voice with the power and theatricality of **Judy Garland** and **Patti La Belle**."

Essential purchases Leading the way are **A Night At The Opera** (with Bohemian Rhapsody) and **A Day At The Races** (with complex arrangements like Millionaire's Waltz, the gospelish Somebody To Love and beautiful You Take My Breath Away).
Underrated The early albums: 1974's **Queen II** includes the likes of The Fairy Feller's Master-Stroke and White Queen, a world apart from your average pop.
You've been warned Best to give **Flash Gordon** and **Hot Space** a miss.

The Ramones
Oh brothers, where art thou?

Although The Ramones never achieved much commercial success, they are now, a quarter of a century after their heyday, one of the world's **most influential** bands.

The Ramones formed in New York in 1974, eventually settling on a line-up of Joey (vocals), Johnny (guitar), Dee Dee (bass) and Tommy (drums). They were not, of course, related, but their image as brothers became one of rock's most enduring brands. They started writing their own songs because, by their own admission, they weren't talented enough to play anyone else's and soon gained notoriety alongside Blondie, Patti Smith and Television on the emergent New York punk scene.

> **They started writing songs because, by their own admission, they couldn't play anyone else's**

Their sound – an unmistakable **revved-up** blend of glam rock, 1960s pop and garage rock filtered through their own skewed sensibilities – served them well on their first three landmark albums, *Ramones* (1976), *Leave Home* (1977) and *Rocket To Russia* (1977). But despite such memorable singles as **Blitzkrieg Bop** and Sheena Is A Punk Rocker, they yielded no hits in America and only minor ones in Britain. Accordingly they employed one of Joey's heroes, **Phil Spector**, to polish their sound for the charts. The resulting album, *End Of The Century*, was a disappointment, both financially and artistically, but it did yield the band's one big hit: a wholly atypical, string-laden romp through the Jeff Barry/Ellie Greenwich ballad **Baby, I Love You**, which reached No.8 in the UK in January 1980. That, sadly, was the Ramones' high-water mark.

They remained a popular concert draw for a further 16 years (Johnny ran the band as a business and insisted they keep touring) but the 1980s saw a succession of increasingly dismal albums. There were good moments – the 1985 single **Bonzo Goes To Bitburg**, attacking Ronald Reagan's visit to a cemetery at which SS soldiers were buried, was their best work since *Rocket To Russia*. The band split in 1996 to **widespread indifference**, but the resurgence in both punk and the New York rock scene meant the deaths of Joey in 2001 and Dee Dee (who wrote a truly scary autobiography) in 2002 led to a reappraisal of The Ramones' importance.

Influences A succession of cartoon **punk bands** have aped The Ramones' style of comedy lyrics allied to fuzzed guitars: Blink 182, Green Day and Bowling For Soup to name but three. U2 and Pearl Jam have also cited their influence.

Essential purchases Don't bother with 'best ofs': they invariably contain too much rubbish later material. Buy the recent reissues of those **first three albums**, all with extra tracks (and, in the case of **Leave Home**, an extra live album).

Underrated If I'm Against It had been on one of the first three albums, it would be considered a classic. But it was on Road To Ruin, so it remains a lost gem of cartoon nihilism ("I don't like summer and spring/I don't like anything/Cos I'm against it"). While Rock'n'Roll Radio is the track everyone cites from the Spector sessions, Danny Says is the better song, an oddly moving ballad about the heartbreak of being a not-very-successful pop singer living in cheap motel rooms.
You've been warned Brain Drain: Any Ramones album from the mid-1980s on could take its place, but this was their first record with no redeeming features.

Johnnie Ray
The prince of wails

To some, Johnnie Ray may be known only as the poor old pop idol recalled at the start of **Dexy's Midnight Runners**' Come On Eileen. Or the man whose 1950s-style hearing aid was briefly adopted by Morrissey. But Ray was hugely influential, a rock'n'roll John The Baptist to Elvis's messiah. You can hear traces of everyone from Elvis to Bowie to Freddie Mercury in his strange, over-the-top vocal style.

The son of an Oregon sawmill worker, Ray suffered a blow to one ear when he was nine, which forced him to wear a hearing aid for the rest of his life. When he became so successful as to irritate the generation reared on Frank Sinatra, critics swore that he switched it off when he sang. Maybe he didn't have a great voice, as his young fan **Andrew Loog Oldham** admitted, "but he acted a great song, sucking you into his three-minute screenplays of shame and pain… he was the male equivalent of a four-hankie movie."

The critical disdain was easy to understand. He often sang as if he were afraid his audience was hard of hearing, using any and every vocal trick to hold attention. A favourite device was to create an artificial crescendo in songs like Cry by bellowing out lines like, "If your heartaches seem to hang around too long" with twice as much power and twice as many syllables as most other singers would dare to.

Yet such was the flaccid state of popular music in the early 1950s that Ray's exhaustingly consistent sense of urgency was just what the industry needed. He was, if such a thing were possible, even more urgent on stage, indulging in the kind of theatrics hitherto associated with black artists and shedding floods of tears.

When he wasn't appalling critics with his vocal audacity (which, sadly, never extended to firing his backing vocalists who marred the chorus of Just Walking In The Rain, a No.1 hit in 1956) he was recording songs like **Such A Night** in such a sultry manner they were banned. He also made some light pop hits, like his gratingly cheerful duet with **Doris Day** on Let's Walk That-A-Way. Let's not, OK?

Ray had refreshingly few illusions about his own talent, once saying, "I've no talent, sing as flat as a table, I'm a human spaniel: people come to see what I'm like.

I make them feel, I exhaust them, I destroy him." Yet Nik Cohn, in his book *Awobpopaloobop Alopbamboom*, says: "He generated more intensity than any performer I ever saw in my life, Judy Garland excepted." When the music he had paved the way for, rock'n'roll, came to dominate, his own hits tailed off. Rumours of drink and drugs problems, and homosexuality, compounded his problems.

Yet he would be remembered by Elvis, **Billy Idol** (in his song Don't Need A Gun), Kevin Rowland et al, and earned a decent living as a cabaret artist almost until his death from liver failure in 1990. Even today nobody can emote like Johnnie – it's one reason you need a rest after listening to a few of his songs.

Essential purchase The Best Of Johnnie Ray (Columbia, 1996) includes makeweights, dross (Faith Can Move Mountains) and all the essential tracks.
Underrated I'll Never Fall In Love Again (not the Burt Bacharach song) is one of Ray's more enduring staccato performances, well arranged and with smarter than average lyrics. It deserved far better than to peak at No.26 in 1959. His version of As Time Goes By is, for Ray, unusually restrained and rather effective.
You've been warned Hernando's Hideaway is even more ludicrous in Ray's grand style than when sung by the likes of Doris Day.

The singing waiter

Frank Paul LoVecchio got his start in showbiz as a singing waiter. He was then discovered by **Hoagy Carmichael** and **Mitch Miller** and became the "rolling, rolling, rolling, keep them beasties moving" legend we know as Frankie Laine.

He hasn't had a chart hit for four decades and, despite selling more than 100 million records, his influence appears negligible. Yet Laine was the first white singer to appear reasonably regularly on the R&B charts. On his classic hits, his vocal delivery ranged from the melodramatic to the apocalyptic and, at a time when most white, male singers had all the dynamism of Perry Como, his urgency was a welcome change. His histrionics on such gems as Jezebel set up a vocal equivalent of a nuclear arms race, with Johnnie Ray determined to outdo such theatrics.

Laine briefly renewed his fame with the spoof theme to **Mel Brooks**'s *Blazing Saddles* in the 1970s. Yet his role as a precursor of rock'n'roll is still not widely known. For proof of his significance seek out *Greatest Hits* Vol. 1 (Laurie, 1992). Move along, Rawhide!

Jim Reeves
The baritone balladeer

Jim Reeves is the only country act to feature in the Top 100 bestselling artists in the UK as measured by weeks in the Top 30. Some feat considering he never toured the UK and died in a plane crash on 31 July 1964 at the peak of his powers.

Reeves began his career, reluctantly, in 1953 as a traditional honky-tonk singer, switching to his natural penchant, ballads, in 1957, after joining RCA Victor. With his producer, **Chet Atkins**, he pioneered the pop-country sound, looking to appeal to a broader, more cosmopolitan audience. His silky smooth baritone and distinctive phrasing, allied to an intimate, close-to-the-microphone technique and careful selection of material, provided the bedrock for his success.

Overseas success began in 1960 with **He'll Have To Go**, which re-entered the UK charts and made No.12. This was the trend for Reeves singles: generally they sold steadily rather than spectacularly. Further successes followed including You're The Only Good Thing (That's Happened To Me) and Welcome To My World. But it was after crooning of the country standard **I Love You Because** – in which, at his suggestion, a distinctive harp introduced the lyric – that Reeves really took off, making No.5 in 1964. The follow-up, I Won't Forget You, got to No.3 that July when tragedy struck, and his private plane went down in heavy rain (the same rain **Marty Robbins** was washing his hair with in his back garden when he heard the crash). But death couldn't stop the bandwagon. Several albums, many rush released in the UK after the tragedy, made the Top 20, and a *40 Greatest* compilation became one of the top-selling albums in the 1970s, appealing mostly to a working class who'd grown up to Elvis.

> 'Gentleman Jim' wasn't always a gent: he had a hot temper and he cheated on his wife

Reeves had also recorded several demos and these, together with unissued recordings, allowed his widow, Mary, to release more singles and albums of 'new' material for a decade. The most successful was **Distant Drums**, a US No.1 in 1966, still impossible not to sing along to when you hear it on the radio. Some of his other material (like the novelty hit But You Love Me Daddy) hasn't aged as well.

The question of what might have been lingers. As Atkins noted, Reeves was fast becoming the world's most popular singer. Today he's less respected than another crash victim, **Patsy Cline**. (The two, through the miracle of technology, duetted after their deaths...it's stunts like this that could bring back Luddism.)

Although known as Gentleman Jim, Reeves had a hot temper, cheated on his wife and his impatience probably contributed to his death – he could have waited for the storm to pass before taking to the skies. But his legacy was a style of intimate baritone

Not so gentlemanly Jim

singing which has influenced countless others.
Essential purchases The Ultimate Collection
is a good place to start, as is The Intimate Jim
Reeves, the first album he recorded with strings.
Underrated Twelve Songs Of Christmas
(1963): don't be put off by the sleeve (or the
sleeves on Jim's top), this is decent festive music.
You've been warned Steer clear of the unofficial
Gentleman Jim: The Hayride Years (Magnum),
marred by appalling sound quality which isn't
improved by the dubbing of fake applause.

Peter Sarstedt   Busker made good

"I looked up from my book and thought: I am a cathedral in the shadow of St
Stephen." Hey, who hasn't? It's the kind of thing that happens all the time – to
Peter Sarstedt. You can accuse him of many things – of looking, as *All Music
Guide* puts it, like someone who'd play the hero in a bad TV movie of the life of
Donovan – but you can't say he's afraid to follow his muse wherever it leads.

The enduring claim to fame of this British former busker (and younger brother
of the early-1960s pop idol **Eden Kane**) rests essentially on his No.1 hit Where Do
You Go To My Lovely? – a folksy portrayal of an Italian girl's rise from gutter to
jet set. Toned down for release (the verse about the girl's body being "firm and
inviting" was deemed too near the knuckle even in 1969), the song still sounds
fantastic today, with its waltzing beat, Sarstedt's mannered vocal (Dietrich
becomes "Dee-trick") and the bit where, after noting how his lovely keeps
a racehorse just for a laugh, he decides to laugh himself. Laughing on record is
never easy to carry off and though Sarstedt sounds more convincing than David
Bowie's chortling on The Laughing Gnome, this is the point where, for many,
Where Do You Go To My Lovely? becomes intolerably smug.

The portrait of a lovely who knows the Aga Khan, keeps a friend of Sacha Distel,
and gets an even suntan on her back and on her legs (thanks to a carefully
designed topless swimsuit) might seem absurd, but **Andrew Loog Oldham**, who
remembers the 1960s, regards this as a fair stab at 1960s jet-set life. Its success
almost persuaded Simon Napier-Bell to record an album of buskers to find the
next Sarstedt. Thankfully, producer Ray Singer tore up the original score for 40
string players and just kept the accordion, Sarstedt's guitar and a couple of cellos.

The follow-up, Frozen Orange Juice, wasn't quite as successful (it made No.10 in
the UK) and success never beckoned in the US, but Sarstedt has continued to record

despite never having another hit (though his younger brother, Robin, reached No.2 in 1976 with his cover of Hoagy Carmichael's **My Resistance Is Low**). Where Do You Go To My Lovely? jointly won the Ivor Novello songwriting award for 1969 with Space Oddity. At the ceremony Sarstedt and Bowie agreed to record together, but pressures of work and all that prevented them teaming up. Given that one of Peter's most famous recent efforts was a 20-minute A to Z of environmental issues called **The Green Alphabet**, Bowie might do well to keep out of Sarstedt's way.

Essential purchase The Best Of is the only decent compilation even if, perversely, it omits Frozen Orange Juice, one of only two of Pete's songs that charted.
Underrated Beirut, from 1979's *PS*, is a genuinely impressive song, and his near-hit, **Love Among The Ruins** (from 1982's *Update*), is almost as good.
You've been warned Watch out for **ropey live versions** of Where Do You Go To My Lovely? where the laughing bit sounds downright sinister.

Peter Sellers The real fifth Beatle

Elvis, Wet Wet Wet, Nick Cave and Engelbert Humperdinck have all covered Lennon and McCartney's songs, but few artists have had the nerve to reinterpret the Fab Four's classics quite so radically as Peter Sellers did when he performed **She Loves You** in the manner of **Dr Strangelove**.

As a member of **The Goons**, a trio of comedians who had more impact on British culture than any pop group before The Beatles, Sellers had almost as many voices as all the male voice choirs in Wales. Best known now as the franglais-speaking Inspector Clouseau, Sellers was a first-rate mimic and recorded a superb album of sharply observant and **satirical** songs with producer **George Martin** at Abbey Road studios in 1959. While Martin would hit the heights producing The Beatles, he first became well known as the creator of comedy records, with Sellers, Spike Milligan and Bernard (Right Said Fred) Cribbins among his alumni. The album, *The Best Of Sellers* (the title a dig at Decca, who would only let Martin release the album as a 10in LP) was released in 1959 and has been a cult classic ever since, especially for I'm So Ashamed, a lament about the plight of the teenypop idol (anticipating the **Gareth Gates** phenomenon) which has the neglected singer crying out plaintively, "What's the matter with me platters?"

Apart from being very funny, the album was **technically innovative**. Martin said: "I could experiment with playing with tapes and 'musique concrete' noises [abstract music achieved by tape manipulation] and so on. I don't think I would have done what I did on *Sgt Pepper* unless I'd done the Sellers album."

The experience impressed The Beatles, who were all *Goon Show* fans, and when

The Beatles met Elvis in 1965, Lennon and Presley bonded in their affection for Sellers, their imitation of his voices and comedy being a highlight of the summit.

Sellers, who also rendered A Hard Day's Night in the manner of a Shakespearean actor, taking it to No.14 at Christmas 1965, went on to become reasonably friendly with The Beatles, and co-starred with **Ringo Starr** in the 1969 movie *The Magic Christian*. By then, Peter's recording career was almost over, although he did make cameo appearances on records by The Hollies and Steeleye Span.

Sellers left behind a body of work which would be drawn on by everyone from the **Bonzo Dog Doo Dah Band** to Spinal Tap and **Monty Python**. Since his untimely death in 1980, time has rather passed him by, but he has left behind a distinctive comic (and musical) legacy which deserves to be better appreciated.

Essential purchases **The Best Of Sellers** (on vinyl or cassette) is his best single album if you can find it. If not, **Classic Songs And Sketches** (Disky) is a good start, although it omits some of his best work.
Underrated The Dr Strangelove **She Loves You** is well worth tracking down.
You've been warned The 67-track, four-CD **Celebration Of Sellers** (EMI) might be too much of a good thing for many, although it does contain all of his classics including more versions of She Loves You (in Cockney and as a chinless wonder).

Del Shannon — Spurned love a speciality

The pathos of Del Shannon's life is summed up by a live recording in the twilight of his career. "Here's Hey! Little Girl" he announces, but he's barely started before someone calls out for Runaway. He'd recorded **Runaway** 20 years earlier and, like the Ancient Mariner and his albatross, had to live with it for the rest of his life.

Previously a **carpet salesman** called Charles Weedon Westover, Shannon was discovered fronting a Hank Williams-influenced band in Michigan. Shortly after, in 1961, Runaway became an instant classic. Fast and dramatic, with Shannon cast as the wronged lover, it showcased his trademark falsetto and was written on stage at a nightclub with his organ player **Max Crook** who ad libbed the brilliant solo at the first attempt. It went straight to No.1. A series of minor hits, each a **minor pop epic of spurned love**, could have led to better things had it not been for the disastrous Cry Myself To Sleep (reportedly the inspiration for Elton John's Crocodile Rock) and a bizarre semi-yodelled cover of **Roger Miller**'s Swiss Maid.

Little Town Flirt was a more contemporary return to form, but by then The Beatles had arrived. Shannon's cover of **From Me To You** was the first Beatles song in the US charts, but like many rock'n'rollers he was fighting a rearguard action and, to compound his problems, fell out with his record company. He tried to

Rock'n'roll suicides

David Bowie wrote a fine song about rock'n'roll suicides (the classic line being, "Time takes a cigarette and puts it in your mouth") but he was smart enough not to become one. So was **Johnny Mandel** who wrote Suicide Is Painless, the *M*A*S*H* theme and a surprise UK No.1 hit. But Mandel's occasional compadre, **Chet Baker**, wasn't, falling out of an Amsterdam hotel while high on heroin in 1988. The miracle, given Baker's habits, was that he'd lived till he was 59. Only the good die middle-aged then, to tweak Billy Joel.

The list of pop and rock casualties is so great and varied – from **Kurt Cobain** and Joy Division's **Ian Curtis** to folkie **Phil Ochs**, Del Shannon and even Cantonese pop icon **Leslie Cheung** – you can see why Morrissey felt moved to croon, "Fame, fame, fatal fame."

Maybe doomed, young pop stars perform the same role as doomed, tubercular romantic poets in Keats's day. The finality of their fate thrills our adolescent souls and we safely romanticise them as we go about the grubby business of getting old. Or maybe it's just a guy thing.

start his own label, but had to return one year and two indifferent singles later.

A collaboration with Stones producer **Andrew Loog Oldham** showed some promise but it lost out in the dawn of psychedelia. He managed a late rally with Keep Searchin' (We'll Follow The Sun) – a UK No.3 in 1965 – but spent most of the 1960s bouncing around labels doing Stones and Monkees covers. He fared better as a producer, working with Bryan Hyland on his US No.3 Gypsy Woman.

Shannon suffered from depression throughout his career, and spent most of the 1970s struggling with alcoholism in the twilight of the rock'n'roll revival circuit. He recorded an album, Drop Down And Get Me with **Tom Petty** in 1981 but, with a certain grim inevitability, it was Runaway that was chosen as the theme tune to the TV series *Crime Story* in 1986. Shannon's friendship with Petty led to rumours that he'd replace Roy Orbison in the Travelling Wilburys but by 1990 he was battling his demons again. On 8 February he ended his life with a .22 rifle.

Essential purchase Del Shannon 1961-1990 has enough for everyone.
Underrated The Further Adventures Of Charles Westover, an endearing piece of sunlit 1968 oddness, suggests he could have had a more rewarding later career.
You've been warned Swiss Maid: should be buried in the Swiss Alps.

The Smiths

With their intentionally prosaic name and darkly monotonous vocals, it was all too easy to dismiss The Smiths as the eternal miserabilists of 1980s pop, but there was much more to them than doom and gloom. With Morrissey's sharp eye and **epigrammatic wit** cradled by Johnny Marr's guitar, The Smiths could be seen as the best British band since The Beatles.

While many of their contemporaries were singing in mid-Atlantic accents about glamorous assignations in exotic clubs, Morrissey projected The Smiths as pop stars who would have been more at home trading custard creams and gossip with Thora Hird. Through him, The Smiths called on the same northern tradition as **George Formby** and **Alan Bennett**, creating a world populated with cross-dressing vicars, girls who would and boys who couldn't.

The debut single, Hand In Glove, was well received, but as a summary of everything the band represented, their follow-up, **This Charming Man**, is unsurpassed. It has all their trademarks: sexual ambiguity that owes more to thwarted provincial librarians than the triumphal glam of Bolan or Bowie; a lyrical flourish ("why pamper life's complexities when the leather runs smooth on the passenger seat?") and the deathless genius of Marr's playing to hold it all together.

The single, and their John Peel sessions, made The Smiths the darlings of the indie circuit, and they made good on their promise with their self-titled debut album. **What Difference Does It Make?** charted at No.12, but it was Suffer Little Children that got the headlines, with its reference to Myra Hindley and the Moors murders. It outraged the tabloids, as did Morrissey's later carefully calculated pronouncements on everything from **eating meat** to the Thatcher government. But as Morrissey said, "At least I'm not Andrew Ridgeley."

Hatful Of Hollow followed, the first of three compilations that would include album tracks alongside singles, B-sides and unreleased material. It included one of the Smiths' rare Top 10 hits, the self-parodying **Heaven Knows I'm Miserable Now**. *Meat Is Murder* was the second studio album; its standout track How Soon Is Now? – a plangent wail with brooding lyrics – is a defining Smiths moment.

If their melancholy often teetered on contrivance, wit always pulled them back. It's this combination that makes **The Queen Is Dead** the perfect Smiths album. Cemetry Gates acts as though namechecking Keats and Yeats is the most natural thing in the world; Vicar In A Tutu takes a winking romp through transvestism; **The Boy With The Thorn In His Side** and Big Mouth Strikes Again were hits, and it all ends with the *Carry-On* sentiment of Some Girls Are Bigger Than Others.

Marr walked out shortly after recording the final studio album, *Strangeways*

Here We Come, but The Smiths' epitaph is a masterpiece. Affected, flamboyant and darkly funny, it reaches its zenith with **Girlfriend In A Coma**. But without Marr, the magic – and the tunes – had gone. The solo careers of Morrissey and Marr have alternately delighted and frustrated, but together the two of them made sublimely clever pop music. And if you've never flounced home from a disastrous date singing Please, Please, Please, Let Me Get What I Want, you haven't lived.

Essential purchases They don't get any more essential than **The Queen Is Dead**, while **Louder Than Bombs** is an eminently worthwhile compilation.
Underrated Strangeways Here We Come has great tunes, a fabulously melodramatic attitude and some truly memorable lines.
You've been warned Avoid the two posthumous, post-Rough Trade label compilations. **Best I** is eclectic and aimless; **Best II** is an oxymoron.

Phil Spector
The Nosferatu of pop

With his shades and helmet of black hair Phil Spector looked like a child of Edgar Allan Poe's imagination and, as the first star producer, brought a suitably intense sensibility to pop with his **Wall of Sound**. A lavish, multi-layered Wagnerian blast of vocals and instruments swelling to a delirious climax, it sounded, noted one critic, like "a thousand drunken angels singing in a subway tunnel."

Spector made an unlikely chart debut in 1958 as one third of vocal trio The Teddy Bears with his song **To Know Him Is To Love Him**. An amiable if saccharine period ditty that went to No.1 in the US (No.2 in the UK), it had a dark twist: the title was the inscription on his father's grave. After The Teddy Bears split, Spector was headed for a job as a UN interpreter when he was hired as an assistant to independent producer Lester Sill. There he worked with Elvis's former songwriters Jerry Leiber and Mike Stoller, co-writing Ben E King's **Spanish Harlem** and playing guitar for The Drifters before forming Philles Records with Sill.

At Philles, Spector quickly built his trademark arrangement, which proved a heady and popular mix. He gave The **Righteous Brothers** a No.1 in 1965 with You've Lost That Lovin' Feelin', but the alchemy worked best with girl groups. The Crystals had hits with **Then He Kissed Me**, **Da Doo Ron Ron** and an iffy paean to the romantic power of domestic violence, **He Hit Me (And It Felt Like A Kiss)**, part written by Carole King. Another girl group, The Ronettes, gave pop music one of its greatest moments with his sassy-but-vulnerable **Be My Baby**. And Spector was so impressed with the Ronettes' Ronnie Bennett that he married her.

The triumphant bombast of **River Deep, Mountain High** marked the zenith of the Wall of Sound. Though officially credited to **Ike & Tina Turner**, it's rumoured

"I like to ride my bicycle, I like to ride my bike..."

Eccentrically yours

The British public (and indeed the critics) have not been kind to pop's eccentrics, greeting them with an innate suspicion normally reserved for estate agents and the like. Here we redress the balance – a bit.

Bonzo Dog Band

The Bonzos (especially Neil Innes and Vivian Stanshall) were the missing link between The Beatles and Monty Python, who spoofed nearly every major pop genre and act and produced Can Blue Men Sing The Whites?, Canyons Of Your Mind and the immortal Tent (with its menacing, yet risible chorus: "I'm gonna get you in my tent, tent, tent..."

If you buy one album Make it The Doughnuts In Granny's Greenhouse.

Half Man Half Biscuit

Amazingly, Birkenhead's funniest export have never had a hit single, not even their ditty about Dukla Prague away kits. But at their best, their sleeve notes are funnier than most TV sketch shows. They are also responsible for the funniest song ever written about an England and Middlesex cricketer, the brilliant "Fuckin 'ell it's Fred Titmus!"

If you buy one album Start with Back In The DHSS.

XTC

Poor old **Andy Partridge** and **Colin Moulding**. Their Swindon roots were often cited as 'proof' of their dullness. In reality, XTC's biggest problem was that Partridge wrote songs that were witty and too intricate for the masses to hum. The charge of dullness bit deep: the cover of their box set *Coat Of Many Cupboards* stars a man in a grey suit holding a gold key. Yet their catchy, nervy, music deserved better. In an era when the charts were full of songs about girls called Sherona, it was good to have someone write a hit about a bloke called Nigel.

If you buy one album Try Drums & Wires.

Orange Juice

Fronted, inspired and destroyed by Edwyn Collins, Orange Juice came close to neo-pop perfection with the beautiful Felicity and the pop-cum-soul of Rip It Up, which combined a moronic chorus with a verse that rhymed boredom and humdrum. Collins' smoothly sung insulting patter is best summed up by the line, "Here's a penny for your thoughts... incidentally, you can give me change."

If you buy one album Try the debut You Can't Hide Your Love Forever.

that Spector paid Ike to stay at home so he and Tina could concentrate on his masterpiece. It reached No.3 in the UK in 1966, but bombed in the US. Angry and burnt-out at 25, Spector went into semi-retirement until 1969 when John Lennon asked him to oversee **The Beatles**' half-finished *Let It Be* sessions. His efforts proved popular with everyone except **Paul McCartney**, who hated them, and Spector later worked on solo projects with John Lennon and George Harrison.

Spector worked only sporadically thereafter, producing *Death Of A Ladies' Man* for Leonard Cohen, and **Baby I Love You**, The Ramones' only Top 10 single, but his erratic behaviour made him more famous than his work. Everyone, including **Stevie Wonder**, seems to have had Spector **pull a gun** on them in the studio, and in his paranoid isolation, his 23-room mansion became Beverly Hills' answer to the House of Usher. By 1974 Ronnie Spector had had enough. She filed for divorce, telling a court that her husband had threatened her life if she contested custody of their three children – and adding that he had also hidden her shoes.

Spector then seemed to reach an equilibrium, but in February 2003 actress Lana Clarkson was found **shot dead at his mansion** and he was charged with first-degree murder. The epitaph to the career of the man described as the "first tycoon of teen" may yet be written by the jury in a Los Angeles courthouse.

Essential purchases The **Back To Mono** four-disc set has most of his best work. The great seasonal **A Christmas Gift For You** LP showcases many Philles artists.
Underrated Go for anything on **Back To Mono** that isn't instantly recognisable.
You've been warned Cohen's **Death Of A Ladies' Man**: as bad as it is bizarre.

Alvin Stardust   Serial teenage sensation

Alvin Stardust can be accused of many things but lack of effort isn't one of them. His real name was **Bernard William Jewry**, but he realised that in the early 1960s Bernard was a moniker for a light comedian, not a pop star. Still, the lead singer of the Tremolos (no relation) had died, so Bernard filled the void as **Shane Fenton**. With and without the Fentones (as the Tremolos became), he enjoyed a few minor hits with songs like Cindy's Birthday. Some of these were produced by **George Martin**, and Bobby Elliott, the Hollies drummer, was an honorary Fentone. Alvin seemed to be on to a half-decent thing, but then Martin discovered The Beatles.

Effectively retiring, Fenton re-emerged in 1973 under the self-parodying name of **Alvin Stardust**. In black leather (a tactic borrowed from Gene Vincent) hair dyed blacker than soot and artificially expanded **sideburns**, Stardust was essentially Elvis-lite, although the influence of 1960s Brit rocker Dave Berry was obvious in the gloved hand which curled rather menacingly around the mike. As the real Elvis was then mostly in Las Vegas, Stardust was smart enough to spot a gap in the market. The release of **My Coo Ca Choo**, unlucky not to top the charts although it hung around the Top 10 for ages, proved there was a market in the gap. Daft as his transformation might seem today, this was the 1970s. Next to **Gary Glitter**, Alvin looked subtle.

The Alvin toy never caught on

My Coo Ca Choo, the title possibly alluding to the "coo coo ca choo" chorus in **Mrs Robinson** was his finest work, with its mysterious invitation to his lover to "lay down and groove on the mat" and a guitar sound reminiscent of Norman Greenbaum's Spirit In The Sky. Legend has it that when he arrived at *Top Of The Pops* to perform it, **Tony Blackburn** challenged him: "Hey, aren't you Shane Fenton?" Stardust allegedly went into a sulk which lasted through his performance. More likely he knew he'd do better playing mean.

The follow-up, Jealous Mind, did climb to No.1. The best of the gradually diminishing hits that followed **Red Dress**, in which Alv was so desperate to click with a girl in a red dress somebody should have put bromide in his tea. Other Top 10 hits included the catchy Pretend and I Feel Like Buddy Holly, even though that was a blatant lie: if he ever felt like any dead rocker, it was **Gene Vincent**.

Stardust must have been tired of Jewry service, because when his 15 minutes of fame (and his marriage to lite entertainer Liza Goddard) ended he didn't revert to his original name. Henceforth eternally Alvin, he became 'a popular showbiz personality', hosting various Christian music shows on the BBC. The sideburns, you'll be delighted to hear, remain as profuse as ever.

Essential purchase Greatest Hits has all his 'classics', though the ideal CD would have just My Coo Ca Choo, Jealous Mind, Red Dress and Good Love Can Never Die.
Underrated My Coo Ca Choo: unjustly ridiculed for its daft title.
You've been warned So Near Christmas could ruin yours. And everyone else's.

Cat Stevens
Singer/songwriter in exile

Cat Stevens (real name: Steven Giorgiou; now known as Yusuf Islam) was the reason **David Bowie** never made much headway on Decca. The label's A&R men were convinced Cat ("I needed a name people wouldn't forget") was the next big thing.

His first song in the charts was the often-covered **First Cut Is The Deepest**, a Top 20 UK hit for the exiled US singer **P P Arnold**. But by 1968, Stevens was a genuine pop star, writing and singing commercial folk/pop hits like I Love My Dog and Matthew And Son. A bad case of tuberculosis forced him into temporary retirement – and to question the music he was making. He returned with the world-weary *Mona Bone Jakon*, which he capped with one of the finest self-penned albums of the late 1960s/early 1970s, *Tea For The Tillerman*, and its smoother successor, *Teaser & The Firecat*. Songs like **Lady D'Arbanville** (inspired by his girlfriend Patti, a New York model, actress and teenage Warhol acolyte) were much subtler and lyrically **more sophisticated**, although he always could cut to the heart of a matter – witness such songs as **Matthew And Son**.

The sense of disillusionment (and the quest for some deeper meaning for life) became more obvious with each album and, although his decision to become a Muslim rather than hang out with a maharishi or the Dalai Lama was something of a surprise, his second retirement from the pop business came as less of a shock than his reported backing for Iran's fatwa on Salman Rushdie (he says he was misinterpreted). He leaves behind a body of classic songs, perhaps as many as 20, and one masterpiece of an album, *Tea For The Tillerman*. Although he was probably most satisfied with his songs seeking **spiritual truth**, his music about relationships still strikes the greater chord.

Essential purchases Very Best Of (A&M) is good: it also includes the rare I've Got A Thing About Seeing My Grandson Grow Old. And **Tea For The Tillerman**.
Underrated Buddha And The Chocolate Box often gets overlooked, but any album which includes Oh Very Young is worth listening to.
You've been warned His concept album **Numbers** which, he advised, was not to be taken "2 seriously" should not be listened to 2 often, although it's not as dire as many said at the time. Avoid the experimental and dodgy **Foreigner** too.

Scott Walker   The Howard Hughes of pop

As mysterious as Glenn Miller's disappearance and as morose as a bedsit CD player programmed entirely with Leonard Cohen albums, **Scott Walker** is one of pop's last great unsullied myths. After a brief mid-1960s teenybop career in The Walker Brothers (he was once treated for concussion after being **mobbed** in Chester), he became a Brel-singing artistic recluse, revered by such individuals as Julian Cope. According to popular myth, he enters a recording studio only slightly more often than it rains in the Atacama desert, usually when he has grown tired of playing darts in pubs. If only every rock star could be as **reticent**…

Walker was born Scott Engel in Ohio and first came to Britain with his 'brothers' – John Maus and Gary Leeds – to avoid being drafted to fight in Vietnam.

The pop biography

The stories of pop idols, before shows like **Pop Idol** distorted them, often bear striking similarities. The overall narrative is familiar enough. The archetypal pop or rock star rises from under-appreciated or neglected childhood (the humbler the better, as far as the marketing folk are concerned) to fame, and then has to face whatever happens next – an untimely but mythologically significant death, the living death that is the 1980s reunion tour (or its predecessor, the Baileys nightclub circuit) or, more recently, the life of millionaire irrelevance exemplified by Mick Jagger, Phil Collins et al.

Within that overall trajectory, other key events recur across pop stars' lives. There is always, as **John Aizlewood** noted in a piece in *Word* magazine, a meeting (Elvis and Sam Phillips; John and Paul; The Beatles and Brian Epstein; Johnny Rotten and Malcolm McLaren; Jacko and Quincy Jones; Rick Astley and Pete Waterman) which changes the course of personal and pop history. And there's usually a parting too (with a symmetry no novelist would dare invent, the names in brackets apply here too).

Some idols, even those who notch up quite a few hits, suffer from the curse that they are never quite as big as their first record. This could be referred to as **Paul Anka Syndrome**, after the diminutive singer/songwriter burst into the world's charts with Diana, a UK and US No.1, which he never really topped – although he racked up 17 other UK hits and was partly responsible for My Way. Other victims of this syndrome include the **Spice Girls**, **Connie Francis**, **Cyndi Lauper** and even **Frankie Goes To Hollywood**, who could never relax knowing their debut No.1 was more legendary than they were.

For most pop stars, fame lasts longer than 15 minutes but not much longer than a few years. A lucky few (Elvis, Lennon, Madonna, Bruce Springsteen) stage a comeback which surprises the critics. Most don't. Since Live Aid, the rock/pop aristocracy has proved more durable as celebrities, but not always musically; even Bono is in danger of being more famous as a moral authority, a thinking person's Pope rather than a musician.

The template pop star life is summed up in the **Peter Sellers** epic I'm So Ashamed. His sorry tale of an eight-year-old pop star fallen out of fashion should be played outside the auditions for the next *Pop Idol*.

Scott Engel and John Maus search for the third Walker Brother, Gary Leeds

Designed to emulate those other non-related fraternal singers the Righteous Brothers, they had their first hit with **The Sun Ain't Gonna Shine Anymore**. It was a flop when first cut by Frankie Valli, but it's impossible now to imagine the song without Scott's **deep, moody, slightly ethereal** croon. Other hits followed (notably the wondrous Make It Easy On Yourself) as did the trio's break-up.

Spurning the prevalent psychedelia, Scott created a musical world full of ennui, longing, pessimism and passion, as he drew on songs from **Jacques Brel** and wrote oblique, even impenetrable, material inspired by Ingmar Bergman movies which commented on Stalinism. *Scott 4*, entirely self-penned, is cited as his best album although it sold moderately – the public preferring the lush, slightly bombastic, orchestration less in evidence here. Apart from delivering some great vocal performances (Joanna, If You Go Away), Scott Walker changed what people expect from a pop song with numbers like **Montague Terrace In Blue**, true to his belief that "people who follow me don't want sugar-coated rubbish". One can intellectualise forever about what makes great popular music but often it comes down to **the voice**, and Walker has one of the best, most soulful, voices in the business. He still hasn't caught on in America though, where England's reverence for him remains as much of a mystery as the French's adoration of Jerry Lewis.

Essential purchase No Regrets has his greatest hits as a Walker Brother and some of his best solo work, such as Jackie and Boy Child.
Underrated Till The Band Comes In has never got the credit it deserved, possibly because one track is sung by Esther Ofarim of Cinderella Rockerfella fame.
You've been warned Tilt is not for those who adore Scott the lush balladeer.

Jimmy Webb
You can name his tunes in...

Frank Sinatra told Jimmy Webb he'd created "the greatest torch song ever written". Yet **Sammy Davis Jr** threw the up-and-coming songwriter out of his hotel room, telling him not to come back till he'd written some happy songs.

The son of a baptist minister, Webb was born in Elk City, Oklahoma, in 1946, but by the time he was 20 he'd moved to LA and written the song Sinatra would later rave about – **By The Time I Get To Phoenix**, a hit for **Glen Campbell** in 1967 (it was turned down by Motown because it didn't have a proper hook). Up, Up And Away was equally successful for The 5th Dimension the same year... two songs, eight Grammy awards and Webb was on his way.

Although he struggled as a performer (he'd earlier been in a boy-girl harmony group called The Strawberry Children), by the early 1970s Webb was the most in-demand songwriter of his generation. Glen Campbell recorded several more

Sweet green icing, anyone?

of his songs, including **Wichita Lineman** (now a modern standard) and Galveston, both hits.

Sadly Webb turned his back on pop and sought something higher. He hasn't been the same since, though paradoxically he's probably best known for leaving his cake out in the rain in the epic **MacArthur Park**. An extraordinary, intensely poetic confection, it was a hit for the late actor Richard Harris in 1968 – astonishing given its unprecedented seven-minute length – and later (in more conventional fashion) for disco queen Donna Summer. Remarkably, Harris's album of Webb songs (*A Tramp Shining*) also spawned the simple, wistful **Didn't We**, now a favourite with nightclub balladeers.

The key to Webb's writing is defying genres. His music is touched by country, musicals, pop, easy listening and rock, and his songs have been covered by artists as varied as Tony Bennett, Urge Overkill and REM. His two sons, Justin and Christiaan, have also had some success with their band, The Webb Brothers.

Essential purchase And Someone Left The Cake Out In The Rain has 18 versions of classic Webb songs by the above artists and more (Judy Collins, Scott Walker…).
Underrated 1996's Ten Easy Pieces is just Webb, a piano and his greatest songs. If you can find them, 5th Dimension's two 1967 albums of Webb material, **Up, Up And Away** and **The Magic Garden**, are fantastic, dramatic pop.
You've been warned Most of Webb's own albums, which generally contain one or two good songs, also feature a great deal of tuneless agonising.

The Wedding Present Out of time

Statistically, at least, **The Wedding Present** are the equal of **Elvis Presley**. Like the King they managed 12 hits, one in every month of one calendar year. Unlike Presley, however, they didn't change the face of popular music. The 12 singles of 1992 – a calculated attempt to equal Elvis's achievement – all reached the Top 30, albeit largely because they were limited-edition releases snapped up by fans, but a chart high of No.10 achieved by the May single (Come Play With Me) was a poor return for a band who had once been hailed as '**the new Smiths**'.

The Wedding Present emerged from Leeds in 1985 and were soon lumped in with the "shambling" movement that dominated UK indie music at the time. But then, thanks to their northernness, leader David Gedge's slice-of-life lyrics and their muscular music, the parallel was drawn with The Smiths (whose final album was released just weeks before The Wedding Present's 1987 debut). That first album, **George Best**, was an instant indie classic and sold well enough to win the band a deal with RCA. But Gedge was so committed to his indie principles that large-scale success was never on the cards (the band's first RCA release was a mini-LP of **Ukrainian folk songs**). The next album proper, *Bizarro*, was a natural sequel to *George Best*, but then Gedge took a sharp left turn, immersing himself in the emergent US underground – a decade before Blur did – working with Steve Albini (he later produced Nirvana's *In Utero*) on 1991's harsh, dissonant *Seamonsters*.

A decade later the album would have sounded much of a piece with any number of bands inspired by US mavericks such as Pavement. At the time it just sounded messy. The 12 singles of the following year – collected on *Hit Parade* – did nothing to ease the band back towards the mainstream and they were soon back on indie labels. In an attempt to step away from his fading legacy, Gedge split them and formed **Cinerama**. It was, perhaps, his misfortune that his peak coincided with a dismal time for UK alternative music. Rather than being seen as someone ahead of the crowd, he was often vilified for the very failings in his contemporaries he was reacting against: parochialism and musical conservatism.

Essential purchases Two stand out – **George Best** and **Seamonsters**.
Underrated Tommy: a collection of early singles and B-sides that shows why RCA wanted to sign them in the first place.
You've been warned **Ukrainian John Peel Sessions** is just what it sounds like.

Robbie Williams
Take that!

When Robbie Williams left **Take That** in 1995, newspapers reported that the Samaritans set up extra phone lines to stop teenage fans committing suicide. It wasn't true, but the story underlines the huge popularity and hysteria surrounding Take That, the group that started the renaissance of the lost art of boy bands.

Once freed from the **Take That** prison, Robbie took to the sex, drugs and rock'n'roll lifestyle with abandon. He was in and out of the tabloids as often as the kiss 'n' tell girls were in and out of his bed. But his ballooning weight had the hallmarks of an indulgent rock star past his prime and he was embroiled in legal battles to extricate himself from the Take That contract. No one imagined then that this **chubby, partying joker** would become Britain's top-selling, male, solo artist. It wasn't just the chubbiness, there's always been a hint of **Norman Wisdom** about his looks. Given that he's the only reigning pop monarch who you can imagine suddenly crying "Mr Grimsdale!", his eminence is even more remarkable.

When the legal battle ended and he was free to record, Robbie chose to cover the

George Michael hit Freedom. It got to No.2 in 1996, but of greater note is that it started a theme to which Robbie has frequently returned: reflecting events from his private life in his songs. On his first album, **Life Thru A Lens,** Ego A Go Go is about Take That's Gary Barlow, while Clean, Killing Me and Old Before I Die all deal with overcoming the addictions that had ruled his life for the previous year.

A classic **attention seeker,** Williams yo-yos between loving life in the public eye and suffering with self-doubts, self-pity and introspection. The feature-length documentary *Nobody Someday* and book *Somebody Someday* both give a behind-the-scenes account of his 2001 European tour with the conflicting sides of his personality fully exposed: the pop king and the insecure, lonely tears of a clown.

> **There's a hint of Norman Wisdom about Robbie which makes his stardom even more remarkable**

But on stage the showman rules. His concerts are as full of **charisma and chutzpah** as they are of belting pop hits. Unlike his sparring partners Oasis (reported as saying, "I hope all of you who sang through Wonderwall die of hypothermia"), Robbie feeds off his fans and enjoys working them into a frenzy of participation and swaying lighters. Catch Robbie Williams live and you'll see why he is a star.

Then again, Robbie would never be such a success had it not been for songwriter **Guy Chambers,** co-writer on all his major hits. They have now parted company and it will be interesting to see if Robbie can maintain his hit rate without him.

Essential purchases The songs you've not heard of are surprisingly varied and catchy, but what you really want with Robbie is to join in with the hits in your living room; on the first two albums, **Life Thru a Lens** and **I've Been Expecting You,** you've got Angels, Old Before I Die, Let Me Entertain You, Millennium, Phoenix From The Flames and She's The One. Listen out, too, for the hidden tracks that pop up at the end of both albums.

Underrated The clue to appreciating Robbie is right there in his song **Let Me Entertain You.** Take it all with a pinch of irony and you've got one of Britain's best entertainers. Just don't go looking for anything more.

You've been warned **Swing When You're Winning** is his homage to the Rat Pack and the big band era. To those who adored Life Thru A Lens, it might sound close to karaoke – although it does have some great tunes and, a decade from now, may well be re-evaluated. Duetting with Sinatra was not one of Robbie's better ideas.

THE LISTS

The bestsellers, Christmas No.1s, what pop stars
did next – all that and much, much more...

DJ Alan Freeman, aka Fluff, had his own theme: At The Sign Of The Swinging Cymbal

"Greetings pop pickers, erm.... not aarf!"
Alan Freeman

You could fill a library full of pop music trivia, so this section can only ever be a primer. But filing away such facts as the full official title for Johnny Mathis's 1970s festive hit – **When A Child Is Born (Soleado)** – can backfire. Handled carelessly, such trivia can lead you into a twilight zone populated by the likes of Jimmy Savile ("and the full title is – opening bracket – O Sole Mio – close bracket – It's Now Or Never; give yourself two points if you got that right") and whoever writes the captions for TOTP2. Still, there are worse things than not knowing where your anorak ends and your personality starts – like owning a Vince Hill album.

Ten Acts With Most Number Of Weeks On The UK Singles Chart

(From *The Complete Book Of British Charts*)
Cliff's chances of narrowing Elvis's lead dipped with the Nike/JXL/Presley smash A Little Less Conversation. But don't write off a man so hungry for chart action that he'll rollerskate around singing, "I've got small speakers." This list includes all UK chart action until the end of 2002.

1.	Elvis Presley	1,185
2.	Cliff Richard	1,152
3.	Elton John	593
4.	Madonna	576
5.	Diana Ross	560
6.	Michael Jackson	508
7.	Rod Stewart	477
8.	The Beatles	456
9.	David Bowie	451
10.	Frank Sinatra	433

They Wrote The Songs

1. Needles And Pins **Sonny Bono**
2. He's A Rebel **Gene Pitney**
3. Georgy Girl **Jim Dale**
4. Simon Smith And His Amazing Dancing Bear **Randy Newman**
5. Living Doll **Lionel Bart**
6. Smile **Charlie Chaplin**
7. Up Where We Belong **Buffy Sainte-Marie**
8. Son Of My Father **Giorgio Moroder**
9. Can't Get You Out Of My Head **Cathy Dennis, Rob Davis**
10. I Tawt I Taw A Puddy Tat **Mel Blanc**

Sonny, Jim Dale, Charlie Chaplin, and Buffy Sainte-Marie co-wrote their hits. Lionel Bart also gave us Little White Bull. Mel Blanc, author of Tweety Pie's song, was also the voice of Bugs Bunny. Rob Davis wore earrings in Mud and Cathy Dennis sang with D-Mob.

Top Ten Bestselling Singles In The UK
(From *Guinness Book Of British Hit Singles*)

When you're talking supergroups, no one can touch Boney M, as this list clearly proves.

1.	Candle In The Wind (1997)/ Something About The Way You Look Tonight	**Elton John**	**4,860,000**
2.	Do They Know It's Christmas?	**Band Aid**	**3,550,000**
3.	Bohemian Rhapsody	**Queen**	**2,130,000**
4.	Mull Of Kintyre/Girls' School	**Wings**	**2,050,000**
5.	Rivers Of Babylon/Brown Girl In The Ring	**Boney M**	**1,995,000**
6.	You're The One That I Want	**John Travolta & Olivia Newton-John**	**1,980,000**
7.	Relax	**Frankie Goes To Hollywood**	**1,910,000**
8.	She Loves You	**The Beatles**	**1,890,000**
9.	Unchained Melody/(There'll Be Bluebirds Over) The White Cliffs Of Dover	**Robson & Jerome**	**1,840,000**
10.	Mary's Boy Child/Oh My Lord	**Boney M**	**1,790,000**

Top Ten Bestselling Singles In The World
(From *everyHit.com*)

There may be a constant influx of new blood in the charts, but at the risk of sounding like an old codger, it seems they really don't make songs like they used to. Either that or we don't buy them like we used to. Originally a hit in 1973, Candle In The Wind is bounds ahead of the pack, with the 1955 Bill Haley classic way behind and not a boy band or Pop Idol in sight.

1.	Candle In The Wind	**Elton John**	**37m**
2.	White Christmas	**Bing Crosby**	**30m**
3.	(We're Gonna) Rock Around The Clock	**Bill Haley & His Comets**	**17m**
4.	I Want To Hold Your Hand	**The Beatles**	**12m**
5.	Hey Jude	**The Beatles**	**10m**
6.	It's Now Or Never	**Elvis Presley**	**10m**
7.	I Will Always Love You	**Whitney Houston**	**10m**
8.	Hound Dog	**Elvis Presley**	**9m**
9.	Diana	**Paul Anka**	**9m**
10.	I'm A Believer	**The Monkees**	**8m**
	(Everything I Do) I Do It For You	**Bryan Adams**	**8m**

Ten Artists With The Most UK Top 10 Singles

(From *The Complete Book Of British Charts*)

Crumbs, as Cliff himself might say. Proof that he's bigger than Elvis, Madonna and U2.

1.	Cliff Richard	64
2.	Elvis Presley	55
3.	Madonna	49
4.	Michael Jackson	38
5.	The Beatles	28
6.	Elton John	27
7.	Queen	26
8.	Rod Stewart	26
9.	U2	24
10.	David Bowie	23

Producers With Most UK No.1s

(From *Guinness Book Of British Hit Singles*)

1.	George Martin	27
	Norrie Paramor	27
2.	Mitch Miller	17
3.	Steve Sholes	15
	Pete Waterman	15
4.	Matt Aitken	13
	Mike Stock	13
5.	Chet Atkins	11
6.	Benny Andersson	10
	Bjorn Ulvaeus	10
	Johnny Franz	10
7.	Mike Chapman	9
8.	Dick Rowe	8
	George Michael	8
9.	Madonna	7
	Norman Newell	7
	Tony Hatch	7

Four Pop Stars Who Found God (And One Who Misplaced Him)

1. Prince

The man who wrote "come inside my sugar walls" for Sheena is now a Jehovah's Witness.

2. Barry McGuire

Possibly affected by the apocalyptic feel of his only No.1 hit, Eve Of Destruction, Barry McGuire quit secular music, became born again and moved to – gulp – Waco, Texas. He now makes occasional gospel records and hosts Christian music cruises.

3. Little Richard

In 1957, Richard Penniman believed the launch of *Sputnik* and the crash of a plane he'd been scheduled to fly on were signs of divine displeasure. He gave up rock for the appropriately biblical period of seven years, but then gave up giving up rock and now denies he ever became a Mormon minister.

4. Al Green

The revered reverend of Memphis soul fell off the stage in 1979, narrowly avoiding serious injury. He took this as a sign from God and retired to preach and sing gospel, not releasing a secular album until 1995.

5. The Singing Nun

Belgian nun Sister Luc-Gabrielle (real name Janine Deckers) recorded plenty of uplifting music for her fellow nuns but one song, Dominique, was released as a single, topping the US charts. The Singing Nun then left the convent to help her spread the Word, although presumably the church wasn't too chuffed when she released the pro-birth control Glory Be To God For The Golden Pill. She committed suicide in 1985.

UK's Top Ten Selling Albums	**Global Top Ten Selling Albums**
(From *everyHit.com*)	(From *everyHit.com*)

UK's Top Ten Selling Albums
(From *everyHit.com*)

1. Sgt Pepper's Lonely Hearts Club Band **The Beatles**
2. (What's The Story) Morning Glory? **Oasis**
3. Bad **Michael Jackson**
4. Brothers In Arms **Dire Straits**
5. Stars **Simply Red**
6. Thriller **Michael Jackson**
7. Greatest Hits (Volume 1) **Queen**
8. Spice **Spice Girls**
9. Abba Gold **Abba**
10. The Immaculate Collection **Madonna**

Global Top Ten Selling Albums
(From *everyHit.com*)

1. Thriller **Michael Jackson**
2. Their Greatest Hits 1971-1975 **The Eagles**
3. Dark Side Of The Moon **Pink Floyd**
4. Rumours **Fleetwood Mac**
5. Come On Over **Shania Twain**
6. Jagged Little Pill **Alanis Morissette**
7. The Bodyguard **Soundtrack**
8. Sgt Pepper's Lonely Hearts Club Band **The Beatles**
9. Led Zeppelin IV **Led Zeppelin**
10. Bat Out Of Hell **Meatloaf**

Eight Pop Acts And What They Did Next

There comes a time in every pop star's life when those cash registers simply stop ringing...

1. Chubby Checker

After The Twist craze had worn out, its chief protagonist marketed beef jerky for a while.

2. Clive Lea (Rocking Berries)

After the hits and the Royal Command Performances dried up, Clive replaced Russ Abbot in the Black Abbots.

3. David Van Day (Dollar)

Famously ran a Brighton burger bar; less famously (and more bizarrely) ran his own Bucks Fizz – 'David Van Day's Bucks Fizz'.

4. Lynn Anderson

She never promised us a rose garden, but this country singer did recently promise us great things if we called a psychic hotline.

5. C W McCall

The creator of the novelty CB radio hit Convoy, responsible for a brief splurge of rubber duck jokes in the mid-1970s, became mayor of Ouray, Colorado.

6. The Capris

The New York doo-wop group, whose There's A Moon Out Tonight hit no.3 in the US in 1961, soon turned to real work. Baritone Frank Reina became an air-traffic controller, lead singer Nick Santo a cop, tenor Mike Mincelli drove a school bus and bass singer John Cassessa worked at a hairpiece firm.

7. Danny Williams

When the kudos from Moon River dried up, Williams taught black-belt karate.

8. Dean Ford (Marmalade)

Became a house painter in Los Angeles. Still, like the song said, la la la la life goes on.

Meanwhile, Over In America...

From soundtracks in the 1950s to, er, soundtracks in the 1980s. That's musical progress for you.

Bestselling Albums In The US In The 1950s

1. South Pacific **Soundtrack**
2. Calypso **Harry Belafonte**
3. Love Me Or Leave Me **Doris Day/Soundtrack**
4. My Fair Lady **Original Cast**
5. The Kingston Trio At Large **The Kingston Trio**
6. The Music Man **Original Cast**
7. Around The World In 80 Days **Soundtrack**
8. Gigi **Soundtrack**
9. Elvis Presley **Elvis Presley**
10. The Music From Peter Gunn **Henry Mancini/Soundtrack**

Bestselling Albums In The US In The 1970s

1. Rumours **Fleetwood Mac**
2. Saturday Night Fever **Bee Gees**
3. Tapestry **Carole King**
4. Songs In The Key Of Life **Stevie Wonder**
5. Grease **Soundtrack**
6. Frampton Comes Alive **Peter Frampton**
7. Bridge Over Troubled Water **Simon & Garfunkel**
8. Elton John Greatest Hits **Elton John**
9. The Long Run **The Eagles**
10. Cosmo's Factory **Creedence Clearwater Revival**

Bestselling Albums In The US In The 1960s

1. West Side Story **Soundtrack**
2. Blue Hawaii **Elvis Presley**
3. More Of The Monkees **The Monkees**
4. The Sound Of Music **Original Cast**
5. Days Of Wine & Roses **Andy Williams**
6. Sgt Pepper's Lonely Hearts Club Band **The Beatles**
7. Mary Poppins **Soundtrack**
8. The Button-Down Mind Of Bob Newhart **Bob Newhart**
9. Exodus **Soundtrack**
10. Modern Sounds In Country & Western Music **Ray Charles**

Bestselling Albums In The US In The 1980s

1. Thriller **Michael Jackson**
2. Purple Rain **Prince/Soundtrack**
3. Dirty Dancing **Soundtrack**
4. Synchronicity **The Police**
5. Business As Usual **Men At Work**
6. Hi Infidelity **REO Speedwagon**
7. The Wall **Pink Floyd**
8. Whitney Houston **Whitney Houston**
9. Faith **George Michael**
10. Whitney **Whitney Houston**

(All US album Top Tens From *Billboard*)

181

The Very First UK Top 10

In more leisurely times, when pop on radio was scarce – an hour a day at lunchtime on the BBC's Light Programme – it was *NME* (not the BBC) who broke the big news about a new No.1, with their Record Hit Parade. Percy Dickins, co-founder of *NME*, had the idea of calling 53 record stores – mainly in London but also in Glasgow, Birmingham, Manchester and Belfast – to compile a list of the week's bestselling singles. The first pop chart as we know it appeared on 14 November 1952, with 15 records spread over 12 places, and Vera Lynn grabbing three of them. In the same year, the Dame became the first British artist to have a No.1 hit in the US with Auf Wiederseh'n Sweetheart, which spent nine weeks at the top.

1. Here In My Heart **Al Martino**
2. You Belong To Me **Jo Stafford**
3. Somewhere Along The Way **Nat 'King' Cole**
4. Isle Of Innisfree **Bing Crosby**
5. Feet Up **Guy Mitchell**
6. Half As Much **Rosemary Clooney**
7. Forget-Me-Not **Vera Lynn**
   High Noon **Frankie Laine**
8. Sugar Bush **Doris Day & Frankie Laine**
   Blue Tango **Ray Martin**
9. Homing Waltz **Vera Lynn**
10. Auf Wiederseh'n **Vera Lynn**
11. Cowpuncher's Cantata **Max Bygraves**
    Because You're Mine **Mario Lanza**
12. Walkin' My Baby Back Home **Johnnie Ray**

The Artists With The Most Hit Singles Without Reaching The Top 40

You have to feel sorry for Gorky's Zygotic Mynci. Actually, it's not compulsory.

1. Gorky's Zygotic Mynci **8 hits**
2. That Petrol Emotion **7 hits**
3. A **6 hits**
   Deus **6 hits**
   Diesel Park West **6 hits**
   Frazier Chorus **6 hits**
   Rick James **6 hits**
   Love And Money **6 hits**
   Ragga Twins **6 hits**

Six Songs That Got Turned Down
1. Don't You Forget About Me
Offered to Bryan Ferry and then, after his refusal, Simple Minds had a smash with it.
2. Yesterday
Chris Farlowe decided the Beatles ballad was too soppy, a decision he says he's never rued.
3. Little Sister
Bobby Darin's loss was Elvis's gain: one of the King's finest rock performances of the 1960s.
4. Son Of A Preacher Man
Fortunately for Dusty Springfield, Aretha Franklin rejected this song, only recording it after Dusty's version had charted.
5. How Do You Do It?
Mitch Murray's song was turned down by The Beatles, but snapped up by Gerry & The Pacemakers for their debut No.1 hit.
6. Raindrops Keep Falling On My Head
Bacharach and David's classic Butch Cassidy theme was turned down by Bob Dylan and Ray Stevens before B J Thomas recorded it.

Old Enough To Know Better; Too Young To Care
(Charts on this page and next based on *The Complete Book Of The British Charts*)
Child stars are nothing new but Louis Armstrong was nearly 70 when he finally got his due.

Oldest Solo Chart-toppers
1. **Louis Armstrong**
   67 years 10 months, in 1968
2. **Cliff Richard**
   59 years 2 months, in 1999
3. **Isaac Hayes (as Chef)**
   56 years 5 months, in 1999
4. **Cher** 52 years 5 months, in 1998
5. **Telly Savalas**
   51 years 1 month, in 1975
6. **Clive Dunn** 51 years, in 1971
7. **Elton John**
   50 years 6 months, in 1997
8. **Frank Sinatra**
   50 years 6 months, in 1966
9. **Charles Aznavour**
   50 years 1 month, in 1974
10. **Ben E King**
    48 years 5 months, in 1987

Youngest Solo Chart-toppers
1. **Little Jimmy Osmond**
   9 years 8 months, in 1972
2. **Donny Osmond**
   14 years 6 months, in 1972
3. **Helen Shapiro**
   14 years 10 months, in 1961
4. **Billie Piper**
   15 years 10 months, in 1998
5. **Paul Anka** 16 years, in 1957
6. **Tiffany**
   16 years 3 months, in 1988
7. **Nicole** 17 years, in 1982
8. **Britney Spears**
   17 years 2 months, in 1999
9. **Gareth Gates**
   17 years 8 months, in 2002
10. **Glenn Medeiros**
    18 years 1 month, in 1988

Most No.2 Hit Singles
1. **Cliff Richard** 10
2. **Kylie Minogue** 9
   Elvis Presley 9
4. **Madonna** 8
5. **Boyzone** 6
   Queen 6
7. **The Beatles** 5
   Tom Jones 5
   George Michael 5
   Sash! 5
   Steps 5
   Sweet 5

Longest Span Of Hit Singles
1. **Elvis Presley** 45.5 years
2. **Frank Sinatra** 44.6 years
3. **Cliff Richard** 43.3 years
4. **Shirley Bassey** 42.7 years
5. **Louis Armstrong** 41.9 years
6. **Nat 'King' Cole** 41.4 years
7. **Rolf Harris** 40.2 years
8. **Perez 'Prez' Prado & His Orchestra** 39.7 years
9. **Eartha Kitt** 38.9 years
10. **The Chipmunks** 37.4 years

Most Weeks On Singles Chart Without Reaching The Top 10

These records are often 'sleepers' – records released by low-profile artists whose fame (or notoriety in the case of Judge Dread) spreads slowly by word of mouth. The result is a record that sells over a long period without ever acquiring enough momentum to crack the Top 10.

1. A Scottish Soldier (Green Hills Of Tyrol)
Andy Stewart with the Michael Sammes Singers 40 weeks
2. He'll Have To Go **Jim Reeves** 39 weeks
3. Somewhere My Love **Mike Sammes Singers** 38 weeks
4. Hi-Ho Silver Lining **Jeff Beck** 29 weeks
5. Big Six **Judge Dread** 27 weeks
6. My Girl **Otis Redding** 25 weeks
7. Higher And Higher **Jackie Wilson** 24 weeks
8. Break 4 Love **Raze** 23 weeks
   My Way **Dorothy Squires** 23 weeks
   Shame **Evelyn 'Champagne' King** 23 weeks
   She Sells Sanctuary **The Cult** 23 weeks

Ten Records With Most Weeks On Singles Chart

If Frank Sinatra's version of My Way seemed to hang about the charts for years, that's because it did – two years and 18 weeks to be exact. Compared to that, Frankie Goes To Hollywood's Relax (59 weeks) and Oasis' Whatever (50 weeks? Pah – not even a year!) are mere here-today, gone-tomorrow ephemera. Respect to New Order, though, who never got further than No.9.

1. My Way **Frank Sinatra** 122 weeks
2. Amazing Grace **Judy Collins** 67 weeks
3. Relax **Frankie Goes To Hollywood** 59 weeks
4. (We're Gonna) Rock Around The Clock
Bill Haley & His Comets 57 weeks
5. Release Me **Engelbert Humperdinck** 56 weeks
6. Stranger On The Shore
Mr Acker Bilk with the Leon Young String Chorale 55 weeks
7. Blue Monday **New Order** 53 weeks
8. Whatever **Oasis** 50 weeks
9. I Love You Because **Jim Reeves** 47 weeks
10. White Lines (Don't Don't Do It)
Grandmaster Flash, Melle Mel & The Furious Five 46 weeks

The Merry Monarchs Of The Christmas No.1 Slot

There are two main popular misconceptions about Christmas No.1s. Firstly that no one hits the Christmas top spot as frequently as Cliff Richard, and secondly, that the Christmas chart-topper usually has a festive angle. But the Spice Girls have had as many Christmas No.1s as Cliff, and while there have been a wealth of 'novelty' Christmas hits (the kindest term we can apply to the festive offerings of the St Winifred's School Choir et al), songs like Another Brick In The Wall or Return To Sender are as far removed from tinsel and turkey as you can get.

1. The Beatles 4 weeks, 4 songs

In the mid-1960s The Beatles virtually owned the Christmas chart. Apart from a Tom Jones interlude in 1966, it was a one-band show with I Want To Hold Your Hand (1963), I Feel Fine (1964), Day Tripper/ We Can Work It Out (1965) and Hello Goodbye (1967), providing the musical backdrop to Christmases across the land.

2. Cliff Richard 3 weeks, 3 songs

Cliff's first Christmas No.1 was I Love You back in 1960. He then had to wait 28 years to taste Christmas success again, with Mistletoe And Wine, but notched up a third – courtesy of Saviour's Day – just two years later. And it could have been so much better: The Young Ones (the solo version) missed the 1962 Christmas No.1 spot by an agonising two weeks; The Next Time/Bachelor Boy hit the top just a week late in 1963; and The Millennium Prayer was sitting pretty in top spot as Christmas 1999 approached, only for Westlife to spoil the party.

3. Spice Girls 3 weeks, 3 songs

In their prime the Spices could seemingly hit the top of the charts at will, and they did precisely that in the late 1990s, repeating the feat achieved by The Beatles some 33 years

earlier with their hat-trick of successive Christmas No.1s – 2 Become 1 (1996), Too Much (1997) and Goodbye (1998).

4. Queen 2 weeks, 1 song

When Bohemian Rhapsody became No.1 at the end of November 1975, even Queen fans didn't expect it to be there at Christmas. It was, and was again – as a double A-side with These Are The Days Of Our Lives – at Christmas 1991, released after Freddie Mercury's death to help fund AIDS charities.

5. Band Aid 2 weeks, 1 song

Band Aid's Do They Know It's Christmas?, part of the 1984 campaign to raise funds for famine relief, had five weeks at the top of the charts, making it to No.1 two weeks before Christmas. Six years later, Band Aid II – different line-up (Jason, Kylie and Wet, Wet, Wet in for George Michael, Duran Duran and Spandau Ballet) but the same aim – took the song to the Christmas No.1 slot again.

6. Al Martino, Frankie Laine, Winifred Atwell et al 1 week each

Some 37 other acts have racked up a single Yuletide No.1, including St Winifred's School Choir who made us want to stuff Christmas pudding in our ears.

Five Greatest Hits Albums That Aren't

A selection of greatest hits compilations with the lowest percentage of greatest hits on them.

1. Ottawan D I S C O (Delta, 1998)
Contains 13 tracks, but one is a remix of another track. Only two were real hits (two more made No.49 and No.56), so two-thirds of the tracks weren't any kind of hits, and 83 per cent never hit the US or UK Top 40.

2. Jennifer Rush Best Of (Sony, 1999)
Contains 14 tracks, two of which charted on both sides of the Atlantic. Oddly, for a woman who racked up just six chart hits in the US and UK combined, this album ignores her only US Top 40 single. So over 85 per cent of the 'hits' aren't hits.

3. Paper Lace Greatest Hits (Music Club, 2001)
With 16 tracks, this album seems good value. Yet more than 80 per cent of the tracks weren't chart hits. And it omits Nottingham Forest's European Cup theme, We've Got The Whole World In Our Hands.

4. The Honeycombs Have I The Right (EMI, 2002)
Some 20 performances, just four of which charted in the US or UK. For the other 80 per cent of the time, it's the same stuff done worse.

5. Dean Friedman The Very Best Of (Music Club, 2001)
The very best of this 1970s singer/songwriter's stuff could surely have squeezed onto an E.P. Sixteen tracks is a bit lavish for an artist who had four hits. Still, we can thank our lucky stars that Dean hasn't released an anthology.

Top Ten One-Hit Wonders

One No.1 debut single and then: nothing, nada, zip. (For which, many thanks in most cases.)

1. **The Archies** Sugar Sugar — **1969** (8 weeks at No.1)
2. **The Kalin Twins** When — **1958** (5 weeks at No.1)
3. **The Simon Park Orchestra** Eye Level — **1972/1973** (4 weeks at No.1)
4. **Partners In Kryme** Turtle Power — **1990** (4 weeks at No.1)
5. **Clive Dunn** Grandad — **1971** (3 weeks at No.1)
6. **Lee Marvin** Wand'rin' Star — **1970** (3 weeks at No.1)
7. **Brian And Michael** Matchstalk Men And Matchstalk Cats And Dogs — **1978** (3 weeks at No.1)
8. **Dreamweavers** It's Almost Tomorrow — **1956** (3 weeks at No.1)
9. **Lena Martell** One Day At A Time — **1979** (3 weeks at No.1)
10. **Matthews Southern Comfort** Woodstock — **1970** (3 weeks at No.1)

Pop Stars Who Almost Made It As Footballers

Those below ultimately took a more conventional route to a pop star lifestyle but, as youngsters, all showed the sort of promise that had football club scouts drooling on their clipboards and could have earned them fame and fortune without singing a note.

1.	**Dr Robert** (Blow Monkeys)	Norwich City
2.	**Rod Stewart**	Brentford
3.	**Nicky Byrne** (Westlife)	Leeds United
4.	**Dave Stewart** (Eurythmics)	Sunderland
5.	**Ian Matthews** (Matthews Southern Comfort)	Bradford Park Avenue
6.	**Owen Paul**	Celtic
7.	**Mark Owen** (Take That)	Manchester United, Huddersfield, Rochdale
8.	**Steve Harris** (Iron Maiden)	West Ham United
9.	**Nicky Wire** (Manic Street Preachers)	Wales Under-16s captain
10.	**MC Harvey** (So Solid Crew)	Aldershot (semi-pro)

Posthumous Chart-toppers

1. **Buddy Holly**
   It Doesn't Matter Anymore (1959)
2. **Eddie Cochran**
   Three Steps To Heaven (1960)
3. **Jim Reeves** Distant Drums (1966)
4. **Jimi Hendrix**
   Voodoo Chile (1970)
5. **Elvis Presley** Way Down (1977)
6. **John Lennon**
   (Just Like) Starting Over (1980)
7. **John Lennon** Imagine (1980)
8. **John Lennon** Woman (1981)
9. **Jackie Wilson** Reet Petit (1986)
10. **Freddie Mercury**
    Living On My Own (Remix) (1993)
11. **Aaliyah**
    More Than A Woman (2002)
12. **George Harrison**
    My Sweet Lord (2002)

Among My Claims To Fame...

Not everyone can have the most No.1s.

Lulu
The first British female pop act to perform behind the Iron Curtain – in Poland in 1966.

Golden Earring
In 1993, 1,000 drummers played Radar Love on pontoons in Rotterdam harbour.

Paul Simon
Once co-hosted Saturday Night Live with his namesake – US senator Paul Simon.

Olivia Newton-John
The only artist to have had a hit single (If Not For You) on which her pet dog can be heard knocking the microphone stand over.

Roy Harper
"...Caught toxoplasmosis while giving mouth-to-mouth to a pregnant sheep," reported *Rolling Stone* on 24 March 1971.

Ten Hits That Never Were

Sometimes songs that seem to have everything going for them inexplicably fail to strike a chord with those required to part with hard cash for them. Other times, it's hard to fathom exactly why anyone wasted good time and money releasing them in the first place. At the end of the day the upshot is the same: crashing disappointment all round.

1. Shelby Lynne Leavin'
Arriving in the wake of Shania Twain's high-kicking country music, fellow Nashville misfit Shelby failed to make the same impression, reaching a lonesome No.73 in 2000. Maybe go with the catsuit next time, Shelby.

2. Soul City Orchestra It's Jurassic
Soul City's unique version of the theme to *Jurassic Park* wasn't quite in the same league as the movie, stalling at No.70 in 1993.

3. Bill You're A Star
Before Chris Moyles arrived, Steve Wright was Radio 1's idea of helping stressed drivers get through rush hour with his own brand of buffoonery. Wright released this under the pseudonym of Bill (one of his show's many characters) but it stalled at No.73.

4. Patti Day Right Before My Eyes
In 1989, Day's debut single failed to get any higher than No.69, thus ensuring it became her only single. To add insult to injury, in 2000 garage act N N' G Featuring Kallaghan reached No.12 with the same song.

5. Blue Melons Do Wah Diddy Diddy (The Wiggle Mix)
A word to the wise – don't release a remix of a popular ditty as your first single, and don't give yourself a stupid name just because you can. Take heed from Blue Melons who made No.73 in 1996, never to be heard of again.

6. Pizzicato Five Mon Amour Tokyo
Rolling Stone magazine says they're the 21st-century Sonny & Cher. The public disagrees: their sole release only got as far as No.72.

7. Lady Of Rage Afro Puffs
Despite help from Dr Dre and Snoop Dogg, and lyrics such as "I rock rough and stuff with my Afro Puffs (RAGE!)/Rock on, wit cha bad self", Afro Puffs fizzled out at No.72 in 1994.

8. Curtis Lynch Jr featuring Kele Le Roc & Red Rat Thinking Of You
Despite the number of people helping Jr, it was his only UK release, solo or otherwise, falling some 30 places short of the Top 40.

9. Frank Stallone Far From Over
He had a famous, multi-millionaire brother. And the song was on the *Staying Alive* soundtrack. But the less-talented Stallone brother still couldn't get past No.68.

10. The Violent Femmes The Blind Leading The Naked
If they had been pre-menstrual women as their name suggests, they might have at least cornered one market. But they were three guys from Wisconsin, hence the No.81 peak.

Ten Acts Who Never Got Past No.40

Unless you're a lifelong resident of the town without pity you have to feel sorry for the acts who spent a single, glorious week in the UK Top 40, never to trouble the chart compilers again. All these just barely made it under the wire. Still, these are all chart giants compared to the likes of Sourmash – one week at No.73 in 2000 with the double A-side Pilgrimage/Mescalito.

1960 Happy Go Lucky Me
George Formby

Within seven months of Formby's 'lucky' chart debut, his wife died, he alienated the public by quickly getting engaged to a young teacher – and then he died.

1961 Don't Jump Off The Roof Dad
Tommy Cooper

Released on the Palette label which, the Classic Comedy 45s website says mysteriously, is believed to have been Belgian in origin.

1964 Um, Um, Um, Um, Um, Um
Major Lance

The sweet-voiced Chicago soul singer only had one UK Top 40 hit (written by Curtis Mayfield), but became a key figure on the northern soul circuit in the early 1970s.

1967 Train To Skaville Ethiopians

A key reggae group of the 1960s and one of the major forerunners to The Wailers, The Ethiopians were more successful in the US, although chart success was scuppered by their label not pressing enough copies.

1973 Natural High Bloodstone

A pivotal black group in the 1970s shift from soul to funk, Bloodstone never acquired more than a cult following in the UK.

1978 Homicide 999

One of Britain's most durable punk bands (lead vocalist Nick Cash studied art under Ian Dury), they had five minor hits spread across three different labels. This was the only one to trouble the Top 40.

1979 You Need Wheels
The Merton Parkas

At least keyboard player Mick Talbot had some consolation for the Mod band's lacklustre chart career – he would form The Style Council with Paul Weller.

1986 The Queen's Birthday
St John's College School Choir & The Grenadier Guards

Proof that the charts were littered with rubbish – even as far back as the 1980s. And the choir needed the aid of the Grenadier Guards to get even this far up the charts.

1993 Cannonball The Breeders

Although the single peaked too early – from The Breeders' viewpoint at least – at No. 40, a sample of this song reached No.1 in 1996 after being used in The Prodigy's worldwide smash Firestarter. And The Breeders did, at least, get some royalties.

1997 You Can't Stop The Reign
Shaquille O'Neal

The basketball star: immoderately gifted on the court but only moderately gifted as a rapper. But Shaq didn't give up. He released his fourth album (not including a rather unselective 'Best Of' selection), called *Respect*, the year after.

Five People Who Could Have Been On The Sgt Pepper Sleeve

1. Jesus Christ
Dropped after the virulent reaction in parts of the American south to John Lennon's "We're more popular than Jesus" statement.

2. Mahatma Gandhi
Vetoed by EMI, presumably worried that his inclusion would offend buyers in Pakistan and those Beatles fans nostalgic for the good old days of the Raj.

3. Leo Gorcey
You may just remember this actor as the befuddled cab driver in *It's A Mad, Mad, Mad, Mad World.* You'd probably remember him better if he hadn't asked for a fee to appear in the back row of heroes on the sleeve. Artist Peter Blake's response was to paint blue sky over him. He wasn't the only one to fail to see the benefit of becoming part of this unique pop cultural moment: Mae West almost turned EMI down too, complaining, "What would I be doing in a lonely hearts club?" She changed her mind when The Beatles wrote her a personal plea.

4. Adolf Hitler
The Führer was discarded at the last minute. His inclusion would have been so provocative it might have overshadowed the strength of the album. Still, the Fab Four kept Aleister Crowley in, who, pre-Hitler, was described in tabloids as, "The Wickedest Man In The World".

5. Elvis Presley
The King was on the original shortlist but didn't make the cut.

The Performers Behind The Hits
The name on the single ain't necessarily a guide to the musicians who played on your favourite hit. Milli Vanilli didn't invent this deceptive art, they just took it a step further.

1. Yellow River
Officially credited to Christie (nothing to do with Tony), but Tremeloes manager George Austin insisted his boys cut this 1970 No.1.

2. Johnny Reggae
Credited to The Piglets, this was one of many fronts for Jonathan King.

3. Gimme Dat Ding
A hit for a fictional entity called The Pipkins, this No.6 hit was sung by session singer Tony Burrows, who had three other Top 10 hits under various aliases in the same month, including...

4. Love Grows
Members of the band Greenfield Hammer became Edison Lighthouse after the group's first hit, about love growing near Rosemary (sung by Burrows), had reached No.1.

5. United We Stand
The Brotherhood Of Man's 1970 debut Top 10 single was sung by, you guessed it, Tony Burrows. The, er, classic Eurovision-winning Abba-lite line-up came later.

6. My Baby Loves Lovin'
White Plains' first hit, charting in spring 1970, was sung by, who else... Tony Burrows.

7. Beach Baby
The hitherto unknown (and hitherto non-existent) First Class had a summer hit in 1974 with this Beach Boys tribute featuring the inevitable Burrows on vocals.

8. Moontrekkers

The creepy 1961 instrumental hit Night Of The Vampire was the work of Joe Meek.

9. Chalk Dust

This dismal piss-take of John McEnroe, released under the name Brat (geddit!), was the work of comedian Roger Kitter, now "much in demand as an after-dinner speaker".

10. Winchester Cathedral

This No.4 hit for the New Vaudeville Band in 1966 was really sung by John Carter (and not producer/songwriter John Stephens). Carter, with partner Ken Lewis, wrote and produced Let's Go To San Francisco, a No.4 hit the following year for The Flowerpot Men who included, yes, Tony Burrows.

12 Odd Origins For Famous Pop Names

Almost every band goes through the prolonged torture of trying to come up with a suitable name for themselves. Often the answer can be found in the works of others, whether it's a book (the flights of imagination offered by science fiction being particularly popular), a movie or a board game. Here are 12 of the more unusual sources for well-known names.

1. Everything But The Girl

The two Hull students saw a shop selling furniture with a sign reading: "For your bedroom needs we sell everything but the girl."

2. Human League

Rejecting ABCD, the Sheffield synth-players adopted their name from a team name in a sci-fi board game called *StarForce*.

3. Hedgehoppers Anonymous

This band of RAF servicemen, formerly The Trendsetters, was renamed because the RAF was notorious for flying low over hedges.

4. Billy Idol

William Broad adopted the name Idol as a riposte to the teacher who marked on his school report that he was "idle in class".

5. Bay City Rollers

Struggling to come up with a name, the Scots hopefuls stabbed a pin blindly at a map of America and landed on Bay City, Michigan.

6. Squeeze

Took their name from an obscure (post-Lou Reed) Velvet Underground album.

7. Tears For Fears

This came from an idea in Arthur Janov's book *Prisoners Of Pain*, which advocates confronting your fears to eliminate them.

8. T'Pau

A Vulcan high priestess in *Star Trek*.

9. UB40

Like many hopefuls, they survived on dole money while getting the band together (their first album was titled *Signing Off*). UB40 was the official code number for what was then the unemployment-benefit claim form.

10. The Boomtown Rats

Taken from the name of a gang in Woody Guthrie's novel, *Bound For Glory*.

11. Duran Duran

The name of a villain in 1968's sci-fi fantasy movie *Barbarella*, starring Jane Fonda.

12. Elton John

Reg Dwight wanted a rock'n'roll name, so he created one from two ex-colleagues in the first band he'd joined, Bluesology – singer Long John Baldry and sax player Elton Dean.

Ten Hit Songs About Real People

There's nothing like writing a song about another person, especially if they're famous – it's one of pop's great pastimes. While Carly Simon remains tight(ish) lipped about the subject of You're So Vain (see page 282), there's less debate about the inspiration of the songs below.

1. Elizabeth Weber (Just The Way You Are, Billy Joel)
Billy wrote this for his wife and manager.

2. Patti Boyd (Layla and Wonderful Tonight, Eric Clapton)
Clapton wrote Layla when Boyd wouldn't ditch George Harrison. She finally left him in 1977 and duly wed Eric. "I'd rather she was with him than with some dope," said Harrison.

3. Angie Bowie (Angie, Mick Jagger)
Angie once said on TV that she found her hubbie and Mick in bed and thought they were writing this song. Keith Richards says he wrote it and "Angie" was the right two-syllable name for the hook.

4. Robin Wright Penn (Thief Of Hearts, Madonna)
Madonna failed to warm to the second Mrs Sean Penn, warning her: "Bitch! You're a thief of hearts and now you'll have to pay."

5. Brian Epstein (You've Got To Hide Your Love Away, John Lennon)
Tom Robinson believes this ballad, penned after Epstein and Lennon went on holiday in Barcelona, is the Beatle's gift to his manager.

6. Billie Jean King (Philadelphia Freedom, Elton John)
A huge fan and later a friend, Elton was given a customised tracksuit by tennis legend King. In return he promised to write a song for her: she is the BJK who appears in its dedication.

7. Guy Burchett (Song For Guy, Elton John)
A rare, celebrity-writing-about-Joe-Public song: Guy Burchett, a messenger at Elton's Rocket Records, died in a motorcycle crash.

8. Patti D'Arbanville (My Lady D'Arbanville, Cat Stevens)
Now best-known for being a US soap queen, Patti was a glamorous, youthful New York model and actress (she appears in Warhol's Flesh) when Cat Stevens began courting her.

9. Janis Joplin (Chelsea Hotel, Leonard Cohen)
Laughing Len's ruthless depiction of an affair with Janis Joplin includes the line: "She told me again she preferred handsome men but for me she'd make an exception." Ouch.

10. Don McLean (Killing Me Softly, Lori Lieberman, Charles Gimble, Roberta Flack)
Folk singer Lori Lieberman saw Don Mclean perform – opinions differ over whether it was Empty Chairs, his song about divorce or American Pie – and was so moved she began writing this classic song about a singer who was strumming her fate with his fingers.

25 Real Names In Pop

Some may class it as vain, but it's not too hard to understand why some celebrities changed their name in their bid for fame. William Bailey, for example, doesn't quite have the same rock'n'roll ring to it as Axl Rose.

	Real name	Stage name
1.	Elaine Bookbinder	**Elkie Brooks**
2.	François Silly	**Gilbert Becaud**
3.	Louis Firbank	**Lou Reed**
4.	Eric Clapp	**Eric Clapton**
5.	Cherilyn LaPier	**Cher**
6.	Doug Trendle	**Buster Bloodvessel**
7.	Christa Pavolsky	**Nico**
8.	William Broad	**Billy Idol**
9.	David Batt	**David Sylvian**
10.	Vincent Furnier	**Alice Cooper**
11.	Evangelos Papathanassiou	**Vangelis**
12.	James Jewel Osterberg	**Iggy Pop**
13.	Reginald Dwight	**Elton John**
14.	Patricia Andrzejewski	**Pat Benatar**
15.	Stuart Leslie Goddard	**Adam Ant**
16.	Rita Crudgington	**Cheryl Baker**
17.	Priscilla Maria Veronica White	**Cilla Black**
18.	Natalie Renee McIntyre	**Macy Gray**
19.	Barry Alan Pinkus	**Barry Manilow**
20.	Adrian Donna Gaines	**Donna Summer**
21.	Henry John Deutschendorf Jr	**John Denver**
22.	Anna Mae Bullock	**Tina Turner**
23.	William Bailey	**Axl Rose**
24.	Steveland Morris Hardaway	**Stevie Wonder**
25.	Trevor Smith	**Busta Rhymes**

25 Original Names Of Groups

This section could have been subtitled 'A History Of Headaches' (a name in fact used at one time by Tears For Fears), such is the awful struggle to find the right name for your band. Here are some famous first attempts.

	Started as	Famous as
1.	Caesar & Cleo	**Sonny & Cher**
2.	The Golliwogs	**Creedence Clearwater Revival**
3.	The High Numbers	**The Who**
4.	The M and B 5	**Moody Blues**
5.	The Pendletones	**The Beach Boys**
6.	The Percussions	**The Stylistics**
7.	The Ravens	**The Kinks**
8.	The Saxons	**Bay City Rollers**
9.	Seymour	**Blur**
10.	Tom & Jerry	**Simon & Garfunkel**
11.	The Beefeaters	**The Byrds**
12.	Rain	**Oasis**
13.	On A Friday	**Radiohead**
14.	The Salty Peppers	**Earth, Wind & Fire**
15.	Tiger Lily	**Ultravox**
16.	Stoop Solo & The Sheet Starchers	**Bad Manners**
17.	Ed, Ted & Fred	**Nirvana**
18.	The N' Betweens	**Slade**
19.	Stiff Kittens	**Joy Division**
20.	The Jennifers	**Supergrass**
21.	Feedback	**U2**
22.	Angel & The Snakes	**Blondie**
23.	Johnny & The Self Abusers	**Simple Minds**
24.	The Executive	**Wham!**
25.	The Lovely Lads	**Kula Shaker**

Ten Other Names Used By Steely Dan

Naming their band after a steam-powered dildo in William Burroughs's *The Naked Lunch* wasn't just a passing fancy for Messrs Becker and Fagan. It was the end of a long and clearly painstaking road. Just imagine asking for a record by any of their working titles…

1. **Penis Whip**
2. **Oceans Of Chocolate**
3. **Marsupial Soup**
4. **Thigh Patties**
5. **Cold Stone Sea Monkey**
6. **The Blabberworks People**
7. **Nabokov**
8. **The**
9. **Saliva, The Movie**
10. **Shredded Brain Compote**

Ten Pop Singers Whose Names Became Rhyming Slang

Of course very few cockneys go around saying, "Lend us a Jann Wenner [tenner] cos I'm too Girls Aloud [proud] to ask me Theatre Of Hate [mate] to stand us a pint of Gary Glitter [bitter]." But on behalf of the Cockney Tourist Board we'll maintain the pretence…

Berni Flint	**Skint**
Leo Sayer	**All Dayer**
Britney Spears	**Beers**
Paul Weller	**Stella [lager]**
Gloria Gaynor	**Trainers**
Nat 'King' Cole	**Dole**
Otis Redding	**Wedding**
Samantha Mumba	**Number**
Stevie Nicks	**Flicks**
Fatboy Slim	**Gym**

From Catwalk To Caterwauling: Ten Model Pop Stars

Actresses who want to sing is nothing new – Marlene Dietrich made a decent fist of it in the 1920s. But the knack of strolling down a catwalk in the latest creation is not, as this list shows, a great guide to your ability behind the microphone. Vanessa Paradis, that's Mrs Johnny Depp to you, managed to parlay the novelty hit Joe Le Taxi into a role with Chanel.

1. **Whitney Houston** Saving All My Love For You — **First of four No.1 songs in the UK in 1985**
2. **Billie Piper** Because We Want To — **First of three No.1s in 1998**
3. **Samantha Fox** Touch Me (I Want Your Body) — **No.3 in 1986**
4. **Grace Jones** Slave To The Rhythm — **No.12 in 1985**
5. **Twiggy** Here I Go Again — **No.17 in 1976**
6. **Caprice** Oh Yeah — **No.24 in 1999**
7. **Quentin & Ash (Leslie Ash)** Tell Him — **No.25 in 1996**
8. **Samantha Janus** A Message To Your Heart — **No.30 in 1991**
9. **Naomi Campbell** Love & Tears — **No.40 in 1994**
10. **Mandy Smith** Don't You Want Me Baby — **No.59 in 1989**

Ten Hits Written By
The Beatles For Others

Sir Macca has had a lot of stick since the Fab Four divided by four, but he did have the nerve to perform with the Frog Chorus himself. Here's ten songs The Beatles gave away to pals.

1. Goodbye **Mary Hopkin**
2. It's For You **Cilla Black**
3. Bad To Me
   Billy J Kramer & The Dakotas
4. A World Without Love
   Peter & Gordon
5. Like Dreamers Do **The Applejacks**
6. Hello Little Girl **The Fourmost**
7. Step Inside Love **Cilla Black**
8. That Means A Lot **PJ Proby**
9. Got To Get You Into My Life
   Cliff Bennett & The Rebel Rousers
10. Thingumybob **Black Dyke Mills Band**

Ten Hits Written By The Bee Gees
For Others

1. Woman In Love **Barbra Streisand**
2. Islands In The Stream
   Kenny Rogers & Dolly Parton
3. Grease **Frankie Valli**
4. If I Can't Have You **Yvonne Elliman**
5. Heartbreaker **Dionne Warwick**
6. More Than A Woman **Tavares**
7. Only One Woman **Marbles**
8. To Love Somebody **Nina Simone**
9. Chain Reaction **Diana Ross**
10. Immortality **Celine Dion**

To Love Somebody was originally written by the brothers Gibb for Otis Redding, but he died before he could record it.

20 Weird Song Titles

No, we haven't made these up. Honest. Just ask Dr Demento.

1. How Can I Miss You When You Won't Go Away?
2. A Woman Is Only A Woman But A Good Cigar Is A Smoke
3. Mama Get A Hammer (There's A Fly On Papa's Head)
4. May The Bird Of Paradise Fly Up Your Nose
5. My Wife Ran Off With My Best Friend And I Sure Do Miss Him
6. Wouldn't Take Her To A Dog Fight, Cause I'm Afraid She'd Win
7. I'd Rather Have A Bottle In Front Of Me Than A Frontal Lobotomy
8. I Don't Know Whether To Kill Myself Or Go Bowling
9. I Live In A Split-Level Head
10. A Bowl Of Chop Suey And You-ey
11. I Like Bananas Because They Have No Bones
12. Jesus Loves Me (But He Can't Stand You)
13. The Buzzard Was Their Friend
14. When There's Tears In The Eye Of A Potato
15. Drop Kick Me Jesus Through The Goalposts Of Life
16. You Can't Roller Skate In A Buffalo Herd
17. Tito Won't Be Dancing Anymore
18. I'm Just A Bug On The Windshield Of Life
19. Her Teeth Were Stained But Her Heart Was Pure
20. Carrot Juice Is Murder

CULT POP

And Stevie Wonder On Harmonica…

Guest solos, bird whistles, extra vocals. Pop people are always helping each other out…

Stevie Wonder

His versatile organ enlivened Eurythmics' There Must Be An Angel, Prefab Sprout's Nightingale, Elton's I Guess That's Why They Call It The Blues. And many, many more.

Toni Tennille

Gave the Captain the slip for long enough to lend her vocals to Pink Floyd's *The Wall* and Elton's Don't Let The Sun Go Down On Me.

Bob Dylan

Bob gave vocal support to Leonard Cohen and Phil Spector on the critically slammed album *Death Of A Ladies' Man*.

Jimmy Page

Nineteen year old session guitarist Page wrote to his American pen pal in 1963: "I was lucky enough to play backing guitar with Jet Harris." The song, Diamonds, reached No. 1.

Rick Wakeman

Before he joined Yes, session man Rick played on three No.1s: Space Oddity, Love Grows by Edison Lighthouse and Grandad by Clive Dunn. And he helped Brotherhood Of Man out on United We Stand. Helpful bloke, Rick.

Elton John

Reg sang the demo of Brotherhood Of Man's United We Stand, played (uncredited) piano on He Ain't Heavy He's My Brother, and arranged a Richard Clayderman album.

My Name Is…
15 Grievously Named Offspring Of Pop Stars Who Really Ought To Have Known Better

When chided about the names he'd given his children, Frank Zappa drily replied that they'd have more problems because of their surname. These parents have obviously forgotten how cruel ridicule in the school playground can get. Can't be long before some popster has a boy named Sue, surely.

1. Chudley Lane
   daughter of Diana Ross
2. Dandelion
   daughter of Keith Richards
3. Elijah Bob Patricius Guggi Q
   son of Bono
4. Giacomo Luke
   son of Sting
5. Heavenly Hiraani Tiger Lily
   daughter of Michael Hutchence & Paula Yates
6. Kecalf
   son of Aretha Franklin
7. Moon Unit Two & Diva
   daughters of Frank Zappa
8. Dweezil & Ahmet Rodan
   sons of Frank Zappa
9. Phoenix Chi
   daughter of Melanie B
10. Tyson
    daughter of Neneh Cherry
11. Fifi Trixibelle, Peaches & Pixie
    daughters of Bob Geldof & Paula Yates
12. Doremi Celeste
    daughter of Justin Hayward

The Four Longest Titles For Hit Singles
(From *The Complete Book Of British Charts*)

1. You Can Make Me Dance Sing Or Anything (Even Take The Dog For A Walk, Mend A Fuse, Fold Away The Ironing Board, Or Any Other Domestic Short Coming) – **114 letters: The Faces (No.12 in 1974)**
2. Calling Occupants Of Interplanetary Craft (The Recognized Anthem Of World Contact Day) – **73 letters: The Carpenters (No.9 in 1977)**
3. I'm In Love With The Girl On A Certain Manchester Megastore Checkout Desk – **68 letters: The Freshies (No.54 in 1981)**
4. Chi Mai (Theme From The TV Series *The Life And Times Of David Lloyd George*) – **59 letters: Ennio Morricone (No.2 in 1981)**

Leavin' On A Jet Plane

"I hope your plane crashes." Waylon Jennings's jesting last words to Buddy Holly after giving up his seat on the plane Holly had chartered (because of defective heating on their freezing tour bus) still haunt him. Here are 13 stars who never arrived at their destinations.

1. Buddy Holly, Ritchie Valens & The Big Bopper
Died 3 February 1959 en route from Iowa to Minnesota when a wing of their four-seater Beechcraft Bonanza hit the ground in snow.

2. Patsy Cline
Died 5 March 1963 in her manager Randy Hughes's yellow Piper Comanche.

3. Otis Redding
Died 10 December 1967 when his private plane plunged into a Wisconsin lake. Most of the band The Bar-Kays also perished.

4. Stevie Ray Vaughn
Died 27 August 1990 when the helicopter in which the guitarist was travelling to Chicago crashed into a fog-shrouded hill.

5. John Denver
Died 12 October 1997 when the experimental aircraft he was piloting crashed in the Pacific.

6. Aaliyah
Died 25 August 2001 when an overloaded light aircraft crashed after take-off in the Bahamas.

7. Jim Reeves
Died 31 July 1964, after his single-engine Beechcraft Debonair hit a thunderstorm and crashed ten miles south of Nashville.

8. Jim Croce
Died 20 September 1973 in a Beechcraft D-18 after it hit trees during take-off in Louisiana.

9. Ricky Nelson
Died 31 December 1986 when a rickety old charter plane once owned by Jerry Lee Lewis crashed in Texas en route to a concert.

10. Steve Gaines & Ronnie Van Zandt
Died 20 October 1977 when the Lynyrd Skynyrd plane crashed en route to Louisiana. By macabre coincidence, their latest album sleeve showed the band engulfed in flames.

Weird Albums: From The Groundbreaking To The Simply Bizarre

There are artists out there who wouldn't dream of trying to make it big with angst-ridden tales of unrequited love or any of the other themes common in pop songs. Among those who eschew the conventional approach are this lot, whose offerings range from corporate propaganda to tips on belly dancing, taking in architecture and psychiatry along the way.

1. Basic Principles Of Kreskin's ESP

Stand-outs on this 1960s album include How To Catch A Murderer and Setting Up The Seance For Table Tilting. Kreskin's eerie style of narration led to him being sampled by modern creators of exotica club music.

2. Conversations Regarding The Future Of Architecture

The Reynolds Metals Company released this delight by Finnish modernist architect Eero Saarinen "for the pleasure of all interested in architecture". Not a typical 1957 toe-tapper.

3. Innovations By Masonite

This 1965 selection by Skitch Henderson and his orchestra was designed to motivate Masonite sales staff to shift even greater quantities of wood-panelling.

4. Love Is A Drag

Never before had songs of love to a man been sung by a man! This barrier-breaking (yet sadly anonymous) effort on Hollywood shows one man (wistful) gazing at another (smoky, sultry).

5. More How To Belly Dance For Your Husband

No collection is complete without this sequel by Sonny Lester & His Orchestra, presented by Little Egypt. With instruction booklet.

6. Music For Washing And Ironing

This Somerset Strings' selection was designed to match the smooth, rhythmic sweep of the typical ironing action.

7. Perspective For The 70s

Corporate propaganda for the Westinghouse Electrical Corporation. The sleeve says it all: "Electric energy, like wine, is a highly valued commodity which everyone wants to have available everywhere – at once – on demand."

8. Seduction!

Another exotica magnet: actor Gregg Oliver narrates a 1961 tale over a jazzy soundtrack. "With a half-smile of possessive pride, I asked for the secluded table for two and assured the captain that we shall dine in authentic Polynesian splendour as the menu dictates."

9. Songs Of Couch And Consultation

Folk singer Katie Lee salutes the popularity of the psychiatrist in the US in the 1950s with a set of tuneful ditties including Repressed Hostility Blues and I Can't Get Adjusted To The You Who Got Adjusted To Me.

10. Truckin' Through The Years

Vance Edwards spent 18 years truckin' before cutting these here country tunes, including gems like Looking At The World Through A Windshield and The Trucker And The UFO.

The Odd Couples: Ten Unlikely Duets

Think of the great double acts: Lennon & McCartney, Laurel & Hardy, fish and chips. Now forget all about them and focus on this list of potentially deadly duos.

1. The KLF & Tammy Wynette
Justified And Ancient

Tammy 'first lady of country' Wynette and the anarchic KLF seemed a match made in hell, but the resulting track, Justified And Ancient, topped the charts in 18 countries.

2. Kylie Minogue & Nick Cave
Where The Wild Roses Grow

"I've always wanted to write Kylie a song, to have her sing something slow and sad," said Cave, showing a more open mind than most arbiters of taste. His murder ballad with the pop princess hit Top 10s worldwide.

3. Prince & Sheena Easton
U Got The Look/The Arms Of Orion

Who could have predicted the purple imp would strike up a relationship with the feisty Glaswegian winner of *The Big Time*?

4. Lil' Kim & Phil Collins
In The Air Tonight

The swearing, blonde-wigged, scantily clad rap diva was not an obviously suitable collaborator for Collins. Is that a middle-age crisis we see before us?

5. Omar & Ol' Dirty Bastard (of the Wu-Tang Clan) Say Nothin'

Omar's seductive There's Nothing Like This seemed to be on the radio constantly in the 1990s. A six-year dry spell, however, led him to head down slightly less Heart FM lines.

6. Dolly Parton & Sylvester Stallone
Stay Out Of My Bedroom

Rocky and Dolly teamed up for the 1984 flop film *Rhinestone* but the soundtrack, with four duets, was a Top 10 hit in the US. But Stallone the singer was as convincing as Sly in goal in *Escape To Victory*.

7. Shane MacGowan & Johnny Depp
That Woman's Got Me Drinking

Depp may not have sung with MacGowan on this 1994 release, but he does play guitar, and even went to the trouble of flying to London to film *Top Of The Pops* with him.

8. Run-DMC & Aerosmith
Walk That Way

Officially it's just a Run-DMC single. But the inspired grafting of a hard rock song on to a hip hop beat broke down the walls – literally in the video featuring the ageing rockers – between two opposing music styles. Rap crossed over and pop history was made.

9. Elton John & Jennifer Rush
Flames Of Paradise

Elton teaming up with Miss Power Of Love wasn't any more outrageous than, say, Elton getting married, and this peculiar combo did at least give Rush her first US Top 40 hit.

10. Don Estelle & Sir Cyril Smith
Trail Of The Lonesome Pine

For once, words fail us.

Ten Top B-Sides

Sometimes the B-side is just better than the A-side, as even Tamla Motown were forced to recognise when the A-side of Stevie Wonder's 1969 single Don't Know Why I Love You became the B-side after a week as DJs preferred the flip side, My Cherie Amour. By the same process, Rock'n'Roll Part 1 is now forgotten while Rock'n'Roll Part 2 glitters in the memory,

1. Ruby Tuesday The Rolling Stones
Let's Spend The Night Together was much too controversial for the BBC to play in 1967. This craftily selected genteel flipside helped the single reach No.3 in 1967.

2. Professional Widow Tori Amos
You couldn't find a club, bar or school disco during the summer of 1996 that didn't play this B-side to Hey Jupiter. Six months later a remixed version was No.1 in its own right.

3. Move It Cliff Richard
Originally Cliff's first hit was supposed to be his cover of the American teen ballad Schoolboy Crush. But Move It had the finger-clicking momentum to reach No.2.

4. Kung Fu Fighting Carl Douglas
Recorded in ten minutes as the B-side to I Want To Give You Everything, but when Pye Records heard it, they flipped (literally). It worked: the song was No.1 for three weeks in 1974, not a bad return for ten minutes' work.

5. Dreams Of Children The Jam
Less well known than Going Underground, but officially a double A-side in 1980.

6. What The World Is Waiting For The Stone Roses
It's probably better known as the B-side to

the ever-popular Fools Gold, but when the single hit the charts in 1989, this was in fact the lead track. Together they made No.8.

7. Little Sister Elvis Presley
This is one of those singles (Kraftwerk's Computer Love/The Model being another) which exist in a twilight zone where not even the label can confidently state if it was a double A-side or, if not, which song was the B-side. As far as the UK charts go, Little Sister was the A-side when it entered at No.4 in 1961, yet His Latest Flame was listed as the record soared to No.1.

8. Mean Woman Blues Roy Orbison
Elvis recorded the rock classic in 1957, with several others following suit, so Blue Bayou became the lead track (and No.3) in 1963.

9. Scooby Snacks Fun Lovin' Criminals
Originally an A-side in 1996, it took another year before "Running around robbing banks/ All wacked off of Scooby Snacks!" became a Top 20 chant in the UK. This time the cult favourite was serving as the B-side to the trio's dodgy cover of 10cc's I'm Not In Love.

10. Fat Bottomed Girls Queen
Teamed up with Bicycle Race, Queen's unlikely pairing made No.11 in 1978.

THE NUMBER ONES
The stories behind the chart-toppers

Jerry Lee Lewis, by his own admission, the meanest piano-playin' son of a bitch who ever lived

Mickey "Man, we are almost on the road to success!"
Mike "We're almost at the top of the heights!"
Davy "We're nearly at the top of the heap!"
Peter "It's all downhill from there!"
The Monkees

Jimmy Webb, who might know a thing or two about pop songs, reckons all songs fall into seven categories. These are: people, places or events in the past, present or future that (may) make us happy, sad or angry; satire (social, personal or political); songs emanating from fictional characters (such as Randy Newman's Rednecks); past events told as a story; silly music (Ray Stevens's The Streak); abstract surrealism (I Am The Walrus); and allegorical tales (The Day The Music Died). **Nick Hornby**, in his book *31 Songs*, insists that "the truly great songs, the ones that age and golden-oldies radio stations cannot wither, are about our romantic feelings." There are obvious exceptions to Hornby's rule – **Walk On The Wild Side** is just one – but many of the No.1s discussed here reinforce his point. And then there's the perpetual puzzle that is **Tight Fit**'s The Lion Sleeps Tonight.

✿ ...Baby One More Time ✿

Britney Spears
No.1 for two weeks from 27 February 1999

The old tricks are often the best ones. So, post-**Spice Girls**, what better way to sell records than a voluptuous teen princess – sexy enough to have men looking for high-falutin' excuses to attach her to a cultural zeitgeist, but not so sexy she'd seem an unrealistic ideal to adolescent girls? Trigger moral outrage with some iffy lyrics and a racy video, and let the media know that the idol at the eye of this hurricane of hype is a God-fearing, possibly virginal gal from Louisiana, and hey presto!

Almost 50 years ago similar tactics had worked wonders for another God-fearing southerner. But times (and levels of outrage) move on. Mere hip-shaking was no longer enough to enrage the moral majority so **Britney Spears** had to pout at the camera with her hair in blonde plaits and her school blouse tied up saucily. As if this were not offence enough, the song's hook encourages the girl's lover, "Hit me baby one more time." Heck, it beats the 'original' idea: presenting Britney as a girl Power Ranger. The cries of misogyny were curiously muted, though chat rooms were vexed by the question of whether Britney's invitation was to be taken literally. Was this a sequel to **Phil Spector**'s 'classic' **He Hit Me And It Felt Like A Kiss** with its line "He hit me and I knew he loved me"?

The debate was slightly beside the point because, as even **New Musical Express** felt obliged to note, "this was a perfect slice of tightly composed modern pop, fizzing with infectious vocals and world-class production." It has everything you would ask of a pop song and Britney sings her heart out, especially when she's complaining about her loneliness while watching basketball. Britney isn't really singing to her baby but to us, desperate to make sure we don't want to let her go and are hungry to ensure that she has hits more than one more time.

She pulled it off too, although none of her later hits compare with her debut. The song, for so recent a hit, has had its share of decent covers, with everyone from Darius to Barenaked Ladies and Travis on a VH1 special, giving their own take. Travis' guitar-propelled acoustic version is proof that, even without world-class production, …Baby One More Time is actually a very decent song.

★**…Baby One More Time** is on **Britney**'s album of the same name (Jive).

❀ Back Home ❀

England World Cup Squad
No.1 for three weeks from 16 May 1970

Elton John's very first No.1 – if you believe the recurring rumour that he was on backing vocals. This record makes 1970 sound like a damn long time ago. The very idea that the 22 players selected to form an England World Cup squad could turn up on **Top Of The Pops** in tuxedos and all but promise to bring the World Cup back 'home' seems risible today. Nor is Back Home the Inger-land No.1 Anglo-Saxons cherish. That honour belongs to **World In Motion**, the collaboration with **New Order** which marked the 1990 World Cup and not a bad record. Yet Back Home is a much fairer representation of the tastes of footballers, the 'boys' being far more likely to listen to Phil Collins than New Order on the team bus.

Back Home was cheesy, stiffly sung and awkwardly presented. The England squad sported their dinner jackets about as naturally as Huckleberry Finn would wear a pinstripe, and the attempt to create a beery singalong with the chorus was another embarrassment. Perhaps none of this should come as a surprise when you learn that the man who persuaded Alf Ramsey to go along with this stunt was **Bill Martin**, author of such **Eurovision** delights as **Puppet On A String** and

Congratulations. Martin is actually a Scot, though any notion he was having a laugh at England's expense can be discounted when you look at what he inflicted on his own nation in 1974: "Yabba dabba do/We support the boys in blue…"

Even so, Back Home is still far superior to the official 1982 effort **This Time**, which began with "We're on our way/We are Ron's 22" – perilously close to being misheard as "We're on our way/ We're the wrong 22." Still, realism isn't what you expect from a World Cup theme, although Scotland's 1998 theme, **Don't Come Home Too Soon** by **Del Amitri**, deserves three points for its painful honesty.

The FA Cup single also first reared its ugly, repetitive head in 1970. This dubious tradition, which brought us such 'classics' as Chelsea's Blue Is The Colour in 1972, reached a crescendo of naffness in 1982 with Spurs' Ossie's Dream. This particular football gem availed itself of **Chas & Dave**'s musical expertise, rhymed 'trembly' with 'Wembley', and proved that Ossie Ardiles couldn't pronounce Tottenham. Without Back Home (and its accompanying album on which Peter Osgood got to sing Sugar Sugar), all this would have been lost to humanity.

★**Back Home** is all too available on **The Ultimate Football Anthems** (Crimson, 2000).

☺ Billie Jean ☺

Michael Jackson
No.1 for one week from 5 March 1983

The oddness, the scariness and the sadness would come later, but there was a time when **Michael Jackson**'s undisputed brilliance was all that counted. There are better songs than **Billie Jean** in Jackson's canon and none quite so dulled by over-familiarity, but it was the moment everything gelled for Michael Jackson. When it flew to No.1 in America on 5 March 1983 (the same day that it became UK No.1), Jackson became the first artist to simultaneously top the US singles and album charts in both pop and black categories, with

its parent album, **Thriller**, well on the way to becoming the world's biggest-selling album.

It's a weird little song on which Jackson takes a full writing credit. Jackson always claimed it was a true tale of a woman (unsurprisingly never named) who had snuck over the wall of his compound to claim he was the father of one – hey, spooky – of her **twins**. Apparently in real life she was conveniently bonkers and, equally conveniently, soon disappeared. In the song,

Oh Mickey he was so fine...

Jackson seems to admit to going to her room after a night of dancing "on the floor in the round". It's a standard Hollywood morality tale, but Billie Jean originally began "she told me I was a lonely guy" and that does have the ring of truth.

Musically, it's weirder still. The introduction lasts for 30 seconds which producer **Quincy Jones** thought too long, but Jackson insisted. The dominant bass line was courtesy of **Louis Johnson**, late of The Johnson Brothers (of **Stomp** fame), and if ever a man deserved credit on *Thriller* it is he, though he says he was just following Jackson's direction. Johnson's circulating bass creates the feeling of paranoia, while **Jerry Hey**'s string arrangement gives it a certain operatic grandeur and jazz man **Tom Scott** added uncredited lyricon. But, as was the case throughout *Thriller*, Jackson was the star, even if Jones was the mastermind.

The constituents – taut bass, paternity suit, pop splashiness, sheer danceability – may be disparate, but they meld beautifully. So what if it's a tall tale and so what if Jackson had more help constructing it than he lets on? It is clearly the work of a man at the peak of his game. With its clipped basslines, its strangely unmelodic melody and its finger-clicking tightness, it altered the course of popular music – ask anyone from Jive Bunny to Justin Timberlake. And the video wasn't bad. **Fred Astaire**, watching Jackson dance through the song for the 1983 Motown 25th anniversary TV special, was so enthused he shouted: "You knocked them on their asses out there kid, you're an angry dancer, you got rage in your feet."

★Billie Jean is available on **Greatest Hits: HIStory, Vol.1** and **Thriller**

☺ Don't Look Back In Anger ☺

Oasis
No.1 for one week from 2 March 1996

It's easy to forget just how great and influential **Oasis** were. That's not to say they don't still make toe-tapping hits, with Liam Gallagher recently coming into his own as a writer with Songbird. But since they found and discarded their own Yoko Onos (Patsy Kensit, Meg Matthews), the **Mad-for-it** Mancunians have, for many, lost some of their spunk. The leering and fighting – not so much rock'n'roll as playground scuffles – are now charted in *Hello!* and *OK!* rather than *NME*.

Hype – not least their verbal sparrings with **Brit-pop** rivals Blur – propelled them to the top of the charts, but hype can only take you so far. Their second album, **(What's The Story) Morning Glory?** had already become the second-fastest seller of all time in the UK (after Michael Jackson's *Thriller*), and its first three singles had reached No.1 or No.2. So it was no mean feat for a fourth single, from an album which seemingly everyone already owned, to reach No.1.

Don't Look Back In Anger may be the most anthemic of Oasis' pop songs. Noel has often been accused of borrowing too heavily from other writers, especially **The Beatles**, and Don't Look Back In Anger is a prime example. You can hear Lennon's influence throughout. The opening bars are a homage to Imagine, while the line, "Gonna start a revolution in my bed" was inspired by the Beatles book *Revolution In The Head* that Noel was reading. Even the cover featured a white piano like that used by Lennon to write Imagine. The name itself is said to be an amalgamation of **Bob Dylan**'s rockumentary *Don't Look Back* and the John Osborne play *Look Back In Anger*, while the video was a lavish affair featuring *Avengers* star **Patrick Macnee**.

Although Noel had always been the driving force of the band, Liam's sneering vocal style had been a key hook of the Oasis sound. But Don't Look Back marked Noel's debut on lead vocals, with Liam playing tambourine, something that didn't sit well with the singer, judging by his schoolboy-tantrum stance on stage. The idea that he might no longer be needed was fuelled when the song reached No.1. It all proved a bit too much for Liam, who quit in the middle of the US tour.

Like Wonderwall, the song has become a firm karaoke favourite. Even **The Wurzels** have released their own unique interpretation as a gesture of thanks for Oasis honouring one of their songs, Morning Glory.

★Don't Look Back In Anger is available on (**What's The Story**) **Morning Glory?**

☺ Eternal Flame ☺

The Bangles
No.1 for four weeks from 15 April 1989

Any young hipsters puzzled by how good **Atomic Kitten**'s 2001 No.1 was need wonder no more. The song was actually a cover of a 1989 No.1 by The Bangles.

In the late 1980s the LA-based female quartet were one of the few acts in the UK charts who didn't stem from a mediocre soap opera or the Stock, Aitken & Waterman battery farm. **Prince**, under the pseudonym Christopher, gave them their 1986 breakthrough song, Manic Monday, his generosity largely due to his infatuation with singer **Susanna Hoffs**. (The song made No.2, kept off the top, ironically, by Prince's Kiss). Seven months later, the quirky Walk Like An Egyptian made No.3, but it was 1989's Eternal Flame which made them – and destroyed them. A huge hit, it was No.1 in both the UK and the US (the fifth-biggest selling single of the year in the latter) but the title proved more ironic than anything Alanis Morissette could have come up with. Within months The Bangles had split up.

Singer Hoffs had always been singled out as band leader, despite protests by founder/guitarist Vicky Peterson and the others. Eternal Flame (written by Hoffs with **Madonna** collaborators Billy Steinberg and Tom Kelly) simply seemed to confirm her pre-eminence. The group had emerged as an energetic rock quartet with sparky guitar tunes and harmonies influenced by The Beatles and **The Byrds**, but Eternal Flame seemed to mark a massive shift to the mainstream. Worse, there was barely any contribution (instrumental or vocal) from the other band members, with only the soft, yielding voice of Hoffs accompanying a lush string section.

Having earlier relied heavily on other writers' material, the band had become determined to pen their own songs, and the success of Eternal Flame only brought **internal tensions** to a head. Overworked, unhappy and resentful that the record company appeared to be grooming Hoffs as a solo artist, The Bangles split at the end of the year. Their label blamed 'creative differences' and for once the industry's oldest cliché was true – though they did get back together in 2003.

★**Eternal Flame** is on **Greatest Hits** (Columbia, 1995) the best of the compilations.

❀ Ghost Town ❀

The Specials
No.1 for three weeks from 11 July 1981

Despair, rising unemployment, riots, to say nothing of a rapidly escalating tension and bitterness in the band – out of it all came The Specials' greatest triumph and that rarest of entities, a meaningful pop song.

While supporting **The Clash** in 1978, The Specials gained an audience, a name (they'd decided before their first show that Special AKA was too long) and their credo. Having seen neo-Nazi skinheads attack the co-support act Suicide, **Jerry Dammers** wanted his music to promote change. The Specials had flirted with social comment in 1980 on **Too Much Too Young**, a pro-contraception song the BBC banned. But Ghost Town caught the mood of a nation's despondent youth, alienated by unemployment and Margaret Thatcher's assertion in 1978 that "Britain might be rather swamped by people of a **different culture**." From 1980 Britain was blighted by riots. Brixton was ablaze in April 1981 and on 10 July 1981 riots spread to Manchester and Liverpool. The next day Ghost Town was No.1.

Ghost Town was conceived on the 1980 More Specials tour, with **2Tone** supremo Dammers appalled by the state of the nation he was seeing, leading to the lyrics, "Government leaving the youth on the shelf/No job to be found in this country." Constant recording and touring was taking its toll on The Specials, but the most contentious issue was their musical direction, with some members worried by the drum-machine elements Dammers was adopting. When the band recorded Ghost Town they could barely stand to be in the same room. Musically, Ghost

The Specials found it easier to agree over pizza topping than music

Town was far more ordered than the nation it described (or the band that made it), Dammers planning everything down to the last beat in an effort to produce a kind of **historical trip** through The Specials' musical style. The song boasted reggae and jazz elements, and a horn section influenced by John Barry.

Despite the song's success, the damage had been done. On *Top Of The Pops* the three singers (led by Terry Hall) announced they were leaving to form **Fun Boy Three** – though Dammers struggled on until 1985 with a series of vocalists.

★Released on its own EP but not on any Specials albums, **Ghost Town** can be surprisingly hard to find. Try the 1991 compilation **The Singles Collection**.

🌑 Grandad 🌑

Clive Dunn
No.1 for three weeks from 9 January 1971

When **Clive Dunn** had finished singing **Grandad** in the studio, his partner in crime (and super session man), **Herbie Flowers**, turned to the actor and said: "I think we've got a monster here, Clive." To which Clive, sadly not familiar with pop music lingo, replied: "I'm awfully sorry – I sang it as best as I could."

Dunn and Flowers were an unlikely duo. Dunn, then just turned 50, had become a household name as the sixty-something Corporal Jones in the BBC sitcom **Dad's Army**. He had met Flowers (a session musician and member of **Blue Mink**) at a dinner after **Ronnie Corbett**'s *This Is Your Life* and the two, meeting again in a Barnes chip shop, decided to make a record. It took Flowers all of five hours to write the saccharine ditty about a grandfather remembering when he was a boy and worrying about motor cars and aeroplanes tied up with string. Still, as the inevitable children's chorus pointed out, despite being even more doddery than Corporal Jones, he was dearly loved by his grandkids.

Flowers played bass on the record and **Rick Wakeman** – who had yet to make his lucrative link-up with Yes – played piano to earn another £20 as a session musician. It wasn't quite like The Traveling Wilburys but, given that Flowers would later play bass on **Walk On The Wild Side** and that Wakeman was already playing in prog-folkies The Strawbs, there was no shortage of musical expertise. In such illustrious company Dunn may have had a point about his vocal – after about one-and-a-half plays, his doleful delivery begins to grate.

But success proved painful for Flowers: "I never lived that song down. My career skidded to a halt. I lost all my cred." Nor did he coin it in to compensate. "The way to make money in this business is to write a huge hit that 20 people cover. But who's going to cover Grandad?" The answer to that, of course, was **Pinky & Perky**. Dunn, at least, got a shortlived BBC TV series named after the song.

★Grandad is available on the two-CD compilation **Chegger's Choice**, a selection of hits picked by **Keith Chegwin**, the professionally lovable, child pop picker and ex-Mr Maggie Philbin. But a word of warning: this 1999 selection (on Global TV) also includes tracks by the likes of **Mr Blobby**, **St Winifred's School Choir** and **Marguerita Pracatan**.

❀ Great Balls Of Fire ❀

Jerry Lee Lewis
No.1 for two weeks from 10 January 1958

This is the kind of record Jerry's cousin **Jimmy Swaggart**, the famed televangelist, had in mind when he warned that rock'n'roll was the devil's music. The very title was (as the snippets of studio dialogue between Lewis and Sun producer **Sam Phillips** suggests), an act of Pentecostal sacrilege, while The Killer hammered the keyboards and sang as if too much love had indeed shaken his nerves and rattled his brain. The laugh with which he introduced the final verse suggested that Jerry Lee, far from feeling guilty about this act of sin, was revelling in it.

Co-written by **Otis Blackwell** (who was also responsible for All Shook Up and

Don't Be Cruel), Great Balls Of Fire is a perfect companion piece to Lewis's other classic, **Whole Lotta Shakin' Goin On**. Such was the productivity of Lewis (and Phillips, aiming to prove, perhaps, that he hadn't erred when selling Elvis Presley to RCA) that both these masterpieces were cut and released in 1957. Just as well, because the following year what should have been a triumphant tour of Britain ended when the newspapers (and the public) were shaken and rattled to find that The Killer had wed his **13-year-old cousin**, thereby confirming all the media's deep-seated prejudices about rock'n'rollers and white southerners.

Jerry Lee's career never recovered, although he found professional and artistic solace in country. In the next 20 years the most famous thing he did was turn up outside the gates of **Graceland**, fuelled by vodka and resentment, and demand a parlay with the fellow Memphis resident who, Lewis felt, had usurped his place as rock'n'roll's reigning monarch. Sadly, he and Elvis never got to have their pow-wow. Jerry Lee has since used his sole survivor status to push his own claims insisting, "Al Jolson, Jimmie Rodgers, Hank Williams and Jerry Lee Lewis – that's your only four fuckin' stylists that ever lived."

But the recriminations, tax evasions and deaths in his family (one son drowned in a swimming pool, another died in a car crash and one wife took an overdose) were all in an unimagined future when Jerry Lee whooped his way through this tribute to the unnerving power of love – or, as is apparent when you hear the lyric, lust. A great live version can be heard on *Live At The Star Club* (on the Bear label), recorded in concert in Hamburg, where his rendition should by rights have set off the smoke alarms. Nearly half a century after it was cut, Great Balls Of Fire is proof that Jerry Lee Lewis was, as he put it, "a rompin', stompin', piano-playin' sonofabitch. A mean sonofabitch. But a great sonofabitch."

★**Great Balls Of Fire** is available on **18 Original Greatest Sun Hits** (Rhino).

☺ His Latest Flame ☺

Elvis Presley
No.1 for four weeks from 9 November 1961

Such is the mythical status of Elvis's Sun Sessions, it's easy to forget that the king of rock could, when willing, play the king of pop to perfection. This **Doc Pomus-Mort Shuman** composition, with its rolling Bo Diddley beat, Latin influence and (for a 1960s pop single) literate lyrics which never descend into stupidity or stale repetition, is light years away from Baby Let's Play House. But as soon as the piano kicks in, it doesn't really matter. This is consummate pop: immaculately made, apparently disposable but very durable indeed.

Coupled with the harder, rocking **Little Sister**, His Latest Flame was the best of Elvis's four No.1s in the UK charts in 1961 – although Can't Help Falling In Love is almost as classy in its way. (Wooden Heart and Surrender, sung in semi-operatic tribute to his idol **Mario Lanza**, were his other two.) He sings this song about betrayal with just the right amount of emotion, never investing too much or too little in any line and letting the beat roll on.

The song sounds effortless but Elvis and his early 1960s all-star band (with **Hank Garland** on lead guitar and **Floyd Cramer** on piano) laboured long and hard, with drummer Buddy Harman even toying with the congas. They were so keen to nail the piano solo, they rang up Doc Pomus in the middle of the night to ask him how he'd played it on the demo. The end result is unusual, Pomus noted, because the intro is just three bars long, not the customary four. The performance is so perfect you wonder why **Bobby Vee** turned this song down in the first place.

Before Presley's recording career became monopolised by the need to fill three movie soundtrack albums a year, he would cut the wondrous **Return To Sender**, a No.1 hit on both sides of the Atlantic in 1962. Yet even that great performance doesn't quite match this, and you can hear why – years later – **The Smiths** decided to reprise a part of His Latest Flame in their stage act (Morrissey has always had a good ear for a fine pop tune), running it into **Rusholme Ruffians**. For any other artist, this classic piece of work might have represented the climax to a career. For Elvis, it's just one of the least known and most underrated of his 18 UK No.1s.

★**His Latest Flame** is probably best found on the 2002 No.1s compilation.

❀ The House Of The Rising Sun ❀

Animals
No.1 for one week from 9 July 1964

Years after **The House Of The Rising Sun** had topped the charts on both sides of the Atlantic, bass player **Chas Chandler** inspected the record company's books and found that it had cost exactly £4 10s to make. The main reason the song was so cheap was because it took only 12 minutes to record. "The first four minutes was the run-through, the second eight minutes was the record," said producer **Mickie Most**. But then the Animals had been experimenting with the song for ages, finally trying it out live when they won a coveted slot to support Chuck Berry on one of his UK tours.

It was assumed that the Animals had discovered the song on **Bob Dylan**'s self-titled 1962 album but, like their debut single (**Baby Let Me Take You Home**), it came from American folk/blues legend **Josh White**. Dylan, by the way, learnt the song from Greenwich Village regular Dave Van Ronk, who said later: "We had a terrible falling out about House Of The Rising Sun. He was always a sponge, picking up whatever was around him and he copied my arrangement of the song."

The song's origins are mysterious, steeped in legend and counter-claim. Country historian John Rumble, in his liner notes to a **Roy Acuff** compilation, says it is derived from a 17th-century British folk melody. Certainly Alan Lomax, in his book *The Folk Songs Of North America*, says a **brothel** called Rising Sun occurs in two British folk songs. He noted it down in 1937 in Kentucky, adapting it to the form used by Josh White. Yet black bluesman **Texas Alexander** had already recorded a song featuring an establishment called Rising Sun in 1928.

The Animals' version featured a new guitar riff from **Hilton Valentine**, but it was driven by **Eric Burdon**'s gravelly vocal and **Alan Price**'s urgent, soulful blues organ. Although rock critic **Dave Marsh**, among others, detects the acoustic influence of Dylan, he says the Animals sang it as if "they'd connected the ancient tune to a livewire." The fact that Burdon's growling, Geordie-accented vocal was almost incomprehensible in America somehow only added to the attraction.

With Burdon singing, the song changed from its traditional form: a complaint by a female prostitute about her lot. Marsh moans that Burdon turned the lyric round, turning himself into a catamite, but as Burdon points out, the words could also apply to frequenters of brothels, prisons or drug-dealers' houses.

Burdon says that the band wanted the song to be their second single but Most didn't. Most, however, maintains he did want the song to be their single but **EMI/Columbia** didn't, complaining that, at four minutes and 29 seconds, it was too long. Most, in his words, asked them: "What difference does it make how long it is? If it's boring then it's too long, and if it's not boring it's got to be right."

★ The **Animals'** rendition of **The House Of The Rising Sun** is on **The Best Of The Animals**, a 20-track compilation which in itself cries out for the band to be re-evaluated. **Josh White**'s version is on his **Complete Recorded Works, Vol 6** (Document, 1998).

❂ I Feel Love ❂

Donna Summer
No.1 for four weeks from 23 July 1977

When God whispered, "You're gonna be famous" to eight-year-old Adrian Donna Gaines during a church recital, the plan probably didn't involve producing orgasmic-sounding tracks such as 1975's **Love To Love You Baby**. The Almighty must have breathed a sigh of relief two years later when I Feel Love was released. "**God** had to create disco music so that I could be born," Summer announced as her fourth album marked a turning point in her music. "I was being treated as

Summer (the first time)

a novelty. I'm multi-dimensional – I don't want to be known for just one thing."

These weren't idle words. Boston-born, she had sung with local rock bands before moving to Germany in 1968. There she appeared in German productions of *Hair* and *Porgy And Bess* before teaming up with dance producers **Giorgio Moroder** and Pete Bellotte in 1975.

For her fifth album they kept close to her disco style, but used only an electronic bass line (created on an old Moog synthesizer) and a drum machine to create the pioneering electro sound which later evolved into **techno**. Moroder almost composed it and recorded it at the same time. "What the hell is this?" was the multi-dimensional Summer's initial response. She finally trusted their judgement, although she later claimed she finished it as a joke.

Originally I Feel Love was the **B-side** to **Can't We Just Sit Down**, but radio stations knew better. Its hypnotic pulse and Summer's almost operatic rendition of its simple lyric made it fascinating. Saturating the airwaves and clubs, it spent four weeks at No.1 in the UK and made No.6 in the US. Summer then proceeded to alienate her predominantly gay audience by declaring that AIDS was divine judgement on homosexuality. "Who told her?" **Little Richard** demanded. "She ain't no prophet." Although she claims she was misquoted, her career has never recovered. Truly the Lord works in mysterious ways.

★I Feel Love is still available in its original setting on **I Remember Yesterday** (Casablanca) but, for most, a compilation like **Endless Summer** (Mercury) will be better value.

❃ I Will Survive ❃

Gloria Gaynor
No.1 for four weeks from 17 March 1979

To many, I Will Survive is simply their karaoke specialty, the kind of song that no matter how out of tune you are, as long as you throw yourself into it and employ plenty of facial expressions no one will jeer you off stage. For **Gloria Gaynor** it was more than that, becoming **the song that shaped her life**.

Gaynor had already enjoyed a few moderate hits prior to I Will Survive, most memorably the groundbreaking 1976 album, **Never Can Say Goodbye**. Aimed at the club scene, it pioneered the seamless mixing of songs long before Fatboy Slim twiddled his first knobs. On the back of this success, Gaynor and her husband/manager, Linwood Simon, were given free reign to sculpt her next album, bringing in **Motown** producer Freddie Perrin, on his condition that he could write the B-side for a single. The result was I Will Survive, penned by Perrin and Dino Fekaris. It was **intended as the B-side** to Substitute, but Gaynor knew a hit when she heard one, although it had to become a club hit at New York's trendy Studio 54 before her record-label bosses agreed to release it as a single.

Although the tune fitted perfectly with the disco vibe sweeping the world, it was the lyrics that attracted fans, leading to covers by **Diana Ross** and **Billie Jo Spears** (a No.47 hit four months after the original) and an Arabic translation. The song became an immediate gay anthem, women connected with the declaration that they didn't need a man to survive and, in June 1998, the **French football team** made it their World Cup anthem. Gaynor, though, saw it as a simple song about survival, regardless of what you had overcome: "**I love the empowering effect**. I love the encouraging effect. It's a timeless lyric that addresses a timeless concern."

No.1 on both sides of the Atlantic, it climbed back to the top for a second time in the US, dethroning Rod Stewart's Da Ya Think I'm Sexy? and winning the first (and last) Grammy Award for Best Disco Recording in 1980. By 1981, the **disco** revolution had died, but the 'First Lady of Disco' is still belting out the song today.
★I Will Survive is still available on the original – and remarkably decent – **Love Tracks**, while **The Millennium Collection** (Polydor, 2000) is the pick of the compilations.

❂ Imagine ❂

John Lennon
No.1 for four weeks from 10 January 1981

John Lennon would have us believe that **Imagine** is simply **Karl Marx**'s *Communist Manifesto* set to music. In life, Lennon was, as **Bryan Ferry** pointed out, as much of a jealous guy as a politician, but his shabby murder led many to see him as a political martyr and this utopian address his political testament.

Lennon was doing himself a disservice. The simple poetry of his appeal for a "brotherhood of man" makes Marx's prose look distinctly lumpen. The Beatle also worried too much about his own family (and his own failure as a father) to subscribe to Marx's idea that families should be abolished too. The final irony is that those countries ruled in Marx's name seemed to regard their ideology as something they should kill or die for as readily as any reactionary.

None of that detracts from the power of the song, especially in the simple setting

Hairpiece, bed peace, all John and Yoko need now is to find the codpiece

Lennon gave it. Apart from the catch in his voice on the "you" which begins the last verse, he keeps things very simple indeed. The performance is now regularly run on VH1, complete with a rather puzzling video in which Lennon is dressed as a **cowboy** and **Yoko Ono** is clad as a native American **squaw**. A subliminal message ("gee, if cowboys and indians can get it together…") or just fancy dress?

Yoko's presence in the video seems superfluous, but Lennon later admitted: "That should be credited as a Lennon/Ono song… the lyric, the concept came from Yoko, but those days I was more selfish, more macho and omitted to mention her contribution. But it was right out of *Grapefruit*, her book – there's a whole pile of pieces about imagine this and that." Renegade Elvis fans believe the song was inspired by a song called **Suppose**, on the King's **Speedway** soundtrack – the Elvis ballad does have lines beginning "suppose there…" but short of Yoko admitting John owned this trashy soundtrack, this row will never be settled.

The song has been covered by those who might be thought to have shared Lennon's dream (**Joan Baez**), by obscenely wealthy divas eager to stress their humanitarian credentials (**Diana Ross**), and by instrumentalists for whom the tune is key (**Chet Atkins, Acker Bilk**). Few versions have the nerve to match the simplicity of Lennon's original: even Baez's is showy and over-arranged. **Randy Crawford**'s well-sung version is marred by a MOR-ish arrangement, while Ross makes it sound like just another Vegas cabaret number. Many covers ignore the fact that Lennon doesn't sound at all confident that what he imagines will come true. **Eva Cassidy**'s cover is suitably fatalistic and quite moving – except when she decides to sing certain lines very, very loud for no apparent reason.

★**Imagine** still sits best on **Lennon's** album of the same name.

⚙ It's Over ⚙

Roy Orbison
No.1 for two weeks from 25 June 1964

There was a time in the 1970s when the Big O's career was a big zero. He was even seen on such Saturday night schedule-fillers as ITV's **Wheeltappers & Shunters Social Club** and if he wasn't performing, a comedian would be getting a cheap laugh at his expense. The stock Orbison gag – for comedians who made Freddie Starr look like Oscar Wilde – was to get up on stage clad in black and then take off a pair of Orbison's trademark tinted glasses to reveal… another pair underneath. This gag – Roy suffered from astigmatism although his widow once claimed he was an albino – was repeated till the audience stopped laughing.

Orbison, one of a handful of rock legends who learned their trade at **Sun**

Studios in the 1950s, staged a comeback in the mid-1980s. The acclaimed **Mystery Girl** album and his membership of the supergroup the Traveling Wilburys (alongside such luminaries as Bob Dylan, Tom Petty, George Harrison and, well, **Jeff Lynne**) put him back on the map. But in 1988, with more of the bad luck that had marred Orbison's life and career, his heart finally packed in.

Even before his death, Orbison had suffered enough to fill a year's Sunday tabloids. His wife Claudette died in a motorcycle accident in 1966, and he lost his two sons in a fire in 1968. Since he'd left Sun, insisting he wanted to record ballads, Orbison had written songs which suggested that he lived with the expectation of imminent tragedy. His debut ballad **Only The Lonely**, which he'd tried to get his friend **Elvis Presley** to record, had been followed by such tearjerkers as Blue Angel and In Dreams. It's Over was one of two No.1s for Orbison in 1964 – not bad for an American singer in the eye of the British beat invasion. Of the two, It's Over (rather than **Oh, Pretty Woman**) was closer to his persona as the romantic loser.

On stage Orbison exerted a strange magnetism. Clad in black more often than Johnny Cash, he would stand stock still, letting the music move and his voice soar. On It's Over the rhythm pounds so urgently it's almost a flamenco. The song kicks off with a line about golden days whispering to the wind – and proceeds to get even more high-flown and poetic. On paper the lyrics look sentimental; as sung, they are chilling. It's Over was the kind of dirge **The Beatles** wanted **Please Please Me** to be – even if their subtext, a plea for oral sex, was hardly the Big O's normal subject matter – before George Martin persuaded them to speed it up.

★It's Over is probably best found on **For The Lonely** (Rhino), a good 18-track career overview which adds the pick of his Sun early days to the best of his balladeer years.

❧ King Of The Road ❧

Roger Miller
No.1 for one week from 13 May 1965

Sometimes songwriters need a prod or two. In June 1964, while on a tour of the American midwest, Miller was driving somewhere near Chicago when he spotted a sign saying, **"Trailers for sale or rent"**.

Realising he couldn't get the phrase out of his head, he did the obvious thing: he tried to turn it into a song. One verse later, he got stuck. It was frustrating, but no great shock for a singer/songwriter who had famously observed: "The human mind is a wonderful thing. It starts working before you're even born and doesn't stop again until you sit down to write a song." Sitting in Boise, Idaho, a few weeks later, he spotted a **hobo in an airport gift shop** and, as he put it later, "labour was induced". The scribbled lyrics of the song, which had taken him six weeks to write (compared to the four minutes he spent writing his previous biggest hit **Dang Me**), now hang in the Country Music Hall Of Fame.

Miller was one of those overnight successes who took more than a decade to break through. Raised in a small Texan town by his aunt and uncle, he picked cotton as a child to raise money to buy a guitar. After a spell in the army he went straight to Nashville, arriving in Music City sans guitar – country great **Chet Atkins** had to lend him one so the young man could audition a few of his songs.

For the next decade he wrote songs (including Del Shannon's **Swiss Maid**), sang anywhere (he was known in Nashville as the '**singing bellhop**' for a while) and did a variety of odd jobs (including a spell as a fireman in Amarillo). His purple patch really started in 1964 after being signed by **Smash Records**, a small but ambitious subsidiary of Mercury. Miller had almost given up country music for acting, asking Smash boss Charlie Fach for a $1,600 advance so he could head to acting school in California. Only when Dang Me and King Of The Road became hits did Miller finally give up on the idea.

Just as Dang Me had a surprisingly cheerful sound for a song where the narrator says the best thing anyone could do was hang him, King Of The Road was an **uplifting, funny, warm** song about being destitute. Miller's lyrics didn't try to create any fake romance of the road but he got the humour and the detail just right. The declaration that two hours of pushing broom would finance an eight-by-twelve, four-bit [ie twice two-bit: 50¢] room is so precise it could only have come from experience. To top it all, there was the fact that halfway through your first listen, you felt compelled to start snapping your fingers.

The song was a crossover smash (providing Miller with his only UK No.1). He even built a King Of The Road motor inn in Nashville in its honour. Miller never again wrote anything that connected with the public in the same way, although My Uncle Used To Love Me But She Died is almost as good and **England Swings** (a rose-tinted view of a quaint Olde England – "bobbies on bicycles two by two") was another UK hit in early 1966. His commendably non-treacly rendition of Bobby Russell's maudlin **Little Green Apples** was his last big hit, in 1968.

Over-exposure and amphetamines then took their toll, although he wrote the award-winning musical *Big River* (based on the **Mark Twain** novel *Huckleberry Finn*) just before his death from lung cancer in 1992. Asked how he'd like to be remembered, Miller said simply: "I just don't want to be forgotten." He isn't. One of his songs was sampled for the Hamster Dance, one of the Internet's strangest musical fads, and King Of The Road has been covered by everyone from **Boney M** to REM. But no one has topped Miller's original.

★**King Of The Road** is included on the mid-priced **The Very Best Of Roger Miller** (Castle).

☼ Lily The Pink ☼

The Scaffold

No.1 for three weeks from 11 December 1968, and for one week from 8 January 1969

Take one poet, a Post Office engineer and a brother of one of The Beatles; add a dash of bass from Cream's **Jack Bruce** and stir in the final ingredient – an old rugby song – and you have the recipe for one of the most unlikely No.1 hits of the 1960s.

The Scaffold were originally **Michael McCartney** (playing as Mike McGear to avoid charges of cashing in on his sibling), engineer **John Gorman** and teacher and Mersey poet **Roger McGough**. Briefly known as the **Liverpool One Fat Lady All Electric Show** they won, as The Scaffold, a stint at Peter Cook's Establishment Club and late-night TV spots with their mixture of poetry and comedy.

There are, as you might expect, conflicting theories about the origins of Lily The Pink. Some insist it was inspired by an American businesswoman called **Lydia Estes Pinkham** who, in 1875, began selling a concoction, 20 per cent of which was alcohol, to alleviate "all those painful complaints and weaknesses so common to the female population." The tonic (the recipe is at *www.mum.org/MrsPink1.htm*) was especially popular in Prohibition America. But **Dave Roberts**, a back-up musician for The Scaffold who would join their successor group Grimms, recalls: "We thrashed it out in John Gorman's flat. I was there the day Roger said, 'I've got these words… it's an old rugger song we used to do.'"

The song (much like The Scaffold's other hits: the ever-puzzling Thank U Very Much and the Boy Scout campfire nonsense of **Gin Gan Goolie**) stuck in your mind instantly but, oddly, never got irritating. The lyrics sounded as if nonsense poet **Edward Lear** had been told to write a hit, and helped cement the song's popularity. Perhaps it was a reaction to hippydom, but that era also marked the birth of bubblegum, with hits like **The Ohio Express**'s Yummy Yummy Yummy.

By 1973, The Scaffold had effectively ceased to exist, although **Liverpool Lou** was a Top 10 hit in 1974. McGough became even more famous as a poet; Gorman appeared on another cult classic, the Saturday morning ITV show *Tiswas*; and Mike McCartney went on to write children's books.

There is a recurring rumour that Mike's brother produced Lily The Pink and Paul certainly attended the Abbey Road session where **Thank U Very Much** was produced, telling Mike the song was too oblique. When Mike disagreed, Paul harrumphed, "Have it your own way if you know so much about it." Later, when the record had reached No.4, Paul rang his brother and admitted, "You were right." Other reports have **Elton John** and The Hollies' **Graham Nash** helping out in the studio. Pinning personnel down to specific sessions is not easy but The

Scaffold certainly rubbed shoulders with rock's elite, working with **Jimi Hendrix**, **Keith Moon** and half of **10cc**. So the possibility that this was Sir Elton John's first UK No.1, rather than the England World Cup squad's **Back Home** (on which he is alleged to have sung backing vocals), cannot be ruled out.

★**Lily The Pink** can be found on **Thank U Very Much**, a mid-price compilation on EMI Gold.

❀ The Lion Sleeps Tonight ❀

Tight Fit
No.1 for three weeks from 6 March 1982

The **Zulus** have not, as a nation, dominated the pop music world but they can claim the, excuse the pun, lion's share of the credit for this novelty No.1.

This number, about a mighty jungle and a dozy lion, started life as a kind of African doo-wop song called **Mbube** (pronounced uyimbube, meaning 'the lion'), complete with a catchy refrain. Recorded and written by the black African artist **Solomon Linda**, the record was a huge hit in South Africa. Linda, in an era and part of the world where copyright was as hazy a concept as Einstein's unified theory of everything, was paid ten shillings for the song and his performance by the Johannesburg recording studio. He didn't earn any royalties, then or later when the song was covered by everyone from **Pete Seeger** and **Bert Kaempfert** to, of course, **Tight Fit**. But he was a local legend and was seldom short of a free drink until he died, of renal failure, in 1961.

The 78 of Linda's song was sent, along with a pile of other African discs, to **Decca**, where it was discovered by American musicologist **Alan Lomax**. He took it to Pete Seeger, then a down-on-his-uppers folk singer, who, after just one play, said, "Golly, I can sing that." With his group **The Weavers** he added some finger-popping rhythm and delivered a howling soaring vocal, and their version entered the US charts in 1952, climbing to the Top 10. The group were fingered as Communist sympathisers at the height of **Joseph McCarthy**'s Cold War witch hunt, but that was not the end of the song. Over the next nine years it was covered by bandleader Jimmy Dorsey, Peruvian singer **Yma Sumac**, The Kingston Trio (America's most popular folkies of the 1950s) and a clean-cut (ie white) New York doo-wop act called **The Tokens**.

The Tokens, recovering from the defection of lead singer **Neil Sedaka**, heard The Weavers' version and wanted to record it. The RCA production duo of **Hugo Peretti** and **Luigi Creatore** enlisted **George Weiss** (the three later co-wrote Can't Help Falling In Love) to devise some lyrics about a sleeping lion which sounded daft but harked back to the song's roots. It was released on the B-side of a cover of the Portuguese folk song Tina, but became the de facto A-side through airplay.

The Lion Sleeps Tonight reached No.11 in the UK in 1961, but the following year the song – rechristened Wimoweh (to untrained Western ears, "uyimbube" sounded a lot like "wimoweh") by Scottish country and western-cum-novelty band **The Karl Denver Trio** – reached No.4. **Denver** (real name Angus McKenzie) and his cohorts also got to play their hit in Zimbabwe. "We'd be doing these open-air concerts in front of 2,000 to 3,000 people and when we'd get to Wimoweh they'd all join in, banging on tin cans and everything… it was a bit eerie."

The song has been a UK hit four times (three times as The Lion Sleeps Tonight and once as Wimoweh), but is now most famous through the soundtrack for Disney's **The Lion King**. The Tight Fit version, the only time the song topped the UK charts, is the least remarkable rendition of this song, certainly less remarkable than the group's leopardskin, off-the-shoulder outfits and shiny trousers. The soaring vocal trembles on the edge of (and finally falls into) self-parody. Still, kids loved it and it was infinitely better than the **Goombay Dance Band**'s Seven Tears which replaced it at No.1. New Tight Fit are still touring and are "available as a full five-piece band or a trio using playback." So now you know.

★The Lion Sleeps Tonight by **Tight Fit** is on **The Best Of Tight Fit** (Emporio, 1995) along with 37 other tracks, mostly 1960s covers. **The Weavers**' Wimoweh is best found on The Best Of Decca Years (Uni/MCA, 1996) while **Solomon Linda**'s original is on Mbube Roots (Rounder, 1987). The song has also been recorded by **Ladysmith Black Mambazo** on Gift Of the Tortoise (Warner Brothers, 1994) and **Brian Eno** on Eno Box II Vocals (Virgin, 1993).

❀ Mack The Knife ❀

Bobby Darin
No.1 for two weeks from 16 October 1959

Mack The Knife is the Mount Everest of popular music, a song which has been tackled by countless performers – from **Louis Armstrong** to **Robbie Williams** – simply because it is there. Often described as the single most influential song of the 20th century, Mack The Knife is a genuine oddity – a song which started life as a satirical warning about a treacherous gangster but which, in Bobby Darin's still unsurpassed rendering, seems like a celebration of the joy of life.

You could write a book about the origins of Mack The Knife, and **Joseph Vincent Mach** already has. (The 'book' is on the web at *http://mobydicks.com/lecture/ Brechthall/messages/70.html*). You don't need to know who the **Macheath** in "Old Macheath, babe" is, to get the song, but his name is a good way in to the song's complexities. Macheath was originally the swashbuckling, sinister star of **John Gay**'s 18th-century musical play *The Beggar's Opera*, a well-dressed consort of whores.

Bertolt Brecht saw the revived play and adapted it to create his political *Threepenny Opera*, in which Macheath becomes a gangster businessman called **Mackie**.

The song was only written to placate the actor **Harold Paulsen** who wanted his entrance as the villainous Mackie built up in the play. Brecht and his musical collaborator **Kurt Weill** created it, initially relying on a hurdy-gurdy, to be sung by a corrupt cop warning about Mackie's evil nature. Sharks, at this time, was a slang term for brothels and the names of the girls which closed the song was originally a list of prostitutes (although one of them, **Lotte Lenya**, was actually Weill's wife).

The hurdy-gurdy ballad was the hit of the show when it premièred in August 1928. The song's voice-only intro, which would attract jazz performers like Louis Armstrong, was actually a mistake: the hurdy-gurdy didn't work the first time. Darin's version was recorded 30 years later, on 19 December 1958, and produced by Ahmet Ertegun, Neshuhi Ertegun and **Jerry Wexler** – who would become famous for records by everyone from Aretha Franklin to Rod Stewart.

Darin is a vastly underrated performer who could deliver (and write) such classic rock'n'roll love songs as **Dream Lover**, yet swing through material like Mack The Knife as well as any Rat Packer. As hard and as loud as the orchestra works, Darin is in control, his voice accentuating the beats and pacing the song as it starts, then rising to a devastating display of vocal control at the end. On the last time around he holds the "ie" in "Mackie" for five perfect seconds then caps it, two syllables later, with a nine-second-long "town". Darin won a **Grammy** for his performance, which draws on a huge variety of vocal mannerisms yet never sounds mannered.

Nobody has done it better, though the line of those who have tried forms on the right. Halfway down the queue is Robbie Williams, who had a reasonable stab until the orchestra overwhelms him at the end. Bizarrely, **McDonald's** created a character called Mac Tonight, a lounge singer who croons the song, in a failed bid to shift more Big Macs. The song also provided the title for a 1989 movie starring **Roger Daltrey** and **Richard Harris**, which was about as awful as the Big Mac promotion. Despite all this, the attraction of Mack The Knife endures.

★**Darin**'s **Mack The Knife** is on **The Hit Singles Collection** (Rhino, 2002) while **The Very Best Of Louis Armstrong** (Verve, 2003) is one of many albums featuring Satchmo's version.

◦ Maggie May ◦

Rod Stewart
No.1 for five weeks from 9 October 1971

Wrinkly rocker, aging lothario, man in need of a haircut – all these images spring to mind at the mention of Rod Stewart's name. But 30 years ago it was his vocal power not his pulling power which hit the headlines. 'Rod the Mod' was universally regarded as one of the best white soul singers in the business.

The years up to 1971 had seen him and his fellow musician/partygoer **Ronnie Wood** replace Steve Marriott as the new faces of The (Small) Faces, but Stewart had also signed a solo deal. At first he became famous with The Faces in the UK and as a solo artist in the US, but his third album, 1971's *Every Picture Tells A Story*, established him on both sides of the Atlantic, *Rolling Stone* calling it the "greatest rock'n'roll album of the last ten years."

Reason To Believe, by the ill-fated Tim Hardin, was the first choice as a single, but Hardin's melancholy folk musings didn't really catch on with radio stations. Led by Radio 1 they opted for the B-side – Maggie May. Promoted to lead track, it quickly topped the charts on both sides of the Atlantic.

Maintaining that "performing is where it's at", Stewart initially saw writing as something for more creative minds, describing his own lyrics simply as "words that rhyme". Maggie May was more than that. Penned with **Martin Quittenton** (who also co-wrote the follow-up No.1 **You Wear It Well**, but had to take the notoriously tight-fisted Stewart to court to get paid), the song is said to tell the story of a schoolboy's ill-fated liaison with a prostitute. The inspiration is rumoured to be from Rod's own experiences, a not wholly unbelievable notion,

The last Stewart monarch in repose

but Stewart's hit shares its title with a Liverpool folk song about a prostitute called Maggie May, which inspired a musical by **Lionel Bart** (best known for *Oliver!*) and appeared, as a snippet, on The Beatles' album **Let It Be**.

Stewart had rarely sung better, but the hook of the song was the mandolin section. Although **John Peel** accompanied Stewart and The Faces on the instrument on the 1971 Christmas edition of *Top Of The Pops*, he was just miming. The melody was originally supplied by Ray Jackson, a member of Geordie folk band **Lindisfarne** (the sleeve notes simply say: "The mandolin was played by the mandolin player in Lindisfarne. The name slips my mind").

Despite his solo worldwide success, Stewart continued to be a member of

The Faces until 1975 when the band finally fell apart. Stewart blamed Ronnie Wood's increasing association with The Rolling Stones for the split, but Wood confirmed rumours that the rest of the band were tired of playing second fiddle.
★Maggie May is available on **Every Picture Tells A Story** (Mercury) and on compilations: **Handbags & Gladrags** (Mercury) offers the best of Stewart's earlier, superior years.

☼ Mr Tambourine Man ☼

The Byrds
No.1 for two weeks from 22 July 1965

Much has been made of the ambiguity and elusiveness of **Bob Dylan**'s lyrics. Dylanologists may be disappointed, then, to find Dylan saying his real inspiration for this classic was a man with a big tambourine. "'Disappearing through the smoke rings in my mind' – that's not drugs. Drugs were never that big a thing with me," he noted, saying he owed the song to Greenwich Village folk guitarist **Bruce Langhorne**. "He had this gigantic tambourine. It was, like, really big. As big as a wagon wheel. He was playing and this vision of him playing just stuck in my mind."

In 1964 **Jim Dickson** was the manager of a Beatles-inspired LA beat combo, **The Jet Set**. He and band members **Roger McGuinn**, **David Crosby**, **Gene Clark**, **Michael Clarke** and **Chris Hillman** wanted to fuse the energy of The Beatles with **Dylan**'s lyrical prowess. Luckily, Dickson was friends with Dylan and his tour manager, who sent him a tape of a new Dylan song, **Mr Tambourine Man**. It was, he thought, just what the band needed, blending thought-provoking, stream-of-consciousness lyrics with a catchy melody. But the band thought it too folksy while **McGuinn**, having been a struggling folk singer in Greenwich Village, resented Dylan: "He was my enemy. I thought anybody could get up and do that." Dickson invited Dylan down to hear them record the track and Dylan's immortal words, "**Wow, man, you can dance to that**," finally convinced them to reconsider.

Changing their name to The Byrds (the misspelling is a homage to The Beatles), the band signed to Columbia/CBS, who agreed to the song on condition that session musicians played on the track. Producer **Terry Melcher** (Doris Day's son) felt their debut would benefit from a group of old hands, so only McGuinn actually played on the record (indeed his distinctive 12-string Rickenbacker is key to its appeal). He also sang the lead vocal – striving for a sound somewhere between Dylan and **John Lennon** – but Melcher graciously allowed Crosby and Clark to sing harmonies.

The song shot to No.1 in the US and the UK in the summer of 1965, its appeal enhanced by the band's Beatle fringes, McGuinn's tiny shades and Crosby's cape. Mr Tambourine Man may mark the **birth of indie rock** and it encouraged Dylan to turn electric, while The Beatles, on *Revolver* and *Rubber Soul,* were influenced by The Byrds' hypnotic sound. Countless bands have imitated those jangling guitars ever since, though rarely with McGuinn's expertise.

Finally, a diverting footnote. Donovan is alleged to have heard the tune on the radio, absorbed it and, when he met his idol Bob Dylan, played the tune to him as his own song with his own lyrics. After a few bars, Dylan interrupted to point out to his mortified disciple that, funnily enough, he already knew that song.

★Mr Tambourine Man features on **The Byrds'** debut album of the same name and on **The Very Best Of The Byrds**. But you'll need to buy the **Mr Tambourine Man** album if you want to hear their version of Vera Lynn's We'll Meet Again.

☼ Millennium ☼
Robbie Williams
No.1 for one week from 19 September 1998

After spending two years in a drunken, drug-fuelled abyss, the cheeky one from **Take That** conjured up – as if from nowhere – Millennium, a catchy song, slice of autobiography and ingenious marketing ploy all rolled into one.

For a while, Robbie Williams was in danger of becoming the Liz Hurley of the pop world, content to hob-nob with pop stars but never actually making a hit himself. Tiring of partying with the brothers Gallagher at Glastonbury (and probably realising they were never going to give him any of their songs), he was back on the Pyramid Stage two years later, this time wowing the crowds with his showmanship and the Steve Wright Sunday love songs favourite, Angels.

Then, in September 1998, Williams released Millennium. Prince may have spotted the musical and marketing potential of the millennium back in 1985, but with less than 18 months till the big day, Williams's effort was beautifully timed. This song and its parent album (*I've Been Expecting You*) represented the new Robbie. With producer Guy Chambers, formerly of World Party, providing the beguiling melodies to Robbie's confessional, often brutally honest lyrics, the pair finally honed to perfection a distinctive Robbie Williams style.

The coming of age of ambitious artists is often marked by the introduction of a string section into their music (think The Verve's Bittersweet Symphony). Williams went one step further, sampling John Barry's memorable strings from the James Bond theme You Only Live Twice, and combining that with candid yet very entertaining lyrics ("Live for liposuction, detox for your rents"). Add in a video showing a new, slimmed-down figure (Gary Barlow was once again the fat one from Take That) who was suited and booted, and you have what amounts to a perfect 007 audition tape. **Angels** may be his most anthemic hit, but Millennium proved Williams was no longer simply playing at being a pop star. ★**Millennium** is on **I've Been Expecting You**.

❂ Paint It Black ❂

The Rolling Stones
No.1 for one week from 26 May 1966

In the early days **Brian Jones** was the lynchpin of The Rolling Stones. By 1967 he was a shadowy, dysfunctional figure whose influence seemed marginal, but his legacy to both the group and rock'n'roll perfectly captured in Paint It Black, a No.1 where the beat was as insistent as ever but with an eclectic sound which would largely vanish from the Stones' repertoire after Jones's death. (It was also one of the last Stones numbers to involve manager **Andrew Loog Oldham**.)

Aftermath – which marked a shift from high-energy interpretations of R&B standards towards a more daring, gritty and experimental sound – was the Stones' first album to feature only **Mick Jagger/Keith Richards** compositions, but it was Jones who gave their sound creative impetus. He had an unnatural gift for learning to play instruments in a few hours – he taught Jagger to play harmonica and even supplied a saxophone solo on The Beatles' You Know My Name (Look Up The Number). It was his fascination with **Moroccan** music that gave the album its psychedelic and Eastern tinges – marimbas on **Under My Thumb** and harpsichord on the olde-worlde **Lady Jane** – but his crowning glory was Paint It Black.

After **Bill Wyman** began tinkering with the track in the studio, jokingly adding an organ line, Jones picked up his **sitar**. He hadn't mastered the instrument, but drew sounds from it which connected brilliantly with the gloomy mood and rhythm of the track. The words weren't bad either, the shocking juxtaposition of death and birth ("like a new-born baby it just happens everyday") being one of Jagger's finer conceits. And as record executive Andrew Wickham recalls, "those early Stones records were beautifully produced. Paint It Black remains unsurpassed as a production 30 years on and still sounds electrifying on the radio."

Aftermath, as it happened, had already been released in the UK before this dark, brooding number was written. But Paint It Black replaced **Mother's Little Helper** on the version released in the US, and duly hit No.1 on both sides of the Atlantic.

When the song was played live, all eyes focused on Jones, sitting cross-legged and playing his sitar. But his revival was all too brief, as **drink, drugs and paranoia** combined to undo him, the last being hinted at in his resignation note from the band which read, "I no longer see eye to eye with the others over the discs we are cutting."

A Rolling Stone out on his own: a suit takes Brian Jones out for a walk

He had already recorded Moroccan musicians on *Brian Jones Presents: The Pipes Of Pan At Jajouka*, but within a month of leaving the band he was found **drowned** – possibly murdered (an anonymous accomplice later confessed to a biographer) – in his swimming pool. Yet, as **Simon Napier-Bell** says, "Nobody could continuously take as many drugs as Brian unless they were searching for an exit from life."

★Paint It Black can still be found on the US version of **Aftermath**, but the compilations **The Singles Collection: The London Years** and **Forty Licks** offer fantastic value.

☼ Papa Don't Preach ☼

Madonna
No.1 for three weeks from 12 July 1986

This is the song that proved there was more to Madonna than blonde ambition and craftily constructed pop videos. The best track on her third album (**True Blue**), Papa Don't Preach, is, Madonna announced before its release, "a message song that everyone is going to take the wrong way." Indeed everyone from **Tipper Gore**, wife of Al (the only president elect never to occupy the White House), to the feminist attorney **Gloria Allred**, who insisted that Madonna acknowledge that abortion was a valid choice for teen mums, assumed that she was referring to an unborn child when she talked about keeping her baby.

Rolling Stone, in its review of the album, refers to this as, "Madonna's Billie Jean" and the song, co-written by **Brian Elliott**, could be interpreted that way. But it could easily refer to a much simpler conflict where dad disapproves of his daughter's boyfriend. Hence the appeal to her dad that if he could only see how "good he's been treating me", he might understand. The good advice she's in search of might, in this reading, simply refer to whether she should marry her baby or live it up as her friends have suggested. But it's part of the song's beauty that both readings work equally well. That said, if you listen to the lyrics of **Oh Father** on her next real album, **Like A Prayer** ("Maybe someday... I'll be able to say you didn't mean to be cruel") you might conclude she had a few issues with her dad.

Papa Don't Preach is as irresistible musically as Into The Groove, yet Madonna sings it, in a perfect blend of innocence and rasp, with the emotional intensity she had poured into her often overlooked cover of Love Don't Live Here Any More on *Like A Virgin*. Recently covered by the wannabe enfant terrible of rock **Kelly Osbourne**, this song is, as Dave Marsh noted, that ultimate rarity: a message song, which opens with Beatle-esque rifling cellos, that you can dance to.

★Papa Don't Preach is still best heard on **True Blue**. While **The Immaculate Collection** does include it, many of the other songs on it have been pointlessly speeded up.

Death Discs

When meeting an untimely end is just the ticket

Love may be the most common subject in pop music, but death comes a close second. Below is our Top 10 of classic death-disc tracks...

1. Leader Of The Pack – Shangri-Las
A classic drama about a girl forced to give up her bad boy only for him to be killed in a motorcycle crash.

2. Dagenham Dave – The Stranglers
Dave was a car worker who became a friend of the band, introducing them to Rabelais and acting as bodyguard. When his body was found in the Thames, they wrote this song for him.

3. Tell Laura I Love Her – Ricky Valance
A cover of Ray Peterson's US hit, the Welshman's only hit was a No.1. Controversial for 1960, the song dealt with the last words of Laura's love after a stock-car racing crash.

4. Johnny Remember Me – John Leyton
After his debut, Tell Laura I Love Her, lost out to Valance, Leyton released this lover's plea from the grave – but only after "the girl I loved died a year ago" had been softened to "lost". It worked, reaching No.1 in 1961.

5. Death Cab For Cutie – Bonzo Dog Doo-Dah Band
Featured in *Magical Mystery Tour*, Death Cab... is a pastiche rather than an actual death disc, with front-man Vivian Stanshall doing his finest and most comical impersonation of Elvis.

6. Pledging My Love – Johnny Ace
The rock'n'roll pianist's biggest hit (US No.1 for 10 weeks in 1955) was a posthumous one. On Christmas Day 1954 he lost a game of Russian roulette backstage in Houston.

7. Shannon – Henry Gross
A founding member of Sha Na Na, Gross's minor UK hit (in 1976) was about the death of Beach Boy Carl Wilson's Irish setter. Spookily, Gross also had a setter called Shannon.

8. Ebony Eyes – Everly Brothers
Don and Phil were reluctant to sing their third No.1 live. Not surprising really: it's about a soldier set to meet his fiancée at the airport only to hear she's been killed in a plane crash.

9. To Know Him Is To Love Him – The Teddy Bears
Written by Phil Spector after seeing the inscription on the tombstone of his father, who'd committed suicide when Phil was nine. The first release by Spector's band, it went to No.1.

10. Honey – Bobby Goldsboro
"See the tree, how big it's grown..." Bobby's musing over the tree (it's symbolic) and missing his dead honey, and we're missing ballads with such immortal lines as, "She'd wrecked the car, but what the heck?"

❀Perfect Day❀

Various Artists
No.1 for two weeks from 29 November 1997, and for one week from 10 January 1998

Perfect Day must be one of the least-likely candidates for a remake as a feelgood No.1 to raise millions for charity. The song, written by **Lou Reed** for his biggest-selling album **Transformer** in 1972, is often said to be about getting stoned in public – hence the final refrain, "You're going to reap just what you sow."

The underground meaning of the song was not, it has to be said, apparent to everyone when *Transformer* was first released. The professionally cynical **Nick Tosches**, in his review of *Transformer* for *Rolling Stone* magazine, called Perfect Day "a soft lilter about spending a day drinking sangria in the park with his girlfriend, about how it made him feel so normal, so good. Wunnerful, wunnerful, wunnerful." Compared to the album's most famous track, Perfect Day was very much a walk on the mild side. But the sweetness was tempered with wistful regret ("I thought I was someone else/Someone good").

The all-star BBC version to raise money for **Children In Need** was as overblown as the original was laid-back. (For a complete run-down of who performs on it and the lines they sing, see *www.teenagewildlife.com/music/collab/PD/Title.html*). Uniting artists as diverse as **Lesley Garrett** and **Shane MacGowan**, it was No.1 in the UK, Ireland (six weeks), Greece (one week), Norway (seven weeks) and Croatia (two weeks). It's nice to think of all those Croatian pop fans watching the video and wondering who on earth the bloke with the rotten teeth was.

Heather Small, the Lesley Garrett of M People, and **Tom Jones** rose to the vocal challenge, making the line about reaping what you sow sound like an immediate threat. Musical bombast abounded in this retelling, but perhaps the most ironic piece of casting was **David Bowie**, who had helped produce *Transformer*, singing, "You make me forget myself." Yeah, right David, as if anything could do that.

The American poet **Robert Frost** used to say that he never dared be radical when young, for fear it might make him conservative when he was old. (This was slightly tongue-in-cheek; Frost didn't really need old age to shove him to the right.) Lou Reed was about to discover a rock'n'roll variation on that same theme. Dare to be an anarchic rebel when you're young and, 25 years later, you find yourself being cherished as a showbiz institution by exactly the kind of schmucks you first rebelled against. No wonder Lou had to hurry off and make an album based on the works of **Edgar Allan Poe**.

★**Perfect Day** is best savoured on **Transformer** (RCA) where the original retains its gentle, purposeful mood. The **BBC** single is also available on CD via the Internet (try *Amazon*).

☀Rock Around The Clock☀

Bill Haley & His Comets
No.1 for three weeks from 25 November 1955, and two weeks from 6 January 1956

A tsunami hitting the studio in which Bill Haley & His Comets were recording wouldn't have seemed out of place considering the obstacles they faced recording Rock Around The Clock. What went on to become the **second-biggest selling rock single of all time** overcame feuding management, technical glitches, acts of God and an apocalyptic blues tune.

Rock The Joint (their debut single as The Comets) had already inspired DJ **Alan Freed** to coin the phrase **rock'n'roll** (although it was black slang for sex) and its success led writer/producer **James Myers** to offer them Rock Around The Clock, a quasi-rhythm and blues parody he had penned with **Martin Freedman** (they later disagreed on Freedman's level of contribution). Their Essex Records boss, Dave Miller, didn't want the band to record it. "Three times I took the tune into the studio," said Haley. "Every time Miller would see it, he'd come in and tear it up." The answer was to leave Essex, and the Comets signed to Decca in 1954.

In due course the band headed to New York to lay down two tracks, Thirteen Women and **Rock Around The Clock**. En route, the ferry they were on grounded in the middle of the Delaware River, holding up the session for most of the day, and reportedly leaving **Sammy Davis Jr** waiting in the lounge for his own session.

On their arrival, producer Milt Gabler elected to record **Thirteen Women** (his own composition) first. A track which might have come from the mind of Hugh Hefner, it recounted the explosion of an H-bomb leaving only one man and 13 women alive. But Haley took six takes to get it right, leaving only 40 minutes for Rock Around The Clock. Fortunately the band knew it inside out, having listened to **Sonny Dae**'s original recording and practised new ideas at Haley's home.

Haley's punchy vocals dominated, along with **Danny Cedrone**'s guitar solo. He'd already used the same solo on **Rock The Joint**, but the limited time schedule meant the band had to use it again. Still, they managed to surpass both Dae's original and Myers's and Freedman's ideas, making the melody stronger and the riffs punchier. The engineers must also take credit: a quick second take allowed them to splice the two versions to make Haley more audible over the instruments.

Thirteen Women was aimed at **Louis Jordan**'s audience, so Rock Around The Clock was **relegated to the B-side**. Sales of 75,000 made it a moderate success, but Myers wasn't satisfied and sent copies to every producer in Hollywood. He had the right idea, but an MGM executive had already played his daughter's copy and commissioned it to play over the credits to **The Blackboard Jungle**. Rock

Around The Clock was re-released, topping the charts in the US and in the UK. In Britain it had peaked at No.17 on its first release, before re-entering the charts in October 1955, becoming a worldwide phenomenon and, bizarrely, re-entering the UK charts in both 1956 and 1957, reaching No.5 in September 1956.

★ Rock Around The Clock is available on **Greatest Hits** (MCA), with the 22-track **Rock The Joint!** (Schoolkids) collecting more material from the immediate period.

☼ Seasons In The Sun ☼

Terry Jacks
No.1 for four weeks from 6 April 1974

"Goodbye to you, my trusted friend…" From the opening words, **Terry Jacks**'s voice was cracking up as if he really were saying his last goodbyes. Although Jacks was Canadian and the lyrics were vague, many assumed it was some sort of mild protest against the futility of war in general and in **Vietnam** in particular.

The truth was very different. **Jacques Brel**, who wrote the song as Le Moribond (literally "The Dying Man") told Jacks he had written it in a Tangiers brothel. "He said it was written about an old man dying of a broken heart because his best friend had been goofing around with his wife," Jacks recalled. Certainly Brel's original lyrics – which bitterly accused his friend of hopping into his bed before he'd be in the ground – are much darker than Jacks's more conventional sentiment. It was Californian poet **Rod McKuen** who first recreated Le Moribond in English (he also adapted, or ruined, according to your point of view, Brel's original of If You Go Away), for American folkies **The Kingston Trio**.

Their version failed to chart but Jacks heard it and, in 1972, tried to persuade **The Beach Boys** to record it at a session he was producing. The group did cut it but never released it. Jacks then recorded his own version, inspired in part by his conversation with a friend on a golf course who had just been told he only had months to live. Jacks had already had a transatlantic Top 10 hit in 1970 with the maudlin **Which Way You Going Billy?**, recorded with his ex-wife Susan Pesklevits as **The Poppy Family**. But despite revamping the lyrics and persuading guitar legend **Link Wray** to add some fine, reverbed guitar work, he hesitated to release it. Industry myth has it that Jacks was only finally convinced by the enthusiasm of his newspaper delivery boy.

Ironically, the single Jacks replaced at No.1 in the UK was a more explicit anti-war song, **Billy Don't Be A Hero**, penned and produced by Nottingham's finest, **Paper Lace** (lace being Nottingham's most famous product). With such couplets as "And as Billy started to go/She said, 'Keep your pretty head low,'" Billy was a tender, teenypop, anti-war song by **Mitch Murray** and **Peter Callander**, taken, to the group's chagrin, to

"Whatever will be will be, the turkey will be stuffed by three, que sera sera"

the top of the US charts by a septet called **Bo Donaldson & The Heywoods**. For a harsher, grown-up companion to Billy Don't Be A Hero, you could do worse than look up **Elvis Costello**'s Any King's Shilling on his album *Spike*.

★**Terry Jacks**'s Seasons In The Sun is available on such compilations as **Walk On The Wild Side** (Columbia, 2001). **Paper Lace**'s **Billy Don't Be A Hero** is available on the band's **Greatest Hits** (Music Club). **Jacques Brel**'s Le Moribond is available on a 34-track CD of the same name released on Universal France.

☀ Secret Love ☀

Doris Day
No.1 for one week from 16 April 1954, and for eight weeks from 7 May 1954

One of Doris Day's friends dubbed her '**Suzie Creamcheese**' and this nickname perfectly sums up the virginal, happy-go-lucky image which made her one of the biggest movie stars of the 1950s and 1960s. The Doris Day sex comedy (the comedy springing from the fact that there was never any sex in these movies) has so overshadowed her genuine gift as a singer, that to listen to her sing Secret Love after a long interval is a minor revelation.

Her co-star **James Cagney** identified the key to her vocal craft when he said: "The touchstone is simplicity, the simple line of performance, directly to you, uncluttered." Day herself admits she learned from **Ella Fitzgerald**: "The subtle ways she shaded her voice, the casual yet clear way she sang the words." By the time she came to sing Secret Love, she had enjoyed a long apprenticeship as one of America's sultriest swing vocalists with the likes of **Bob Crosby** (Bing's brother) and **Les Paul**, with whom she recorded her first classic, Sentimental Journey.

Doris Mary Anne Kappelhoff originally sang Secret Love as a cross-dressing tomboy called **Calamity Jane** in the 1953 movie of that name – the cross-dressing may help to explain the song's appeal as a gay classic. But Day's performance isn't simply a matter of technique: there's an emotional simplicity to her vocal that even Ella didn't always achieve. But then behind the Suzie Creamcheese image was a passionate woman who lived through **four marriages** (one husband beat her; another poured her millions into bad business ventures leaving her $500,000 in debt when he died), who had her right leg shattered in a car accident when she was just 17, and who confessed to an adulterous affair with an unnamed actor (her very own secret love) in her tell-(almost)-all memoir *Doris Day: Her Own Story*.

In other words, it's possible that the passionate Secret Love, the subtly sexy **Move Over Darling** (Britney please note) and the husky, yearning Sentimental Journey are truer to the real Doris Kappelhoff than the cheery infectiousness of

Whatever Will Be Will Be (Que Sera Sera). Secret Love, written by **Sammy Fain** (hitherto mainly famous for his contribution to the soundtracks for such Disney classics as *Peter Pan*) and **Paul Francis Webster**, has been covered by everyone from **Engelbert Humperdinck** to **Sinead O'Connor** but nobody has yet topped Doris's version. For her part, she now devotes most of her energies to a not-so-secret love: her animal sanctuaries (*www.ddal.org*).

★**Doris Day**'s **Secret Love** is on such greatest hits albums as **Daydreaming** (Columbia) or, for the real fan, on **Golden Girl: The Columbia Recordings 1944-1966** (Columbia/Legacy).

❀ Shakin' All Over ❀
Johnny Kidd & The Pirates
No.1 for one week from 4 August 1960

Is Shakin' All Over the finest British rock'n'roll single ever? It's hard to think of anything better before The Beatles. **Cliff**'s Move It comes close – but it lacks the genuine fire of Kidd's vocal, and session man **Joe Moretti**'s lead guitar blisters through Kidd's record in a manner which bears comparison to some of **Scotty Moore**'s work for Elvis at RCA.

Seminal is an overused adjective in popular music writing, but London-born Kidd (real name Fred Heath – you can't blame him for changing it, can you?) was an enigmatic and influential figure in the history of British rock by the time he died (just 27 years old) in a car crash in 1966. He started out in the unpretentiously named skiffle group **Five Nutters** alongside partner and lead guitarist **Alan Caddy**. Their first (minor) hit was the energetic Please Don't Touch in 1959. As is the way with Pirates, the crew changed, with **Brian Gregg** (bass) and **Clem Cattini** (drums) joining for what would be The Pirates' finest two minutes and 19 seconds. Presumably some of the previous members got tired of wearing those pirate uniforms. Kidd, just to show what an innovator he was, wore an eye-patch – a whole decade before **Dr Hook**.

Shakin' All Over is a mysterious, even contradictory, record. It's a song on which you can hear many echoes of stars and styles, past and future (**Gene Vincent**, rockabilly, hard rock, even **The Shadows**), yet it sounds utterly distinctive. The stop-start tempo, which could have sounded like a gimmick, felt utterly natural, stamping the song as a true original. Kidd's vocal is powerful, passionate yet subtle, not as insufferably cheery as, for example, **Brian Poole** on The Tremeloes' Do You Love Me? And Johnny, unlike Cliff, makes the word "lust" sound like it's not just something he looked up in a dictionary.

It was always going to be hard for Kidd to write or sing another song as good as Shakin' All Over and he never quite did. By 1963, trying to resist the tidal wave from the **Mersey**, The Pirates sounded almost like Merseybeaters on hits like I'll Never Get Over You. There were more defections with **Mick Green** lending his guitar skills for a while before leaving for The Dakotas and then, ten years after Kidd's death, re-forming The Pirates (he was last seen supporting Bryan Ferry on tour). Kidd re-formed The New Pirates in 1966 but his comeback ended in tragedy.

But Shakin' All Over is one of a handful of British rock singles which still don't sound dated, unlike many of the Merseybeat hits which followed. Canadian band **Guess Who** covered the song in 1965 (as did The Who, on **Live At Leeds**, 1970) reaching No.22 in the US. Some critics, notably Dave Marsh in his book *The Heart Of Rock & Soul*, insist Guess Who's version is better. They are, of course, wrong.

★**The Complete Johnny Kidd** is probably the best way to own **Shakin' All Over**. The record is also on tons of compilations such as **Totally Number 1 Hits Of The 60s** (EMI).

✿ Smoke Gets In Your Eyes ✿

The Platters
No.1 for one week from 20 March 1959

The Platters were the first black vocal group to top the British charts and they did so with a soaring sublime rendering of a **Jerome Kern Tin Pan Alley** classic which would be covered by almost everybody – including **Bryan Ferry** who had a Top 20 hit with his remake in 1974.

Ferry and The Platters should be grateful to lyricist **Otto Harbach**, who found the tune in the unrevised score for Kern's 1934 Broadway show *Roberta*. Originally, Kern had written it as an up-tempo, instrumental tap-dance routine. Harbach suggested that with some modification it could make a decent ballad. The show struggled until the nation began humming or whistling the song, and four different versions were soon in the charts, with bandleader **Paul Whiteman**'s the most popular – although a version by troubled songstress **Ruth Etting** (the character played by Doris Day in the film *Love Me Or Leave Me*) reached No.3.

Harry Belafonte, the first black singer to have a British No.1 (with Mary's Boy Child), cut the song in 1950, but it was The Platters, led by the lush, unrestrained vocals of **Tony Williams**, who topped the charts on both sides of the Atlantic with their version. Set, as critic **Dave Marsh** put it, "in a pool of echo", the song "winds up as one long crescendo, a Broadway bolero." Williams has shaken off the restraint he'd shown on such early hits as Only You and invests the melodramatic lyrics with such tragedy you're so overwhelmed you forget the occasional awkward rhyme (chafed/laughed). It was all something of a shock for Kern's widow who threatened to sue.

Ferry's version, cut when he started wearing the white tuxedo, doesn't try to top

Williams's falsetto crescendo, but he brings the appropriate tone of lovelorn adolescence to a rendition which, in its different way, possesses all the urgency of the original. Patti Austin – best known in the UK for her duets with James Ingram (the 1982 Top 20 hit, Baby Come To Me) and Michael Jackson (on *Off The Wall*) – has cut a superlative version on her 1988 album *The Real Me* (Qwest).

★**The Platters'** version is best found on the 1998 compilation **Enchanted** (Rhino, 1998) while **Bryan Ferry**'s is on **Another Time Another Place**. For a different spin, try the version by **CoCo Lee** (aka the Asian Madonna) on her album **Brave Enough To Love**.

❀ Something's Gotten Hold Of My Heart ❀

Marc Almond and Gene Pitney
No.1 for four weeks from 28 January 1989

This coupling wasn't as unlikely as it seemed at the time. Almond, freed from the constraints imposed by teen fans of **Soft Cell**, had begun to cut minor hits with titles that sounded right out of the Gene Pitney songbook: The House Is Haunted (By The Echo Of Your Last Goodbye), Tears Run Rings, Bitter Sweet and, after this duet, A Lover Spurned and The Desperate Hours. Pitney had made his name with such dramas as Town Without Pity, In The Cold Light Of Day and Backstage (I'm Lonely), which wouldn't have been a bad title for Almond's memoirs.

Almond was a former art student at Leeds University who had wanted to create music for the theatre. Pitney had started out as a songwriter (penning such pop hits as **Hello Mary Lou**) before becoming a singer, breaking through in the UK in 1963 with the typically dramatic 24 Hours From Tulsa. He might have looked like a middle manager for an American corporation, but he was a canny judge of material. He was the first American singer to chart with a **Jagger/Richards** song (That Girl Belongs To Yesterday), returning the favour by playing piano on Under Assistant West Coast Promotion Man on the **Rolling Stones'** album *Out Of Their Heads*. Critic **Dave Marsh**, trying to sum up his career, said simply, "Gene Pitney is a very strange case" – a verdict which applies equally to Almond. What the two shared, as solo artists, was a heartfelt approach to balladeering which could be called the 'everything and the kitchen sink' style.

Pitney sings with such intensity (**Nik Cohn** compared his voice to the whine of an electric saw) that the listener is physically and emotionally exhausted after just a few numbers. But Something's Gotten Hold Of My Heart was one of his subtler hits, penned by British duo **Roger Cook** and **Roger Greenaway**, which describes the exaltation of love in a slightly trippy way. Pitney delivers it with his customary conviction and it deserved better than to peak at No.5 in 1967.

Fast-forward a couple of decades and Almond, establishing his second, rather less camp career as a **torch singer**, decided to cover the classic song by a singer he loved. Then someone suggested it might be fun to get Pitney to help out as a guest vocalist. Before long the song had become a full-blown duet. Because of Almond's touring commitments, he and Pitney (who is clearly a good sport) had to record their parts separately, but they did meet in Las Vegas to make the very funny video, with Almond taking the opportunity to get his idol to sign some of his old Pitney albums.

Their duet rocketed to No.1 in the UK and other parts of Europe (amazingly it was Pitney's first chart-topper) and became the bestselling record in Britain in 1989. Pitney noted that the song introduced him to a new audience: "The first tour after we had that big hit with that record, I was seeing orange-spiky-haired people in my audience, who were never there before and stood out like a sore thumb."

★**Something's Gotten Hold Of My Heart** is on such compilations as It Takes Two (Columbia 1996). It's not on **Marc Almond**'s album of the time, Stars We Are (1988), but as his best solo work it's worth buying. For **Gene Pitney**'s original, try the Very Best Of Gene Pitney.

✿ Space Oddity ✿
David Bowie
No.1 for two weeks from 8 November 1975

When a young hopeful called David Bowie met producer Tony Visconti to discuss recording his song called **Space Oddity**, the meeting didn't go very well. "David was writing these beautiful acoustic songs like Memory Of A Free Festival," Visconti recalled later, "and then he comes along with Space Oddity. Of course, they're scheduled to land on the moon in a few weeks and I said to him, 'This smells of blatant commercialism and it isn't like you at all.'" Visconti was so unimpressed he suggested that if Bowie really wanted to record that song, he do so with Gus Dudgeon.

Bowie did just that, although he told Visconti that Dudgeon hadn't got that involved and what made the record was Rick Wakeman busking on the Mellotron. Bowie had his hit although, coming three months after the 1969 moon landing, it only reached No.5. Maybe Visconti, who later admitted that he learned to like the song, had a point.

It was another three years before Bowie bothered chart compilers again, becoming the first **sci-fi pop star** with hits like Starman and Life On Mars, and playing a character (Ziggy Stardust) whose backing group were called The Spiders From Mars. Bowie has never completely escaped from sci-fi, possibly because there is something genuinely otherworldly about his persona, a strangeness that goes deeper than him having one green and one blue eye. **Nic Roeg** would capitalise on this in The Man Who Fell To Earth (by far Bowie's most convincing turn as an actor), and Bowie

"Eyeliner, whitener, colour the eyes"

himself would return to the theme with Loving The Alien (on 1984's *Tonight*), tongue-in-cheek on Hallo Spaceboy (on 1995's *Outside*) and, perhaps resignedly, on the cover of his 2002 album *Heathen*.

It was not until Space Oddity was re-released in 1975 that it got to No.1, just as Bowie was reinventing himself. For an artist anxious to move on (the Berlin trio of *Low*, *Heroes* and *The Lodger* would be next), Space Oddity was threatening to become an albatross, and so **Major Tom** returned to No.1 in 1980's **Ashes To Ashes**. Visconti did produce this one, calling it "the most conventional pop song ever written, with a cute verse, a cute chorus and the devastating stab where he tells the world that Major Tom's a junkie, and kills off the character he created all those years before. He'd been sardonically looking for some way to get rid of Major Tom once and for all."

For all Bowie's ambivalence, Space Oddity is a decent pop song. The observation of the astronaut's **celebrity status** ("the papers want to know whose shirt you wear") was sardonic and prophetic, while the rhyme about not daring to leave the capsule provided a killer emotional punch. And Bowie did care about the subject. He and Visconti spent hours debating whether there was **life on Mars**, possibly why he sings it with such conviction. Or maybe that's the sound of a gifted, young man feeling that his life's ambitions are just one song away from being fulfilled.

★Space Oddity is on most of the numerous **Bowie** compilations. To hear it in its historical context, try 1969's **Man Of Words, Man Of Music**, re-released as **Space Oddity**.

☼ Spirit In The Sky ☼

Norman Greenbaum
No.1 for two weeks from 2 May 1970

When Norman Greenbaum's third single, California Earthquake, peaked at a barely tepid **No.92** in the US Hot 100, no artistic tantrums were thrown. "Well, I'm not a rock'n'roller," he said. "I've got money – fuck it. And I went into the **dairy**

business." Sensible guy Norm. Alas, other popsters with less talent have not emulated him. The charts can get pretty competitive, but the dairy business can generally always find room for one recently enriched pop millionaire.

Greenbaum had always had his own take on life ever since he picked up a guitar in a Massachusetts high school in the late 1950s. His earlier jugband-style singles featured deadpan humour under titles like The Eggplant That Ate Chicago (a minor US hit in 1966 for Dr West's Medicine Show & Junk Band) and **Gondoliers, Shakespeares, Overseers, Playboys And Bums**. Even Greenbaum admits he doesn't know what the latter was about, beyond confiding in typically droll style: "I can tell you it had nothing to do with **Bob Dylan**."

Spirit In The Sky was pretty direct for Greenbaum. Like the song says, it's all about **God**. Well, God and country singer **Porter Wagoner** (see below). Wagoner had a 30-minute TV show in LA on which he sang a religious song. Greenbaum was entranced by a glimpse of Wagoner, in embroidered country gear, standing in front of a stained glass window, singing about a miner who goes to church for the first time in 20 years – only to find a sign saying the preacher is on vacation. "I knew then that, God almighty, I needed a religious song," Greenbaum told **Wayne Jancik**, author of *The Billboard Book Of One Hit Wonders*.

The man behind the hits

When Norman Greenbaum was moved by Porter Wagoner to write **Spirit In The Sky**, it wasn't the only time the country singer inspired a No.1 smash. Remembered for his ostentatious attire and 'old before his time' demeanour, Wagoner pushed **Dolly Parton** into the limelight and tried to pull her back out again when she became too big.

Pairing up with the then unknown Dolly in 1968, Wagoner was already a 17-year country-music veteran and had had a country hit with **Green Green Grass Of Home** in 1965, a year before Tom Jones's hit version.

Dolly (replacing one Norma Jean) was hired to boost the ratings of his TV show. The duo were rarely out of the country charts but split in 1975, parted by Porter's jealousy and Dolly's ambition. Parton wrote **I Will Always Love You** to soften the blow. It may not have worked, as he's rumoured to have brandished a gun at her. Parton will say only, "Even if that was the truth, it's not a thing the public should know."

Parton was also once asked whether she and Wagoner had ever had sex. "Hundreds of times," she replied, "but never with each other."

The record, with its driving guitars, groovy female chorus and simple yet vague lyric, reached No.3 in the US and went two places better in the UK. Greenbaum summed up the effect when he said, "With that success I failed." He never wrote anything as compelling as Spirit In The Sky again, and after he gave the farm to his ex-wife in a divorce settlement, he was spotted living in a converted chicken coop. Still, his story has a happy ending. His song has been used by American Express (although they refused to give him a gold card), and covered by **Dr & The Medics** and **Gareth Gates**, both of whom took it to No.1 – in 1986 and 2003 respectively. And Greenbaum himself returned to music in 1995 with a companion piece to Spirit called Day They Sold Beer In Church. We recommend you visit his website (*www.spiritinthesky.com*) where his sense of humour is still in full working order.

★Spirit In The Sky is on **The Best Of Norman Greenbaum** (Repertoire) – all those songs about gondoliers, canned ham and the ditty about beer in church, for less than a tenner.

☼ Sunny Afternoon ☼
The Kinks
No.1 for two weeks from 7 July 1966

By the middle of the 1960s, the idea that rock'n'roll was exclusively for the young and swinging had become almost an article of faith. Yet **Ray Davies**, who with his brother Dave founded **The Kinks**, never really bought into this. "I wrote **Sunny Afternoon** when I was 21 years old and I wrote it so my grandad could sing it. And I don't believe **Pete Townshend** hated old people and wanted to die before he got old, because he got along really well with his dad."

Davies wasn't as cute as McCartney and didn't quite have Lennon's edge, but he did write some of the most listenable, intelligent pop songs of the 1960s. **Sunny Afternoon** is a remarkable piece of work, a song about an aristocrat happily sipping an ice-cold beer while contemplating the fact that he's been impoverished by his taxman and is about to be squeezed by a mysterious obese mama.

"At the time I wrote Sunny Afternoon, I was playing the greatest hits of Frank Sinatra, Dylan's Maggie's Farm, Glenn Miller and Bach," he recalled later. You can hear echoes of all these in Sunny Afternoon which, although some would say it's Davies's meisterwork, he describes as being almost an accident: "It was made very quickly, in the morning. The bass player went off and started playing funny little classical things on the bass and Nick Hopkins, who was on piano at that session, was playing something to get us in the feeling of the song."

The Kinks' work has been much more influential than you might expect from a group which hasn't graced the UK Top 10 since 1970. The raga sound of **See My**

Friend, released in August 1965, anticipated The Beatles' eastern experiments. All Day And All Of The Night was reworked by **The Doors**. Classic songs like Days have been picked up by such artists as **Kirsty MacColl** while **The Sex Pistols** included a few Kinks B-sides in their early live act and **The Jam** covered David Watts. But their streak of English whimsy – which made them less marketable in America than The Beatles, the Stones or The Who – also led to some dreadful 1970s concept albums. Asked to justify 1968's **Village Green Preservation Society** (actually a pretty good album), Davies's list of influences was fascinating: "I like **Donald Duck**, Desperate Dan, draught beer, Frankenstein."

Sunny Afternoon was the last of The Kinks' three No.1 hits and, with the greatest respect to the other two – You Really Got Me, with its heavy garage riff, and the mellower Tired Of Waiting For You – probably their finest. The 1970s, although starting brightly with Lola, weren't kind to The Kinks or to Ray Davies's liver, as he stumbled drunkenly through too many concerts. A minor 1980s comeback with **Come Dancing**, from the soundtrack of *Absolute Beginners* (and their biggest hit ever in the US), helped revive their influence. By the mid-1990s they were being namechecked by the likes of **Damon Albarn**. This song shows why.

★Sunny Afternoon is best found on 1966's **Face To Face** (Essential) one of the great 1960s albums. On **Live At Kelvin Hall** (1968), you can hear it being sung by a concert hall full of Glaswegians, a curiously uplifting experience.

⊛Telstar⊛

The Tornados
No.1 for five weeks from 4 October 1962

A pop-trivia teaser for you: name the **first British group to top the US charts**. No, not The Beatles. Nor The Springfields (though they were the first British group to crack the US Top 20). Not even The Shadows, but George Bellamy, Roger LaVern, Alan Caddy, Clem Cattini and Heinz Burt, aka the **Tornados**, who achieved the feat with an instrumental inspired by and named after the first telecommunications satellite, Telstar. Not bad for a band whose previous claim to fame was that they had backed **Billy Fury** in Great Yarmouth (though Caddy and Cattini had also been in Johnny Kidd's Pirates).

Yet distinctive as their stylised sound was, with LaVern's cinema organ firmly in the lead, most of the record's success was due to its producer **Joe Meek**. A former studio engineer who became one of the first independent pop producers, he created most of his records in the same London flat where, four years later, he is supposed to have killed his landlady and then himself.

One of the mysteries of Telstar was where the money went. Meek (who wrote the tune) died penniless, although Decca had paid him the royalties from this worldwide smash which racked up sales of more than five million. The smart money suggests that the money got eaten up in a legal dispute with the composer of the soundtrack to the French film *The Battle Of Austerlitz*, who alleged that Meek had stolen his melody. The case was still in progress when Meek died.

One day Joe will inherit the earth

The other mystery is how Meek, who overcame deafness to produce some of the finest British pop of the 1960s (though few actual hits), created it. He relied on others, among them a young **Ritchie Blackmore**, to create the soundscapes he imagined. The big record labels accused Meek of "making stars by twiddling knobs". His collaborator **Geoff Goddard** says, "Joe would mix the sounds up, pumping them through different amps and coming up with a mushy sound that would lead to hands raised in horror at major studios." The young **Tom Jones** was briefly signed to Meek – possibly one of the most fascinating 'what ifs?' in British pop history.

The Tornados had a few other hits, including Globetrotter and Robot, which adhered closely to the formula of their first smash, all too closely. **Heinz**, the bass player, got fed up and went solo, securing a No.5 hit in 1963 with **Just Like Eddie**, his tribute to Eddie Cochran. Heinz has since had, yes, 57 varieties of 'civilian' jobs, including delivering potatoes, selling advertising on the *Southend Evening Echo* and working in a bakery. The Tornados soon ran their chart course, but Meek's mysterious exit (his suicide marked the anniversary of Buddy Holly's death) continues to obscure the genius he exhibited in life.

★**Telstar** is best found on **It's Hard To Believe: The Amazing World Of Joe Meek** (BMG) with the added bonus that you also get **Heinz**'s big solo hit, **Just Like Eddie**.

☸ That'll Be The Day ☸

Buddy Holly
No.1 for three weeks from 1 November 1957

Buddy Holly was just 22 when the plane he had chartered fell to earth in an Iowa cornfield. At that age, Bruce Springsteen hadn't even released an album, David

Bowie was in serious danger of becoming a one-hit wonder and John Lennon had just signed, with his three mates, for Parlophone.

Yet in the space of a professional career which lasted barely two years, **Charles Hardin Holley** – Buddy to the world – had written and sung at least four classics: That'll Be The Day, Peggy Sue, Not Fade Away and, well, take your pick from Think It Over, Rave On or Everyday (bizarrely never a Top 20 hit for anyone in the UK; Don McLean's version peaked at No.38). All of them have stood the test of time, fashion and some pallid cover versions.

Strangely, rock's first great white singer/songwriter is in danger of being over-praised in death. **True Love Ways** might be the one treacly ballad that deserved to be massacred by David Essex and Cliff Richard, but part of his fallibility was due to **the breadth of his influences**. He once opened in concert for Elvis and said generously, "We owe it all to Elvis," but he was being too generous. Holly (born in Lubbock, Texas) drew on rockabilly, Tex Mex, big-band ballads and country, and it's a mark of his range that the title of his first smash, **That'll Be The Day**, was taken from a phrase muttered cynically by **John Wayne** in the John Ford western **The Searchers**. The phrase was later incorporated into the chorus for **Don McLean**'s tribute to Holly in particular and American pop in general, **American Pie**.

Astonishingly the single (officially credited to The Crickets: Holly's business life was a contractual mess) was only released as a favour to Coral record executive Bob Thiele. **Decca**, which owned Coral, may have had Bill Haley on its books but it didn't really like rock'n'roll. Holly's case of hiccups and the staccato guitar give That'll Be The Day its drive, creating a sound that would inspire The Beatles. Like Elvis's early Sun records, many of Holly's classic tunes didn't actually feature drums: in the studio, The Crickets' **Jerry Allison** would often play the drum part on the inside of a cardboard box.

The words may be mean – he's mocking his girl's idle threats to leave him – but his voice isn't. Although well-crafted mush like **It Doesn't Matter Anymore** is among his most-covered songs, Holly was at his best when he was, in his polite way, letting his lover know where she stood. A devoted husband (at least to his second wife), in song he was always encouraging his partner to think over what she'd just said, reminding her that hearts grow cold and old. Or, in **Not Fade Away**, laying down the law with an arrogance that inspired **Mick Jagger**.

If Holly didn't have it all, he damn near had it all until he died on 3 February 1959. Nearly half a century later, his influence is still with us. If, despite the efforts of Paul McCartney (who now owns his publishing), Holly's music does just fade away, we should all be very worried and break open the whisky and rye. Because that will be the day pop music dies.

★That'll Be The Day is available on **From The Original Master Tapes** (MCA).

Tie A Yellow Ribbon
❀Round The Old Oak Tree❀

Dawn featuring Tony Orlando
No.1 for four weeks from 21 April 1973

Musicologists will tell you that this song dates back as far as the **American Civil War**. The story – in which a homecoming man asks his significant other to tie a yellow ribbon around a tree to show she still loves him – is simple and generic enough to have started out as a folk song. But this version was, co-writer **L Russell Brown** insisted, inspired by a real story involving a returning convict that he'd read about in a local paper. The heartwarming tale ended with a tree festooned with ribbons and a whole bus full of passengers breaking into cheers.

It's more likely the story had become an urban myth, common in 1950s America. Brown changed the story a bit – the apple tree became an oak, the ribbon changed from white to yellow and the Civil War train became a bus. The result was that **Dawn** (or 'Dawn featuring **Tony Orlando**') had a worldwide hit in 1973 with it. Dawn, in case you were wondering, consisted of two backing vocalists **Telma Hopkins** and **Joyce Vincent**: Orlando had been drafted in to front on **Candida**, their first big hit. Tie A Yellow Ribbon was played three million times on the radio in 18 months and is said to be the most-covered song in the world after Yesterday.

Dawn's version is cheery, infectious and insipid, with Orlando (real name: Michael Anthony Orlando Cassivis) more influential for his hairstyle and his clothes than his vocal style. Countless British footballers and the lead singer of British soundalikes **Brotherhood Of Man** would ape the Orlando look. In 1981, the song had a new lease of life when Americans started tying ribbons around trees as a kind of public prayer for the hostages to come home from **Iran**. By then Dawn had lost Orlando (who had given up showbiz in favour of God), and would have been lucky to get a gig in a nightclub in Orlando.

★ Tie A Yellow Ribbon is on **The Very Best Of Dawn Featuring Tony Orlando**(Camden), complete with an alternate raw, gutsy, acoustic version of Tie A Yellow Ribbon. Just joking.

❀Unchained Melody❀

Jimmy Young
No.1 for three weeks from 24 June 1955

Unchained Melody was No.1 for **Jimmy Young** for three weeks in 1955, for **The Righteous Brothers** for two weeks in 1965 plus another four weeks in 1990, for

Robson & Jerome for seven weeks in 1995, and for **Gareth Gates** for four weeks in 2002. It's the only song to top the UK singles charts five times – and by four different acts. Although it has been covered by everyone from **Al Green** and **Roy Orbison** to **Peter Sellers** and **Melanie**, it's usually topped the charts when sung by a current teen idol. The exception to this rule, The Righteous Brothers, were already working from memory when they soared to No.1 in 1965 (OK, they were 25), then repeated the performance 25 – spooky! – years later when their version was included in the soundtrack to the Demi Moore weepie *Ghost*.

To some, Unchained Melody epitomises the genre immortalised by **The Beautiful South** in One Last Love Song: "Those bloody great ballads we hated at first." Yet what has come to be seen as pop's quintessential expression of romantic yearning was written for a long-forgotten 1955 movie about a California prison farm, called *Unchained*. The music was written by **Alex North** and the lyrics by **Hy Zaret**. The song was sung on the film's soundtrack by blind, black singer **Al Hibbler**, but his version lost out in the US to **Les Baxter**'s instrumental which topped *Billboard*'s charts for two weeks. In the UK, both versions lost out to Jimmy Young's, the future housewives' favourite racking up his first UK No.1. Hibbler stuck at No.2, Baxter ran out of steam at No.10, while **Liberace**'s version peaked at No.20 – his first (and biggest) UK hit.

Ten years later, The Righteous Brothers provided dramatic proof of the song's enduring magnetism by topping the UK charts with their version, now widely regarded as definitive. **Bobby Hatfield**'s lead vocal was powerful, full of romantic hunger, yet ethereal, even ghostly, long before Hollywood thought of including it in that **Demi Moore** blockbuster.

The elaborate orchestral arrangement is usually credited to **Phil Spector**, although Hatfield's fellow Righteous Brother **Bill Medley** insists it's his work. "Phil asked me if I would produce the album tracks because it was too time-consuming for him, and the song was produced for the album. It was on the B-side of Phil Spector's track Hung On You and the minute it released just went through the roof." Twenty-five years later, Hatfield had a call from his tour manager saying that *USA Today* wanted to interview him about the film *Ghost*. "I said I'm not even in it, but he said that our recording of the song was. Actually, it sold more the second time around."

Some great singers have recorded the track, notably the legendary black singer **Roy Hamilton**, whose version inspired Elvis to perform it in the 1970s, and **Al Green** (for a full listing, visit the song's best fan site on *http://home.earthlink.net/~charlieharvey*). Less memorably, **Leo Sayer**'s No.54 'hit' in 1986 marked his last appearance in the UK charts with a new single.

Since then this mournful melody has topped the charts twice, by **Robson & Jerome**, joint stars of a hit TV drama called *Soldier Soldier*, and **Gareth Gates**. The latter is a must for fans of truly bad records. Hearing Gates croon about lonely rivers and the sinister power of time is a bit like watching a seven-year-old beauty queen. You're left feeling unconvinced, slightly nauseous, and blaming the parents. The arrangement doesn't help, slowing the song down to a pace where every vocal misjudgment is painfully obvious. Maybe the Peter Sellers estate should release his frankly mad version, although it must be said it isn't one of his more inspired re-readings of a popular classic.

★Unchained Melody is on **The Very Best Of The Righteous Brothers**, Roy Hamilton's **Anthology**, **The Best Of Jimmy Young**, **Love Songs** by **Robson & Jerome**, and Gareth Gates's album **What My Heart Wants To Say**. A fine soulful version by **The Sweet Inspirations**, female backing singers for Elvis and Aretha Franklin, is on their **Best Of** album.

❀ Wannabe ❀

Spice Girls
No.1 for eight weeks from 20 July 1996

The Spice Girls' debut single is usually analysed in terms of statistics: No.1 in 23 or 31 countries (depending which estimate you believe); **four million** copies sold worldwide; the first debut single by a UK girl group to stay at No.1 for eight weeks… All of which kind of forgets to note that Wannabe is, whatever else it might be, a very catchy pop record, appealingly made and sung.

The **Girl Power** bit was always misleading. In *Rolling Stone*'s very sniffy review of the first album *Spice*, **Christina Kelly** noted the "girls don't get bogged down by anything deeper than mugging for promo shots and giving out tips on getting boys into bed." As **Chris Herbert** (who promoted the audition which led to the girls being cast Monkees-style), says, the point was that "the teen-band scene was saturated by boy bands. If you could put together a girl band which was sassy for the girls and with obvious sex appeal for the boys, you'd double your audience."

Wannabe was written with **Clive Stannard** and **Mat Rowe** (who had worked with **East 17**), recorded in just 20 minutes and jumps into life with the Spices sounding like a load of ladettes on a night out. The line about the girls really wanting to "zig-a-zig-ahhh" prompted much debate on the Internet. Everyone agreed it was a euphemism for sex (it was suggested by Mel B, after all) but many were appalled at the group's inarticulacy, obviously having forgotten that some of pop's greatest songs (eg Get A Job by **The Silhouettes**) were built on the eloquent juxtaposition of such meaningless sounds as "sho no no no" and "yip, yip, yip".

Virgin and the Spice Girls' first manager **Simon Fuller** didn't want this to be the group's first single. Virgin tried remixing it, before the girls rejected these versions, insisting on the release of a beefed-up version of the original demo. Replayed today, Wannabe sounds sadly prophetic. The advice to forget the past if you want (if you really really want) to be part of their future never really caught on with the tabloids, and as for that bit about "friendship never ends"…

★Wannabe is available on the **Spice Girls'** debut album **Spice**.

☺A Whiter Shade Of Pale☺

Procol Harum
No.1 for six weeks from 8 June 1967

Whiter Shade Of Pale has been analysed, dissected and scrutinised for clues to its real meaning as if it was a set of **Egyptian hieroglyphics** or an allusive literary masterpiece like T S Eliot's *The Waste Land*. Yet in *Melody Maker* in June 1967, lyricist **Keith Reid** explained where he'd got the title: "Some guy looked at a chick and said to her, 'You've gone a whiter shade of pale.' That phrase stuck in my mind – I wish I'd said it." Composer/singer/pianist **Gary Brooker** admitted the hymnal organ sound and fervent vocal were clear nods to his R&B roots and **Percy Sledge**'s When A Man Loves A Woman. He also drew on **Bach** (though, he still maintains, as much on the cantata Sleepers Awake as on Air On A G String).

The lyrics certainly seem to come with significant trappings. The allusion to the miller's tale is not a reference to **Chaucer** – Reid admitted he'd never read any. But references to 16 vestal virgins certainly gave the listener the sense they were getting a much richer cultural experience than they'd get from **Engelbert Humperdinck**'s Release Me, which also topped the charts for six weeks that year. Yet ultimately, this record is about the hoariest of situations: a bloke on a date using alcohol to give himself the nerve to make the first move – only to discover, as the porter in *Macbeth* could have told him, that alcohol makes a man and mars him.

Less well known is that there is a missing verse (and a further optional one) cut by producer **Denny Cordell** to keep the single to airplay length. If included it would have made the song much less enigmatic and far less effective. It includes a schoolboy allusion to Shakespeare ("If music be the food of love"), and is as clumsily obvious as the rest is appropriately subtle. Full details can be found in Mike Butler's book *Lives Of The Great Songs*, but be prepared to be disillusioned.

The song has been covered by **Annie Lennox** and **Noel Harrison**, the son of Rex Harrison, who renders it like a Monty Python upper-class twit in a trance which, oddly, works quite well. Yet Whiter Shade Of Pale, a soul ballad with a progressive rock feel, is one of the **most influential singles of all time**, its legacy obvious on **Stairway To Heaven** and **Bohemian Rhapsody**. But for Procol Harum this was as big as it got, though the follow-up **Homburg** was good. **Nik Cohn**'s verdict on the group was: "They made one classic record and kept reviving it in different names and disguises until everyone got sick to death of it." Harsh. But not entirely unfair.

★**A Whiter Shade Of Pale** is available on **Procol Harum**'s **Greatest Hits**, but real fans may want **Anthology** (Westside, 1997) which contains alternate takes of both big hits. **Noel Harrison**'s rendition is available on **Golden Throats** (Rhino, 1988) and you can find **Annie Lennox**'s gentle reading on her solo album **Medusa** (RCA, 1999).

❀ The Winner Takes It All ❀

Abba
No.1 for two weeks from 9 August 1980

Abba's final No.1 single was both an extreme statement of **fatalist philosophy** and a **heartbreaking love song**. The fact that even the most ignorant listener knew there was some secret heartbreak involving Anni-Frid, Agnetha, Benny and Bjorn didn't do the song's commercial prospects any harm either.

Benny (facial hair; keyboards) and **Bjorn** (clean shaven; guitar) may have been folkies for a time, but they'd also paid their dues to psychedelia and classic American pop like **Paul Anka**'s Diana, and even maudlin stuff like **Elvis Presley**'s Ink Spots tribute, That's When Your Heartaches Begin. **Agnetha**'s first role model was **Connie Francis**. Somehow, you can hear all this in The Winner Takes It All

because it is, above all, a beautifully constructed classic which doesn't sound as if it was created in Sweden or any other country with recognised boundaries, but in the universal kingdom of pop.

The backing track started out as a song called The Story Of My Life, which Bjorn recorded with a nonsense French lyric. The music changed a lot: the first version was up-tempo with a persistent beat. Benny later threw in a **descending piano line** which made the song feel more like a French *chanson*. Feeling that the lyrics would need to be suitably **melodramatic**, and not convinced he'd deliver, Bjorn cracked open a bottle of whisky – which did the trick. "I was drunk," he admitted later, "and the whole lyric came to me in one hour."

Abba went their own Swede way

Je T'Aime... Moi Non Plus

"Jane was such a lovely English, upper-class schoolgirl," said **Marianne Faithfull**, as she pondered how sleazy **Serge Gainsbourg**, the "dirty old man of popular music", had persuaded **Birkin** to groan to such devastating effect on a song which sold six million copies, probably led to the conception of as many babies and contained such mysterious lines as, "I come and go between your kidneys."

Gainsbourg, a French professional provocateur who had already recorded the song with his ex-lover **Brigitte Bardot**, seduced Birkin physically and professionally. All this wooing and froing must have exhausted poor Serge as his song owed a clear musical debt to A Whiter Shade Of Pale.

Je T'Aime was the UK's first foreign language No.1 – in October 1969 – helped by a BBC ban and not harmed by Gainsbourg's record company Philips dropping the single for "moral reasons" (it finally topped the charts on the Major Minor label). But it stalled at No.58 in the American charts (not, as is usually reported, No.69).

Thousands of British schoolboys became disillusioned when they bought Gainsbourg albums and realised they were a) in French, and b) not full of orgasmic groans.

His lyrics were driven by his break from Agnetha but he recognised, despite some talk that he might actually sing the song himself, that it would need all his former partner's vocal talents to carry it off. Agnetha loved the song, calling it "**a small masterpiece**", and claiming "singing it was like acting a part." It was a part she played beautifully; this is, by common consent, her finest performance.

Musically, The Winner Takes It All is simple ("There are only two different melody lines in it," Benny noted) but it develops a **pounding momentum** which accentuates Agnetha's litany of lost illusions ("building me a fence, building me a home"). The song was an instant No.1 in Europe although it didn't make the US Top 10. In many ways, this really was Abba's farewell – they split in 1981.

But they never really went away. Erasure reached No.1 with an EP of Abba covers in 1992. U2 made Dancing Queen a feature of their Zoo TV tour. **Mamma Mia: The Musical** has been a box-office hit (even in the United States), an Oz soundalike group called **Bjorn Again** seems to be perpetually touring the world, and an Abba routine is one of the highlights of the Australian comedy **Muriel's Wedding**. If the world seems fuller of Abba than ever, The Winner Takes It All may help explain why.

★The Winner Takes It All is still probably best enjoyed on Abba Gold.

The Best No. 2 Ever

Strawberry Fields Forever/Penny Lane – The Beatles

It is hard to overstate the shock that descended on the pop world in February 1967. The new **Beatles** single changed not only received wisdom of what they were about, but also the very nature of the pop music business. "No one I think is in my tree," sang John Lennon, and he was absolutely right.

Strawberry Fields Forever marked The Beatles' great change from live band to recording artists. It appeared (as a double A-side with **Penny Lane**) at precisely the time when people were whispering that the band might be finished, burnt out, gone to ground and in disarray. In fact, they were deep into experimental sessions with producer **George Martin**, piecing together the new album that was to become **Sgt Pepper's Lonely Hearts Club Band**.

Brian Epstein, worried that the band's image was slipping, brought forward a new single and packaged it audaciously to make a statement about The Beatles' new direction. Strawberry Fields was released with a picture sleeve (almost unheard of) and had a prototype music video, filmed at Knole Park in Kent and directed by **Peter Goldmann** using weird techniques such as backwards film and negative shots, with the moustachioed band in military tunics or candy-striped blazers.

But it was the music that shocked the most. "Quite honestly," said Derek Johnson in **NME**, "I don't really know what to make of it." With its combination of Mellotron, flutes, cellos and harpsichord, its bustling crescendo and crisp bass, the record became, he said, "more spellbinding with every play."

The familiar version is a composite of two separate takes, reflecting Lennon's desire to reach for perfection in new effects and editing/overdubbing techniques. Yet in its original form, released on the **Beatles Anthology**, a beautiful acoustic version encapsulates the spirit of the piece. And for the first time, the words take centre stage. "Living is easy with eyes closed, misunderstanding all you see," is as profound today as ever it was.

But a confused public stuttered in its response and, for the first time in four years, a Beatles single failed to make No.1, hitting the buffers behind Engelbert Humperdinck's Release Me. But rarely has a band reinvented itself so completely; **Strawberry Fields** is the sublime single that marks the Rubicon between two eras of pop history.

WIRED FOR SOUND
The technology, the formats,
the instruments, the fads

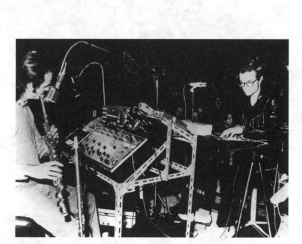

Kraftwerk get in the Moog with a synthesizer the size of a small telephone exchange

"It's quite untrue that the English people don't appreciate music. They may not understand it but they absolutely love the noise it makes"
Sir Thomas Beecham

Thomas Edison didn't create pop music, but he did create the means for pop music to exist. As he also assisted in the birth of movies, Edison can, more than anyone, be seen as the genius behind the development of mass entertainment. Yet Edison was not, noted his fellow scientist **Niko Tesla**, a great problem-solver. Tesla said that if Edison were asked to find a needle in a haystack, he would simply inspect each straw until he found one with a needle attached. Nor was he a great judge of music, telling one interviewer that **Mozart** was one of the least inventive composers who ever pored over a stave. Having done the hard bit (proving a human voice could be recorded), Edison sat on the phonograph for a decade. The German scientist **Emile Berliner** would supersede him with the **gramophone**, for which it was easier and cheaper to produce discs.

Pop music wouldn't be the same if the right technology hadn't fallen into the right hands. At the turn of the 20th century, recordings by an Italian tenor called **Enrico Caruso** (for the **Victor Talking Machine Company**) helped popularise recorded music. In the 1970s, albums like **Pink Floyd**'s **Dark Side Of The Moon** made some feel, if only briefly, that they needed a full-blown quadrophonic sound system to fully appreciate the music. At the same time, technology has changed pop, for the better. Would Satisfaction be as satisfying if **Keith Richards** hadn't discovered the Gibson Maestro **fuzz pedal**? And would **Frankie**'s pleasure dome have been quite so pleasurable without a **digital reverb** unit?

The purpose of this chapter is not to explore the mysteries of technology – in the studio or the home – but to point to where it has changed popular music for good or ill. To debate the various merits of mono, stereo, Digital Audio Tape, compact discs etc is, in the context of pop's development, to miss the point slightly. The one piece of technology which has done most to shape pop is the 7in vinyl **45 single** which has prospered because, as critic **Dave Marsh** put it, "it gave the consumers a single song and performance, with nothing they presumably didn't want."

In an age where vinyl is a cult object, and multinational 'entertainment'

And now for something
completely different...

Vegetable orchestras
The first **Viennese vegetable orchestra** isn't really pop but work with us. This unusual orchestra "consists exclusively of vegetable-based instruments" although "where necessary, knives or mixers are employed" and has played the Royal Festival Hall. The added bonus, for the audience, is that the instruments are made into a soup after the performance.

Cigar box guitars
Eight year old **James Marshall Hendrix** wanted so much to play the guitar he used a broom to strum out the rhythms in his head until he crafted a cigar box into his own guitar. He used rubber bands for strings. Other legends who played cigar box guitars include **Carl Perkins** and **George Benson**.

Prepared piano
John Cage, a massive influence on **David Sylvian**, invented a grand piano in which such items as bunches of keys and tin cans have been hung on the strings, so that all sorts of clangs and bangs accompany the usual sound. Cage also issued the most famous silent record (4 Minutes 33 Seconds).

conglomerates dominate the music industry **the single** seems increasingly out of fashion. But as the furore over MP3s and downloading music from the Internet shows, the appeal of a single song remains as strong as ever. The recording industry might do better to stop bleating about piracy and admit that its basic product is a song. Trying to persuade us we must buy songs in batches of ten or 12 is no more logical than a bookseller insisting we buy novels ten at a time.

There's also the matter of **price**. With new albums on CD costing anything up to £18, buying an album by a new artist represents a hefty financial gamble. In contrast, a single in 1972 cost 30p (£2.26 at today's prices).

Since Edison, new technology has often helped **widen our access** to music. At first we could only hear recorded music in our homes through the gramophone. Now we can hear it at home, on the move (through the Walkman or MP3, successors to the transistor radio), in our cars (cassettes, CDs or radio) or at work (on our computers). In other words, wherever, however and whenever we want.

The magic of mono
In the beginning there was **mono**, and mono was good. One of the main reasons mono was so good was that it had a monopoly. Its single speaker also made concerts by touring bands sound more powerful than they actually were. Mono may, today, seem like the Dark

THE TECHNOLOGY

Ages of pop music but the **microphone** and the Fender electric guitar were enhanced and invented in this era.

The arrival of the microphone in the 1920s changed the craft of popular singing. **Gary Giddins**, author of the biography *Bing Crosby: A Pocketful Of Dreams*, says: "The condenser mic allowed the intimate nuances of the baritone voice to be projected, you can sing in a normal tone, interpret the lyrics and, with the microphone, you get an erotic undercurrent in popular music that hadn't existed, outside of the blues and certain regional musics."

Bing Crosby (who cut his first record with a carbon mic in 1926) learnt from jazz singers like **Louis Armstrong** who, encouraged to practise rhythmic flexibility, virtually invented scat singing, a massive influence on rock. (Armstrong once said of his friend and rival that Bing had a voice. "like gold being poured out of a cup.")

The **Fender guitar**, the invention of a former radio repair man called Leo Fender, would enable guitarists to play louder than ever, without feedback or distortion. Fender made his first guitar in 1948, capping a decade which had seen **T-Bone Walker** use the electric guitar as a lead voice in his fast jump blues, **Merle Haggard** use his guitar as a kind of stringed pianoforte in country music, and **Les**

And now for something completely different...

Taps

Bryan Ferry decided that his retread of the standard When Somebody Thinks You're Wonderful just needed that little something extra so he called on American jazz and ballet dancer **Tobias Tak** to provide the taps which round off Ferry's cover on his As Time Goes By album.

Castrato

The process of whipping a boy's testicles off so their voice could soar a few octaves was outlawed in 1870 in Italy. So the only castrato whose voice is preserved on disc is **Alessandro Moreschi**, the last surviving castrato in the Pope's choir, who recorded for the Gramophone Typewriter Company in the 1900s. The Gibb brothers achieved a similar effect by wearing terribly tight trousers for Staying Alive.

Bullfrogs

A chorus of bullfrogs helped exotica legend **Martin Denny** to a No.4 US hit in 1959 with a cover of Les Baxter's classic Quiet Village. Is this where Macca got the idea?

1

TV, radio, stereo, drinks cupboard... a 1960s home entertainment 'system'

Paul launch his own solid-body electric guitar. The steady trickle of guitar boogie records soon swelled into a flood and, in 1950, Fender launched a new, better guitar. The foundations of **rock'n'roll** were being laid – it's hard to imagine rock without loud guitars – and popular music would change forever. As Frank Zappa later put it: "The guitar can be the single most blasphemous device on the face of the earth."

Stereo was discovered long before World War II, but came into its own in the 1950s as the pace of technological change quickened. In the standard version of rock'n'roll history, pioneers like Sam Phillips at Sun (and Ahmet Ertegun at Atlantic) receive most of the glory. They fully deserve their place in the record producers' hall of fame, but some of the pioneer work was done, less famously, by people like Les Paul and, crucially, **Patti Page**.

In 1948 Page released a record in which she sang four-part harmony with herself. She did this by persuading the engineer to record a vocal on four different acetates (the soft lacquered disc on which studios recorded songs) and play them back simultaneously to be recorded on a fifth. In 1950, she would do the same with a ballad called Tennessee Waltz. The distinctive sound was imitated by (among others) Les Paul, but Page's version sold six million copies. She only had a cameo part in the melodrama of pop, but the unusual feeling she achieved through such technical ingenuity would inspire vocalists like **Elvis Presley**.

The invention of **magnetic tape** as a recording medium made it easier for others to ape Page and allow producers like Phillips to create the 'slap-back' echo effect that made **Sun**'s records so distinctive. Phillips's mastery of the studio had financial benefits too. He could create a big sound with fewer musicians. Whenever **Elvis**, guitarist Scotty Moore and bass player Bill Black turned up for their first gigs, promoters who had heard their records invariably demanded to know where the rest of the band was.

Transistor radios were invented in 1954 (the first ones cost $49.95), although they wouldn't take off until the 1960s when they became essential for kids who wanted to listen to music when they were supposed to be asleep in bed. The transistor radio sounded tinny but then they weren't really invented to play music. The first manufacturer, **I.D.E.A Co.** of Indianapolis, thought Americans would need them to survive the aftermath of the forthcoming nuclear conflict with the **Soviet Union**.

If the new generation of rock singles seemed to jump out of the airwaves, that was no accident. Sam Phillips at Sun and Elvis's producers at RCA aimed for just that effect, as would **Phil Spector** and **Joe Meek**, the latter inventing his own sound compressor to give his No. 1 **Telstar** more oomph. The next step was real **multi-track**

Why 33⅓ and 45 rpm?

33⅓ was developed around the early sound movies. A 78 might hold a few minutes of sound, but a film reel lasted about ten or 11 minutes and the sound had to be synchronised by the projectionist.

In 1927, 33⅓ revolutions per minute was chosen, after a study to match signal-to-noise ratio with playing time, by **J P Maxfield** of Bell Laboratories, showed it was the best compromise. This soon became the industry standard, and Columbia engineers developed the LP simply by adjusting the dimensions of the groove to get good results on vinyl.

It comes as something of a shock to learn that the source of so much pop pleasure – the **45** – owes its existence to something that has caused so much suffering among the young – **calculus**.

The public wanted its favourite songs in single doses and it wanted them with good sound, so in **1948** RCA used calculus to discover the optimum way. This was found to be when the inner diameter of the recording was half that of the outer. RCA then developed the 7in 45rpm format, which entered into combat with Columbia's format for a while, specifically to get the best out of the music. The fact that 78 minus 33 equals 45 is just one of life's great coincidences.

Variations on the vinyl theme

45rpm 7in single

Lighter, more compact and better sounding than the fragile shellac 78 it replaced, this is still the classic pop format. When RCA introduced it in 1949 even the recommendation that shops stock two **Perry Como** singles didn't put people off. The first 45s were colour-coded: red for classical; midnight blue for light classical; green for country; yellow for children's; cerise for blues and sky blue for international. Black was for pop. Within three years, however, most singles were black. Vinyl is actually clear and, as **punk labels** would find in the 1970s, cleaning the tanks between pressings was time consuming and expensive.

33^1/3rpm 12in long player

The first longer-playing record was launched by RCA in 1932, but the pick-up heads of the day were so heavy they simply cut through the vinyl after a few plays. After years of research (including new playing equipment), Columbia relaunched the LP in 1948. A battle of the speeds ensued, with RCA trying in vain to persuade the public that four minutes was best for classical music (then the whole point of a long-player). Soundtracks to such musicals as **South Pacific** (still one of the bestselling LPs ever) helped to establish the LP, but as far as pop music was concerned it didn't come into its own until the late 1960s when bands like **Led Zeppelin** decided to concentrate on albums.

12in single

Anything longer than three or four minutes of music on a 45 invites technical problems, so the 12in single was developed by **disco** labels of the 1970s for DJs, allowing longer tracks, giving better sound quality and preventing needle-jumping.

EP

Largely a late-1950s/early-1960s phenomenon, Extended Play records saw four tracks crammed onto the 7in format. They looked great in their laminated picture sleeves, but their squeezed-up grooves could be a tad suspect. The format retains a certain style however, and artists as varied as New Wave bands and **Bryan Ferry** have paid homage to it.

16rpm, 8rpm

16rpm records were developed in the late 1950s for the spoken word, though some African and Eastern European countries used it for music too. In the 1970s there were even 8rpm 'talking books' in the US.

recording, pioneered by **The Beach Boys** on *Pet Sounds* and **The Beatles** on *Sgt Pepper's Lonely Hearts Club Band*. Good Vibrations, Brian Wilson would say later, was his "pop symphony". At the same time, the **fuzz pedal** and new **amplifiers** expanded the realm of the guitar. All of this could be heard with greater accuracy as mono was replaced by stereo, first on albums and then on singles. Stereo also favoured the new sounds, as many of the older mono pop classics were, at first, remastered by engineers with tin ears.

Ubiquitous and influential as *Sgt Pepper* was in 1967, there was a backlash. **Bob Dylan**, especially, would react by turning to a simpler, **rootsier sound**, remarking of The Beatles' most famous album: "It was self indulgent… though the songs on it were real good, I don't think all that production was necessary." This wasn't just sour grapes. As **Jim Miller** points out in his rock history *Flowers In The Dustbin*, such "toying with sounds and song forms at whim in expensive recording studios" was the prerogative of **white supergroups** like The Beatles and The Rolling Stones. Many **black artists** were still "stuck in an earlier mode of musical production", manufacturing the "sound of young America" to tight, production-line schedules. Although artists like **Marvin Gaye** and **Michael Jackson** would challenge these restrictions, black music was not much worse off for not treating the studio as a sixth-form common room. The 'liberation' of black musicians from the industrial approach would come with house, techno and hip hop. As Dave Marsh notes, more was at stake with the album as-art-form movement than recording technology: "Entire genres of pop – R&B, dance music and country – have never been oriented to anything but singles."

New adventures in hi-fi

But technology waits for no man, not even Bob Dylan. Two years before Dylan's lament, a young physics graduate by the name of **Robert Moog** had already showed off an electronic device called the **synthesizer**. Although its initial success lay in replacing the temperamental pre-recorded tapes of the Mellotron as a way to produce a more realistic imitation of a string section, its versatility – as popularised by **Kraftwerk** and Giorgio Moroder's disco hits – would enable groups like Japan and **Depeche Mode** to develop a sound that wasn't reliant on thrashing guitars. On albums like **Computer World** (1981), Kraftwerk would presage (and heavily influence) house music and techno. Mind you, in the early days, the instrument had an intriguing flaw – according to **Simon Napier-Bell**. In his racy memoir **Black Vinyl White Powder**, **Keith Emerson** told him that the first models would go out of tune if the surrounding temperature changed; a bit of a drawback if you were playing one in concert.

The mini-Moog enabled producers and bands to produce big sounds for little

The format wars

Vinyl's big drawbacks are surface noise (poor-quality pressings) and the ease with which it scratches, attracts fluff and warps near heat. The search for the perfect format has become the industry's holy grail.

Cassette

Introduced in 1963, the compact cassette – small, convenient, decent sound – had its heyday in the late 1970s/early 1980s. Malcolm McLaren even released **Bow Wow Wow**'s Your Cassette Pet only on tape in 1980. Bands and small labels could now sell their music easily, and in the early 1980s the music papers carried 'cassette culture' columns. But tape's propensity for getting chewed up in recorders meant it wasn't ideal either.

Eight-track cartridge

The Betamax to the cassette's VHS proved that size does matter. Great sound quality didn't help this clunky format which died with the 1970s. Aficionados and nostalgists should visit **www.8trackheaven.com**.

Compact disc

Early hype about indestructibility has been tempered by the fact that many do now stick, skip or cut in and out, especially if played on cheaper in-car systems or office computers. If you do have problems, you can find an impressive list of diagnoses at **http://entertainment.howstuffworks.com**. Compression means sound isn't as true as it might be, but there are 1.5 billion CD players in the world, so the CD is not about to die any time soon.

DAT, DCC

Briefly a contender in the mid-1980s, **Digital Audio Tape** is still used in some studios. Its commercial kin, the **Digital Compact Cassette**, is much smaller than a usual cassette and so far has had a much smaller appeal.

MiniDisc

For sheer portability and ease of recording, Sony's digital format seemed the natural successor to the cassette but has been superseded.

MP3

MPEG Audio Layer 3, to give it its full name, is a way of reducing the amount of data needed to reproduce sound without the listener noticing the difference. Although it does enable users to download music as files much more quickly, MP3 is not without imperfections (some claim the sound quality isn't great after repeated plays), but it is convenient and, crucially, a format in which a lot of good music is now available.

money, but technology didn't just change the sound, it changed traditional demarcations in the studio, enabling artists like David Bowie to take over **mixing** from sound engineers. On *Diamond Dogs*, Bowie wasn't just credited as singer and songwriter, he also took the credit for the mix, alongside producer Tony Visconti.

The 1970s gave consumers their first real choice of formats since the invention of vinyl. The handy, portable compact cassette was perfect for playing in cars – companies like Chrysler had toyed with record players in cars in the early 1950s but somehow the idea never caught on. The clunky **eight-track cartridge** –as oversized as the decade's flared trousers – was soon consigned to history, a fate which also befell **quadrophonic stereo** – you didn't really need four speakers to play punk – and other industry great white hopes such as Digital Audio Tape (DAT), although this is still used in studios.

The single fought back with such novelties as the flexidisc. You had to tape a coin to the player head to make sure the needle didn't jump out of the groove but this didn't stop **Bhutan** making a range of stamps in this format, while **Quaker Oats** launched one called Rising Stars Of Video Music in 1987 to sell bars of Granola Dipps. Other attempts to make the single more versatile include the shortlived maxi-single (an EP at 33rpm) and the gaudy, irrelevant yet glorious picture disc.

Hi-fi was celebrated by Cliff Richard in his 1981 No.4 hit **Wired For Sound**, in which the unforgettable video helped you overlook just how odd the lyrics were. "Stereo, out on the street you know" is rhymed with "Oh oh oh woh woh woh", and when he tells his girl that his music is dynamite she replies: "I am a girl who demands that her love is amplified, switch into overdrive." Quite.

let's get digital...

The Walkman wouldn't have existed without the cassette, but those little tapes never really threatened vinyl's supremacy. The **compact disc**, though, would wound vinyl, possibly fatally. Digital technology, we were promised in the 1980s, would be more accurate, clearer and more portable than scratch-prone vinyl – or mangle-prone tapes – had ever been. As **Giles Smith** put it in *Lost In Music*: "A pet is for life but a CD is for ever. You could heat them up, roll them into little tubes, stuff them with prawns, serve them as hors d'oeuvres at cocktail parties and they still sounded brilliant." Almost the only way you could damage one, according to a 1980s urban myth, was to draw a line across them with a green felt-tip pen. Why it had to be green was never explained, you were just supposed to know.

To fans reared on vinyl's more emphatic sound, the **compression** of sound used on early CDs could make them sound flat. They also proved far trickier to coax out of their box than vinyl records. Mercifully the words 'digitally remastered' no longer imply that the music has been converted from one

Unlock the jukebox

Pop and jukeboxes were made for each other. What better way to market a song than a machine that plays it each time you put a coin in the slot? It's the invention that the contemporary music industry, beset by digital anxieties, desperately needs to reinvent.

Trouble is, no digital downloading iPod could ever have the appeal of a real **jukebox**. Jukeboxes are about vinyl, and in particular the classic three-minute 45rpm disc. With their visible mechanisms, whirring cylinder moving to your selection – **P4: You Really Got Me** – and the thud of the needle landing heavily enough so it wouldn't jump from people dancing, jukeboxes were pure pop romance.

They also sounded great. There was a warmth about a vinyl jukebox, with its big central speaker, that was perfectly attuned to the horns and twangy guitars of 1960s R&B and pop. By the 1970s, with the rise of album bands and disco productions, the heyday of the jukebox was over.

That said, you can still find CD versions in the odd bar, if you can be bothered to scroll through all the unwanted album tracks. You can even buy a CD-playing replica of the most famous jukebox of all, the Wurlitzer 1015 – 'the bubbler', as it was known, from its lava-lamp side panels.

But if you really want a jukebox, it has to be a 45-vinyl machine, and that means buying one for yourself. Fortunately, that's not too hard. Jukeboxes are big, impractical things that don't fit neatly into front rooms, so although classic models are highly collectable, collectors are few and the entry level is pretty low. You could walk off (OK, you couldn't exactly walk) with a working-order 1970s 200-selection 'box' for around £250.

Not that you'd settle for such 1970s tat. If you have space for a jukebox, splash out on one of the prize items of the post-war years from AMI, Seeburg or Rock-Ola. With their revolving coloured lights and chrome deco features, these will look great, sound like a dream, and won't often go wrong if they have been decently reconditioned. Jukeboxes were built to sustain tough treatment.

The best port of call for researching purchases is the Internet. One of the best introductions is the Incomplete Jukebox (www.tomszone.com), which has Web links for machines, accessories and discs, while eBay (www.ebay.co.uk, www.ebay.com) always has jukeboxes for sale on both sides of the Atlantic. Jukebox sites in the US tend to have wider (and cheaper) selections, but you need to arrange specialist shipping. In the UK a reliable outlet is Jukebox Services (**www.jukeboxservices.co.uk**), who recondition classic boxes from the US, Africa and the Caribbean.

But be aware that jukeboxes are big, heavy bastards who like to live on ground floors – and they don't get along with flat conversions. You may avoid a lot of grief by settling for a diner wallbox, which connects to your own speakers and a clever box (about the size of a washing machine) that holds your 45s.

You should know, too, that owning a jukebox will drive you into a lifetime's obsessive pursuit of vinyl 45s. You will never again walk past a pile of discs in a charity shop, and you will find yourself making lists of songs that you will email late at night to New York's House Of Oldies (**www.houseofoldies.com**) to see if they might just have them in their million-plus stock that stretches below two blocks of Manhattan.

You have been warned.

Buy a jukebox – and you'll never walk past a pile of 45s in a charity shop again

format to another by a pasty-faced kid on work experience – but the second flaw has still to be rectified. As for the issues of squeezing the sleeve booklet past the tabs, or trying to read teeny-weeny type lyrics without an electron microscope, don't get us started. Despite grumbles from audiophiles, compact discs have swept all before them; if the single – the ultimate pop artefact – were a species, the World Wildlife Fund would have stuck it on the critically endangered list.

Some bands, notably Portishead on their album **Dummy**, deliberately created low-fi distortion to recreate vinyl's ambience, but digital technology was't all bad. The digital reverb unit (used by Trevor Horn to such effect with Frankie Goes To Hollywood), the sampler, the drum machine and the computer-based sequencer (without which Pete Waterman would still be a Midlands DJ) have made their mark. Even in this digital age, bad singers still sound, at best, marginally competent, no matter what Pete Waterman does.

But **digital technology**, combined with the awesome power of the **Internet**, has given 'home taping' (started by the cassette recorder) a new lease of life. We may not want to buy over-priced CD singles, but we're happy to download single tracks we like to compile our own 'albums'. The major labels have greeted this with an impressive combination of hysteria, inconsistency and genuine head scratching. You can shut down a site like **Napster** but you can't pretend that doing so solves the problem. The recording industry, once the most entrepreneurial of businesses reliant, with a genius for spotting talent in very unlikely places, seems to have lost faith in the open market. Surely, if we could buy any performance of any song at a decent price, we would own more music, not less? A few labels, notably **EMI**, have begun to face the inevitable, selling songs over the Web.

Slowly but surely, digital technology is **taking over our homes**. The technology itself is sophisticated, the sound is to die for, the flexibility of use simply incredible. The size of the all-singing, all-dancing, home-entertainment system – with its widescreen TV, DVD player, multiple speakers and possibly a computer – can seem pointlessly elephantine, especially when the size of the average new house is shrinking almost daily. But when today's kids are sent to bed, what is it that they turn on furtively under the sheets? A **MiniDisc** or **MP3** player.

Looking ahead, the only certainty is more change. Another quantum jump in sound quality seems unlikely, but as technology will throw up one splinter development after another, so expect more format wars between bewildering acronyms (SACD, DVD-Audio etc). More significantly, in a debate about MP3 on BBC Online, Bob Massey from Essex noted, "Within the next ten years **affordable hard drives** will be available which will be capable of storing every piece of music ever recorded. The sort of record collection which was once the domain of major record libraries will be within reach of everybody."

UNCHAINED MELODIES

A K-Tel-style compilation of stories and pop trivia

With one bound, Cat Stevens was free of Carly Simon and all her songs about Warren Beatty

> **"Because the lyrics of the recording Louie Louie could not be definitely determined in the laboratory examination, it was not possible to determine whether this recording is obscene"**
> *FBI field-office report to director J Edgar Hoover, 1962*

Pop music wouldn't be pop music without the urban legends, 'well-known facts' and heavily embellished anecdotes which form such an essential part of its mythology. This section is devoted to the exploration of a few of those legends, and to such endlessly debated topics as the song lyrics which most warrant the attention of the rhyming police, the musical ambitions of one **Charles Manson** esquire and what exactly **Spandau Ballet** were banging on about in their most famous ballad True when they sang so fervently of "seaside arms". All that and a quick look at the musical carnage wreaked by **Sgt Pepper** or, to be more precise, by all the Pepper 'me-too's. In other words, this is the literary equivalent of those 1970s compilations on labels like **K-Tel** with such energetic titles as **20 Power Hits!** or, to update the allusion, Now That's What I Call Pop Trivia 54!

★

The **FBI's pursuit of the 'obscene' Louie Louie**

Thanks to the upright moralists of America, an innocent lament of homesickness became one of the most notorious songs in pop history. **Louie Louie** was written in 1956 as a Caribbean calypso by **Richard Berry**, a little-known R&B singer in Los Angeles. After being given a rock'n'roll makeover, the song became popular at dances and was eventually recorded as a demo (for a cruise-ship entertainment roster) by an Oregon garage band called **The Kingsmen**. Released in 1963 as their debut single, it went nowhere (local rivals Paul Revere & The Raiders' version got there first). Yet six months later the song was getting column inches in every American newspaper and climbing to No.2 (and to No.26 in the UK).

Ironically the band had considered the muffled recording a failure (singer **Jack Ely** had had to yell Berry's pidgin English at a mic suspended near a 15ft ceiling) and didn't want it released. But, in a classic case of Chinese whispers, some fevered imaginations now interpreted lyrics such as "I tell her I'll never leave again" as "tell her I'll never lay her again", and concluded that the indecipherable vocals were designed to obscure obscenities. Letters from irate parents followed and in months the record was banned in Indiana by Governor **Matthew Welch**, his press secretary stating the words were, "indistinct but plain if you listen carefully".

The fuss didn't stop there. Much to the shock of The Kingsmen (a nice bunch of clean-cut boys, unlike the Raiders who really were suggestive), The National Association of Broadcasters, the US Department of Justice and the Federal Communications Committee (FCC) each undertook their own investigations. So while some **FBI** agents were investigating the disappearance of **civil rights activists** in Mississippi, others – under the federal law prohibiting Interstate Transportation of Obscene Material – were busy tracking down **Richard Berry** to find out just what he'd really meant by: "Three nights and days me sail the sea/Me think of girl constantly." The FBI's most dogged G-Men even slowed the 45rpm down to 33⅓rpm in case the obscene messages had been cleverly hidden.

After two years and a 120-page report, the FCC finally concluded that Louie Louie was in no way pornographic. The vocals were "unintelligible", they said, and the "dirty" lyrics supplied by several citizens were branded "**imagined filth**".

By the time The Kingsmen's version became a hit, singer Ely – who had actually taught the band the song, accidentally speeding up the riff in the process – had been the victim of a coup. Drummer **Lyn Easton** sneakily copyrighted the name of the band and lip-synched Ely's vocals in riotous concerts across the nation. Ely had to go to court to get him to stop. The Kingsmen's version is best found on the 1989 Rhino compilation *The Best Of The Kingsmen,* while the whole story of the song is neatly told on Ace Records' multi-version collection *Love That Louie.* Alternatively, **John Belushi**'s cheery, boozy rendering can be found on the soundtrack album to *National Lampoon's Animal House* – but remember: you'll only really enjoy it if you've drunk as much as Belushi's character Bluto in the film.

★

David Hasselhoff: King of German pop?

Among those who like to pretend that the Germans' taste in music is as stodgy as their national diet, the idea that David Hasselhoff reigns supreme over that nation's singles charts is virtually an accepted fact. Sadly, it's not quite true. Actually **Austria** was the first nation to embrace Hasselhoff the pop singer.

Not content with 148 countries watching him rescue damsels in *Baywatch*, Hasselhoff launched a singing career in 1989 with the aid of German producer and songwriter **Jack White**. While the American was making an easy transition, from TV star to pop idol, White – real name **Horst Nussbaum** – had started out as a footballer, playing (as an amateur) for Tennis Borussia Berlin, at one time a Bundesliga club. (Nussbaum would even serve as club president, from 1992 to 1995.) Nussbaum/White wrote eight of the songs on Hasselhoff's first album, *Looking For Freedom*, and the title track (cunningly coined to coincide with the end of the Cold War) became an anthem for the reunited Germans, topping the chart for eight weeks. That year he was the bestselling artist in Germany, and was even invited to perform **Looking For Freedom** atop the Berlin Wall.

Hasselhoff's follow-up releases weren't quite that successful, but he had enough fans to ensure they all made the Top 20, with the imaginatively titled Do The Limbo Dance spending ten weeks in the charts in 1991, thanks to lines like "Let's go to Jamaica/We can limbo on the sand/To the sealband…" Mind you, lest we forget, his single **If I Could Only Say Goodbye** reached No.35 in the UK in 1993.

★

The war between The Monkees and The Beatles

Although the irrepressible Monkees were manufactured by American TV to cash in on the success of The Beatles, John, Paul, George and Ringo never felt threatened enough to physically square up to them. But in the **Philippines** The Monkees regularly went to war with The Beatles.

Towards the end of the 1960s, with the war in Vietnam all too close at hand, a paramilitary group calling itself The Monkees carried out a number of assassinations and operations against Huk units (the armed wing of the Filipino Communist Party). The Huks, in turn, soon decided to score a propaganda victory by calling themselves The Beatles. In *Waltzing With A Dictator*, Raymond Bonner's classic account of the relationship between the US government and the Filipino dictator Ferdinand Marcos, he notes that The Monkees were essentially Marcos's version of the El Salvador death squads. Conflict between the groups became such a regular feature of Filipino society that, Eduardo Lachica notes in *HUK: Philippine Agrarian Society In Revolt*, "When children engage in their war games, one side inevitably calls itself The Monkees and the other The Beatles."

★

The pop music career of Charles Manson

You've probably heard the 'well-known fact' that Charles Manson unsuccessfully auditioned for The Monkees. It's a rumour that continues to endure, largely because of the extreme contrast between the prefabricated four's innocent larks and one of America's most notorious criminals, but it's simply not true: Manson was actually in prison at the time for parole violations (he already had 'previous'

for car theft and cheque forgery). The unsuccessful soon-to-be-celebrity was actually **Stephen Stills**, later of Buffalo Springfield and Crosby, Stills & Nash.

Manson, however, did harbour serious musical ambitions, and, after his release from jail in 1967, tried to become a singer/songwriter. He made a demo tape with **Terry Melcher**, Doris Day's son and the producer of the early **Byrds** albums. In his book *Neil And Me*, **Neil Young**'s father says Manson also pressed Young to record one of his songs. Young even recommended Manson to Warners for a recording contract and gave him a motorbike. Manson later attached himself to the Beach Boys' black-sheep drummer **Dennis Wilson**, and the song **Never Learn Not To Love** (credited to Wilson) on the Beach Boys' 1969 odds-and-ends album *20/20*, is a retread of a Manson song, **Cease To Exist**. For his pains, Dennis received death threats from Manson's followers.

While Manson was in jail for masterminding multiple murder (victims included Sharon Tate, the eight-months pregnant wife of Roman Polanski), a tape of his music was released on the Awareness label via fellow jailbird **Phil Kaufman** (later road manager for Emmylou Harris). The appearance of Manson followers outside his house was enough to ensure its swift transfer to the avant-garde ESP label, which folded in 1974. The album has been pirated since but is not worth seeking out for its musical value. Manson's music did finally achieve commercial success, but for all the wrong reasons: **Guns N' Roses** included one of his songs (Look At Your Game, Girl), unannounced, on their 1993 album *The Spaghetti Incident...* the kind of cheap notoriety which even **Malcolm McLaren** might have balked at.

★

The alternative Sgt Pepper albums

Sometimes records can be just too darn influential. And *Sgt Pepper's Lonely Hearts Club Band*, great as it was, became an open invitation to every other act to ignore all the rules – and many did... for good or ill. Spare a thought, though, for **The Beach Boys**, whose 1966 album, **Pet Sounds**, inspired The Beatles' famous opus. **Brian Wilson** was keen to top *Revolver* and it's hard to imagine *Sgt Pepper* without Wilson, who, in his desire to expand rock'n'roll's sonic universe, captured bicycle bells, barking dogs and the clatter of Coca-Cola cans. The other, often overlooked, irony about *Sgt Pepper* is that although Lennon is supposed to be the far-out, creative Beatle, the album is mostly Macca's work. Producer **George Martin** recalls Lennon protesting, as the sounds got more ambitious, "I don't do this – I'm just a teddy boy." *Sgt Pepper* also inspired a dreadful movie of the same name 'starring' the Bee Gees. Mind you, **Henry Edwards** had insisted on three conditions before he wrote the script: it couldn't be set in England (or in the 60s) and couldn't feature The Beatles.

The Hollies Evolution and Butterfly (1967)

Despite The Hollies proclaiming, "We're about as psychedelic as a pint o' beer wi' the lads," the shirts worn on the cover of Evolution were a pretty obvious hint that they felt it was no longer enough to sing about umbrellas, bus stops and carousels. It wasn't quite the Great Step Forward they were hoping for, despite some nifty arrangements by **Mike Vickers** (of Manfred Mann), possibly because the vocal on Lullaby To Tim, **Allan Clarke**'s ode to his son, was given a warbly underwater effect. Still, **Kenny Everett** liked it. Four months later, they went one better with *Butterfly*, the track Maker displaying the band's prowess with the sitar and trippy lyrics ("Days of yellow saffron lighting purple skies"). The public weren't convinced, but then the Hollies don't sound that certain either.

The Rolling Stones Their Satanic Majesties Request (1967)

At the very least, the Stones' attempt at delving into psychedelica is fascinating. On its release, Beatles fans dismissed it as a '*Sgt Pepper* me-too', while Stones purists thought they should stick to the blues. Letting **Bill Wyman** sing on 2000 **Light Years From Home** was probably a mistake, leading many to overlook the fact that, for a band who would become leading members of the rock geritocracy, they took some incredible risks. The memorably named **Brian Jonestown Massacre** would release their homage (**Their Satanic Majesties Second Request**) in 1996, garnering better reviews than any Stones album of the 1990s.

Nilsson Pandemonium Shadow Show (1967)

Clever, offbeat pop writing (often with a dark side), some weird effects and Nilsson's version of She's Leaving Home are some of the nods to the Fab Four on this versatile, playful album which the Beatles (especially Lennon) loved.

Cream Disraeli Gears (1967)

In their short life, Cream – Eric Clapton, Ginger Baker and Jack Bruce – helped to create a new musical genre. Having established themselves as credible blues men with a neat line in pop (I Feel Free), the trio released the psychedelic *Disraeli Gears*. Tracks like Strange Brew and SWLABR (She Was Like A Bearded Rainbow) featured weird lyrics by ex-beat poet Pete Brown, while Clapton helped to pioneer the extended guitar solo.

The Jimi Hendrix Experience Are You Experienced (1967)

Hendrix had backed Little Richard and the Isley Brothers but the Tutti Frutti man didn't like the loudness of his shirts and fired him. Chas Chandler, ex-bass player of **The Animals**, then spotted Jimi in New York and brought him to London. This debut album excludes (as was the fashion) the hit singles Purple Haze and The Wind Cried Mary, but tracks like **Red House** and **Third Stone From The Sun** are a reminder that Jimi was more expressive playing his guitar than setting fire to it.

The Small Faces Ogden's Nut Gone Flake (1968)

After the druggy overtones on Itchycoo Park, the ex-Mods went into overdrive. Packaged (to resemble a tin of tobacco) in a circular sleeve that required kid-glove handling, Mensa membership and the patience of Job to unfold, the album's more ambitious second half is linked by comedian Stanley Unwin, who burbles on in his own lingo about Happiness Stan and his quest for the other half of the moon.

Frank Zappa & The Mothers Of Invention
We're Only In It For The Money (1968)

Sgt Pepper re-imagined as a nightmare, complete with a spoof cover which replaced such beloved icons as Marilyn Monroe and Fred Astaire with Lee Harvey Oswald and Rasputin. The Fab Four were reportedly not amused.

★

The greatest 'mondegreens' in pop

If you heard Macy Gray wail "**I wear goggles when you are not here**" in **I Try**, you weren't the only one. Pop lyrics are commonly misinterpreted. 'Mondegreen' is the word for such events, coined in 1954 by writer **Sylvia Wright** who, for years, believed a line in the Scottish traditional ballad **The Bonnie Earl Of Moray** was "**They had slain the Earl of Moray/And Lady Mondegreen**". The actual words left the Earl alone in his plight ("**And laid him on the green**"). Here is a compilation of some of pop's more amusing mondegreens, not including **Steve Miller**'s Abracadabra – you don't have to be a literary critic to note that the magic of her sighs sounds a lot like magic of her thighs, and the magical sensation of touching her dress might be taken to sound as if he were touching her breast.

Mulligan's tyre/Mull Of Kintyre
Wings Mull Of Kintyre
Hold me closer Tony Danza/Hold me closer tiny dancer
Elton John Tiny Dancer
Gonna use my sausage/Gonna use my sidestep
The Pretenders Brass in Pocket
Edith was troubled by a horrible ass/Egypt was troubled by the horrible asp
REM Man On The Moon

Christians are a burden/Questions are a burden
Iron Maiden Back In The Village
She's a paper towel/She's a Femme Fatale
Duran Duran Femme Fatale
And there's a wino down the road /And as we wind on down the road
Led Zeppelin Stairway To Heaven
Doughnuts make my brown eyes blue/Don't it make my brown eyes blue
Crystal Gayle Don't It Make My Brown Eyes Blue
In a west end town in Denmark/In a west end down a dead end world
Pet Shop Boys West End Girls

★

They haven't stopped dancing yet...

Dancing is the one part of the pop performance where artists can't cheat. Fancy studio techniques and industry svengalis can't disguise the fact that, no matter what the song says, all God's children ain't got rhythm.

Bryan Ferry
He may be the prince of lounge-lizard pop and the king of cool but a dancing queen Bryan Ferry isn't. Despite being as chilled as an Inuit village in December, Ferry jerks in an arrhythmic style that *Q* magazine once called "endearingly white".

Rick Astley
He emerged from the same intricately choreographed camp as Bananarama and Mel & Kim, but he made Jason Donovan look like John Travolta. Maybe it was his suits or the fact that he looked like a bank manager. Maybe it was both. But Rick was easily one of the worst dancers of the 1980s, some accomplishment when you consider the frightening dance moves both on and off screen in that era.

Andy McCluskey
While one could only admire his wholehearted commitment and apparently endless stamina, the way McCluskey swung his arms and flung his legs about (sometimes bending 90 degrees at the waist when he got particularly carried away) suggested he really ought to have performed all such manoeuvres in the dark.

Sting
Despite Sting's incessant public boasting that, thanks to a strict regime of yoga and tantric sex, he is one of the fittest and most supple fifty-something men

Leo feels like dancing, we feel like wincing

around, on stage he has not learned any moves more complex than bobbing up and down on his heels, a limitation he tries to obscure by taking his shirt off.

Robert Palmer

Perhaps it was the bevy of stone-faced beauties behind him, but you couldn't help notice how ill at ease Robert Palmer looked in the Addicted To Love video. Yet he was only doing the classic parents' dance, stepping from one side to another.

Leo Sayer

He invariably felt like dancing. But then, disguised as a clown when he first rose to fame, he always seemed to feel like moving his hands in a manner which suggested not so much a nervous twitch as a psychotic tic. But he does a great macarena.

★

Offences in the name of rhyme

There's a simple reason why you don't hear many pop songs about oranges. Rhyming isn't a pop prerequisite, but a fair few songsters seem to have stuck with the skills they had aged ten, baring their souls in rhyming verses which chime, say, lazy and crazy and hazy. They're not all this easy – witness the Bonnie Raitt song which rhymes amoeba and sheba. Oasis are disqualified from this selection because, on **Supersonic**, their successive rhyming of Elsa/alka seltzer, doctor/helicopter and laugh/autograph proves that the Gallagher brothers were just trying too hard. That logic, alas, disqualifies Frank Sidebottom's **Estudiantes** with its immaculate combination of brother/mother/aunties/Estudiantes/black panties. If anyone tells you that real songwriters – ones with names like Cole Porter and Ira Gershwin – never rhyme that badly, point them to Gershwin's **Embraceable You** where the master chimes, "encore if I love" and "glorify my love". A rhyme topped only by **Boney M**'s sublime chiming of "love machine" and "Rasputin".

Billy Mac is a detective down in Texas
And though he knows just exactly
what the facts is
He ain't gonna let those two
escape justice
He makes his livin' off of other
people's taxes
Steve Miller Band
Take The Money And Run

Look at you – you're a pageant
You're everything – that I've imagined
Split Enz I Got You

Princes stand in queues they
stand accused
Death in solitude like Howard
Hughes
The Teardrop Explodes Reward

When I met you in the restaurant
You could tell I was no debutante
Blondie Dreaming

Would you find that a risk to
your health?
Would you put me up on the bookshelf?
Adam Ant Desperate But Not Serious

I know what democracy is and I know
what's fascist!
I know what's good and I know what
trash is
ABC Many Happy Returns

I like to singy singy singy
Like a bird on a wingy wingy wingy
Madonna Impressive Instant

This is my time, this is my tear
I can see clearly now
That this is not a place
For playing solitaire
Red Hot Chili Peppers Tear

Baby, you know I ain't no Queen of Sheba
…You know we ain't no amoeba
Bonnie Raitt Thing Called Love

So Bermuda Triangle
Try to see it from my angle
Barry Manilow Bermuda Triangle

And the people that I met, oh were all
…Covered in treacle
UFO Treacle People

Every day a little sadder
A little madder

Someone get me a ladder
Emerson, Lake & Palmer
Still… You Turn Me On

What's it like to be a loon
I liken it to a balloon
Marc Bolan Cosmic Dancer

She used to be a diplomat
But now she's down the laundromat
Spandau Ballet Highly Strung

I couldn't live without my phone
But you don't even have a home
Mel C If That Were Me

I would rather wear a barrel
Than conservative apparel
Spice Girls My Strongest Suit

Promises me
We're as safe as houses
As long as I remember
Who's wearing the trousers
Depeche Mode
Never Let Me Down Again

I don't wanna see a ghost
It's the sight I fear the most
I'd rather have a piece of toast
Des'ree Life

I'm as serious as cancer
When I say rhythm is a dancer
Snap! The Power

I'm gonna write a classic
Gonna write it in an attic
Adrian Gurvitz Classic

It means nothing to me: puzzling song lyrics

Most of the time we accept whatever singers are prattling as if we also drop lines like "Tuna, rubber, little blubber in my igloo" (**Tori Amos** in **Maryann**) into our everyday conversation all the time. Spandau Ballet's **True** is even more mysterious because we know exactly what's going on until, in the third verse, Tony Hadley suddenly croons: "Take your seaside arms and write the next line." This seems to spring out of a (frankly overused) metaphor about the sands of time running out, but it may just be the effect of too many nights spent with a pill on the tongue and Marvin on the stereo. Mind you, even such old hands as **Leiber & Stoller** can mystify. **Pearl's A Singer** is a great song, but why exactly does she stand up when she plays the piano? You wouldn't want to work in her nightclub. Such puzzles make you pine for the strangely articulate **Get A Job** by the **Silhouettes** in which the 1950s harmony group utter 61 inarticulate noises before you get to a proper word. As your dad would no doubt say, they don't write them like that any more…

Furry mussels marching on, she thinks
she's Kaiser Wilheim
…Or a civilised syllabub to blow
your mind
Tori Amos Mr Zebra

I got my head checked
By a jumbo jet
Blur Song 2

Her name was Pauline
She lived in a tree
The Sex Pistols Pretty Vacant

Don't want to go in public
My head is full of chopstick I don't like it
Duran Duran (I'm Looking For)
Cracks In The Pavement

Clowns in my coffee
There are clowns in my coffee
Janet Jackson Nasty

I know I know for sure
A ling dang bong dang ding a bong
dung day
Red Hot Chili Peppers
Around The World

Red dogs under illegal legs
Elvis Costello
Watching The Detectives

Solar Prestige a Gammon
Elton John
Solar Prestige a Gammon

We ran along walking across the rooftops
in my chair
Status Quo In My Chair

Some kinds of love are mistaken for
fishing poles
Velvet Underground
Some Kinda Of Love

Guilty pleasures

Dean Friedman, Elkie Brooks, Barry Manilow; these aren't exactly seminal figures in pop music. Yet that doesn't mean that they haven't made a decent record. So, no post-modern irony intended, here is a list of 'good' records by 'baaad' artists.

Barry Manilow II

Unlike that other housewives' favourite (Sir Cliff), Bazza has never taken himself too seriously. And he has a real, if shlocky, feel for the unlucky in love and life. The best-known track here is Mandy which, in its soppy way, is as authentic an expression of adolescent romantic angst as **Janis Ian**'s At Seventeen.

Vinegar Joe

Elkie Brooks's vocals on this album will come as something of a shock to those who know her from her screeching performance of Nights In White Satin. But Elkie started out as someone seen as the British Janis Joplin. United with **Robert Palmer** in the short-lived Vinegar Joe, she earned rave reviews and almost no sales; the exact opposite of her fate as a solo singer. Still, her version of Lilac Wine is a genuine, against your will, hair standing up on the back of your neck experience

once you've drunk a few bottles of wine, lilac or otherwise.

Dean Friedman

Debut album by thick-haired, thin-voiced New Jersey songwriter which is far better than the later soppy stuff ("Lydia, Lydia, how come you understand me?"; "I may not be all that bright/But I know how to hold you tight") might lead you to expect. Ariel, the best track here, is a well-made, literate pop song.

Very Best Of Matt Monro

Don Black, who co-wrote Born Free for Monro, reckoned the crooner must have had three lungs. Perhaps because of his slightly formal phrasing, Monro didn't really benefit from the lounge revival, even though he is probably the only British singer who could have held his own in the Rat Pack. His **Very Best Of** (on Music For Pleasure), while too long, is still an essential purchase.

Suzi Quatro

The first riot 'girrrrl', her self-titled first album features the innuendo-laden Can The Can (no, we haven't figured out what sexual practice it refers to either) and an All Shook Up cover which Elvis approved of.

The princess of wails: Elkie Brooks in her Vinegar Joe days

Who's so vain? The endless debate...

Pop is full of songs written about other people. Indeed, statisticians have recently calculated that 19.7 per cent of **Joan Baez**'s songs from the late 1960s onwards are about **Bob Dylan**. Bob himself wrote a song called Went To See A Gypsy which tells the story of a possibly apocryphal trip to Vegas to see the King ("He smiled when he saw me coming and said, 'Well, well, well'"). But few songs have been as debated as **Carly Simon**'s You're So Vain. Trying to fit the lyrics to a particular person is like sharing a piece of very juicy gossip, made all the more satisfying because we can delude ourselves that our curiosity is purely musical.

To recap, the runners and riders in the You're So Vain chase are:
Mick Jagger "A lot of people think it's about Mick Jagger and that I fooled him into singing on it," Carly noted once. The hat, scarf and the womanising all sound like the man Truman Capote declared, "moves like a cross between a majorette girl and Fred Astaire." But Mick happened to just drop into the studio; **Harry Nilsson** was originally on backing vocals but let Jagger take over. And, in 1983, Carly flatly denied to the *Washington Post* it was about the Stones' front man.

James Taylor Carly had just married James when, in January 1973, the song began to dominate the airwaves. Carly told *Rolling Stone* magazine: "It's definitely not about James, although James suspected it might be because he's so vain. He had the unfortunate experience of taking a jet up to Nova Scotia."

Kris Kristofferson Another of Carly's squeezes (shocking, isn't it?), Kris was the favourite in a listeners' poll run by a Los Angeles DJ. But heck, what do they know?

Cat Stevens There's a great photograph of Carly and Cat sitting on a pavement, looking as if they're taking a break from busking. Cat may have written **Sweet Scarlet** about Carly, and she may have written **Anticipation** and **Legend In Your Own Time** about Cat. But Stevens isn't famed for his vanity, owning racehorses that win at Saratoga, or flying Lear jets.

Warren Beatty The popular choice. Asked outright by the *Washington Post*, Simon admitted, "It certainly sounds like it was about Warren Beatty." The great lover did ring her and thank her for the song. And she was quoted in *The Book Of Lists* as saying: "There's nothing in the lyric that isn't true about Warren Beatty."

EPHEMERA
Welcome to the wonderful world of pop paraphernalia

 Nancy Sinatra, ephemeral disposable pop icon, but the boots she walked in are worth £500

> "Best of! Most of!
> Satiate the need
> Slip them into different sleeves!
> Buy both, and feel deceived"
> *Paint A Vulgar Picture, The Smiths*

You've bought all the records by your favourite group or artist. You've even nailed down all the alternate versions of every track they ever made and, with your friends, you've thoroughly analysed their relative merits – "The Halifax Romeo & Juliet nightclub live version of **Save Your Kisses For Me** has so much more feeling than the Eurovision studio cut, don't you think?" You've dredged the bootleg pool dry – your prize possession being the one where **Peter Noone** and **Elvis** discuss the Los Angeles Police Department and the rain (featured on a real rare bootleg).

The only thing left is to start collecting memorabilia. This can start innocently (posters, magazines, a few books, a rare concert ticket), but soon you'll be wondering how much to bid for that **Neil Diamond soap-on-a-rope microphone** (a trade promo item for **The Jazz Singer**), whether a cheque signed by **Ringo Starr** is worth £1,000 (probably more than the cheque was made out for), or how you'll tell your partner you've raided the holiday fund to buy one of the 18 microphones **Roger Daltrey** broke during The Who's New York stopover in 1967.

The temptation (and the justification) is to say that you should keep everything. Which is fine as far as it goes, but if you're hoping your collection will become a nest egg, you're probably best not banking on a sudden revival of interest in, say, **Brian & Michael**. You can never tell what's going to happen in pop, but the odds on a renaissance of interest in a duo famous for making a nation hate the matchstick paintings of **L S Lowry** are slim indeed.

There is such a wealth of merchandise available that this chapter can never really be more than a starting point. So view it as a springboard for diving into a world full of rare recordings (such as **Joan Collins**'s version of Imagine or Elvis's rare third Sun single), reference books to peruse when you have finished with this one, the **crazee world of Noddy Holder**, the **paintings of Donna Summer**, the special **Boy George-style Snoopy** and the websites where you can cybermeet the likes of Peter Noone, Supergrass and Bow Wow Wow.

Quick Guide To Collecting

To save you time, space and an ear-bashing from your partner, we spoke to Helen Bailey, a specialist in the Popular Entertainment Department of Christie's in London, for a few tips to point you in the right direction.

1. Always buy from **reputable** auction houses and dealers, particularly if serious money is involved. Otherwise you're in danger of buying Joe Bloggs's eternity ring rather than **Elvis**'s.

2. Learning the **provenance** of items adds value both in terms of meaning and money. Best case scenario: it was given directly by the star to be sold.

3. **Posters** Hold on to posters rather than programmes or tickets. Posters are made to hang on walls, and few survive in good enough nick to be sold.

4. **Autographs** Higher prices are paid for signatures on merchandise – tour programmes, records and posters – than on unrelated pieces of paper. You could spend thousands (although Beethoven and Mozart still fetch better prices than any of the Beatles), yet you could also, for example, buy an authenticated Elvis autograph for £500.

5. **Clothing** That cerise angora cardigan may have been worn by **Nancy Sinatra**, but it's not as collectable as the kinky boots she wore on the Boots cover. Stage clothing – or items where there is documentary proof of ownership – fetch far higher prices.

6. **Instruments** The same rules as clothing apply. If it was used on stage or on an album, it's worth more. The 1956 Fender Stratocaster used by **Eric Clapton** on the Layla album fetched a record $497,500 at a recent auction.

7. In terms of pop eras, artists from the 1950s to the 1970s fetch the highest premiums. **The Beatles** remain top sellers but look out for anything relating to **The Rolling Stones**, **Jimi Hendrix**, **The Doors**, **Elvis**, **Eric Clapton**, **Bob Dylan** and **Buddy Holly**. Do keep an eye out for genuine oddities: **Sugar Ray Robinson**'s 1950s Hot Soup EP could be worth $100.

8. Predicting who will still fascinate the public in 20 years is tough, but stars such as **Michael Jackson** and **Madonna** are pretty good bets. The latter's pink corset worn on the Blonde Ambition tour sold for £12,650.

9. If your interest lies in groups from the 1960s and 1970s who are still going, look out primarily for vintage material featuring **original line-ups**.

10. Above all, buy items you like; you'll get far more pleasure when you find your favourite **Phil Collins** drumsticks are worth a bob or two.

★Records★

Thanks to the World Wide Web, record collecting is more popular than ever. Having transcended the notion that record collector equals anorak, everyone is a potential buyer, and knowledge is easy to acquire from books (we recommend *Collecting Vinyl* by John Stanley), fairs and the Internet. Records' enduring charm is that they hold both a practical and aesthetic appeal. Many collectors focus on tunes that affected or changed their lives. Others hunt for an artist or musical era, or become novelty junkies, hunting for rare recordings, limited editions or items with a story behind them. If you did own the only acetate of a recording by The Quarrymen, John Lennon's pre-Beatles skiffle group, you would have a record worth £100,000. The lists below are designed to suggest what people will buy and what they'll pay for it.

78rpm single
Used until the emergence of the less fragile 45. Despite their age, few 78s are worth collecting, the exception being jazz and rock'n'roll numbers from the 1950s and early 1960s. Often, 78s are worth less than the same singles on 45.
Watch out for:
1. **Frankie Avalon** Why £50
2. **Cliff Richard** Living Doll £100
3. **Gene Autry** Back In The Saddle Again £80
4. **The Seven Dwarfs** The Seven Dwarfs' Washing Song £14
5. **Elvis Presley** That's Alright Mama £4,000

★

45rpm single
Introduced in the UK in the early 1950s, the 45 had all but extinguished the 78 by 1961. The earlier the better is the best way to view the market. Elvis's **Milkcow Blues Boogie** was his third Sun single: it sold fewer copies than the others and is thus rare and prized. The Black Dyke Mills Band's Thingumybob didn't even chart – its value is due to its rarity and its label, The Beatles' Apple Records.
Watch out for:
1. **Blondie** X Offender/In The Sun £750
2. **Elvis Presley** Milkcow Blues Boogie £3,225
3. **Julie Andrews**
   Super-cali-fragil-istic-expi-ali-docious £16.50
4. **Bill Haley & His Comets** Birth Of The Boogie £40
5. **Black Dyke Mills Band** Thingumybob £75

12in single

A product of the 1970s (they were made to give DJs better reproduction quality), they came into their own in the 1980s with the emergence of dance music, which has done most to keep the format alive. It's one of the more recent formats and was vastly over-hyped, so don't buy expecting to make a quick, massive profit.

Watch out for:

1. **Wonderland Disco Band** Wonder Woman Disco £8.50
2. **Monie Love** Don't Funk Wid The Mo £9
3. **Nirvana** Smells Like Teen Spirit £28
4. **Iggy Pop** Iggy Pop Sampler £18
5. **Donna Summer** Breakaway £25

★

EP

Short for Extended Play. These were first used in the 1950s to add extra tracks to 7in hits, and – unlike the singles of the day – had picture sleeves. After almost dying out in the album-oriented hippie era, the format was revived by punk bands and independent labels and artists in the 1970s, and is a favourite with collectors.

Watch out for:

1. **Dickie Pride** Sheik Of Shake £200
2. **The Drifters** Greatest Hits £40
3. **Duran Duran** Careless Memories £1.50
4. **The Clash** Capital Radio £40
5. **The Who** My Generation Live At Wembley £15

★

12in album

Value is placed on early editions, picture discs and limited-edition sleeves. Even something as odd as a misplaced label (in the case of The Beatles' Apple Records) can add more than £100 to an LP's value. And before you rush out to celebrate your riches because you own a copy of The Beatles' *Revolver*, make sure it's a UK stereo release – with a yellow-and-black label. The devil is in the detail.

Watch out for:

1. **Dion** Presenting Dion & The Belmonts £275
2. **The Beatles** Revolver £135
3. **Joy Division** Still £30
4. **Dean Friedman** "Well, Well", Said The Rocking Chair £15
5. **Robert Plant** Manic Nirvana White £20

★Top Of The Pops Albums★

Long before the *Now* albums, **Top Of The Pops** dominated album sales with its unique brand of hit compilations. These albums had nothing at all to do with the powerful TV show – the title was simply 'borrowed' by budget label Pickwick Records when they found the BBC hadn't registered the name. Nor were the original artists involved: the label simply employed session musicians to do cover versions, providing a cheap way to own the hits of the day as long as you weren't too bothered about who sang them. The brainchild of producer **Alan Crawford**, the series churned out one of these albums every six weeks from 1967 to 1979.

In 1970 a regular team of session players was enlisted. Thus singer **Tony Rivers** (of The Castaways and later Harmony Grass) was used to impersonate everyone from Mud to The Sex Pistols, while Donny Osmond, Freddie Mercury and The Stylistics were all really **John Perry**. The use of the same singer time and again had its obvious drawbacks and the team only had up to four days to record each album, so you get some idea of the standard involved. With none of the real artists singing, producers also faced the problem of who or what to put on the cover. The result? One 'fashionable' girl after another, all bearing the same fixed, pearly-white grin.

The series came to an end in 1979 when original-artist compilations took over. Your local charity shop probably has a few copies, now no doubt even cheaper than their original cover price of £1, but the only ones with any value at all are those very few cherished by, say, connoisseurs of Merseybeat who simply must have everything ever recorded by future members of **Liverpool Express**.

★Pop Art★

When, in 1968, **The Beatles** chose a plain white cover with only their name embossed at a crooked angle for their latest release, they hadn't considered it as art. Dubbed *The White Album* by fans, the clean design and the stark cover reflected the album's overall reversion to a simpler approach.

It wasn't the first time a Beatles album had made an impact with its cover design. For *Sgt Pepper's Lonely Hearts Club Band*, artist **Peter Blake** was commissioned to surround the 'Fab Four' with their heroes and influences, and the design included, controversially, a garden of marijuana plants. But the sleeve (the first gatefold) caused a fair old furore. When **Sir Joseph Lockwood**, head of EMI, heard the design cost £1,500, he groaned: "Fifteen-hundred pounds? I could hire the London Symphony Orchestra for that!" Two years on, a Detroit radio caller began the myth that the *Abbey Road* cover represented a funeral procession for Paul. The sleeve contained, he believed, clues to the 'fact' that Paul had died three years earlier (he has bare feet, for example) and been replaced by a look-a-like.

The Beatles weren't the only stars with ideas about art. The cover of **Velvet Underground**'s 1966 debut, *The Velvet Underground & Nico,* featured a sticker which peeled off to reveal a flesh-coloured banana (see right). Production problems with Andy Warhol's design put its release back almost a year. (The first version, with peel-off banana and band photo framed by a male body, is worth £200.)

Hippie albums used everything from the drawings of Swiss artist **H R Giger** (on Emerson, Lake & Palmer's **Brain Salad Surgery**) to nightmarish medieval paintings

by **Hieronymus Bosch**. The Rolling Stones' *Sticky Fingers* was another by **Andy Warhol** (original copies of the crotch shot featured a working zip), and Patti Smith used an unknown **Robert Mapplethorpe** (later famous for his gay S&M and black male nudes) for *Horses.*

Some album covers are cherished for their design, others for the 'meaning' behind the images, and some are famous for the stories behind the making. Below are a few of the most notorious.

Nevermind **Nirvana** (1991)
The main image was suggested by Kurt Cobain and Dave Grohl after seeing a documentary on underwater births. The dollar bill on a fishhook was Cobain's idea, creating one of the most widely recognised album covers of recent years.

Cheap Thrills **Big Brother & The Holding Company** (1968)
Controversial cartoonist Robert Crumb agreed to do the artwork for *Cheap Thrills* on condition that, "when I meet Janis [Joplin], I want to be able to pinch her tit." She agreed, leaving Crumb to create a series of panels, each representing a different song.

Garden In The City **Melanie** (1972)
The first scratch-and-sniff 'scented' sleeve to stink out its owner's collection. The idea was parodied by Stiff Records in 1978: the sleeve of their compilation of artists from industrial Akron, Ohio, smelled of burning rubber tyres.

Electric Ladyland **Jimi Hendrix Experience** (1968)
The UK cover featured 18 nude women (many shops refused to stock it) while the US version used a psychedelic graphic. It was done without Hendrix's knowledge (his 'presence' is a superimposed photograph) and he didn't approve.

But is it an album cover?

These plucky pioneers weren't content to stick to the usual square, one-dimensional, album sleeve.

The Velvet Underground & Nico, Peel Slowly And See, Verve, 1967 The gatefold sleeve had a banana sticker on it, with the words "peel slowly and see" next to it and an arrow pointing to it. When peeled, a pink fleshy fruit was revealed. Lou Reed called this "an erotic art show".

Dan Hicks, Striking It Rich, Blue Thumb, 1972 The maverick Hicks struck on the bright idea of making his sleeve resemble a book of matches.

Cheech And Chong, Sleeping Beauty, Warners, 1976 The 1970s vogue for funky covers peaked with this 'sleeve', shaped like a giant pill. Presumably, it was too hard to create a cover which looked like an ounce of pot.

Public Image, Metal Box, Virgin, 1979 John Lydon's band had considered sealing this album in a sardine can but played safe, encasing it in the kind of metal box used to protect film reels. The cost? A mere £1.10p an album.

Unfinished Music, No.1: Two Virgins John Lennon and Yoko Ono (1968)
A shot of a naked John and Yoko outraged many and perplexed even more. EMI boss Sir Joseph Lockwood told Lennon: "You should have put Paul on the front – his body would look better naked than you."

★Memorabilia★

Talk of money may offend those who collect pop memorabilia out of devotion. But as crass as it may sound, you can put a price on your Monkees commemorative talking hand puppet from 1967 (£95) or your Cliff Richard *We Don't Talk Anymore* album (£2). Clearly, not everything to do with pop is worth keeping, but some items are so unusual they should never be left on the shelf. Here are just a few of the most valuable and the most unusual collectables out there.

Autographs

Steven Spielberg once quipped that he had to stop giving autographs because he was devaluing his own name. Today's pop stars should take note. Fortunately for the market for the original pop collectable, stars haven't always been so prolific. Below are a few of the best places on the Web to find those John Hancocks.

Autographs For Sale http://store.yahoo.com/autographsforsale/
Head to the music section for signatures of past and present rockers, from Elvis and Don Henley to Madonna and Destiny's Child.

Memorabilia UK www.memorabilia-uk.co.uk/links.html
Offers more than simple 7in x 5in shots. It has signed albums, instruments and discs from artists from the 1950s through to the present day.

Odyssey Publications www.autographs.com
The listings are slim but when we visited, this site was offering a get-well card from Janis Joplin for $1,300, while $1,100 would get you a drumhead signed by Ringo Starr. If this is too steep, for $25 you could get a signed photo of Bo Diddley.

Top Star Signs http://dspace.dial.pipex.com/town/plaza/df01/tss/erol.html
Nothing to do with astrology but authentic signed photographs: £12 will get you signed photos of Bruce Springsteen, Britney and Bono among others.

Moving from the general to the specific, here are five examples of what's out there:
1. Chubby Checker $25
A bargain considering how well known his name is 40 years after the Twist craze.
2. Elton John $95
This may seem a little steep judging by the number of cheques he signs so freely.
3. Hear'say $142
We've only included this ludicrously priced item as an example of how it's worth holding on to autographs by even the most transient of acts.
4. Frank Zappa $349
This signed CD cover is described on the website as 'super scarce' and is bound to increase in value now that the man himself has left the building.
5. Buddy Holly $3,500
An all-time great and, as with Zappa, there are no more where that came from.

★

Going, going, gone
Six pop collectables to suit every budget:
1. A lock of Elvis's hair £82,150
Sold for this amazing sum to an anonymous buyer at an Internet auction.
2. One village hall stage (as used by The Beatles) £50,000
The stage from St Peter's Church Hall in Wootton, where John Lennon first met Paul McCartney, is more cumbersome than most items of pop memorabilia.
3. Madonna's bra £14,100

The black, satin, conical bra worn by Madonna on her famous Blonde Ambition tour, went for even more than her pink corset.

4. Prince's Purple Rain guitar £12,000
The instrument on which Prince strummed "Purple rain, purple rain" was sold for this modest sum to the comedian Ed Byrne.

5. Ronan Keating's boxer shorts £1,610
Mother of three Justina Berman extended her overdraft to make sure she snapped up Keating's underwear at auction. Well, they were Yves Saint Laurent boxers.

6. The Best Of Marcel Marceau album £16
Nineteen minutes of silence on the Gone-If label. Priceless really.

★

Posters

Posters are very collectable but need to be in mint condition if you want to sell them on. Encore Rock'N'Roll Nostalgia (*www116.pair.com/encore/*) and E Rock (*www.erock.net/alphadex.html*) are both good places to pick up posters.

1. Andy Warhol design for **Velvet Underground** at the Fillmore Auditorium, San Francisco (1966), £960

2. Bob Marley & The Wailers at the Santa Cruz Civic Auditorium (1979), £340

3. The Clash 16 Tons tour poster (1979), £46

4. The Beatles Black Light Peace poster (1967/68), £23

5. Bob Dylan Don't Look Back poster (1970), £125

★

Clothing

Clothing worn by the artists themselves commands the top prices. Rock'N'Roll Goodies (*www.rocknrollgoodies.com*) has a host of star garments to choose from.

1. George Harrison's navy blue blouson jacket worn on the cover of **Somewhere In England** (1981), estimated £3,500

2. Guns N' Roses bomber jacket given to them by Geffen Records (worn), £250

3. Ozzy Osbourne's black, velvet, military style coat worn in 1976, estimated £700

4. The Who's long-sleeved hessian gown from the film **Tommy**, estimated £600

5. Drape jacket worn by members of **Sigue Sigue Sputnik** in 1985, £40

★

Instruments

Most musicians harbour a deep-seated affection for their instruments, so if you must have the Fender Telecaster owned by Jimmy Page, best try an auction house such as Christie's, or specialist websites such as Rock Buys (*www.rockbuys.com*).

1. Kurt Cobain Fender Stratocaster guitar used at the London Astoria in 1989. Smashed up on stage and therefore in partial state, estimated £1,500
2. Lenny Kravitz signed, white Galveston Stratocaster, £2,600
3. Pete Townshend candy-apple red Kramer Focus guitar, £650
4. Chad Smith (Red Hot Chili Peppers) drumsticks, £48
5. Bob Dylan silver Pocket Pal Hohner harmonica, estimated £800

★

Miscellaneous novelties

Hold on to those Elton John fridge magnets – you never know what will prove valuable. Here are a few of the more unusual items we found on the Net.
1. Rare Snoopy in **Boy George** hat and dreadlocks (1985), £56
2. An original artwork by the 'Queen of Disco', **Donna Summer**, £1,300
3. Michael Jackson sleeping bag, £145
4. Tina Turner *Break Every Rule* stand-up cut-out, £60
5. Grateful Dead afghan throw, £40
6. Abba Fernando mirror featuring Fernando picture sleeve, £250
7. The Monkees 1967 talking hand puppet, £95
8. Beach Boys Hot Rockin 'Woody' model car, £23
9. Donny Osmond guitar pick from 1989 tour, $30
10.Dolly Parton *Dollywood* two-seater buckboard wagon, $2,820

★Books★

This is one of the most saturated areas of memorabilia; we've edited the reams of teen-star biographies and left you with a small selection of the better reads.

General

Who sang what, when it was released, chart positions – that kind of thing.
This Is Uncool: The 500 Greatest Singles Since Punk And Disco
Garry Mulholland *Cassell Illustrated*
You may not agree with all his selections, but Mulholland's reasoning behind even the most controversial inclusions makes for interesting, informative reading.
The Great Rock Discography Martin C Strong *Canongate Books Ltd*
Very useful (though far from error-proof) discography, with artist profiles, track listings, release dates, and UK/US chart placings for singles and albums.
The Billboard Book Of Number One Albums Craig Rosen *Billboard Books*
The inside track on how some of the most influential albums of all time came

about, with enough good behind-the-scenes photos to
keep even casual fans interested.

The All-Time Top 1000 Albums Colin Larkin *Virgin*
A useful guide to some of the best albums, with track
listings and fascinating facts. We love how critics aren't
allowed to be fans or experts!

**The Encyclopedia Of Record Producers Eric Olsen,
Paul Verna & Carlo Wolff** *Billboard Books*

A pretty face doth not a singer make, and managing to
make a tone-deaf singer sound good is truly an art in
itself. The producers profiled here include twiddlers as
diverse as George Martin, Phil Ramone and Dr Dre.

**The Rolling Stone Index: Twenty-Five Years of Popular Culture, 1967-1991
Jeffrey N Gatten** *Popular Culture*
Not bang up-to-date (the years 1992-1996 are also now available) and one of the
pricier reference books, but *Rolling Stone* titles are usually on the money. This is the
most comprehensive with thousands of reviews, features and profiles.

**In Cold Sweat: Interviews With Really Scary Musicians
Thomas Wictor** *Limelight Editions*
Unabridged chats with Gene Simmons (Kiss), Peter Hook (New Order), Jerry
Casale (Devo) and Scott Thunes (Frank Zappa): none afraid to speak their mind.

Rock & Roll's Most Wanted Stuart Shea *Brassey's UK*
Irreverent trivia and assorted weird facts.

The Virgin Illustrated Encyclopaedia Of Rock Colin Larkin *Virgin Books*
Concise, knowledgeable but reassuringly low-brow overviews of artists who have
affected pop and rock'n'roll with their music or infamous behaviour (or both).

Guinness World Records: British Hit Singles David Roberts *Guinness Records*
Needs no introduction from us. An essential work of reference for pop fans.

Critical works

Too many trees have died in vain in the rush to publish books about pop. Academic
tomes by the likes of Simon Frith can often be intriguing but they can also make
a fun subject seem desert-dry. For starters, we'd recommend **Mystery Train** by **Greil
Marcus**, **Revolt Into Style** by **George Melly** (if you can find a copy) and the
splendid **Awopbopaloobop Alopbamboom** by **Nik Cohn**, and then…

The Sound Of The City Charlie Gillett *Souvenir Press*
Still the definitive account of the rise of rock.

Flowers In The Dustbin James Miller *Simon & Schuster*
Gillett's only real rival, strong on the 1960s and 1970s and the cultural context.

Country Nick Tosches *DaCapo Press*
Not for those who are starry-eyed about country singers: a series of opinionated, brutally frank profiles of country greats.
Deep Blues Robert Palmer *Penguin*
Engrossing history of America's most influential musical genre.
Crosstown Traffic: Jimi Hendrix And Post War Pop Charles Shaar Murray *Faber*
Read it and you'll end up spending a fortune on CDs.
Sweet Soul Music Peter Guralnick *Mojo Books*
The inside story of southern soul amidst the dream of freedom.
England's Dreaming Jon Savage *St Martin's Press*
The greatest book on punk, more entertaining than some punk bands.
Psychotic Reactions And Carburetor Dung Lester Bangs *Serpent's Tail*
As funny, quirky and unpredictable as the title; essential rock criticism.
American Roots Music Brown, George-Warren & Santelli *Harry N Abrams, Inc*
A great book about the great American musics.
Where Do You Go My Lovely? Fred Dellar *Star Books*
Fantastic profiles of forgotten 1960s stars; worth seeking in second-hand shops.

Pop fiction

The great pop music novel has not yet been written, but there are already a few contenders. The accomplished **Don DeLillo** had a go in his early novel *Great Jones Street*, though as soon as you learn the star is called Bucky Wunderlick it's hard to carry on. Arguably the best pop novel is **I Am Still The Greatest Says Johnny Angelo** by Nik Cohn, sadly out of print. Cohn has the nerve and insight – some of the novel was inspired by interviews with P J Proby – to carry it off. Michael Thelwell's **The Harder They Come**, the novel that inspired the classic reggae film, has real literary merit. Alan Arlt's **The Carpet Frogs** is a brilliant tale of one star's ambition to make the greatest album ever. Iain Banks' **Espedair Street** starts well (with the star explaining why he won't kill himself) but the band is called Frozen Gold – straight out of Eurovision! Kevin Sampson's **Powder** has its fans, but others found it "toxically boring". Christopher Sorrentino's **Sound On Sound** is insightful and, get this, it's structured as a multi-layered recording session. **Salman Rushdie**'s *The Ground Beneath Her Feet* is marred by daft groupie scenes but it did get him a gig with **U2**. Part of the problem with most of pop fiction is that novelists simply daren't be as strange as the truth, as a flick through Simon Napier-Bell's **Black Vinyl, White Powder** will show.

Artist biographies

We no longer really need biographies to find out about our heroes. The 15 biographies below offer real insight. The *Mojo Heroes* series and **Rough Guides** to Elvis and the Beatles are also worth seeking out.

Take It Like A Man Boy George *Pan*

The sex, the drugs and the music from Britain's most famous David Bowie fan. An entertaining read even if you weren't a child of the glorious 1980s.

A Riot Of Our Own Johnny Green *Orion*

Few people were as close to The Clash as their erstwhile tour manager Johnny Green. Some of his tales are on the hazy side (a few too many drugs perhaps) but it remains informative stuff. Worth it for the wild cartoons of Ray Lowry alone.

The Complete David Bowie Nicholas Pegg *Reynolds & Hearn*

For once 'complete' isn't an exaggeration: a comprehensive analysis of his songs title by title (even The Laughing Gnome), his acting career, his tours and his life.

Lennon Remembers John Lennon & Jann S Wenner *Verso Books*

Lennon shatters the myths behind the band (and creates a few more), including reasons for their split: "We were fed up of being sidemen for Paul."

Faithfull David Dolton & Marianne Faithfull *Penguin Books*

Mick Jagger, Bob Dylan, Mars bars, heroin and rock'n'roll. You won't find many more interesting reads than the life of a pop-princess-cum rock-chick.

Who's Crazee Now? Noddy Holder *Ebury Press*

A comparatively light and amusing read for a pop star biography, bringing new depth to one of the most successful glam rock acts of the 1970s.

Madonna: An Intimate Biography J Randy Taraborrelli *Pan*

One of the better biogs of Madge, possibly because Taraborrelli has actually met her. Highlights include Prince plastering (as in building) Madonna's wall.

Divided Soul: The Life Of Marvin Gaye David Ritz *Omnibus Press*

It's all here, from the revelation that, as a teenager, Mr Let's Get It On was obsessed by his brother's bigger endowment (he used to steal Freddie's underpants in a futile attempt to prevent him from going out) to insights into his troubled marriage to an older woman – Motown boss Berry Gordy's sister, Anna.

The Legendary Joe Meek John Repsch *Cherry Red Books*

Definitive biography of one of the most enigmatic figures in British pop.

The Cheese Chronicles Tommy Womack *Dowling Press*

The true, funny story of what it's like to be in a struggling American rock band.

Dino Nick Tosches *Minerva*

This has the best-ever subtitle for a pop biography: 'Living High In The Dirty Business Of Dreams'. Essential to really understand Dino and the Rat Pack.

Poison Heart: Surviving The Ramones Dee Dee Ramone *Omnibus Press*
You want sex and drugs and rock'n'roll? Here's where to find it. A gripping – and at times very scary – frontline account by a man who wouldn't survive much longer.
Praying To The Aliens Gary Numan *Andre Deutsch Ltd*
Typically blunt – and highly readable – autobiography of an unlikely pop star. The episode where his plane's engine cuts out over the Pacific is a real page-turner.
Stoned Andrew Loog Oldham *Vintage*
The ex-Stones manager tells all; more fun than his protégés have been recently. The sequel, *2 Stoned*, features Oldham and mates talking about 50s and 60s pop.
You Don't Have To Say You Love Me Simon Napier-Bell *Ebury Press*
Hilarious behind-the-scenes anecdotes from the pop impresario who's seen it all, from writing hits in a taxi to being rescued by Keith Moon in a Moroccan brothel.

★Where To Buy★

Auction houses

They may not be the coolest places to shop, but auction houses are great places to find rare or personalised rock and pop items. Head to the entertainment sections for info; otherwise their experts are usually on hand to help with enquiries.

Bonhams www.bonhams.com
Regular items to be found include instruments, stage clothing, rare recordings, autographs and posters.
Christie's www.christies.com
This is the auction house that sold Eric Clapton's 1956 Fender Stratocaster for $497,500. Not all items are this extravagant, with an array of autographs and recordings from such stars as Madonna, Buddy Holly and The Sex Pistols.
Sotheby's www.sothebys.com
In conjunction with eBay.com, Sotheby's now offers online auctions. When we visited, bids were being taken for a black-and-white photo of Muhammad Ali standing over The Beatles, a snip at $862.

The Internet

Record collecting no longer need involve spending every weekend at car-boot sales and record fairs, ploughing through random boxes of vinyl in search of that rare single which has a B-side not on any album. Nowadays you can browse and buy from the comfort of your own record-laden living room. Here are some top sites, but you'd be surprised what a general query on a search engine can turn up as well.

All Vinyl www.all-vinyl.com

Download this US-based catalogue of 30,000 titles or browse it online. Both sleeves and records are graded for condition, the selection is huge and there's a money-back guarantee.

Intoxica www.demon.co.uk/intoxica

Based at a London shop, this site specialises in rare albums and 7in singles, with a very varied catalogue from surf to soul to psychedelia. Buy, sell or exchange.

Music Stack www.musicstack.com

Worldwide site for buying and selling LPs, 45s, 78s, 7in, 10in and 12in vinyl. You can search by artist, song or format, or post your own want list for others to read.

Simply Vinyl www.simplyvinyl.com

Stylish UK site selling everything from The Beach Boys to Snoop Doggy Dog to lovers of vinyl. Old originals or modern issues.

Sweet Memories www.sweetmemories.mcmail.com

Easy-to-use, search-based UK site, with a database organised by format or artist. Useful 'just in' list too. Looking for Elvis's *40 Greatest* on pink vinyl? A snip at £15. Even better, a 1960s single by Acid Gallery (Roy Wood and Jeff Lynne) for £100.

★

General memorabilia

Most of these sites are rock-oriented rather than pop, but keep searching and you can find all manner of treasures, whether you're after a Police key ring, a Donny Osmond doll or a Bobby Darin vinyl LP.

Cooper Owen www.cooperowen.com

Cooper Owen auctions all sorts of valuables (vintage fountain pen, anybody?) but its Rock Legends sales are held three times a year to sell items – often from personal collections – such as Jimi Hendrix personal effects and artwork.

Music Lovers Auction www.musicloversauction.com

Easy-to-use general music store site, with memorabilia to be found among instruments and tickets. Interesting items on offer when we visited included a Lynyrd Skynyrd-autographed $100 Confederate bill for $200, and a limited-edition Elvis Are You Lonesome Tonight? certified platinum disc for $250.

Peace Rock www.peacerock.com

Specialises in original posters from the 1960s and 1970s (including music-related protest ones), but also sells some modern ones from artists as diverse as Jefferson Airplane, B B King and Tori Amos.

Push Posters www.pushposters.com

Despite the name, Push also sells T-shirts, calendars and poster flags of both contemporary pop stars and major rock acts. Serious collectors should head for the signed screenprints section.

Recollections www.recollections.co.uk

Artists range from AC/DC and Howard Jones to Frank Zappa, with a diverse selection of items – from ticket stubs to magazine covers, from hand drawings of Pete Townshend in concert (£35) to a Pink Floyd tour programme from 1967 (£200). Search by artist or item.

Rockmine www.rockmine.music.co.uk

Very rock-oriented but head to the Rock Shop for tour programmes, posters, books, magazines and promotional items, plus the odd more personal piece. How about a 1969 Isle Of Wight Festival programme for £500, or a one-off Jimi Hendrix doll, a bargain at £185? There's an entertaining (if rather limited) rock trivia section too.

Sounds Travel www.soundstravel.demon.co.uk

The perfect site for those who believe vinyl will never die. Sells LPs and singles by artists from every era and genre, along with memorabilia, books and more.

Visionary Memorabilia www.visionaryrock.com

Offers everything from autographs to 45s to drumsticks, involving artists of both the past (Jim Morrison, Carole King) and present (*NSYNC, Michael Jackson).

★Websites★

In cyberspace, pop music is almost as important as movies. Shedloads of websites are dedicated to particular stars or the music industry in general. Of the three-and-a-half million or so sites dedicated to pop music alone, we've included a few of the best.

General

All Music Guide www.allmusic.com

One of the best Web-based music resources, this has well-informed artist profiles and discographies, plus useful links to related artists and genres.

Bob Shannon's Behind The Hits www.bobshannon.com

A well-organised site packed with fascinating inside stories about pop classics, eg who the real Mr Tambourine Man was, plus links to artists' sites from Lesley 'It's My Party' Gore to Norman Greenbaum (be sure to play his Racing Goat game).

Classic Bands www.classicbands.com

Specialises in artists' biographies but has a sideline in pop trivia and chart facts.

Click Music www.clickmusic.co.uk

The latest news, reviews and gigs, plus games, competitions and a channel for free music videos and downloads. Links to lyrics and guitar tabs for songs too.

Dotmusic www.dotmusic.com

Magazine-style site with up-to-the-minute news and features on a whole range of music – from rock and pop through indie, dance and hip hop to folk and jazz. Plus fan forums, free no-commercials radio and licensed (ie paid-for) downloads.

everyHit www.everyhit.com

Database of chart hits and No.1s since the 1950s, with statistics galore. Most siblings in one group? Teenyboppers The Jets (they had a hit with Crush On You in 1987), comprising eight of the highly fertile Wolfgramm's 17 children.

Nostalgia Central www.nostalgiacentral.com

Pop culture by decade, with brief but informative summaries of music.

Oldies Music Calendar www.oldiesmusic.com/cal.htm

Dates from 'this week in rock'n'roll history', plus trivia, chat room, charts etc.

The Rocking Vicar www.rockingvicar.com

Highlights of the cult spoof parish newsletter, featuring irreverent thoughts and assorted foolishness (such as imagined football results between record labels) from parishioners (ie subscribers), including the disgruntled winner of a signed copy of John Lennon's *Plastic Ono Band* album – signed by Tony Blackburn.

Rolling Stone www.rollingstone.com

A livelier, more up-to-the-minute version of the magazine. This is one of the most

comprehensive music resources online, with videos, movie trailers and animation in addition to news, features and artist profiles, plus reviews with – hey! – feedback from readers.

Songfacts www.songfacts.com

Did you know Bob Dylan wrote the Manfred Mann hit The Mighty Quinn after seeing Anthony Quinn play an Eskimo in *The Savage Innocents*? Head to Song Facts for more such fascinating trivia, in a searchable database.

Super Seventies www.superseventies.com

If you were there, this isn't so much a trip down memory lane as a trip down an eight-lane

Norman's spirit's on the Web

freeway. If you weren't there, you'll feel like you were after perusing this site, which is full of reviews, trivia and stories about the music of the era.

Who Does That Song www.whodoesthatsong.com

Searchable database that can match hit song with artist and year. It's limited, however. Select The Twelfth Of Never, for example, and you'll get Cher, Johnny Mathis and Donny Osmond, but no mention of Cliff Richard or Elvis Presley.

★

Artists' websites

Perhaps the hallmark of real stardom is when your fans build a website in your honour. If you're Abba, these sites proliferate like a virus. Here's a quick sample of some recommended sites for pop acts over the last five decades.

★★ 1950s ★★

Bobby Darin www.geocities.com/thecurtainfalls/thecurtainfalls/index.htm
Curiously for a man whose life was dogged by medical problems, Darin died after a trip to the dentist. This memorial includes everything you need to know about the underrated singer (his is the essential version of Mack The Knife) and actor.

Elvis Presley
http://host.elvisnumberones.com
With hundreds of sites to choose from, The Virtual Elvis is a welcome bit of light relief. Kit him out to match your favourite era and hear him sing. If it's Elvis news and gossip you want, then head to the best fan-club site on the Net: Elvis Information Network (**www.elvis.com.au**).

Pat Boone
www.theonionavclub.com/ avclub3830/avfeature_3830.html
The second most popular artist of the 1950s (after Elvis), Boone epitomised squeaky-clean squaredom. Find out how he risked alienating his Christian fans by embracing heavy metal in 1997.

Vera Lynn www.theiceberg.com/artist.html?artist_id=1117
Includes biography, discography and other essential Vera-ness.

★★ 1960s ★★

The Animals www.animals.mcmail.com
Standard official site (biography, merchandise, news etc) enlivened by links to

Eric Burdon's and Hilton Valentine's personal homepages. Valentine conducts his own memorabilia auctions (for backstage passes, T-shirts etc) via eBay.

Del Shannon www.d21c.com/Spacebeagle/delshannon.html
Simple, succinct biog of the tragic singer/guitarist, with discography.

Led Zeppelin www.buckeye-web.com/ledzeppelintrivia.html
Nearly ten years in the making, this site offers list upon studious list of Zeppelin trivia. Representative sample: Roy Harper's song Evening Star was written for Robert Plant's daughter Carmen on the occasion of her wedding to Charlie Jones.

Peter Noone www.peternoone.com
This site is a work of genius. In contrast to most official sites, it's very, very funny with Noone mocking his old photos ("the illegitimate son of Mick Jagger") and offering much autobiographical hilarity. What other pop star would tell tales of setting fire to cornfields age six and then being forced by his grandmother to punch his best friend on the nose for snitching on him to the cops? Apart from the usual merchandise, this site also offers a chance to chat with Herman and links to other vintage pop stars' sites. Guaranteed to send Noone soaring in your estimation.

★★ 1970*s* ★★

ABBA www.abbasite.com
The band's official site is one of the most informative and easy to navigate. If it's cyber karaoke you want, head for **www.users.globalnet.co.uk/~wingnut/**.

The Bay City Rollers www.baycityrollers.de
A German fan site (with the homepage carrying a large warning about poor quality bootlegs when we visited) offering discography, news (Nobby Clark is making a comeback with Pilot's Dave Paton!), videos and a song (by new member Duncan Faure) of "hope, freedom and supporting the troops that will touch your heart."

The Sex Pistols www.sex-pistols.net
Fan site carrying news, reviews, movie clips and features (eg producer Mike Thorne interviewed, and a transcript of the notorious TV appearance that cost Bill "say something outrageous" Grundy his career), plus links to the individual members' sites (including one which asks whether Sid was a villain or a victim).

X-Ray Spex www.terrapin.co.uk/xrayspex
Representing the more thinking side of UK punk with a site which includes peace meal recipes (Hare Krishna vegetarian, naturally) alongside lyrics, audio clips and the usual news (last updated September 1997!) and biographies.

★★ 1980*s* ★★

Adam & The Ants www.geocities.com/antliberationfront/
"Official website of the most co-operative Antpeoples' organisation in existence!"

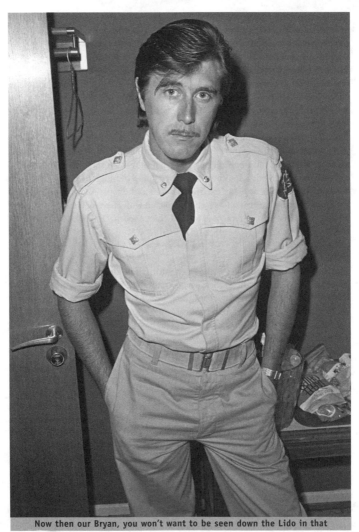

Now then our Bryan, you won't want to be seen down the Lido in that

Fashion! Turn to the left!

Sartorially, the pop charts have got a lot to answer for. No one's teenage years would be complete without adopting some accessory – or even entire outfit – that was deemed in by the in-crowd. A quick look back through the old photo albums provides a salient reminder of the true horrors.

The Beatles' early appearances spawned a rash of dodgy haircuts. The mop-top seems tame now, but back in 1963 just having a man's hair touch his ears was enough to induce apoplectic rage in a generation reared on National Service haircuts. In the 1970s, music appreciation demanded total devotion. Mercifully, not many blokes could afford to follow Bryan Ferry's white tuxedo phase. But after **Ray Stevens** hit No.1 in 1974 with a song about an American college fad called The Streak, naked folk were suddenly everywhere, at sports events, festivals and parks. The following year people were covering up again – this time with anything as long as it was tartan. **The Bay City Rollers** sparked a craze for tartan-trimmed flares and shirts that were unfeasibly tight. Parents despaired, but would look back on all that with great fondness a year later when punk rock arrived, causing all items of clothing to disappear beneath rips and safety pins.

By the time the 1980s got going, pop music and fashion were inextricably linked. New Romantic music demanded make-up, frilly shirts and dramatic hairstyles (a fad which **A Flock Of Seagulls** took to extremes). **Madonna** persuaded us to adopt fingerless gloves; then **Michael Jackson** suggested we only wear one glove, which at least saved wear and tear. **Bros** sparked one of the weirdest crazes by attaching Grolsch bottle tops to their shoes, but the **The Beastie Boys** were not far behind when they made stolen VW car badges a must-have accessory. Meanwhile a gladioli-waving **Morrissey** made the mosh pit at some concerts look like the Chelsea Flower Show.

In the 1990s decisions had to be made. Did you just wear plaid shirts, never wash your hair and go for the Seattle grunge look? Turn your clothes back to front like child-rappers **Kriss Kross**? Or glam up with a feather boa and check out a **Manic Street Preachers** gig? It was tough staying ahead of the crowd – and some things never change. **Gareth Gates**' spikey hair-do caused sales of hair gel to rocket for the first time since the 1950s, while **Craig David**'s collection of woolly hats is helping a lot of fashionable folk avoid bad hair days. You never know what might come next – although we wouldn't bet on the return of **Bryan Ferry**'s gaucho look.

It's understandably coy about Adam's recent troubles, but this site – and his dedicated fans – are still behind him. Ant Lib Online is packed full of stuff.

Aerosmith www.geocities.com/SunsetStrip/3364/

Box Of Fire may not have the most sophisticated design but it does have all the essentials: biography, discography, sound/video clips, guitar tabs for musicians and tour info. Best of all for dedicated fans, it has a bootleg information section.

Bow Wow Wow http://thorin.adnc.com/~pwb/

"The ultimate links" claims this fan site, and it's not kidding. Apart from a few blurry photos, a biography and some facts, it consists almost entirely of links (frustratingly, many no longer work), ranging from a mad fundamentalist's list of dead rock stars ("the years of the wicked shall be shortened") to media downloads.

The Name www.thename.tv

This obscure British band may have only lasted from 1979 to 1981 but the strong sense of community among Mods (lots of good links here) keeps fans logging in.

★★ 1990s ★★

Dee-Lite www.geocities.com/the_grooveweb

A rather bare site for such a visual, funky band. It offers the usual biography, discography, lyrics, photos and links to similar fan sites, but there are also audio files for all songs, including the timeless Groove Is In The Heart.

New Kids On The Block http://members.lycos.co.uk/Tracey/nkotbuk.html

A well-organised and up-to-date UK fan site with some impressive content.

The Stones Roses www.thestoneroses.co.uk

Clean and clearly organised (if rather impersonal), this site offers the usual staples plus merchandise (mugs, T-shirts, mousemats etc), a link to auction site eBay for items for sale, and a link to sister site **www.ianbrownonline.com**.

Supergrass http://supergrass.densitron.net/mainmenu.htm

What a difference a sense of humour makes. This imaginative, award-winning yet engagingly self-deprecating site (run by the band) is hugely entertaining as well as informative. Apart from the usual news/tour dates/biog basics, its features include a tour diary and games (eg be their tour manager trying to round up his crew against the clock in an Alpine bierkeller… without punching the locals).

★ Music videos ★

Learned scholars could spend months debating which was the first music video. Was it **Elvis Presley** dancing to the *Jailhouse Rock* (1957)? How about **The Beatles'** *Yellow Submarine* (1968), a full-length animated movie that was a great way to repackage songs and oddments for a new album? Or *Tommy* (1975), **The Who**'s rock opera – an assault on the senses if watched all the way through, but in five-minute song-bites entertaining enough to make you buy the double CD?

But when Buggles talked about video killing the radio star in 1979, they weren't referring to two-hour movies. Their beef was with those one-song clips that brought music onto our televisions. In the 1970s, music videos were purely a promotional tool. A band that was too busy to appear on some godforsaken German pop show could stand in front of a camera, mime their song and send the tape off, rather than turn up in person. But as video technology became more advanced, so did the pop video, and record companies realised that if you made a flashy video that *Top Of The Pops* wanted to play, it certainly wouldn't hurt the band's chances of getting to No.1.

Among those quick to realise the advantage of spending time in front of the camera were **Bryan Ferry** (his strange video of A Hard Rain's Gonna Fall, in which he appears side on with white theatrical make-up at the piano, still seems ahead of its time), **Queen** (whose Bohemian Rhapsody is still often included in 100 Best Music Video lists almost three decades after its release) and **David Bowie** (whose love of art and dressing up, not necessarily in that order, shines through in **Ashes To Ashes**). Likewise **Olivia Newton-John** gave herself an image change, and a huge hit, via the video for Physical, while former punk rockers **Adam & The Ants** influenced fashion with their dandy highwaymen outfits in the Stand And Deliver video.

As the 1980s dawned, directors realised there was art to be made too. And that art got its own channel in 1981 when MTV (music television) launched in the US (the British channel followed six years later) to broadcast 24 hours of rock and pop videos every day. New artists like Culture Club, Cyndi Lauper, Duran Duran and a young Italian-American gal named **Madonna Ciccone** soon realised that their efforts would stand out if their videos did. Video soon became as important as the song itself, as **Duran Duran** guitarist John Taylor recalls: "Video was a great tool and had a real impact in America. We couldn't understand why, in every interview we'd do, people talked about the videos. With songs like Hungry Like The Wolf it was because you saw them first. The music and visuals were one to most people." (Godley and Creme, according to Simon Napier-Bell, even made a special porn version of the **Girls On Film** video to be shown in clubs, which was a key to the song's success.) And no one understood the fusion of sound and image better than Michael Jackson, who hired directors like **Martin Scorsese** (Bad) and **John Landis**, whose *An American Werewolf In London* so impressed Jacko he hired him to make a 14-minute mini horror movie, with Rick Baker monster effects, for Thriller.

The videos didn't just make stars of the artists (many believe Madonna owes her success to memorable videos). Video directors often graduated into movies.

Russell Mulcahy, who directed Bonnie Tyler in Total Eclipse Of The Heart, Elton John's sunny I'm Still Standing and Duran Duran videos including Rio, took the helm for *Highlander*. David Fincher, director of Express Yourself and Vogue for Madonna (arguably her best videos), is now better known for stylish movies like *Fight Club*. And let's not forget Spike Jonze, whose groundbreaking videos for the Beastie Boys (including Sabotage), Fatboy Slim (Praise You) and Bjork (Oh So Quiet), laid the groundwork for a film career that has already garnered an Oscar nomination as best director for *Being John Malkovich*.

Some songs became hits because of the video that promoted them. Would Peter Gabriel's **Sledgehammer** have been such a hit without its stop-motion, claymation video (made by director Stephen R Johnson, the Brothers Quay and Wallace & Gromit man Nick Park)? What about Robert Palmer's Addicted To Love, featuring identikit leggy models as his backing band? Or Shania Twain's Man! I Feel Like A Woman!, with its answering video with identikit himbos? And a-ha would certainly not have got as much airplay for Take On Me without its animated/live-action video – the song had been released several times previously.

Videos become so popular that *Top Of The Pops* producers, sick of being sent videos instead of the artists, effectively banned promos from the show in a bid to get flesh-and-blood acts back on screen. But the videos were still made for MTV and the multitude of other music channels that had sprung up (including **VH1**), and they became so much a part of everyday life that award shows were devoted to them and celebrities lined up to appear in them (see list below).

The 1990s saw extra TV channels devoted to emerging artists and different music (rap, hip hop etc). Hiring a top director such as Mark Romanek – K D Lang's Constant Craving – or Hype Williams – Aaliyah's Rock The Boat (it was the return flight from its Bahamas location that killed her) – has become a rite of passage for new stars. The videos have become more innovative and, for some artists, more raunchy (yes, Christina Aguilera, Holly Valance, we mean you). Mind you, there's a lot to be said for simplicity. The Flying Pickets' video for **Only You** was shot on a budget which didn't reach beyond a few pints at the local Nags Head and, with a focus that never shifts from the bar or the pool table, it's much, much better than the song. While The Police's mono video for Every Breath You Take, courtesy of Godley and Creme, matches the neurotic intensity of the song.

Ten best performances by actors in music videos

And, laydeez and genullmenn, the nominations are...
1. Christopher Walken in Fatboy Slim's Weapon Of Choice
He dances! He flies across the room! Trained dancer-turned-movie star Christopher Walken proves he is the coolest actor alive.

2. Keanu Reeves in **Paula Abdul**'s **Rush Rush**

Anyone who can pretend to be besotted by Abdul in this homage to *Rebel Without A Cause* gets our vote.

3. Danny Aiello in **Madonna**'s **Papa Don't Preach**

Aiello is the strict Italian dad unimpressed by his daughter Madonna's wild ways.

4. Donald Sutherland in **Kate Bush**'s **Cloudbusting**

Sutherland plays the free-thinking scientist taken away by the government for moving clouds around (or something), leaving weirdly wigged Kate behind.

5. Robert Downey Jr in **Elton John**'s **I Want Love**

Elton, no longer a spring chicken, hires a hunky actor to lip-synch his lyrics. Genius.

6. Joan Collins in **Badly Drawn Boy**'s **Spitting In The Wind**

The ex-*Dynasty* star shows she has a sense of humour by flouncing around a fancy apartment and ending up escorted out on the town by the woolly-hatted one.

7. Johnny Depp and **Faye Dunaway** in **Tom Petty**'s **Into The Great Wide Open**

We're not entirely sure what's going on in this young-man-lets-ego-cause-his-downfall tale, but Johnny and Faye make it look cool.

8. Alicia Silverstone and **Liv Tyler** in **Aerosmith**'s **Crazy**

Daddy Steven gets daughter Liv and her mate (a then unknown Silverstone) to

cavort in his band's music video. Smart move.

9. Helena Christensen in **Chris Isaak**'s **Wicked Game**

Once seen, Helen's frolic in the surf is never forgotten. By men, anyway.

10. Courteney Cox in **Bruce Springsteen**'s **Dancing In The Dark**

A pre-*Friends* Courteney is the 'fan' pulled on stage by Brucie to dance.

★

Best videos to buy

Madonna The Immaculate Collection

Watch Madonna change from pudgy girl with big earrings to sleek, sexy video star in this collection of her first decade of videos, from Lucky Star and Express Yourself up to Vogue. Completists should also buy *Madonna: The Video Collection 93-99* (note that neither contains Madonna's raunchiest pieces of cinema, the videos for Erotica and Justify My Love).

Michael Jackson Thriller

First released (but now deleted) on video, as the Thriller video plus 'The Making

Of Michael Jackson's Thriller'. Now John Landis's pop movie is part of *Michael Jackson – HIStory – Video Greatest Hits*.

Beastie Boys Video Anthology

The DVD of this includes all the mad Beastie Boys videos, from the acclaimed Sabotage (directed by Spike Jonze) to the impressive Intergalactic.

Eminem Eminem

Uncut versions of Eminem's videos from his *Slim Shady* and *Marshall Mathers* LPs, including Stan (co-starring Dido, whose song Thank You is sampled), The Real Slim Shady, My Name Is… and a documentary on the making of Stan.

Kate Bush The Whole Story

Some videos – like Wuthering Heights, in which she twirls around manically while some sad 1970s lighting effects go bonkers – have dated, but Bush also created clips that made points rather than just looked pretty (eg Cloudbursting with Donald Sutherland).

George Michael Freedom 90

The *Ladies And Gentlemen: The Best Of George Michael* DVD also includes Too Funky (more supermodels), the sexy Fastlove and mickey-taking Outside.

Duran Duran Rio

The suits. The cavorting models. Simon Le Bon hanging off the end of a sailboat but not falling in. The video to Rio summed up the excesses of the 1980s and can be reappreciated on video as part of *Duran Duran Greatest – The Videos*.

Adam & The Ants Antvideo

Mr Ant may now be a few sandwiches short of a picnic, but in the early 1980s he and his band of merry men rocked and became video stars with lavish mini-movies like Stand And Deliver, Prince Charming (with the lovely Diana Dors) and Ant Rap.

from bad to verse

The potency of cheap music has fascinated many a wordsmith, but rarely with happy results. **Thom Gunn** wrote two stream-of-consciousness poems about Elvis, which even he admits he doesn't like now. **Philip Larkin** memorably dated sexual intercourse to around the time of the Beatles first LP in his poem Annus Mirabilis. American poet **Etheridge Knight** wrote As You Leave Me, probably the finest poem ever written about Johnny Mathis's dulcet tones. Actually, it's about the poet watching his partner sell her body, but she relaxes by listening to the singer: "How you love Mathis – with his burnished hair and quicksilver voice." Inspiring this heartfelt poem may be the best thing Mathis has ever done.

★Pop on the box★

"My own TV series is something I'm really excited about," **Marc Bolan** confided modestly to readers of his **Record Mirror** column on 6 August 1977. "Granada's big chief Johnny Hamp wanted someone to host a rock show which would bridge the gap between today and tomorrow and generate a genuine feeling for young people. Someone who would be accepted by the new wave, the old wave, the supernovas, the black holes in space and skateboarders."

Mystified? Well Bolan went on to reveal that the show would be directed by **Mike Mansfield**, the man who'd given us the Bay City Rollers's **Shang A Lang** (now there was a great series) and who, in Bolan's words, had fulfilled his destiny on **Supersonic** by burying "the likes of me up to me earoles in foam, balloons and bubbles." Finally, Bolan promised to do his new single, **Celebrate Summers**, "against a background of a **genuine skateboard team** called The Benji Boarders", thereby hoping to bring back "real fun and fantasy into those tired old presentations on early Top Of The Flops."

And there in a nutshell, or a small forest littered with nutshells, you have the history of pop on TV. Bolan's TV show was chiefly famous because some kids assumed he was **Mick Robertson** (the fuzzy-haired dreamboat who co-presented ITV's *Magpie*) and because Bowie turned up to sing along and Marc, to celebrate, fell off the stage. The marriage of pop music and TV has not been one made in heaven, the bad genes of both partners winning out over the good.

Television's one positive contribution to the history of pop was to bring its one essential star, **Elvis Presley**, into America's living rooms. In the 1960s, programmes like *American Bandstand*, *The Ed Sullivan Show* and light-entertainment series like *The Smothers Brothers Show* introduced British acts to America. The Who became a legend after a performance of **My Generation** on *The Smothers Brothers Show* which was supposed to end with a small gunpowder blast. **Keith Moon** filled his drums with far too much explosive and as the number ended – this was live on air – the blast was so great that Moon flew backwards, his arm sliced open by a cymbal, and Pete Townshend's hair was briefly ablaze.

In the UK TV has seldom been that helpful, although the BBC's all-day-and-all-of-the-night coverage of Live Aid helped make that charidee concert an epochal moment where, until normal service is resumed, it was possible to hope that famine could be ended by the combined efforts of Bono, Sir Bob Geldof and Phil Collins. The late 1950s through to the early 1970s was possibly the golden age of pop on TV. In the 1950s, we had **Jack Good**'s **Six Five Special** hosted by that swinging cat **Pete Murray**. In the 1960s, there was **Top Of The Pops**, the groovier

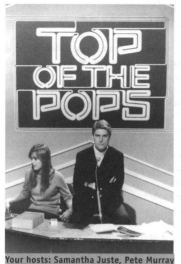

Ready Steady Go!, and the grimly fascinating **Juke Box Jury** hosted by **David Jacobs**, his persona summed up by Jack Good: "smooth as liquid paraffin, and just as colourless."

And in the 1970s, we had a profusion of weekday afternoon shows like **Marc, Shang A Lang**, and **Get It Together**, in which an ex-straight man for Basil Brush called **Roy North** performed pop hits, a visual equivalent of all those **Top Of The Pops** albums made by me-too musicians. In the evenings, **Whisperin' Bob Harris** was our guide to the more serious stuff. Today, along with dedicated music channels like MTV and VH1, we still have Top Of The Pops, and we have Jools Holland's **Later** (a good idea grown self-congratulatory) and the curse of the

Your hosts: Samantha Juste, Pete Murray

Channel 4 *Top 10* although, strangely, we've not yet had one called *Top 10 Ways To Fill The Saturday Night Schedule Very Cheaply And With Bugger All Effort.*

The wise Monkees

Made to shift records and breakfast cereal, The Monkees's TV series was far funnier than it's usually given credit for. The proof? Well since you asked...

Ben Cartwheel Hey, uh, water my horse, will you son?
Davy Water your horse? I'm not a stable boy!
Ben Cartwheel I don't care about your mental condition; water my horse!

Tony It's no good, Babyface, you're a has-been.
Micky No, Tony, I WAS a has-been. Now I'm an AM-IS!

Micky So this is the world of television.
Peter That's funny; it doesn't look like a vast wasteland.

POP GOES TO THE MOVIES
Charting the celluloid highlights and horrors

One Leningrad Cowboy goes to America in one of the more unusual, affecting, pop movies

> **"A chip on your shoulder, an H-bomb in your pants – it's you against the world, baby, and the world loves you for hating it"**
> *Laurence Harvey to Cliff Richard in* **Expresso Bongo**

Cynical, reductive and cheap though it sounds, it's tempting to say that any chapter which looks at **pop on celluloid** should be headed pap on celluloid. The marriage of pop music and movies has seldom been happy or fruitful. Critic Joe Queenan, in his essay 'The King And His Court', has a simple explanation: "Rock stars suck [and] are not especially pleasant to look at, so they can't get away with being terrible actors for as long as **Don Johnson**… Moreover, they rely on broad, vulgar, **exaggerated gestures** designed to transfix the very last, drug-crazed teenager in the very last row of the very darkest, multipurpose civic center [but which] look ridiculous in close-up."

Certainly, vanity has often hindered pop stars' progress in movies. What pop stars really want to do is act just as, eventually, all that successful actors really want to do is direct. Often, Hollywood attracts because it is deemed to represent a **challenge** that is missing in their day job, which could be one way of saying that the movies are a luxurious diversion if you're worried about cutting it in the studio. Yet movies, for every idol from Elvis to **The Beatles**, from Peter Noone to Britney, have also seemed a logical alternative to both the repetitive business of touring and as some kind of insurance against the fickleness of pop fashion.

It's easy to blame **Frank Sinatra** for all this. The Chairman is one of the few to make the transition from teen idol to Oscar-winning actor (for his supporting role in *From Here To Eternity*). But even he was following a route mapped out by Bing Crosby (who won an Oscar for his turn as a loveable yet tuneful priest in *Going My Way*) and, less profitably, by **Rudy Vallee**, the 1920s band leader and crooner.

Vallee once said, "People called me the guy with the cock in his voice. Maybe that's why in 84 years of life I've been with over 145 women and girls." Starting in adolescence, that only actually works out at around two a year, so perhaps Vallee's bedroom skills were on a par with his acting ones. His movie career – in which he co-starred with everyone from Betty Boop and Bela Lugosi to **Elvis** (in the King's bid to revive the screwball sex comedy, *Live A Little, Love A Little*) – was decidedly iffy.

Sadly it's Vallee's dodgy cinematic career, not Crosby's or Sinatra's, which has set the pattern for most pop stars, but it's too simplistic to blame this on the stars themselves. **Hollywood** has been remarkably consistent when it comes to exploiting the latest teen sensation. Remarkably, consistently, crass. **Elvis**, as the character Deke Rivers in his second film, *Loving You*, sums up the approach when he says to his agent: "That's how you're selling me, isn't it? Like **a monkey in a zoo**." For every half-decent effort like *Jailhouse Rock* or *A Hard Day's Night*, there's been a slew of *Clambake*s. Movies where the formula of a light romantic comedy, peppered with just enough opportunities for the star to tax their tonsils, has been followed with such moronic zeal that star and audience are insulted.

Then again, even the *Clambake*s of this world can be easier to watch than the more ambitious efforts of Bob Dylan, Sting or **Madonna**. Madonna's performance as an S&M-loving murder suspect in *Body Of Evidence* is often cited as some kind of **all-time low** in the pop movie canon (it might have been more fun if she'd been an M&S-loving murder suspect). But even that pales alongside **Bob Dylan**'s *Hearts Of Fire*, a film about a reclusive **rock-star-cum-chicken-farmer** in which Rupert Everett and Ian Dury are also implicated. The most charitable explanation for *Hearts Of Fire* is that it's Dylan's attempt to make a worse movie than his idol Elvis: cinema buffs still debate the respective demerits of *Hearts Of Fire* and Elvis in *Paradise Hawaiian Style*. Still, it's just possible that *Take Me High*, **Cliff Richard**'s soppy, mid-1970s **romantic travelogue** set in Birmingham, is worse than either.

Yet good movies have helped change the course of pop for the better. Hollywood's 1950s movies about rock were often so cynical about the business (witness **Jailhouse Rock**, *The Girl Can't Help It* and *Expresso Bongo*) that they almost form a genre of their own, a genre you could call the great rock'n'roll swindle, yet they helped to popularise both the music and stars like Little Richard. **The Beatles** might never have become quite the same force without the, er, help of *Help!* and *A Hard Day's Night*. **Saturday Night Fever** helped make **disco** a global phenomenon, and *Grease* gave us You're The One That I Want, the ultimate rock song in a fairground sequence.

The most successful pop movies have often been **biopics** of the stars themselves (be they lightly or heavily fictionalised, or as blatant as **Prince**'s *Purple Rain*) or of other stars (such as **Diana Ross** as Billie Holiday in *Lady Sings The Blues* or Bette Midler as **Janis Joplin** in *The Rose*). At least in the best of these films the scriptwriters have not felt obliged to try and concoct a plot, relying instead on the traditional rise and fall (or rise, fall and rise again) of the **traditional showbiz** biopic, such as *A Star Is Born*.

Here, for your delectation and delight, is our alphabetised guide to the sharp, the flat and the often **off-key history** of pop in the movies.

If you only watch one movie starring...

★The Beatles★
Go for *A Hard Day's Night*, although *Yellow Submarine* comes close.

★David Bowie★
Make sure it's *The Man Who Fell To Earth*, perfect casting because Bowie genuinely does seem alien.

★Cab Calloway★
Try *The Blues Brothers*. You also get Belushi, Aykroyd, Ray Charles and James Brown. And Aretha.

★Jimmy Cliff★
Opt for *The Harder They Come*.

★Bob Dylan★
Try *Pat Garrett And Billy The Kid*.

★Alan Freeman★
Pick *Absolute Beginners*, in which Fluff plays Call-Me-Cobber.

★The Leningrad Cowboys★
Make sure it's the first one, *Leningrad Cowboys Go America*, in which the quiff-toting Finnish rockabilly musicians take the home of rock'n'roll by storm. Sort of.

A is for Aruba Liberace, the flamboyant Polish pianist's contribution to the soundtrack of *When The Boys Meet The Girls*. Liberace also appeared in this mid-1960s musical, one of those films which never quite manages to live up to the incongruity of the cast; it also starred Peter Noone, Sam The Sham & The Pharaohs, Louis Armstrong, Connie Francis and Sue Anne Langdon – the only actress to appear alongside Liberace, Peter Noone (twice) and Elvis (twice).

A is also for *Abba: The Movie* (compelling if you're one of those people who never tire of looking at Agnetha's bum) and *Absolute Beginners*, Julien Temple's underrated take on a 1950s pop movie.

★

B is for beach-party movies. Naff they may have been, but they kept Frankie Avalon out of music-making mischief for much of the 1960s. Kicking off with *Beach Party*, in an era before the words "skin" and "cancer" ever appeared next to each other, Frankie got the sand between his toes throughout *Muscle Beach Party*, *Bikini Beach*, *Beach Blanket Bingo* and *How To Stuff A Wild Bikini*. Not that these films were formulaic – there's *Ski Party* too, where "the HEs meet the SHEs on SKIs, and there's only one way to get warm!" In other words, the beach-party movie where snow stands in for sand.

★

C is for *Catch Us If You Can.* John Boorman's 1965 debut is an obvious cash-in on (and homage to) *A Hard Day's Night,* in which The Dave Clark Five are a team of stuntmen working on TV ads. Despite a dubious sequence involving a romp in a Roman bath, some maintain this is better than the film it's cashing in on.

★

D is for *Don't Look Back,* the D A Pennebaker documentary about Bob Dylan's 1965 tour of Britain which made Bob seem cool at the time. Watch it today and you might, despite the fine moments, end up agreeing with Roger Ebert, himself a Dylan fan, who watched it on re-release and concluded: "What a jerk Bob Dylan was in 1965. What an immature, self-important, inflated, cruel, shallow little creature, lacking in empathy and contemptuous of anyone who was not himself or his lackey. Did we actually once take this twerp as our folk god?"

★

E is for *Expresso Bongo.* Cliff's second film (and his first real starring role) is stolen by Laurence Harvey, who plays the sleazy agent manipulating Cliff's rock'n'roll idol (the ludicrously named Bongo Herbert). The film had a huge impact on rock not because of its own merits (not inconsiderable, actually) but because of its influence on a young bloke called Andrew Loog Oldham, who managed the Rolling Stones to fame and of whom Stones biographer Philip Norman said: "His ideal was Laurence Harvey in *Expresso Bongo.* That was the blueprint." Oldham even quoted Harvey's lines from the film in his daily life as a rock impresario.

★

F is for *Flame!* Some critics will tell you that this is the best rock biopic ever, which is probably overstating things somewhat. But Wolverhampton's finest, Slade, are shown to good effect in this rock flick which includes a generous number of canal towpaths, and which one reviewer described as "a cross between *Get Carter* and *Stardust.*" Even Noddy Holder recalls watching it on TV and thinking, "Bloody hell, this is quite good."

★

G is for *The Ghost Goes Gear.* This 1966 movie – an attempt to do for The Spencer Davis Group what *A Hard Day's Night* and *Help!* had done for The Beatles – never quite recovers from the curious decision to cast Nicholas Parsons as their haunted, upper-class manager, Algernon Rowthorpe Plumley. As a result it's only for diehard fans of the group, Stevie Winwood, Parsons and Acker Bilk (who has a cameo role).

That said, it didn't stink out the cinema quite as much as the 1965 sci-fi/musical *Gonks Go Beat!* Starring Kenneth Connor (as Wilco Roger), Frank Thornton, Terry Scott, Ginger Baker, Jack Bruce and Lulu (with

If you only watch one movie starring...

★Madonna★

It has to be *Desperately Seeking Susan*. At least by playing herself, Madge is portraying someone she can relate to.

★Mick Jagger★

Try *Performance*, in which James Fox, playing a gangster, tells Mick: "You'll look funny when you're 50."

★Elvis Presley★

Make it *That's The Way It Is*, the rockumentary with rock's ultimate star at the centre.

★Cliff Richard★

Stick to *The Young Ones*.

★The Rubettes★

Pick *Never Too Young To Rock* – and fast-forward to the bit where they play on the back of a lorry.

'original music' from Marty Wilde), it has been called Britain's revenge for *Santa Claus Conquers The Martians*.

★

H is for *Head*. This 1968 Monkees movie sank without a trace on release, with more discussion of the title than the plot. (Rumour has it the name was chosen in anticipation of a sequel, where the posters could read: "From the people who gave you *Head*.") To say the script was written by Bob Rafelson and Jack Nicholson is pushing it (it was mainly the product of a semi-continuous brainstorm at a California motel), but then to say the script was written is probably an exaggeration to start with. To fully understand this film you'll need to be taking whatever they were on at the time, but the music still holds up and, as a whole, the movie still exerts a certain period fascination.

★

I is for *It's Trad Dad!*, director Richard Lester's 1961 debut, which did for trad jazz what the Village People's *Can't Stop The Music* did for disco – ie stopped it in its tracks. The movie's definition of 'trad' was never going to find favour with purists, embracing as it did Acker Bilk, Del Shannon, Helen Shapiro and Chubby Checker. Still, it does have a genuine sense of fun and is worth seeing if only because so many legendary figures are on show, including John Leyton (who, after a hit with Johnny Remember Me, was soon forgotten),

Gary 'US' Bonds and actor Arthur Mullard, who'd later cover You're The One That I Want with Hylda Baker.

★

J is for *The Jazz Singer*. The Neil Diamond-Laurence Olivier version isn't actually about a jazz singer at all, but about a sensitive Jewish singer/songwriter (Diamond) who performs a few half-decent songs (including Love On The Rocks) and manages not to wince whenever Olivier speaks in a Jewish accent so terrible it dominates the film.

★

K is for *King Creole*. It's easily the King's most monarchical musical, and worth watching just to see him growl through Trouble when challenged by the local mobster (played by Walter Matthau). Director Michael Curtiz, who had been slated to make the film with James Dean in the title role, told Presley to cut his hair and lose weight, hoping to provoke a tantrum which would lead the star to pull out. Instead, Elvis knuckled down and delivered a performance which convinced even the *New York Times* that he could act and knocked out Curtiz, who told everyone that Presley could be a great movie star. It never happened but the potential is obvious here.

★

L is for *Light Of Day*, with Joan Jett of The Blackhearts (and formerly of all-girl group, The Runaways) who was a bit of a goddess in her day – or,

as the *New York Times* put it, "godmother to female musicians with loud guitars and idealistic dreams", though she probably prefers the catchier, 'Girl Elvis'. In Paul Schrader's 1987 movie, Jett is the ambitious Patty who, with Michael J Fox as her rocking (ahem) brother, is determined to make her rock band The Barbusters succeed. Sadly the soundtrack only features a few Jett songs, including the unusually titled Rabbit's Got The Gun. Fox sings the self-penned You Got No Place To Go but soon goes back to his day job, leaving the field clear for such rock alumni as Steve Tyler, Bon Jovi and Bruce Springsteen. The film was to be called *Born In The USA* with Springsteen supplying the title track but he liked his song so much he kept it. The rest, as they say, is history – of a very lucrative kind.

★

M is for *Mrs Brown, You've Got A Lovely Daughter*. Hard as it is to believe now, Peter Noone was chosen as the lead singer in Herman's Hermits because producer Mickie Most thought that he resembled John F Kennedy. Sadly, the resemblance isn't obvious in this musical comedy – one of the few films to be named after a pop song – described by an admirer as "bad but interesting". The tag line says it all really: "You've got to sing, swing, and do your own thing… And no one does it better in merry young London than Herman's Hermits."

★

POP MOVIES

Take it away Ringo

When The Beatles split in 1970, rather than try hairdressing (his original fall-back if drumming didn't pan out), Ringo Starr turned to acting. Which he took to like a born hairdresser. The highlight of Starr's acting career is his narration of *Thomas The Tank Engine*, which made Starr to tank engines what John Wayne was to westerns.

★Blindman (1971)★
Facial hair does not a Mexican bandido make, yet bizarrely this was all Ringo and director Ferdinando Baldi felt he needed for the role of a hyperactive Mexican bandit who has to go *mano mano* with a blind gunslinger whose horse tells him where to shoot. Pity the horse didn't read the script.

★Son Of Dracula (1974)★
Ringo's first production venture outside of Beatles films starred Harry Nilsson as Count Downe, a substitute for David Bowie who, wisely, declined the role. Ringo also played Merlin The Magician with such aplomb that Sir Ian McKellen must have nightmares about being usurped as Gandalf. Not.

★Lisztomania (1975)★
This may be a Ken Russell film, but surely even Russell fans must have found it hard to swallow the idea of Ringo as the Pope.

is for Norman Rossington, the British character actor (you'll know the face even if the name doesn't ring a bell). He's the only actor to have co-starred with The Beatles (*A Hard Day's Night*), Elvis (*Double Trouble*), Tony Blackburn (*Simon Simon*) and Bob Todd, the Benny Hill regular immortalised in Half Man Half Biscuit's song Why Do 99 Per Cent Of Gargoyles Look Like Bob Todd? (Go For A Take).

★

is for Old MacDonald, the farmyard classic ("with a moo moo here" etc) sung by Elvis on the back of a truck in *Double Trouble*, his film about touring swinging Europe shot entirely on the MGM lot. Film historians, fans and rock critics often cite this as the nadir of the King's career on film – probably because they've forgotten the scene in *Paradise Hawaiian Style* where he has to watch a nine-year-old girl in a grass skirt murder Won't You Come Home, Bill Bailey?

★

is for *Purple Rain*. Before the diminutive purple one preferred people to draw, rather than spell, his name, he made this 1984 film which is essentially an extended music video. The dialogue and storyline can easily be discarded in this biopic with Prince playing himself in the story of 'The Kid' who just wants to play music. It's the Prince songs that drive the film – which is not without its absurdities,

321

as Giles Smith crossly noted in his book *Lost In Music*: "I've never forgiven Prince for the scene where he arrives late for a rehearsal, scoots up on to the stage, apologises crisply, slips his guitar strap over his neck and off they all go into perfectly mixed, effortlessly disciplined pop heaven."

★

Q is for *Quadrophenia*. The presence of Sting, Toyah Willcox and a cameo by Ben Elton (sipping a beer) wasn't enough to sink this largely improvised movie which even the professional cynics at *The Onion* website describe as a "near definitive portrayal of teen angst". Phil Daniels stars as the *Catcher In The Rye*-style teenage hero, member of a Mod clique in 1960s London. Even if you find the hero a bit irritating (not an uncommon reaction), it's worth watching just for the songs, which run from The Cascades' Rhythm Of The Rain to The Who's My Generation.

★

R is for *Rock'n'Roll High School*. The Ramones revisit the 1960s teenage beach-party film, only this time the high-school kids go to the extreme of burning their school to the ground while The Ramones play on in the background. The songs include such classics as Sheena Is A Punk Rocker, Pinhead and Teenage Lobotomy ("I'm going to have to tell 'em/That I've got no cerebellum") and the script ain't bad either. One pupil, asked to explain why he's never opened his algebra book, replies: "I only use it on special equations."

★

S is for Spinal Tap. Three cheers for *This Is Spinal Tap*, a spoof so accurately observed and so well done, it went on to influence the very scene it sent up and is regularly quoted by musicians of all kinds on tour.

S is also for *Shining Star*, a portrait of music-industry discrimination, with Harvey Keitel playing a (pre-disco) record exec keener on an Earth, Wind & Fire-type group (played by Earth, Wind & Fire) than an act closely resembling The Carpenters who are the record company's big priority.

★

T is for *That'll Be The Day*, the first of two movies about the resistible rise of a rock star called Jim Maclaine (David Essex) and his band The Stray Cats (no relation). The story is entertainingly told, with support from Ringo Starr, Keith Moon, Billy Fury and, further down the cast, Vivian Stanshall. The sequel *Stardust* is often dismissed, but is not without merit: the film's portrayal of a rock star driven mad by fame is well-observed, chilling and quite prophetic.

★

U is for *Up In Smoke*, Cheech & Chong's drug rock comedy in which Cheech announces, "We're going to be bigger than Ruben & The Jets," a reference to the name of a doo-wop parody album by Frank Zappa & The Mothers Of Invention.

Take it away Ringo

★Sextette (1978)★
As Tony Curtis, George Hamilton and Timothy Dalton were also cast, Ringo wasn't the only thespian to be implicated in this mess. Mercifully, Mae West got the worst reviews.

★Caveman (1981)★
So bad it's a must-see, with Starr as caveman outcast Atouk, trying to outsmart the leader of another caveman clan with the help of his band of outcasts which include a dwarf, a blind caveman and a gay caveman couple.

★Give My Regards To Broad Street (1984)★
Ringo's appearance can charitably be explained as an act of misguided loyalty to an old mate. Or maybe by appearing in it Ringo was subtly implying to audiences that, even if he'd appeared in some turkeys, he'd never made anything as boringly smug as Macca's magnum opus.

V is for Village People who, despite having some of the dodgiest costumes outside of your local charity shop, managed to convince Hollywood to bankroll a truly awful two-hour pseudo-biography of the group (called *Can't Stop The Music*) in 1980. How bad was it? Well, it ended co-star Valerie Perrine's hopes of being a first-rank movie actress and sent the promising career of Steve Guttenberg into doldrums so deep he was forced to star in four *Police Academy* movies. For a wonderfully scathing and very funny review of this witless disaster, read Jason McIsaac's scene-by-scene dissection at *www.jabootu.com*.

★

W is for *The Wiz*. But if ever a wiz there was, he wasn't a wiz in this one, because because because the very idea of an African-Americanised version of the *The Wizard Of Oz* was a bit naff (though it worked better in the Broadway musical from whence it sprang). Among the challenges for the viewer was accepting 34-year-old Diana Ross as Dorothy, as she whined her way along the yellow brick road.

Talking of bricks, W is also for *The Wall*, the Pink Floyd extravaganza starring Bob Geldof. Alan Parker (who quit as director) called it "the most expensive student film ever made."

★

X is for *Xanadu*, which would have cemented Olivia Newton-John's place in pop history even if she hadn't already earned a kind of immortality by hanging around Sir Cliff for longer than any other female (apart from Sue Barker and Una Stubbs). *Xanadu* unites the disparate talents of Newton-John, Gene Kelly and Jeff Lynne (the sinister force behind ELO), but sadly the only stand-out scene is the moment in the ballroom-dance number where you can see the camera crew in the mirror. The theme song was a No.1 hit for Olivia, but the movie's biggest achievement was that, on a double bill with The Village People's *Can't Stop The Music*, it inspired John Wilson to launch the Razzle awards for the worst films of the year.

★

Y is for *Yentl*, which is probably summed up best by Joe Queenan: "Eastern Europe circa 1904, the way western Hollywood, circa 1983, imagined it: more songs, fewer pogroms." Barbra Streisand stars as the girl pretending to be a boy to get ahead, although her rendition of

Papa Can You Hear Me? is so mawkish you wouldn't blame the neighbours if they did start a civil disturbance.

Y is also for *Yellow Submarine*, as entertaining and downright charming as *Yentl* is excruciating. Even without the Fab Four, any film which unites the vocal talents of Dick Emery with those of Lance Percival and Geoffrey Hughes (Eddie Yeats in *Corrie*; Twiggy in *The Royle Family*) deserves respect. Astonishingly, Erich 'Love Story' Segal was among the writers.

★

Z is for *Ziggy Stardust And The Spiders From Mars* which, if you feel a burning need to understand glam rock (or just to go on a nostalgia trip), is essential viewing. Directed, not always successfully, by the ubiquitous D A Pennebaker, it's a revealing record of Bowie's final bow as Ziggy, complete with big hair, cracking songs and some mime sequences that were old when Marcel Marceau was born.

THE FINAL COUNTDOWN
The last 50 years of pop music in a nutshell or two

Some of us have time on our hands, but Public Enemy's Flavour Flav...

1952

November: Al Martino tops the first singles chart with Here Is My Heart.
In the real world: King George VI is found dead in bed by a servant delivering the king's morning tea.

1953

April: Frankie Laine's I Believe is No.1 for nine weeks from 24 April, goes back to No.1 for five more weeks from 3 July, yields top slot to Mantovani for a fortnight and then returns to No.1 for three weeks from 21 August – a convoluted performance still unmatched.
In the real world: The Tuskegee Institute in Alabama announces that, for the second year in a row, there were no lynchings in the US.

1954

February: When the Stargazers quintet's single I See The Moon climbs to No.1 they become the first (and only) British group before The Beatles to rack up two No.1 hits.
In the real world: Roger Bannister becomes the first man to run a mile in less than four minutes.

1955

June: Las Vegas has a new headliner: Noel Coward live at the Desert Inn for $35,000 a week. Frank Sinatra declares: "If you want to hear how songs should be sung, get the hell over to the Desert Inn."

In the real world: Albert Einstein dies.

1956

June: Having just heard Be Bop A Lula on the radio, Elvis Presley's mum Gladys mistakenly congratulates her son on his latest single, actually performed by Gene Vincent.
In the real world: The first contraceptive pill is introduced.

1957

December: Barry Gibb, and his five-year-old brothers Robin and Maurice, make their singing debut in the interval at Manchester's Gaumont cinema.
In the real world: Dr Seuss's first *Cat In The Hat* book is published.

1958

January: Paul McCartney appears at the Cavern Club with the Quarrymen.
In the real world: Vice-president Richard Nixon is stoned, booed and spat upon on a tour of Latin America.

1959

November: Oh Neil – Carole King's answer to Oh Carol, the hit Neil Sedaka had written for her – flops. She shelves solo work for two-and-a-half years to concentrate on writing songs with Gerry Goffin.
In the real world: Barbie is born.

1960

July: Rolf Harris releases Sun Arise, the record that persuades Leo Sayer

that he wants to enter showbiz.
In the real world: Science takes two
giant steps with the invention of the
felt-tip pen and the aluminium can.

1961
November: The BBC refuses to
broadcast The Moontrekkers' novelty
record **Night Of The Vampires**,
declaring it "unsuitable for those
of a nervous disposition."
In the real world: Communist East
Germany builds the Berlin Wall.

1962
Mike and Bernie Winters turn down
an agent's offer to manage four young
lads who were "big up north". But they
were to run into the Fab Four later on
in life – when The Beatles appeared on
Mike and Bernie's *Big Night Out*. **John
Lennon**, Bernie insists, found his She
Loves You spoof hilarious.
In the real world: Peter Parker gets
bitten by a radioactive spider.

1963
December: **Jerry Lee Lewis** records
Lincoln Limousine, a tribute to
assassinated **John F Kennedy**,
which includes the immortal line:
"Oh Lord, it would have been better
if he'd stayed at home."
In the real world: Soviet Russia's
Valentina Tereshkova becomes the
first woman in orbit.

1964
April: **The Beatles** hold the top five

positions on the Billboard US singles
chart. On 4 April Can't Buy Me Love
is at No.1, followed by Twist And
Shout, She Loves You, I Want To Hold
Your Hand and Please Please Me.
In the real world: Designer **Rudi
Gernreich** launches the world's first
topless swimsuit.

1965
October: The Beatles' **Yesterday**
becomes their tenth US No.1. With
some 2,500 cover versions, this may
be the world's most recorded song.
In the real world: Ray Bradbury's
sci-fi short story **The Rocket Man**,
believed to have inspired both **David
Bowie**'s Space Oddity and **Elton
John**'s Rocket Man, is published in
a collection of Bradbury short stories
entitled *R Is For Rocket*.

1966
March: David Jones leaves for the new
Deram label and changes his name to
David Bowie to avoid being confused
with the singer in The Monkees.
In the real world: Anthony Newley
and Terence Stamp turn down the
title role in *Alfie*, so **Michael Caine**
wins the role with which he will
forever be identified/confused.

1967
December: **The Monkees** sell more
records than The Beatles and the
Rolling Stones combined and become
the only band ever to have four No.1
US albums in the same year.

Eurovision-winning Dana (Mark I)

In the real world: Paul McCartney, defending the Boxing Day screening on British TV of the critically mauled *Magical Mystery Tour*, says, "The Queen's speech was hardly a gasser."

1968

January: New York police confiscate 30,000 copies of the **Two Virgins** album saying the cover, which shows a naked John Lennon and Yoko Ono, is "pornographic".
In the real world: James Brown appears on television to try to calm America after Martin Luther King's assassination.

1969

November: The decade ends with Rolf Harris's Two Little Boys at No.1 and a self-titled debut album by **The Stooges**, now seen as laying the roots for punk.
In the real world: In the US, the first series of *Star Trek* is cancelled.

1970

June: Ray Davies flies from Los Angeles to London to change the lyrics to The Kinks' single **Lola** so the BBC won't ban it. Not because the song is about a transvestite but because one line mentioned **Coca-Cola**, which Auntie saw as advertising. It was changed to "cherry cola". Phew!
In the real world: Apollo 13 makes it safely back to earth. Just.

1971

December: The **New Seekers**' version of a Coca-Cola advert jingle is not banned by the BBC and I'd Like To Teach The World To Sing goes to No.1.
In the real world: Idi Amin seizes power in Uganda.

1972

January: Frank Sinatra's version of **My Way** re-enters the charts an eighth time, notching a 122nd week in the charts, still a record for a UK single.
In the real world: Sir John Betjeman becomes Poet Laureate.

1973

March: Columbia's top A&R man, **John Hammond**, suffers a non-fatal heart attack after watching his discovery, **Bruce Springsteen**, live.
In the real world: Roger Moore makes his debut as James Bond.

1974

May: Ireland loses the Eurovision Song Contest (Abba's Waterloo wins), partly because its entry only includes 78 "la la la"s. Spain's 1968 winner,

La La La (sung by a woman called Massie who looked like Nana Mouskouri's naughty younger sister), had a record 138 "la la la"s.
In the real world: Heiress **Patricia Hearst** is kidnapped by US guerrillas, the Symbionese Liberation Army.

1975

November: Queen's **Roger Taylor** locks himself in a recording studio cupboard till Freddie Mercury agrees that his I'm In Love With My Car can be the B-side to Bohemian Rhapsody.
In the real world: Pong, a video-game version of table tennis, is sold to home users for the first time by Atari.

1976

June: **The Wurzels**, at No.1 with a cover of Melanie's Brand New Key, introduce most of Britain to the musical microgenre known as **Scrumpy & Western** for the first time. As Adge Cutler and the Wurzels, the band had released several singles from 1966 to 1974, most notably **Drink Up Thy Zider** (No.45 in 1967).
In the real world: The filming of *Star Wars* begins.

1977

August: **Billy Joel** decides that Just The Way You Are should not, after all, be cut from his album *The Stranger*, after protests from **Linda Ronstadt**.
In the real world: BT unveils the Trimphone, the first luxury phone with buttons (instead of a dial).

1978

September: The soundtrack to *Saturday Night Fever* tops the US album charts for 24 weeks and **The Police** appear in a chewing-gum ad.
In the real world: Sweden becomes the first nation to ban aerosols – a whole nine years before a worldwide ban on CFCs is put in place.

1979

July: A **Disco Demolition Night** is held at the Chicago White Sox baseball stadium, Comiskey Park, for the disposal of unwanted disco records. During a double-header against the Detroit Tigers, the crowd chant "Disco sucks!", records are hurled through the air and a bonfire is lit on the pitch, causing so much mess the White Sox have to forfeit the points from the second game.
In the real world: **Josef Mengele** dies, aged 68, in poverty in Brazil.

1980

September: Robert Palmer's **Johnny And Mary**, a minor but enduring hit, features the boy's and girl's names most often mentioned in hit singles.
In the real world: **Alan Parker**'s movie *Fame* provides the format which will spawn a soppy TV series and later provide the blueprint for *Pop Idol*, *Fame Academy* et al.

1981

August: MTV begins broadcasting from a temporary studio in Fort Lee,

New Jersey, with a video of **Buggles'** Video Killed The Radio Star.
In the real world: Britney Spears is born in Kentwood, Louisiana.

1982

October: Dexy's Midnight Runners perform Jackie Wilson Says on *Top Of The Pops*, in front of a big picture of… Scottish darts player **Jocky Wilson**.
In the real world: John DeLorean is arrested for selling cocaine to undercover cops, but found not guilty as a victim of entrapment.

1983

March: New Order's Blue Monday becomes the biggest-selling 12in single of all time.
In the real world: Derby-winning racehorse **Shergar** is kidnapped.

1984

Joan Rivers, hosting her own *Audience With* special on LWT, announces that "Mick Jagger has child-bearing lips."
In the real world: The first Apple Macintosh computer goes on sale.

1985

June: Jennifer Rush's The Power Of Love is the first single by a female artist to sell a million in the UK.
In the real world: Bob Geldof tells Britons, "just give us your fucking money," as pop unites for the Live Aid concert to fight famine. Sequels include Ferry Aid (a single, not a concert), Farm Aid (nothing to do with the Countryside Alliance: **Bob Dylan** and co do their bit for America's poor small farmers) and Sweet Relief, an album to raise money for **Victoria Williams**, the American singer/songwriter who suffers from multiple sclerosis.

1986

July: Wall Of Voodoo member **Stan Ridgway** has an out-of-nowhere No.4 hit with his Vietnam War ghost story, Camouflage. In a spoof called **Geoffrey Howe**, which gets some airplay, "I was awfully glad to see this big marine" becomes "he was an awfully big MP."
In the real world: Student Britflick *Withnail And I* is a cult hit.

1987

January: The Beastie Boys become the first act to be censored on the American **Bandstand** TV show.
In the real world: Jon Marsh, of British ambient dance band Beloved, appears as a contestant on *Countdown* for nine successive weeks.

1988

December: CDs now outsell records.
In the real world: Iranian **Merhan Nassen** gets stuck at Terminal One of Charles de Gaulle airport in Paris without his passport or a UN document identifying him as a refugee. Initially he is seen as a victim of uncaring bureaucracy; a decade later the consensus grows that Nassen actually likes living at the airport.

1989

April: Bright Eyes, a song written about a rabbit by a bat – well, Mike Batt, the man who urged us all to remember Wombles – stays at No.1 in the British charts for six weeks, giving Art Garfunkel his biggest solo smash.
In the real world: *The Simpsons* premières on US TV channel Fox.

1990

October: For the first time since March 1986 there is no **Stock, Aitken & Waterman** single in the UK Top 40.
In the real world: Nelson Mandela is released from **Victor Verster** prison.

1991

July: (Everything I Do) I Do It For You, **Bryan Adams**'s *Robin Hood: Prince Of Thieves* theme, tops the UK charts for 16 weeks. Britain is soon awash with urban legends of a bride who wanted to walk down the aisle to the Bryan Adams song, but instead got the jaunty theme to the 1950s TV series *Robin Hood*: "Robin Hood, Robin Hood, riding through the glen…"
In the real world: On Halloween, Doristine Gipson twice meets a strange, wolf-like entity at a road junction in Delavan, Wisconsin. Two years earlier, another local had met a hunched, lupine but humanlike figure half a mile from the same junction.

1992

March: Spinal Tap finally tap into the UK singles charts with the release of

Bitch School, which peaks at No.35.
In the real world: A Chicago judge approves rebates of up to $3 to anyone who could prove they bought a Milli Vanilli record before the lip-synching scandal began on 27 November 1990.

1993

April: Antonio Romeo Monge and Rafael Ruiz's dance number, inspired by a dancer they saw in a Venezuela night club, becomes a hit in Spain. In the next four years the Macarena by Los Del Rios will occupy the No.1 spot in the US for 14 weeks, become the bestselling single in America in 1996 and reach No.2 in the UK.
In the real world: Czechoslovakia splits into two separate republics.

1994

March: Madonna's obscenity-laced appearance on David Letterman is dubbed "a battle of wits with an unarmed woman" by Robin Williams.
In the real world: Ice skater Nancy Kerrigan is clubbed on the leg by an assailant hired by rival Tonya Harding.

1995

May: Robson and Jerome survive a mini-boycott by radio stations to hit No.1 with their version of Unchained Melody, the third (but not final) time the song has topped the charts.
In the real world: Russia almost launches a nuclear attack on the West after finding a Norwegian scientific missile in its airspace.

1996

December: Novelty singer **Tiny Tim** dies on stage while singing his biggest hit, Tiptoe Through The Tulips, at a women's club meeting in Minneapolis.
In the real world: Swampy becomes a celeb as environmental activists try to stop the Newbury bypass being built.

1997

September: Elton John's Diana-ised version of Candle In The Wind sells 33 million copies worldwide.
In the real world: **Dolly**, the world's first cloned sheep, is created.

1998

May: Dana International becomes the second Dana (and the first transsexual) to top the Eurovision Song Contest, winning the competition for Israel.
In the real world: Julian Cope publishes his monumental survey of megalithic Britain, *The Modern Antiquarian*, which includes the couplet: "Atop Knot Hill I eat my snot/For 'tis the only food I've got."

1999

March: Andy Williams's Music To Watch Girls By is a Top 10 hit 32 years after it was first released, kicking off the 'easy listening' boom. Jitterbugging stages a mini-comeback when ex-Stray Cat **Brian Setzer** has a minor hit with Jump, Jive An' Wail.
In the real world: Francisco Manuel, a Lisbon furniture restorer who claims that he is descended from a secret love child of the Duke of Wellington and **Queen Victoria**, threatens to sue the Queen if she refuses to recognise his lineage.

2000

November: The theme to **Bob The Builder** is the year's bestselling single.
In the real world: Y2K does not crash every computer in the world.

2001

April: Emma Bunton becomes the fourth ex-Spice Girl to reach No.1 – on **Tin Tin Out**'s What Took You So Long. It's the first time four members of a band have individually reached No.1 – The Beatles remain one short, with **Ringo Starr**'s Back Off Boogaloo having only made it to No.2.
In the real world: Afghanistan's cricket team begins its first foreign tour – losing by 80 runs in a one-day game against a Pakistani XI.

2002

March: James Carter, the ex-convict whose voice leads the chorus on the opening track of the soundtrack to *O Brother, Where Art Thou?*, is told he is top of the American album charts. Sales of the soundtrack album soon exceed five million.
In the real world: Philippines president Gloria Arroyo appears on the cover of her country's version of *Tatler* magazine with her top officials dressed up in black suits and shades like agents in the hit movie *Men In Black*.

"Would you mind awfully falling into three lovely lines?"

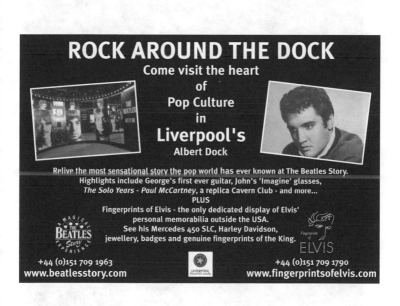

"I never get aggro. I'm pretty butch. Like the guy came up
to me at the airport and said, 'My girlfriend fancies you.'
So I say, cool, I'm probably a better lay than you are"

Marc Bolan, glam rock legend, philosopher prince